First published in Great Britain in 2007

British Library Cataloguing-in-Publication Data
A CIP record for this title is available from the British Library

ISBN 978 1 84114 537 2

Halsgrove House
Lower Moor Way
Tiverton, Devon EX16 6SS
Tel: 01884 243242
Fax: 01884 243325
email: sales@halsgrove.com
website: www.halsgrove.com

Printed and bound by CPI, Bath

Dedication

This book is dedicated to the memory of
my uncle

John Morgan Hosking

The Violinist, Walter Barnes *by Stanhope A. Forbes.* Penlee House Gallery and Museum, Penzance

Contents

Foreword

As the Mayor of Penzance I am very fortunate to be able to attend concerts performed by its many thriving musical organisations, but who could imagine that a town the size of ours could boast its own symphony orchestra. For one hundred years the Penzance Orchestral Society has nurtured natural talent in the town's young people, supported our Choral and Operatic Societies and performed some of the most challenging works in the classical repertoire. Its contribution to the cultural life of Penzance and West Penwith has been immense.

This book, written by Margaret Williams, a local girl and niece of Morgan Hosking who conducted the orchestra for thirty-five years, has been a labour of love and I am delighted to commend it to all who appreciate our town and its music, and to those who have made it such a special place. I congratulate the Penzance Orchestral Society in its centenary year and long may it continue to flourish.

Councillor Dennis Axford
Mayor of Penzance

A Message from the President

There is much to be told of the Penzance Orchestral Society and now, after one hundred years, the time is ripe for telling. On behalf of all members of the Society I welcome *The Food of Love* as a tribute to all those musicians, past and present, who have given so freely of their time, skill and enthusiasm to present live music in Cornwall during the century of our existence.

As we celebrate this auspicious anniversary, the Penzance Orchestral Society will continue to look to the future in anticipation of many more years of happy and successful music-making and thereby bring continued pleasure to our much valued, loyally supportive and appreciative audiences.

Rose Tempest
President, Penzance Orchestral Society

Preface

The impetus to write this book came directly from my uncle, Morgan Hosking, who felt strongly that the Penzance Orchestral Society's history was worthy of a permanent record. He loved to talk about it and I was his willing and fascinated audience.

For some years I was the privileged custodian of Walter Barnes' collection of programmes and cuttings loaned to me by his daughter, Enid Truman, before they were deposited in the Morrab Library, Penzance. The pleasure of working with this archive was immense and re-acquainting myself with it recently, after many years, was like meeting an old friend.

Without the help and encouragement of Morgan and Enid my task would have been very difficult. It is too late now to ask for their approval of my work but I seek their blessings from above for they are its inspiration.

Living in Wales, so far from my subject, I am acutely aware of two things. Firstly, that I have been unable to tap every source of information and memory available among so many people who have been associated with the Society. Secondly, that my excursions into aspects of the history of Penzance, its organizations and its citizens are made with deference to those who have greater knowledge than mine. My research has not always been as exhaustive as I would wish but is, I hope, acceptable for the purposes of this book.

In addition to Morgan Hosking and Enid Truman this book would not have been completed successfully without the help of the staff of the institutions listed below:

The Bolitho Estate; The Cornishman (Jeremy Ridge); The Cornwall Centre, Redruth; The George Lloyd Music Library, Kendal (William Lloyd); Gorseth Kernow (Barbara Shaw and Ann Trevenen Jenkin); The Photographic Department of the Hugh Owen Library, University of Wales, Aberystwyth (David Jenkins); Lloyds TSB Archives and Lloyds TSB, Penzance (Jeannette); The Minack Theatre (Roger Salter and Philip Jackson); The Morrab Library, Penzance (Jan Ruhrmund, Photographic Archive); The National Library of Wales, Aberystwyth; The National Portrait Gallery (Bernard Horrocks); Penlee House Gallery and Museum (Katy Herbert and Jonathan Holmes); Penwith District Council; Penzance Choral Society (Shirley Carey); Penzance Public Library; The Royal Philarmonic Society (Rosemary Johnson); the Western Morning News (Nicola Holdgate).

The following people have made important contributions by allowing me to record their memories of the Penzance Orchestral Society or by providing information, advice and help in other ways:

Edith Angove; Marian Badcock; Judith Bailey; David Ball; Hugh Bedford; Alison Bevan; Jennet Campbell; Dr.Cyril Cannon; John Care; Helen Caseley; Allison Coleman; Marjorie Farnham; David and Irene Flaxman; David Frost; Christine and Mike Grigg; Nic Hale; Jackie Hopwood; Chris Horton; the late Lambert Ivey; the late Ivan James; Alan Gwynedd Jones; Prof. Ieuan Gwynedd Jones; Russell Jory; Peter Kingswood; Margaret Kingsley; John Laity; Piers Lane; Sheila Lanyon; the late George Lloyd; Jane Lofthouse; Hugh Miners; the late Mary Page; John Philpotts; the late Paddy Pinchen; Joyce Preston; Phoebe Proctor; Sheila Richards; Roger Salter; Geoffrey Self; Deborah Sharp; Liz Smith; Rosemary Stanley-Jones; Ann Tempest; Rose Tempest; Jackie Thompson; the late Gladys Tranter; Rosemary and Michael Tunstall-Behrens; Tommy Waters; Douglas Williams; Eileen Woolmington; Cynthia Yates.

For permission to use quotations I am grateful to the authors of books listed in the bibliography and to the editors of *The Cornishman* and the *Western Morning News* newspapers.

Photographs and illustrative material have been acknowledged where possible but in the cases where attribution or copyright ownership has proved unobtainable I trust that their inclusion will not cause offence. I shall be glad to try and resolve any omissions if information is forthcoming.

I am greatly indebted to those who have transformed my handwritten manuscript into an acceptable text. Sylvia Kingswood has devoted her precious time to the project with diligence and patience and has earned my sincere thanks. To Janet Nicholls, called in to reach a 'deadline', I owe another debt of gratitude. Martin Fitzpatrick has provided not only his computer skills but informed musical and editorial comment and advice. His interest and support has been maintained over many years but has been especially valuable and greatly appreciated during the final stages of creating *The Food of Love*.

The officers and committee members of the Penzance Orchestral Society have been consistently supportive and encouraging. They have coped with phone-calls and last minute requests for information with unfailing good humour. I am most grateful to them all.

To my many good friends who have borne my long preoccupation with the Orchestral Society and its history so uncomplainingly, 'thank you' is inadequate, but it is heartfelt.

The publisher, Simon Butler, and his staff at Halsgrove have been a pleasure to work with.

Financial support towards the publication of *The Food of Love* has been given by:

Awards for All (Lottery grants for local groups)
Penwith District Council
Penzance Town Council
Gorseth Kernow

Thank you One and All!

Margaret Williams
November 2006

1 The Story Begins

Prologue

Penzance – 1906 – Population 13,000, 'Dense fog' it is said, 'infested the coast from May to August' – unprecedented! But the sights were clearer than they knew for the five young men who met in a room, now a store and a workshop for furniture repair in St Philip Street, that part of Penzance known as 'The Battlefield', a fitting birthplace for a musical venture! There, Walter Barnes, born musician and leader, born fighter, became conductor of the enfant Orchestral Society and set it on its course.

So wrote Gladys Tranter in 1966 on the occasion of the Diamond Jubilee of the Penzance Orchestral Society. In 1927, when the Society had grown into adulthood and was celebrating its twenty-first birthday, Walter Barnes, the founder-conductor tells us more about the birth of the orchestra:

In the years 1904, 1905-6, there existed a small club of musical amateurs who had named themselves 'The Clefs'. They consisted of the late E. A. Gordon Rogers (of Falmouth), Alfred W. Robinson, Osbert Howarth, Barrie B. Bennetts, George H. Shakerley and myself. We met at each others houses, and played such music as could be obtained to suit our somewhat peculiar constitution, viz – pianoforte, four violins and viola. At the end of this period, Howarth, who was always agitating for the formation of an orchestra, prevailed on the others to do so and offered the use of his large workshop for practices. A decision was made, and we set about the task of collecting enough men to form a small orchestra, and rehearsals were commenced. As can readily be imagined our first efforts were very crude, but genuine enthusiasm for orchestral music was evident and on 8th April 1907, we essayed our first public performance in St John's Hall. The programme was a modest one, but the audience was very kind to us – blind to our teeming imperfections and seeing only the good of having an orchestra, such as it was, in our midst.

More will be told later about this first concert, but already there are questions to answer. Why was Walter Barnes chosen as their leader? What were his qualifications for such a position? Who were the others gathered to form an orchestra? What music did they perform? Where and what was St John's Hall? Was the concert reported in the press? How did the orchestra develop? These are just a few of the queries that come to mind when attempting to fill out the picture of this infant orchestra which matured into healthy old age and now celebrates its centenary.

Setting the Scene

In February 1897 a concert was held in Penzance in aid of the St Mary's New Schools. This was a Bazaar concert and one of the items on the programme was a violin solo by 'Master Barnes'. In view of his later acknowledged talent as a violinist we can safely assume that this was the young Walter Barnes, then aged twelve.

On Friday 3rd November 1905 he was leading the orchestra for an important musical celebration in Penzance. This was a concert given by the Penzance Choral Society (established in 1858) to mark the re-opening of the organ in St John's Hall and was also 'In Memoriam' as a musical tribute to the Choral Society's late conductor, Mr John H. Nunn. The programme consisted of various choral and vocal items accompanied by the orchestra and an organ recital by Dr Daniel J. Wood, organist of Exeter Cathedral. The orchestra totalled 35 players, including ladies among its ranks, and was augmented by members of the Penzance Military Band and

'The Clefs', 1907.

their Bandmaster, Mr Alex Corrison. Only six of these players re-appear in the infant Penzance Orchestral Society where, as we shall see, ladies were not included.

During the early years of the twentieth century Walter Barnes made regular appearances either as a violin soloist or leader of a group of instrumentalists in the many and varied musical events which took place in and around Penzance and remained the Principal Violin for the Choral Society orchestra.

Of particular significance is a concert which took place on 30th November 1906 in the National Schoolroom in Lelant because 'The Clefs' were performing in public at a concert in aid of the Lelant Brass Band. Precisely how many instrumentalists there were on this occasion is not known, but they played works by Manfred Gurlitt, Richard Wagner, Schubert, Beethoven and Edward German, and Walter Barnes also played some violin solos. If the restricted range of instruments among 'The Clefs' was as Walter Barnes stated, then the scope and variety of their contribution is impressive.

The year of 1906 was to be the 'Annus Mirabilis' in the annals of orchestral music in West Cornwall because, according to Walter, it was in the November of that year that rehearsals of the newly formed 'Penzance Amateur Orchestra' began. They took place in the loft of Osbert Howarth's carpenter's workshop in St Philip's Street. Walter Barnes was elected as the conductor of the group and, as he himself said, his qualifications for this position were "a colossal ignorance of everything pertaining to the conducting of an orchestra."! However, his leadership qualities must have been very apparent to the rest of the musicians, especially in view of his age which was just twenty-two, and their faith in him was amply rewarded as the years passed.

Many problems were encountered from the outset, some more amusing than others. For example, the first cornet player fell downstairs and dislodged some very necessary front teeth. His absence from rehearsals with no explanation led the orchestra to find a new player, and on the evening of the arrival of the new member the former one re-appeared complete with new teeth. Walter described the situation by saying that "All the explanation in the world could not solve the difficulty or appease the wrath of the original cornet player at finding himself superseded. Matters were settled by his leaving in high dudgeon and remaining forever our avowed enemy". Shortly after this a flautist also left the group, his part not being full enough for his liking, saying that "he could count bars rest at home as well as at rehearsal."! Surviving these minor disasters the fledgling orchestra carried on and in just under six months it was ready for a public performance.

The First Concert

Their first concert was advertised as a 'Grand Orchestral Concert' and held on Sunday 7th April 1907. Why a Sunday was chosen is not known, but according to Walter Barnes' daughter, Enid, this decision caused uproar among some sabbatarians in the town. But the following Sunday the congregational minister, a Rev. Hamilton, said in his sermon that he saw nothing wrong with giving a serious concert on a Sunday evening.

The printed programme for the concert in Walter Barnes' programme books is a small, bright pink, single sheet of paper announcing itself as 'Programme of Concert of Penzance Amateur Orchestra' held in St John's Hall at 8.15 p.m. In view of the late start and the length of the programme it is anyone's guess as to the time it ended!

A long newspaper report appeared in the *Evening Tidings* for Monday 8th April 1907. The article was headed 'Penzance Amateur Orchestra; opening concert at St John's Hall', and it began "Our congratulations are due to the Penzance Amateur Orchestra which, though only of six months growth, by its opening performance at St John's Hall on Sunday night at one bound established its popularity in the Borough". A large audience was reported, and that nearly every item drew an "irresistible encore".

High praise was given to the performers and the "easy and graceful conductorship" of Mr Walter Barnes. The writer regarded 'The Caliph of Baghdad' as the best executed item on the

programme and the singer, Mr Davey, was described as a singer of "rising popularity in local circles with an excellent bass voice". Osbert Howarth was noted as the person principally responsible for the formation of the orchestra. His song 'My Lady's Garden', which was sung by Mr J. C. Truscott with an orchestral accompaniment, was described as "full of movement and whilst of refined composition is 'catchy' and possesses the elements of great popularity, and Mr Howarth, who personally conducted its rendering, is congratulated". Mr Alf Robinson was given a special tribute for his accompaniments on the piano and organ, and as being fully justified in his reputation as one of the best accompanists in Penzance. Walter Barnes received a glowing tribute, and the report ended with the news that the orchestra intended further performances and "since there is room and to spare for such an excellent company we welcome their performance and success".

Fortunately the newspaper report also listed the orchestral players as their names did not appear in the programme nor was Walter Barnes named as the Conductor. The instrumentalists were as follows:

First Violins
Messrs O Howarth
Rogers
Hoblyn
Richards
Nutt

Second Violins
Messrs Champion
W. Trounson
Warren
A. Hurley

Viola
Mr Barrie Bennetts

'Cellos
Messrs Nicholls
Short

Double Bass
Mr Hofler

Bassoon
Mr Baker

Oboe
Mr C. L. Taylor

Flute
Mr A. Corrison

Euphonium
Mr A. Nicholls

Trombone
Mr R. Nicholls

Clarionette
Messrs F. Latham
Bacher

Cornets
Messrs M. Blewett
Flynn

Drummer
Mr Hosking

Accompanist, Piano and Organ
Mr Alf Robinson

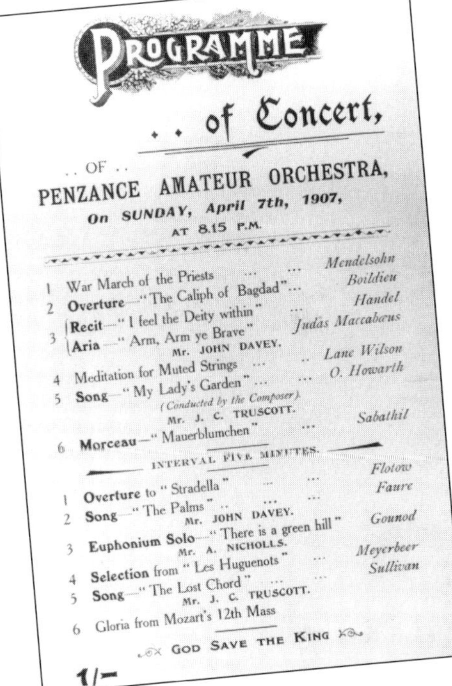
PROGRAMME
. . of Concert,
. . OF . .
PENZANCE AMATEUR ORCHESTRA,
On SUNDAY, April 7th, 1907,
AT 8.15 P.M.

1 War March of the Priests ... ... *Mendelsohn*
2 **Overture**—"The Caliph of Bagdad"... *Boildieu*
3 **Recit**—"I feel the Deity within" ... *Handel*
Aria—"Arm, Arm ye Brave" *Judas Maccabæus*
MR. JOHN DAVEY.
4 Meditation for Muted Strings ... .. *Lane Wilson*
5 **Song**—"My Lady's Garden"... ... *O. Howarth*
(Conducted by the Composer).
MR. J. C. TRUSCOTT.
6 **Morceau**—"Mauerblumchen" ... *Sabathil*

INTERVAL FIVE MINUTES.

1 **Overture** to "Stradella" ... ... *Flotow*
2 **Song**—"The Palms" .. .. *Faure*
MR. JOHN DAVEY.
3 **Euphonium Solo**—"There is a green hill" *Gounod*
MR. A. NICHOLLS.
4 **Selection** from "Les Huguenots" ... *Meyerbeer*
5 **Song**—"The Lost Chord" ... ... *Sullivan*
MR. J. C. TRUSCOTT.
6 Gloria from Mozart's 12th Mass

GOD SAVE THE KING

1/-

Programme of the first concert by Penzance Orchestral Society, 7th April 1907. Morrab Library, Penzance

The newspaper report ended: "The conductor and members of the Penzance Amateur Orchestra Band beg to thank the appreciative audience for their patronage at the concert at St John's Hall last night; also the many friends who helped make the concert a success".

This was a modest though well received beginning for an orchestra which was to become known as the Penzance Orchestral Society. Before continuing the story of its development, growing confidence and achievements over the ensuing decades, it would seem timely to look at the character of its founding conductor, Walter Barnes, in more detail. For over forty years the success of the orchestra was due to his driving force, inspiration and enthusiasm. Also, the venue for the Society's concerts is briefly described.

Walter Barnes

Walter Barnes was born on St Patrick's Day, 17th March 1884. Little is known of his parentage, but it seems that his mother, Catherine Barnes, was unmarried. She moved from Penzance to Liverpool where she married Alexander Campbell in 1891, had another family and died in 1915. (Author's note: for this information I am indebted to David and Irene Flaxman from Liverpool who have researched the Barnes family history. David is the great-grandson of Catherine Barnes – MW.)

Rumour has it that Walter's father was a solicitor in the town, but whatever the circumstances of his birth we know that he was brought up by his grandparents. The family background was humble, his grandfather, John Barnes, was a cobbler and they were not at all well to do. Details of his schooling are not known, but a photograph exists of Walter in a school group at the National School in Queen Street.

We shall probably never know the true facts as to where he acquired his skill as a musician, but his daughter, Enid, recollected that he was known to have carved violins out of wood at the age of about eight years old. She also remembered an old man telling her of his memory of Walter, as a boy, playing the violin in a funeral procession in the town, and we know that he was performing in public at the age of twelve. Another memory is provided by eighty-seven year old John H. Marshall who wrote to *The Cornishman* from America in 1950 recalling his schoolteachers in Penzance. Among them was Mr Vingoe, a member of a musical family, one of whom, Miss Vingoe, "first taught the late Walter Barnes the violin".

Walter Barnes as a boy.
Richards Bros., Penzance

More light is shed on the subject with the help of an article of 16th June 1934 in the *Western Morning News* series 'Musicians in the West' which featured Walter Barnes:

> *...there was nothing of the infant prodigy in Mr Barnes' entry into music. He was sent to a teacher for the ordinary schoolboy lessons, and, to use his own words, 'hated it like the very devil'. Later his attitude towards the subject underwent a change, and since the age of twelve he has been playing the violin all over the west of England.*

Where the money came from to pay for the early lessons, and how he acquired a violin remains a mystery because the straitened circumstances of his family background were such that many lessons or a formal musical education were out of the question. It can only be surmised that after some basic tuition he continued to teach himself, possibly with the aid of a published tutor of some kind.

One of Walter's pupils in years to come, Morgan Hosking, felt that Walter's left-hand technique as a violinist was not as good as it should have been, and the composer, George Lloyd, a close friend of Walter Barnes, felt that: "the pity was that Walter, when young, never got away to be classically trained. With his personality he would have done great things". If there were limitations, there is also plenty of evidence of his skill, authority and popularity as a violinist in the many press reports of performances in which he was involved.

On leaving school, probably at about the age of fourteen, Walter was employed as a clerk in the office of Mr Bodilly, a solicitor in Penzance. From 1900 onwards Walter's own programme and cuttings books provide ample proof of his youthful concert appearances. For example, he appeared in 1903 at the Working Men's Club in St Just where he played a 'Caprice in G Minor' by Paskevitch and the famous 'Romance' by Svendsen. It is not difficult to imagine this good-looking young man working in his office by day, but with his heart and soul devoted to his music-making.

His repertoire was already varied and demanding and it is fascinating to note that some of his pieces, for example 'Souvenir' by the Czech composer František Alois Drdla (1869-1944) had only been written in 1904 and Walter was performing it in October 1906. There were music shops in Penzance where he could buy music but his awareness of newly published works for the violin must have been acute and indicates his keen interest and diligence in his chosen instrument.

While in his early twenties Walter met and married Christiana Simons, known as Chrissie, in St Mary's Church on 13th May 1906. Her father was a shoemaker and the family were originally from Newlyn, but living in Penzance. The couple had three children, Enid, born in 1910 and her two brothers Kenneth and John.

During the early decades of the twentieth century an event occurred in Penzance which was to have a great effect on the life of Walter Barnes. In 1912 electricity came to the town and the decision was made to open a cinema. The borough architect, Frederick George Drewitt, was asked to prepare a design for the adaptation of the Victoria Hall in Causewayhead. This building was converted to "the handsomest and most luxurious picture theatre outside London" according to *The Cornishman* newspaper. It opened in November 1912 as the Savoy Cinema and after a detailed description of its facilities and décor *The Cornishman* report states that "the orchestra will leave nothing to be desired". At the time that this and other exciting developments were taking place in the town, for example, the opening of The Pavilion on the promenade in 1912, a man called Robert Thomas appeared on the scene. From humble begin-

nings as a buttons boy and billiard marker in Redruth he had prospered and moved to Penzance where he took on the role of 'entrepreneur extraordinaire' in the area of public entertainment.

He bought the Regent Hotel in Chapel Street, splendidly refurbished it and lived in an apartment there. He became involved in the establishment of both The Pavilion and The Savoy Cinema as well as other cinemas in the town. Robert Thomas was a man of considerable taste and all his enterprises had to be of the highest standard. He was not content to have pianists providing the music to accompany the silent films in his cinemas and for the Savoy he invited Walter Barnes to form a cinema orchestra. Walter's orchestra is thought to have comprised eight to twelve players including himself and May Stewart as violinists, violist George Shakerley, 'cellist Mr Hoskins, G. Howard White playing double bass, clarinettists William Clay and George Lawrence, bassoonist C. J. Baker as well as flute and brass players. The pianist was E. Fugler Thomas, the organist at St Paul's Church in Penzance.

The Savoy Cinema orchestra quickly established itself as a vital ingredient to the enjoyment of cinema going and people travelled to the Savoy to listen to the music just as much as to watch the films. The late Ivan James, himself a pupil of Walter Barnes and a member of the Penzance Orchestral Society, remembered many visits to the cinema in Causewayhead to listen to "Mr Barnes' band". Music to accompany the films was often sent to Penzance with the films and this contributed to a large library of music which accumulated in Walter's home. It was housed in the attic and looked after by his wife, Chrissie. She would prepare the music prior to performances and woe betide her if anything was missing or forgotten! This is just one of the many ways in which Walter depended on his wife for support and help 'behind the scenes' in all his endeavours. His working hours at the cinema were from 8 p.m. to 11 p.m., so his working day was a very long one.

Despite his busy life he nurtured and developed the fledgling Penzance Orchestral Society through its formative years. When rehearsals were held on a weekday they took place in the early evening and ended promptly at 7.55 p.m., allowing Walter just enough time to get to the cinema for his evening work. His daughter, Enid, remembered that after his work at the cinema he would often call in at The Penzance Club at the top of Morrab Road for a drink (for he was known to be a man who enjoyed his beer). He would then go home and read in bed until about 2 a.m., for he was also known to be a voracious reader. Sometimes rehearsals were held on Sunday afternoons when there was more time, so that even his 'day of rest' was not always a complete one. On such occasions Walter's gregarious nature came to the fore because after the Sunday rehearsals his friends in the orchestra would be invited back to Walter's home for tea and an evening of cards and relaxation.

In the nineteen twenties the 'talkies' arrived which meant that the cinema orchestra became obsolete. Robert Thomas, though aware that he had to move with the times, was reluctant to lose his fine cinema orchestra. How its end came is not known, whether it was a gradual process or an abrupt change, but as a result Walter was faced with decisions about his musical career and lifestyle. It is reasonable to assume that music had become the 'raison d'être' of his life and he could see the potential for making his living by music alone and decided to give up his job in the solicitor's office. He joined forces with two of the leading instrumentalists in the cinema orchestra, May Stewart and George Shakerley, and they set up in business in Clarence Street in Penzance.

It is very likely that they were taking over an existing business because there had been a music shop established in Clarence Street for many years, firstly as White's and later as W. H. Carnes' Music Depot. The new business was named The West Penwith Music Shop and sold sheet music, gramophone records, instruments and other musical requirements. Over the years the two chief assistants were Miss May Paul and Miss Rita Tregenza, and above the shop were rooms where the three partners were able to teach, all of them being well known string teachers in the town.

In order to supplement his income and achieve a reasonable standard of living, bearing in mind that he had three children to provide for and educate, Walter took on any professional engagements that came his way. They were many and varied and included such events as wedding receptions, garden parties, mayoral banquets, flower shows and other social events. One particular engagement that he undertook during this period involved a lady who was one of the most colourful characters to appear throughout the history of the Penzance Orchestral Society, namely Her Highness, Margaret, Dowager Ranee of Sarawak, widow of Sir Charles Brooke the second 'White Rajah of Sarawak'. She had a cottage in Lelant and was a brilliant

Walter Barnes in maturity.

pianist and especially enjoyed accompanying. As soon as she became aware of Walter's reputation as a violinist she asked him to accept a weekly engagement, on a Thursday afternoon, to come to her house and form a violin and piano duo.

Their musical relationship led to the Ranee being invited to play a piano concerto with the Orchestral Society in 1927. Her friendship with Walter did not survive a second invitation for her to perform a concerto because they had a row during a rehearsal.

This seems a good point at which to consider, more fully, Walter Barnes the man. There are many personal memories and recollections of him as a conductor, teacher and friend. They are culled from those who worked closely with him and mostly reflect him in maturity. He was short and heavily built, but his stoutness was relieved by his noble head with its fine crown of hair. Always smartly dressed he relied on his devoted wife acting as his valet, tying his tie etc, and at concert performances in white tie and tails he was a handsome figure commanding authority and respect and his stoutness went unnoticed.

Despite his fiery temperament he had great charm and was highly companionable; his wide and varied range of friends bore witness to this. Apparently he was very fond of cats but had little time to pursue hobbies or leisure pursuits. He did enjoy playing golf, usually at Sancreed, with a friend who tried to discourage this because he knew that once Walter took up a hobby seriously he would want to master it, and thought it was more important that he devoted his time to his music! He also took great interest in other events, musical and otherwise, going on in the world around him.

Walter was not a greatly travelled man, but he enjoyed visits to London, often staying with the Lloyd family, to go to the opera at Covent Garden or attend concerts. During the course of his musical engagements he journeyed throughout Cornwall and went to Falmouth, where he had violin pupils, on a weekly basis.

As a violin teacher Walter Barnes was highly regarded, though his methods would be considered inadequate by today's standards as he taught largely by example, playing alongside his pupils. If there were deficiencies in technical aspects of his teaching there is no doubt that his inspirational qualities and abilities as a teacher produced instrumentalists who were able to hold their own in many orchestras and go on to pursue successful musical careers. One of his pupils, Ivan James, recalled that Walter never dated his pupils' music after lessons, but merely marked them with a large 'B'! Pupils would often be invited to his home to play sonatas with his daughter, Enid, an accomplished pianist, and Ivan remembered playing Beethoven's 'Kreutzer' and 'Spring' Sonatas at these sessions. This experience was much appreciated by them and provided greater insight and understanding of musical interpretation and ensemble playing.

Memories of Walter Barnes as a conductor abound and newspaper reports provide ample evidence of his publicly acknowledged skill, his clear and decisive beat and a left hand that was graceful and effective. Despite his own admitted 'colossal ignorance' at the outset of his conducting career his natural leadership qualities and diligent reading of the subject gained him an unquestioned authority on the rostrum, which was essential in creating cohesion within an orchestra of mixed ability amateur musicians.

This cohesion was not achieved without difficulties at times for Walter was a severe conductor when there were shortcomings of any kind among his players. If a person was late for rehearsals he would halt the proceedings, wait in silence with his arms folded until they had reached their place and then say, "Thank you, perhaps next week you will arrive before we begin the rehearsal", or some other remark designed to quell the latecomer. He was not only a stickler for punctuality, but intonation, too, was an area where he allowed no backsliding. His hearing was acute and he could pick out any wrong or inaccurate playing from individuals even in the middle of complex passages. One look from him was usually enough to make a player aware that something needed attention, but failing this Walter would sometimes make individual instrumentalists play their part alone until he found the culprit, a terrifying ordeal for any ensemble player.

Even real tantrums from Walter were not unknown and there is a memory of him becoming so exasperated during a rehearsal that he threw his score at some poor unfortunate player. His daughter Enid, playing the 'cello, remembers catching the music but who it was aimed at has, happily, not been recorded! One of the people who could stand up to him when his temper and impatience got the better of him was his leader, Mrs Crosbie Garstin. She became so fed up with his habit of stamping his feet to make a point that she threatened to leave the orchestra. This quickly resolved the problem!

However unpleasant these incidents were, once the rehearsal was over they were quite forgotten by Walter and he was able to go for a drink or relax with his players and hold no grudges. The ability to 'forgive and forget' seems to have been reciprocal for he inspired great feelings of affection and respect among the orchestral members. Under his direction the orchestra became, in reality, a 'Society' and was therefore most aptly named by its founding fathers.

One cannot help wondering where Walter Barnes acquired his knowledge of the orchestral repertoire and how works should be performed. In his early days as a conductor the opportunities to hear live performances of orchestral music would have been very few and far between in the west of Cornwall. Radio broadcasts and gramophone records would have been of interest and help as they became available. He would have bought scores and studied them as well as reading reviews and accounts in the press of concerts in London and other large centres, and his visits to London would have provided much insight. We know that he was a great reader so that most of the works of major composers would have been known to him as well as the theoretical interpretations of them, but this still does not readily answer the question as to how his confidence in what to perform and how to conduct it in practice was established at so early an age.

He certainly lived in an unusually cosmopolitan society for such a remote area. Many artists and writers lived and worked in and around Penzance and he had friends amongst them. Some were even members of his orchestra from time to time. For example, Stanhope Forbes, leader of the Newlyn School of Artists played the 'cello during the first decade of the Orchestra's existence, and Frank Heath, another leading artist, was a regular violinist throughout the twenties and thirties. Also the leader of the Orchestra from the middle of the nineteen twenties onwards, Mrs Crosbie Garstin, was a cultured person and a professionally trained violinist. The Lloyd family, William and Primrose and their son, George, were all musically and intellectually sophisticated and had homes in London and Cornwall where all three played in the Penzance orchestra, William as a flautist, Primrose and George as string players.

The Bandmaster

The technical qualifications for a successful conductor may be summed up as follows:

A good ear.
A quick eye.
A perfect sense of time.
A quick perception of places where mistakes are likely to occur.
A keen sense for musical expression, phrasing etc.
An enthusiastic temperament.
A fine sense of tone balance, accentuation.
The power to convey his ideas intelligently to his forces.
The power of controlling his own emotions by keeping cool.
The capacity of beating time accurately.

The duties of a conductor may be put thus:

To direct his band or chorus how to obtain the effects the composer requires.
To beat time so as to help, not confuse, his forces.
To observe every lead and anticipate any possible slip.
To look up the 'part' concerned in taking up any new phrase, however reliable the performer may be.
To beat time in an orderly manner, so that performers can instantly recognise any beat in the bar.
To induce his forces to observe his movements at all important points of the score.

Advice:

Gesticulate as little as possible.
Don't make all the beats of the bar downbeats, which is an affectation.
Don't sway your arms and body about in sympathy with the mood of the music – the expression should come from the orchestra, which cannot result from simultaneous movement with the music.
Don't generally conduct with both hands – reserve your left hand for occasional lead indications.
Don't dangle your hands so that the baton flops loosely about, and the players cannot perceive the actual point of the beginning of the beat.
Remember that the conductor should not attract attention to himself from the audience.
Don't try to conduct from memory – it is a foolish vanity merely, and unnerves your players.
Watch most carefully the wind players in their attack of new phrases; insist upon their beginning absolutely together, if so required.
Insist that phrases are quitted simultaneously so that one player does not slip out before, or stick on longer than his neighbour.
Be particularly watchful of the violins at the close of phrases – they have a bad knack of slipping off the last note in a careless diminuendo manner, which leaves a very untidy effect.
See that the 'cellos are not allowed to unduly hug their notes in cantabile passages – they have a relentless tendency to drag.

This advice was pasted inside the front cover of Walter Barnes' programmes and cuttings book.
Morrab Library, Penzance

West Cornwall was almost unique in its atmosphere of artistic creativity and the life of the artists' colonies in Newlyn and St Ives has been well documented revealing that they held musical and theatrical events within their own circles. The artists also took part in local societies and groups where they combined their talents with amateur musicians in public performances. Walter Barnes was also very friendly with other musicians in Penzance and throughout the county, for example, Dr Charles Rivers, a medical man from Truro who founded the Cornwall Symphony Orchestra in 1922 and Richard White, the organist at St Mary's Church in Penzance. Such friends no doubt influenced Walter and could offer him informed advice.

There remained, however, limits to his musical awareness and embrace. Some members of the orchestra persuaded Walter to rehearse the Sibelius Symphony No. 1 and he reluctantly agreed. The Symphony opens with a long solo for clarinets and at the first rehearsal this did not go well. Walter became impatient and lost his temper saying, "I just don't understand this b★★★★★ music, and I'm not going to have it in my concert" and flung the score aside!

Following this débâcle Walter Barnes never conducted a Sibelius symphony or concerto during his many years with the orchestra. Was this because of an awareness of his musical limitations? Or did he feel that the orchestra was incapable of playing them? We shall never know, but he did not dismiss Sibelius from the orchestra's repertoire, performing 'Finlandia' and 'Valse Triste'on many occasions. It was during Morgan Hosking's conductorship that major works of Sibelius became a regular feature in concert programming.

We shall never really know how this man, in a far-away corner of England, was able to develop his natural talents as a musician to become probably the greatest and best-known musician in Cornwall between the two World Wars. Most of the musical organisations in the county depended on his support and involvement in some way. He was even, on occasions, to be found performing beyond the county border when in 1932 he went to Plymouth to lead the orchestra for the Plymouth Orpheus Choir's performance of Elgar's 'The Dream of Gerontius'.

Walter Barnes was once asked why he had not gone to London to seek his fortune as a musician and he is said to have replied that he would "rather be a big noise in a small town than a small noise in a big town"! His decision to remain in Penzance may have been a loss to the greater musical world, but was an inestimable gain for Penzance and for the county of Cornwall. His memory should never be forgotten in the annals of the town's history, and though he was admitted to the Cornish Gorsedd of Bards in 1931 it seems a great shame that he never received the Freedom of the Borough that he served so well and loved so dearly.

St John's Hall

From its very beginning the Penzance Orchestral Society held its concerts in St John's Hall, within the municipal building of the borough of Penzance. After years of discussion the foundation stone for a new public building was laid in April 1864. Designed by John Matthews it was opened three years later in September 1867. The ceremony took place over two days and the celebrations were lavish involving many public events. Among these was a concert by the Choral Society and "an ascent of a fire balloon from the building with fire works attached which emitted brilliant colours as it rose high above the town".

Built of granite quarried from the nearby valley of Lamorna, its imposing appearance reflects the civic pride of the mid-Victorian period. As originally conceived the accommodation comprised the central auditorium, known as St John's Hall, and two wings. The west wing housed the Geological Society and the east contained many of the municipal departments and public offices of the time. The top step of the impressive entrance was reputed to be the largest piece of dressed granite in the country.

St John's Hall was an impressive but charming setting for concerts and other public events, with its splendid organ installed in an arched alcove at the back of the stage. A gallery around the three other walls gave a feeling of intimacy and embrace; the audience capacity was about five hundred and fifty. This, then, was the venue for the Orchestral Society in 1907 and continues to be so, though the hall has been radically altered over the years.

The municipal building, Penzance (St John's Hall). Richards Bros., Penzance

The Infant Orchestra 1907-1918

Early Concerts

Following the success of their first concert in April 1907, Walter Barnes' newly-born orchestra presented another in July 1907, just over two months later. Calling themselves the Penzance Amateur Orchestral Society this concert was held on Sunday 28th July in St John's Hall and the programme was, again, a mixture of orchestral items and instrumental and vocal solos.

Two of the soloists are of particular interest, Harold Stanislaus, 'cello and Horatio Stanislaus, oboe. Little is known about them except that Horatio was a friend of Walter Barnes and had a home in Penzance. The programme records that he was a member of the Queen's Hall Orchestra in London and he went on to become the principal oboe with the world famous Boston Symphony Orchestra.

Harold was an Associate of the Royal College of Music and was, presumably, a relative of Horatio. Neither of them appears to have been a regular member of the Orchestral Society, but Horatio formed part of an instrumental trio with Walter Barnes, violin and C. L. Taylor, cor anglais, which played in a local concert at the Gulval Parish Harvest Festival concert in 1910.

It fell to the Penzance Choral Society to open the 1908 musical year in the town with their Golden Jubilee Celebration concert.

There were two works performed on Monday 27th and Tuesday 28th January, Handel's 'Messiah' and Mendelssohn's 'Elijah'. The orchestra (or 'band' as it was described in the programme) comprised forty-two players. With Walter Barnes in his usual place as Principal Violin, a choir of about one hundred and fifty singers, soloists, an organist, and the conductor, Richard White, the advertised '200 performers' was virtually accurate. Walter Barnes was on the committee of the Choral Society at this time along with many other well known names in the town.

Richard White was great friend of Walter Barnes. That Walter appreciated this fellow musician is evident from his tribute to him in the orchestral concert programme in April 1927 "... I want to thank our distinguished musician, Mr Richard White, for his encouragement, advice and practical help. Always our friend, he will ever have a warm place in the hearts of the members of the Society."

The third concert of the infant Orchestral Society was given on Friday 28th February, 1908. The programme had expanded to four pages and recorded the names of the Society's Hon. Secretary, J. F. Brock and Hon. Treasurer, Osbert Howarth. With its title including the word 'Society' and officers listed on the programme, the orchestra had lost no time in formalising its organisation. The proceeds of the concert were given to the West Cornwall Infirmary which had been re-housed in an entirely new building during 1907. This gesture by the orchestra is an early example of the many opportunities it took, over the years, to raise money for local needy causes.

Ticket prices for this concert were raised from 1/- to 3/- perhaps to reflect its charitable function as did the programme, which was of a mostly popular character with Lehar's 'Gold and Silver' waltz from 'The Merry Widow' and a selection from Lionel Monckton's 'A Country Girl' among the orchestral items. There was also a xylophone solo played by bassoonist C. J. Baker. The programme is a valuable document in its own right, notable for the seventeen advertisements of local traders in the town which surround the concert information, and for the decorative nature, generally, of its design.

The items in the programme amounted to fourteen in all – certainly a good evening's entertainment! The press report in *The Cornishman* on Thursday 5th March was very complimentary and encouraging:

> *It was soon manifest that there is little of the amateur about the band as the term is generally understood – except the name…for years we have had in our midst an admirable band of outdoor musicians, but it has remained for Mr Walter Barnes to weld these and the growing number of string instrumentalists into one body. The result of his efforts has been to produce a band which for balance and merit has never been surpassed in the town's history and will challenge comparison with any town of a similar size, certainly in the West of England.*

Praise indeed for an infant orchestra, but the response to the Fourth concert on Friday 11th December 1908 was equally glowing, regarding it as an "undoubted success" and reporting many encores being played throughout the evening.

A Portrait of West Cornwall Music 1909-1911

The year 1909 provides a good picture of the busy musical life which occupied Walter Barnes and his fellow musicians throughout West Cornwall at this time. On the 27th January he was leading the orchestra for the Penzance Choral Society performance of Mendelssohn's 'St Paul'. A few days later, on 4th February, he was in Redruth, as part of the fourteen strong orchestra providing music for a farcical comedy, 'Facing the Music' at the St David's Hall, a fundraising event for Redruth Hospital, presented by Mr Stanley Rowse. The leader of the orchestra was Miss Gwen Carling L.R.A.M., who reappears later in the Penzance Orchestral Society.

In April, Walter assisted Mademoiselle Panzé, soprano, of Penzance in a concert involving her pupils given in the Concert Hall in Truro. He was the violin soloist along with Mr John Davey, baritone and Miss Mary Pender, pianist. Mademoiselle Panzé was a former pupil of the celebrated Madame Blanche Marchesi (1863-1940), a French soprano who appeared at Covent Garden as Elizabeth in Wagner's 'Tannhäuser', Elsa in 'Lohengrin' and in other major operatic roles throughout Europe. This concert, though under the distinguished patronage of the Lord Bishop of Truro, was not well attended according to the report in the *West Briton* on 26th April, but was "of a high order" and Walter Barnes' contributions were highly praised.

Back in Penzance at the end of April, Walter was leading an orchestra of twenty-two players for a presentation of three plays by 'The Arcadians', the Penzance Amateur Dramatic Society founded in 1906 of which the President was Sir Arthur Conan Doyle. The orchestra played suitably light music to open the proceedings and between each play. An unidentified newspaper report listed the orchestral players, many of whom were Penzance Orchestral Society members and stated that "the most critical were reassured when they saw Mr Walter Barnes, the talented violinist conducting".

All this while rehearsals would have been continuing for the next Penzance Amateur Orchestral Society's concert, their fifth, which took place on Monday 17th May 1909 in St John's Hall. The programme listed Mr Frank Latham as the Society's President, and the names of the instrumentalists were printed in the programme for the first time, Osbert Howarth leading an orchestra of 28 players. One of the founder members, E. A. Gordon Rogers was missing but the others remain.

Among the players was Frank G. Heath, well known as a member of the Newlyn School of Artists. He played, with some breaks, for many years and his handsome features are clearly identified in a photograph taken of the orchestra in 1922. Another member of the artistic community playing in this concert was Mr C. Gilardoni. His family lived in Newlyn, the most notable figure of whom was Madame Gilardoni who had been a professional singer. Her portrait was painted by Stanhope Forbes and portrays her as an old lady seated at her piano. She had sung with the famous Italian soprano Giulia Grisi and also at a dinner party given in honour of Charles Dickens.

The music played at the concert was varied and demanding and included the 'Vorspiel' from Wagner's 'Lohengrin', a two-part selection from Mascagni's 'Cavalleria Rusticana' and a selection from Bizet's 'Carmen' as well as an overture, 'Marche Militaire' by Schubert, three songs by the contralto soloist, Miss Gertrude Sellers, a cornet solo, two harp solos and Schumann's 'Träumerei' played by a String Quintet.

This concert merited three press reports in Walter Barnes' cuttings book. We learn from them that the 'Vorspiel' was played by Messrs O. Howarth, Barrie Bennetts, P. Polglase and C. Spear Cole, violinists, and that there was an extra soloist not listed in the programme, Miss Hilda Lucas, a violinist from Birmingham who is described as "an accomplished amateur". Also, Mr C. J. Baker "the well known bassoon artist of the Royal Marine Band" was unavoidably absent

and his part was played by the President of the Society (Mr Frank Latham), who "proved a worthy exponent of that difficult and trying instrument". A large audience was reported and the *Western Morning News* stated that it was the first occasion on which a full selection of 'Cavalleria Rusticana' had been heard in Penzance.

The musical year ran merrily on for Walter Barnes and his musicians, and on 23rd June he and three other string players were among the artistes at a concert given in the Marazion Drill Hall in aid of the Marazion and St Michael's Mount Regatta. On the 4th August a Farewell Benefit concert was given for Mr C. Gilardoni which involved Walter Barnes both as a soloist and conductor of a small twelve part orchestra. Among the other performers were three other members of the Gilardoni family and Miss Phyllis Gotch. Stanhope Forbes was playing the 'cello in the orchestra, and Miss M. Palmer (later to become his second wife) was at the piano. Phyllis Gotch, singing folksongs on this occasion, was the daughter of the artist Thomas Cooper Gotch.

After, apparently, a restful month or two another benefit concert, this time for Mr Alex Corrison, conductor of the Penzance Military Band was given on Friday 1st October. Held in St John's Hall, the Orchestral Society provided seven of the eighteen items in the programme. Alex Corrison was the flautist at Walter Barnes first orchestral concert. He was obviously well thought of and an unidentified newspaper report indicated disappointment that the audience was not more substantial in view of Alex Corrison's services "having been fully and frequently placed at the disposal of any worthy cause in the Borough". Only a few days later Walter Barnes was once more playing the violin for Mademoiselle Panzé in her concert at St John's Hall in aid of the West Cornwall Infirmary.

Walter was again violin soloist and director of a small orchestra for "a capital concert" given under the auspices of the Penzance Horticultural Society on Thursday 4th November. Later in the month his musicians again joined the local artists at a Conversazione at the Passmore Edwards Art Gallery in Newlyn on the afternoon of Friday 26th November 1909. The minutes of a Committee Meeting at the Gallery on 13th October 1909 record that the idea was discussed "of having a conversazione. Mrs Forbes was deputed to ask Mr Barnes to bring his orchestra or part of it and to have a concert". The *Evening Tidings* for 27th November reported a "large and fashionable gathering on this occasion".

With the Penzance Orchestral Society's sixth concert looming, Walter and members of his orchestra still made time to play in Redruth Amateur Operatic and Dramatic Society's performance of 'The Mikado' from Tuesday 7th to Thursday 9th December. Presumably the Friday and Saturday were busy with final rehearsals and preparations for the Society's concert on Sunday 12th December in St John's Hall, Penzance. The word 'Amateur' was dropped from their title by this time, perhaps indicating growing confidence following the complimentary press reports received so far. But the orchestra was still small, only twenty-seven players in this concert including, among the 'cellists, Stanhope Forbes, his first appearance as a member of the Orchestral Society.

This concert was interesting for the fact that the 'Tympani' section is mentioned for the first time, played by Mr W. H. Nicholls. It also seemed a little more modern in style, opening with Schubert's 'Rosamunde' Overture and including his Symphony in B Minor ('Unfinished') for which programme notes were given. The orchestra also performed an arrangement by Walter Barnes of Ambrose Ward's 'The Farewell'.

Three press reports following this concert were lengthy and wholly congratulatory towards both the orchestra and soloists saying that it was a pity that the public did not have more opportunity to appreciate the talent of the orchestra "which Mr Walter Barnes so skilfully directs". But as a full and well rehearsed orchestra two concerts a year were as much as could have been expected from these busy and much sought after musicians. Still their year was not over because Walter Barnes was, as usual, leading the orchestra for the Penzance Choral Society's Grand Concert in St John's Hall on Friday 17th December 1909, when a performance of Flotow's opera 'Martha' was given.

The following year, 1910, proved just as busy for Walter Barnes. His programme and cuttings book records many musical events at which he either led an orchestra or was a violin soloist. But, curiously, there were no concerts given by the Orchestral Society in their usual Spring and Autumn routine. Their only appearance during the year was on Monday 28th March, Easter Monday, when a Grand Symphony Concert was given in St John's Hall where they combined with the Principals of the Royal Marine Band, Plymouth.

The Royal Marine musicians numbered ten, being the principals in all string sections, woodwind and French horn. Mr Wellington, 1st violin, Mr Wells, 2nd violin, Mr Dalling, viola and Mr C. G. Pike, 'cello, gave a performance of the Andante Cantabile movement from Tchaikovsky's String Quartet Op. 11. C. G. Pike was the 'cello soloist in this concert and in 1922 became a regular member of the orchestra and a well known and popular soloist in West Cornwall.

The guest soloist at this concert was Miss E. Inglewood Jenkins, a contralto from Redruth who was accompanied by her teacher, Mr H. Dennis. She was described in the press reports as a "girl artiste" with "her hair falling over her shoulders" but her voice was well developed for one so young and gave promise for the future. Substantial programme notes were provided for the orchestral items, and the programme was printed by a Plymouth firm, Hoyten and Cole. Three items in the programme were played by request, all performed by the Penzance Orchestra during 1909 – Schubert's 'Marche Militaire', the Symphony in B Minor, and Mascagni's selection from 'Cavalleria Rusticana'.

This concert received good coverage in the press and was regarded generally as a great success. The *Evening Tidings* for Tuesday 29th March, under the heading "Easter Monday Musical Treat" said that this exceptional concert had been made possible by "the great progress made by the members of the Penzance Orchestral Society". The Mayor and Mayoress of Penzance, Mr and Mrs A. K. Barnett, were present and Lord and Lady St Levan had come over from St Michael's Mount so it was obviously regarded as a special occasion in the town, both musically and socially.

The impact that the orchestra was making in the district is also endorsed by the press report of the Penzance Choral Society's Concert on Wednesday 13th April 1910, conducted by Richard White, in which Walter Barnes was the Principal Violin. In addition to two choral works, the 'band', in the second half of the programme, played Balfe's Overture 'The Maid of Artois' and Elgar's 'Imperial March' (by special request). The *Evening Tidings* reported that:

> *...the nature of the second part of the programme was undoubtedly due to the recognition on the part of the executive of the Choral Society of the great advance which has been made in recent years in Penzance in orchestral music and the more general attention paid to stringed instruments.*

This all seemed to be very encouraging for the Orchestral Society and makes an entry in a well known musical magazine, the Musical Times, under 'Cornwall' rather puzzling. It noted the performance by the Choral Society on 13th April, calling it an "excellent rendering", but also includes the following remarks: "The Orchestral Society formed in Penzance three years ago, under the conductorship of Mr Walter Barnes, has made a fresh start, and at a concert on 28th March proved to be an excellent combination, augmented to forty performers, and led by Mr F. Wellington, the programme including Schubert's 'Unfinished' Symphony".

The phrase "made a fresh start" defies explanation but this remark, alongside the fact that the orchestra's regular concerts were suspended for the year, makes one wonder what was going on to cause this hiatus in routine. There is no doubt that the orchestral players were still active as a group because apart from the two occasions already mentioned they were playing in various combinations throughout the year. We find them at the opening of the Landithy Hall in Madron on Easter Tuesday, 29th March and the 248th Anniversary Concert of the Congregational Church Penzance on Sunday 10th April. Of particular importance was their contribution to the solemn memorial service on the death of King Edward VII, in St Mary's Church, Penzance. *The Cornishman* for Thursday 26th May records this day in great detail, with business in the town suspended and all flags at half mast.

This was a very important occasion, being a ticket-only event attended by all the major municipal and military organisations of the town. The organist, Mr Alan Thorne, was assisted by "a number of skilled instrumentalists" all of whom were Penzance Orchestral Society members and Walter Barnes played Mendelssohn's 'O Rest in the Lord' arranged as a violin solo, followed by Chopin's 'March Funèbre' performed by the organ and orchestra. The musical portion of the service was reported to be "of high order". The service ended with the organ and orchestra playing the Dead March from Handel's 'Saul'.

Through the autumn the musicians were in action at a performance of Spohr's 'Last Judgement' at the United Methodist Chapel in Penzance on 2nd October, and in Redruth on the 9th and 10th November to support the Redruth Amateur Operatic and Dramatic Society once more in their performance of 'The Princess and the Rose'. Finally the Choral Society gave a performance of Gounod's 'Redemption' on 16th December and although the 'orchestral band' was not listed in the programme it is fair to assume that with Walter Barnes as Principal Violin the other instrumentalists would have been from his orchestra.

So what created the gap in regular concerts between the sixth concert in December 1909 and the seventh in January 1911, and why the strange remark in the Musical Times in May? It could not have been due to lack of players because in the 'extra' Symphony Concert on 28th March the players from the Royal Marine Band only totalled ten, which meant that the regular orchestra had increased by four or five players. As there are, to date, no minutes existing for the early years of the Society these questions must remain unanswered.

The year 1911 began with "Mr Walter Barnes' String Band" making an appearance on 2nd January at a Ballad Concert in St Buryan given by Colonel and Mrs Paynter, another collaboration between the local musicians and artists for the soloist was again Miss Phyllis Gotch. The orchestra "kept the audience spellbound" and reflected "very great credit on Mr Walter Barnes and the members of his band".

The winter season of rehearsals resulted in the seventh concert of the Orchestral Society on Friday 13 January 1911. The inauspicious date had no effect on the event because the *Evening Tidings* for the following day regarded the concert as "the finest which this progressive Society has given". Three other newspaper reports give high praise to all involved, especially to Walter Barnes both as conductor and for his work with the orchestra, without which "many of the finest orchestral works of today would have as yet remained unheard in Penzance", and for "developing and broadening the musical tastes of the district".

Proceeds from this concert were used to raise money for a new set of tympani and "was in the nature of a personal appeal, and the large amount of support which it was accorded showed that the end in view had the sympathy of a music-loving public."

Just a week after their seventh concert the Orchestral Society were again on the stage of St John's Hall as part of a Musical and Dramatic Entertainment in aid of the Penzance Cricket Club, held on Friday 20th January, when the orchestra was described as the "celebrated" Penzance Orchestral Society. Throughout the spring and summer of 1911 Walter Barnes, either as violin soloist or leader of a group of musicians, sometimes both, continued to take part in a varied number of events, including the Penzance Choral Society concert on 3rd May, and Redruth Wesley Church Choir Services on 11 May.

A slightly more unusual engagement for Walter Barnes and his "Bijou Orchestra" was providing the musical entertainment at a Mayoralty Banquet, held at the Riviera Palace Hotel on Thursday 9th November 1911. The Mayor was Councillor Howell Mabbott, and the printed menu kept by Walter Barnes indicates that it was, indeed, a banquet:

Oysters; Clear Ox Tail; Purée de Tomato
Boiled Turbot (Lobster Sauce); Fried Fillet Soles (Tartare Sauce);
Sweetbreads à la Toulouse

Compote of Pigeons; Sirloin of Beef; Saddle Mutton;
Boiled Turkey (Celery Sauce); York Ham;
Roast Geese; Pheasants; Wild Duck

Mascotta Pudding; Charlotte Russe;
Fruit Jellies; Trifle
Cheese Straws
Ice Pudding; Dessert; Coffee

They were not the only artistes, sharing the musical honours with the 'St Ives Quartette Party' who, along with Walter as violin soloist, interspersed musical items between the formal toasts and speeches. Whether the musicians were able to partake of the feast is not known but it is to be hoped that their efforts were rewarded with some crumbs from the table!

Ladies are admitted

The concert on Friday 8th December 1911 by the Orchestral Society, their eighth, is notable for the fact that ladies appeared among the string players for the first time. According to Walter

Barnes in his 'Retrospect' of the orchestra in the concert programme commemorating twenty-one years of its existence in April 1927, the admittance of lady players produced "a decided improvement in the ability of the string section of the orchestra". He added, in a later account, "their willing help and ability has been a feature of the Society since that time". Among the first violins were Miss Biles, Mrs Mayne, Miss Violet Nunn, Mrs A. W. Robinson, Miss May Stewart, and only three gentlemen. The second violins remained totally male, but among the violas appears Miss Stapley.

In an orchestra numbering thirty-six players, six ladies may not seem too much of a revolutionary event, but according to the 'remembrancers' their introduction caused a huge furore! In fact, one member's wife was so upset that she forbade her husband ever to play again, and rumour has it that the violinist in question was Osbert Howarth, a founder member and leader of the orchestra. He did play in this concert and the following one, but his name disappears from the lists after this apart from an isolated appearance in November 1922.

The soloist was Miss Amy Tyndale, mezzo soprano of Queen's Hall, London and provincial concerts, who sang an aria from Saint-Saëns' 'Samson and Delilah' in the first half. Sibelius's tone poem 'Finlandia' was the major work in the second half of the programme, and prompted the following note: "This striking and inspiring work by one of the modern school of composers is performed (by request) for the first time in the County by an orchestra".

Sibelius had only completed this work in 1900, so with this work we find the still youthful Penzance Orchestral Society indicating its growing confidence both in its own capabilities and the awareness of its audience. The newspaper write up on Thursday 14th December reported a "huge and highly appreciative audience" and goes on to praise the performance, but apart from listing the members of the orchestra makes nothing of the introduction of lady members which was such a momentous decision for the orchestra itself.

It is clear from the musical events in West Cornwall between 1909 and 1911 that the formation of the Penzance Orchestral Society had created a vital and competent body of instrumentalists which contributed greatly to them, providing the area with concerts of high standards which had hitherto been unknown.

1912-1914

The years 1912 and 1913 continued in a similar pattern with the Orchestral Society giving its two concerts a year in the spring and autumn months.The first of these on Friday 3rd May 1912 was a "Complimentary Concert" to the conductor, Walter Barnes, the orchestra wanting "to mark in a tangible manner their appreciation of the services of their conductor", according to *The Cornishman* for Saturday 11th May. The autumn concert in December 1912 is interesting in that Eric Coates' 'Miniature Suite' was performed, only having been composed the previous year, and also for the fact that already the first violin section consisted entirely of ladies.

This, the tenth concert, was also the first one for which there are any financial figures available and the expenses totalled £16. 3s. 8d. The soloist, Miss Minnie Searle from Plymouth incurred a total of £3. 3s. 10d for her fee and hotel expenses, the cost of hire of St John's Hall was £3. 1s. 0d and printing and advertising costs totalled £5. 5s. 9d. Income from ticket and programme sales was £23. 14s. 5d, so a profit of £7. 10s. 9d was made and despite unfavourable weather, according to *The Cornishman*, it was another success for the orchestra.

During 1912 the Penzance Pavilion was opened on the promenade. The formal opening took place on Monday 5th August, and though no local musicians appear to have been involved because of professionals being engaged to provide the music, the occasion is relevant to our story because of the use to be made of it by the Penzance Amateur Operatic Society in years to come.

Among the memorabilia kept by Walter Barnes is a programme of the Annual Dinner of the Cardiff Cornish Association which took place in Cardiff City Hall on Tuesday 17th October 1912. It was an elaborate programme containing illustrations of institutions in Cardiff and of Richard Trevithick and his locomotive. A programme of music was provided by the Redruth String Band conducted by Mr H. Dennis. Details of the menu of "pasties despatched from Redruth this morning", a wine list including champagne, lists of toasts made, the musical items and a list of members and guests is provided, but no mention of who the instrumentalists were. It can only be assumed that as he had kept the programme Walter Barnes was among them, and was probably the leader of the string orchestra. The event was reported in *The Cornishman* on Thursday 24th October, revealing that copies of Herbert Thomas's song 'Pasties and Cream' were distributed among the guests by "young ladies in Welsh costume".

This is recorded as part of the Penzance Orchestra's history mainly because Walter Barnes' daughter, Enid, took great delight in recounting the story of a 'cello which was lost returning from a trip to Cardiff. Whether this was the occasion or not is lost in the mists of time, but it provides a little cameo of West Cornwall musicians having musical adventures outside their home territory!

The Cornwall Music Competition had been inaugurated in 1910, but was suffering from a lack of financial success, and there were debts to be paid. According to the *Western Morning News* for Wednesday 7th May 1913, three weeks before when the Competition was held in Penzance, the Orchestra had been invited to take part. For various reasons they were unable to do so but promised to devote the proceeds of their spring concert to the funds.

This took place on Monday 5th May 1913, and was attended by the Mayor and Mayoress of Penzance, Councillor and Mrs Barnett, Lord and Lady St Levan, Sir Clifford Cory, Bart., M.P., the Mayor and Mayoress of Truro, Lady Jane Vivian and Mrs Bolitho. Lady Mary Trefusis, the founder and Hon. Secretary of the Competition and her husband Colonel H. F. Trefusis were prevented from attending by the breakdown of their motor car but the competition committee was represented by its Hon. Treasurer, Mr Horton Bolitho. The soloists were Mademoiselle Fifine de la Cote, soprano, of Albert Hall and provincial concerts fame and Miss Ethel Tonking, who had studied in Leipzig and also with Percy Grainger.

The concert was reported at great length in the press and received some contrasting reactions. The *Western Morning News* reported that though the audience was good the cold and wet weather probably prevented many from attending. Though generally supportive of the performances the writer had many criticisms to make of both orchestra and soprano soloist. The *Evening Tidings* for Tuesday 6th May, on the other hand, goes into verbal raptures over the whole thing and the delightfully verbose mood of this report and the initials at the end – "H.T." – must point to the writer being Herbert Thomas, the Editor and proprietor of *The Cornishman* and *Evening Tidings*.

The Market House, Penzance, 1925. The Penzance Orchestral Society rehearsed in the Dome Room of this building in its early years. LLoyds TSB Group Archive

The orchestra now numbered nearly forty and was led by Miss May Stewart, Medallist R.A.M., and the conductor, Walter Barnes receives a vivid portrayal in Herbert Thomas's account who notes his "rhythmical gestures", and "certain sweeping motions". Herbert Thomas was a loyal and long-time supporter of the Penzance orchestra and his wordy, hyperbolic concert reports and articles over the years are unique and full of his remarkable character and personality.

The Annual General Meeting of the Orchestral Society took place during the spring in the Dome of the Market Building, their rehearsal venue at this period. A press report of the meeting stated that following the May concert, profits of £15. 10s. 2d (from an income of £43. 8s. 2d) has been passed on to the Cornwall County Music Competition funds and a letter of appreciation had been received from Lady Mary Trefusis, and Mr Horton Bolitho. The balance sheet for the year ending May 1913 revealed Cash in Hand of 15 guineas and total outgoings of £52. 11s. 7d, including the purchase of a trombone for £1. 15s. 0d and a harmonium for £2. 10s. 0d. Rent of the Dome was £4. 0s. 0d and piano tuning and repairs had cost £6. 8s. 10d.

An interesting piece of information also emerged in the press report. It seems that the President of the Society, Mr Frank Latham, on behalf of the members, presented Walter Barnes with a large portrait of himself, to acknowledge the high efficiency to which Walter had brought the orchestra and the regard in which he was held. Mr Barnes, "taken with surprise", expressed his thanks for the gift and said that it would have an honoured place in his house. No one now seems to have any information about this picture, all attention having been concentrated, in more recent years, on the Stanhope Forbes portrait of Walter Barnes painted in the 1930s.

By the twelfth concert on Monday 13 December 1913 the orchestra had grown to forty-four players, many of whom had 'settled' into positions where they would remain for many years. The main work in the concert was Beethoven's Symphony No 7. This was announced, as at the Queen's Hall the previous week, as a 'centenary' performance, marking its first performance on the 8th December 1813. The lengthy newspaper reports are full of interest and congratulate the Society in continuing "its educational work in symphony playing" and regarded the second movement as the most appealing. The soloists were praised, and Mr C. L. Taylor's performance on the oboe was especially remarked upon, as "this instrument is but little known in the town" and Mr Taylor "is undoubtedly the most skilful soloist west of Plymouth". The 'cello soloist, Miss W. Blight, who like Mr Taylor was a member of the orchestra, produced "a surprisingly big tone for a lady"!

In addition to the two orchestral concerts, and other engagements during the year, Walter Barnes took on work at the newly opened Penzance Pavilion when asked. There had been a change of management during 1913 and it was now being run by Mr Ellis Slack, who was the proprietor of cinemas throughout Cornwall, with Mr Alex Corrison, former bandmaster of Penzance Military Band as his assistant manager and deputy.

As they rehearsed through the winter of 1913 and early spring of 1914, the Society could not have known that their next concert, on Monday 4th May, was to be the last before the dark years of World War One had to be endured. But for other reasons this concert opened on a sombre note, with the playing of Chopin's 'Marche Funebre', "In memoriam Andrew Kitchen Barnett, late Mayor". In *The Cornishman* the following Thursday Herbert Thomas wrote, in an article surrounded by a black border, that the orchestra:

> *...played it so beautifully that all its wistfulness, all its haunting harmony, its sadness and its gleam of sunlight, was realised by the audience, which – needing no call – rose instantly and stood, like the musicians, until the last strains died away. It was worth coming many a mile, if only to hear such a great composition played with such sympathy and artistry... the concerts of the Penzance Orchestral Society must certainly be ranked among the musical treats of the year.*

Although this concert made a small loss of 9s. 2½d the orchestra was in good shape on the eve of the outbreak of war. They had expanded to over 40 members, audiences were plentiful and appreciative, their reputation as the only full orchestra in the county was established, and their confidence in themselves was reflected by increasingly ambitious programming. This had been achieved in just seven years, but how did this still maturing group of musicians, and their enthusiastic conductor survive the four years of war? And was Penzance to continue receiving its 'musical treats' for its duration?

The War Years 1914-1918

The First World War broke out on 4th August 1914, and there are no further concert programmes in Walter Barnes' cuttings book until December 1919. Fortunately other sources of information such as the Society's Account Books, Walter's 1937 'history' of the orchestra and the press do provide evidence that concerts were held during the early war years.

One of the first effects of the war to be felt in Penzance was the arrival of Belgian refugees into the town following the German invasion of their country. The first contingent arrived early one Friday morning in November, and was welcomed at the railway station by the Mayor and Mayoress, Alderman and Mrs George Poole and others, including the Chief Constable. This group of sixteen refugees consisted mainly of family groups, but also of a few young men awaiting call-up and accommodation was provided in various large houses around the town. More refugees continued to arrive and many of the concerts that took place at this time donated their proceeds towards their welfare. For example, a successful concert in St Just given by the Penzance Male Voice Choir, conducted by Mr Ernest White, L..R.A.M., A.R.C.M. of St Ives, raised twenty-five pounds for the "brave Belgians".

Penzance Orchestral Society was no exception, and their fourteenth concert on Friday 11th December in St John's Hall was held in aid of the Belgian Refugees Distress Fund. Among the soloists was Monsieur De Bever from the Brussels Conservatoire and the Keersaal, Ostend, who played two 'cello solos in the first half of the concert and Bruch's 'Kol Nidrei' in the second half, a most pertinent choice of work, which was encored. He was among those taking refuge in Penzance and his presence on stage must have added to the emotional atmosphere of the evening.

The programme opened with the Belgian national anthem, played by the orchestra and also included the Russian national hymn "played with solemn grandeur never before so beautifully educed in Penzance". The overture 'Britannia' by Mackenzie, a breezy nautical composition interwoven with 'Rule Britannia', Walford Davies' 'Solemn Melody' and the French and British National anthems all contributed to the patriotic mood of the concert. The other solo work, Wieniawski's Violin concerto in D Minor, was played by Miss May Stewart, Med. R.A.M. Her performance received "vociferous applause" and she received a bouquet of chrysanthemums. The press reported that this was the "first time a work of this nature has been undertaken in the town" which was a "striking testimony to the progress of the orchestra", presumably referring

to the fact that it was a popular, romantic violin concerto performance, a rarity in Penzance. In the Society Accounts for this concert one of the items of expenditure was "Hire of Town Band £4. 0s. 0d". The part they played in the proceedings is not recorded but with four national anthems during the evening there was plenty of opportunity for their services! A profit of £39. 4s. 7d was made and the sum of £40 given to the Belgian Refugee Fund.

The proceeds of the next concert in the spring of 1915 were also devoted to the needs of the war. This time the cause is described in the Accounts Book as "the purchase of Christmas comforts for local men serving in the Army and Navy", which in view of the time of the year, Friday 7th May, seems rather strange. It is probably more accurately described in *The Cornishman* for Thursday 13th May as "the funds of the Penzance Soldiers Entertainments Committee" and for the comforts of "the Penzance boys at the R.G.A. Tregantle." The programme was a return to the old mixture of orchestral works, vocal and instrumental solos, mostly of a popular nature. The members of the orchestra are not recorded, but the press report states that "Despite the loss of so many members due to war and other changes the Society maintains high standards.... adding to the scope of instrumental parts, the latest introduction being a harp played by Mr A. W. Robinson." The concert made a profit of £16. 13s. 0d and this was divided between "the Soldiers Recreation Committee £10. 10s. 0d" and "R.G.A. Tregantle £6. 6s. 0d."

The orchestral accounts show that members paid their subscriptions for the following season 1915-1916, but there are no records of any more concerts being given until 1919. There is a balance sheet dated 30th June 1916 – 1st January 1919 which shows the on-going expenses of the Society during this period, but no concert accounts.

It has been the proud boast that the Penzance Orchestral Society had an unbroken record of performances, even during the two World Wars, and while this is true for the years 1939-1945 it looks as if there may have been a cessation from May 1915 to January 1919, but it seems certain that it was always the intention to resume the Society's activities as soon as possible.

Walter Barnes would have been thirty years old at the outbreak of World War I but did not take part in war service. It is possible that he was regarded as too old, or perhaps the heart problems which were to be the cause of his death in 1941 were already apparent. Whatever the reason, there is little doubt that he would have given his time and talents wherever he could to money raising and morale boosting musical events during the war years.

The war ended on 11th November 1918, but it was to be over twelve months before the orchestra was deemed ready for its first post-war concert.

3

Coming of Age 1919-1929

It is not hard to imagine the problems with which the conductor and committee of the Penzance Orchestral Society were confronted in the months following the end of World War I. In the midst of victory families would have been adjusting to war time losses, and men who had survived the years of war service and were returning home needing to re-establish their patterns of working life were, perhaps, affected by war injuries. So it is not surprising that many months were to pass before the orchestra could be reassembled and rehearsals resumed in the early autumn of 1919.

On Monday 20th October of that year a terrible accident occurred at the Levant Tin Mine, located on the West Penwith cliffs near St Just. A vertical rod with platforms at twelve foot intervals, powered by the famous Cornish 'man-engine', transported miners up and down from the mine head to the shaft bottom. This rod snapped while in the process of transporting one hundred and fifty men, and thirty-one of them were killed.

The communities of the surrounding area, shattered by this rare tragedy, responded by fund-raising for the bereaved and distressed families, and the first post-war concert by the Penzance Orchestral Society on Sunday 7th December 1919 was in aid of the Levant Mine Disaster Fund.

A. W. Firth, Hon. Treasurer for over thirty years.

Information on the programme records the names of some of the officers and other leading personalities of the Society in 1919 who were to retain their importance and influence for some years. Frank Latham continued as President but now had the title Capt. Frank Latham, R.E. Further evidence of his war service is found later on in a press report for the twenty-third concert of the Society in 1922. Although he was listed as one of the bassoonists in this concert the press report reveals that he did not play due to "his war and accident injuries". Mr Firth was the Hon Treasurer, and Mrs Georgina H. Main, Hon. Secretary.

Albert Williams Firth was the Secretary of the Penzance Cooperative Society from 1910 until 1922, and a staunch supporter of the Penzance Silver Band, becoming its President for a period, and he served on the Allotments Committee of the Penzance Corporation for over twenty years. He was Treasurer of the Orchestral Society for more than thirty years. Less is known about Mrs Main, but she was a violist for over twenty years and played an active role in the administration.

On the musical side Walter Barnes was in his accustomed place on the rostrum with Miss May Stewart as his Principal Violin and Mr A. W. Robinson was still "at the Piano and Organ". When he was required to play the harp, Mrs Main could be found playing the organ and there were a number of other competent keyboard players Miss Violet Nunn being the most notable.

According to *The Cornishman* for Wednesday 10th December the concert was, "A Brilliant Success". In his review, 'H.T.', the inimitable Herbert Thomas, commented "It was a matter of joy and thankfulness that they were permitted to assemble there, in St John's Hall, to render this beautiful programme of music to the glory of God and in such a worthy cause". It was "good to know that all the members of the Society had gathered there from different parts of England, except that their drummer, Mr Jack Edwards, had made the supreme sacrifice in the war from which other members had been spared to return". The Society "sets the standards for the rest of Cornwall and for towns beyond the Tamar".

In eulogistic mode 'H.T.' portrayed Walter Barnes as "the keystone of the arch" and:

> *...the embodiment of the music from all the instruments. Every chord seemed to pass through his brain and body... I have heard that in rehearsals Mr Walter Barnes does not cloy the palate of members of the Society with meringues of sugared flattery. I can believe that when I glimpse*

the statuesque features of the conductor in repose; but whether he gets results by the velvet hand or the eagle eye or Napoleonic voice, we will leave to the privacy of the practice room.

He concluded:

This first peace concert will remain in my paradise memories ...but I wish – just for the credit of Penzance... that Sir Henry Wood, Sir Landon Ronald and a few other musical celebrities could have dropped into St John's Hall on Sunday evening to hear those waves of melody vibrating near the remote Land's End, in the Country once known as West Barbary, but now more justly entitled to be designated a Land of Song.

The "waves of melody" mostly consisted of many previously played works, including 'Finlandia', but also Gounod's 'Meditation on the 1st Prelude of J. S. Bach, performed by May Stewart, violin, C. G. Pike, 'cello, A. W. Robinson, harp, with Mrs Main, Med. L.C.M. at the organ. Thirty-eight pounds was donated to the Levant Mine Disaster Fund.

So many words devoted to one concert necessitates a mere outline of the concerts which followed. Three concerts took place in 1920, the usual spring and autumn ones with the addition of an extra one in June in aid of the Penzance War Memorial Fund. This second 'extra' concert in the orchestra's schedule seemed to have caused some concern over the running total of concerts given, because the concert on Sunday 5th December 1920 is listed as the 'eighteenth' concert, but the next spring concert on Saturday 14th May 1921 is recorded as the 'twenty-first' concert. Presumably the powers that be decided that as the two 'extra' concerts, i.e. 28th March 1910 with the Principals of the Royal Marine Band, Plymouth and 6th June 1920 just mentioned, involved the full orchestra they should be added to the total resulting in twenty-one concerts being performed by the spring of 1921.

This May 1921 concert is interesting because although there is no programme available for it, *The Cornishman* report lists a work by Matthew Clemens, "Orchestral Variations on an Original Air" which was personally conducted by the composer. Mr Clemens was, "a distinguished Cornish musician from Redruth" whose work showed "undoubted merit" and he was recalled for an extra round of applause. This was to be the first of numerous examples of local composers having works performed by the Society.

The Christmas spirit was very much to the fore in December 1921 when the proceeds of the concert, augmented from the funds of the Orchestral Society were used to give a Christmas Party for all the poor children of the town. It seems that the Mayoress, Mrs Howell Mabbott and Mrs Main, Hon Secretary, had arranged to get a Christmas tree for the needy children and the idea of a party grew from this. Walter Barnes recalled it as "the happiest childrens' party possible" and his daughter, Enid, remembered it being held in a room under the Market House. She helped with the tea and said there were a lot of children who all had a wonderful time, each one given a balloon.

An account of this occasion indicates that perhaps as many as 326 children attended because one of the entries reads: "Money Gifts to children, 1/- x 326 = £16. 6s. 0d". No expense was spared, the food costing £16. 9s. 6d; toys £13. 8s. 3d; crackers £2. 1s. 0d; oranges £1. 17s. 6d and sweets £2. 18s. 4d. Decorations and twine accounted for £1. 10s. 10d and the food and drink cost £18. 9s. 6d. The Mayor's Fund received £5 and a "Gift to destitute children per the School Attendance Offices" totalled £4.17s.1d. This generous gesture by the orchestra was much appreciated by leading members of the town and district who patronised the concert; one gentleman had paid £2 for his concert ticket!

Penzance Orchestral Society concerts in 1922 were interspersed with performances by the Cornwall Symphony Orchestra who combined with Redruth Choral Society to give two choral and symphony concerts in May and three orchestral concerts in Camborne, Falmouth and Truro in November 1922. The history of the Cornwall Symphony Orchestra has been well recounted in Geoffrey Self's admirable book *Music in West Cornwall; a Twentieth Century Mirror* published by the author in 1997. Here it is sufficient to note its foundation series of concerts in 1922 and the fact that Walter Barnes was the leader of the orchestra. Dr Charles Rivers, the founder conductor, was a remarkable man, a notable physician and surgeon and a man very proud of his association with the town of Redruth. The Cornwall Symphony Orchestra, under his baton, came to an end in 1932 from lack of funds, and its existence for those ten years was in no small part due to Dr and Mrs Rivers' personal financial support.

This much larger orchestra, of whom about a third were members of the Penzance Orchestral Society, engaged professional musicians to swell its ranks including ladies from the British Women's Symphony Orchestra in London. It would have made further demands on Walter Barnes' already busy life, but it also provided him with opportunities to experience large-scale music-making, as well as introducing him to some first-class soloists. It is noticeable that soloists who appeared with the Cornwall Symphony Orchestra often re-appeared playing with the Penzance Orchestral Society.

Morgan Hosking told one amusing, possibly apocryphal story about the Cornwall Symphony Orchestra. On one occasion, in a rehearsal, the orchestra was going to overrun the time for a train to Penzance used by the Penzance musicians. To overcome the problem Dr Rivers conducted the last movement of the final work at double speed so that the players didn't miss the train!

It appears that during 1922 the venue for the Penzance orchestra's rehearsals changed from the Dome Room over the Market House. Though it is not certain, the new practice room may have been in the Mounts Bay Academy, which was housed in a building in Chapel Street just below the entrance to Custom House Lane. The Society's accounts for the year ending December 1922 include entries under expenditure for rent of Mounts Bay Academy for three weeks £1. 2s. 6d and for three months £5. 0s. 0d, and also "Removing from Dome Room to New Room 10s. 0d". Unfortunately the "New Room" is not specified, so we cannot tell whether use of the Mounts Bay Academy was a temporary measure or if this was, in fact, the "New Room". The annual statement of accounts for 1923 just refers to rent of a "Band Room".

The music chosen for the March and December concerts in 1923 included Grieg's Piano Concerto in A Minor, performed by pianist Miss Violet Nunn, 'The Dream Pantomime' from Humperdinck's opera 'Hansel and Gretel', Edward German's Welsh Rhapsody' and Symphony No. 36 in C by Mozart. The programme notes for the Mozart Symphony began "The Society has much pleasure in presenting, for the first time in Cornwall, this Symphony, the work of one of the greatest musicians the world ever saw".

The programme for the concert on Wednesday 19th December was the first to state on the title page, "Penzance Orchestral Society. Founded 1906". Following his death in 1941 this was amended to "Founded in 1906 by Walter Barnes" and has been included in concert programmes every since. At the back of the December 1923 programme was the following statement:

The Penzance Orchestral Society was founded in 1906, and since that time has filled a useful place in the musical life of the neighbourhood, not only by its concerts during the winter season, but in rendering assistance to almost every local charity and religious institution. The members readily give their services to performances, and the use of the Society's library, and also the library of its conductor, is freely given. Any money which is found at the end of the financial year to be to the credit of the Society is expended in the purchase of music and instruments, and it is of interest to note that at this concert trumpets are for the first time used in an orchestral performance in Penzance.

Penzance Orchestral Society in the early 1920s. The artist, Frank Heath, is the white-haired violinist in the bottom right of the picture. Opie, Redruth

The Society is slowly but steadily acquiring a library of music, and wishes to place on record its appreciation of the gifts of the following works:-
Overture 'Semiramide', Rossini, presented by Percy Crutwell, Esq.
Hungarian Rhapsody (No. 2), Liszt, presented by Percy Crutwell, Esq.
The Welsh Rhapsody, Edward German, presented by Richard White Esq.
Serenade, Jadassohn, presented by Thomas Carr, Esq."

The Cornishman report for this concert mentions that the stage had "a charming appearance with holly giving a Christmas touch to the front of the platform." One of the trumpets played at this concert was the property of the Society itself, purchased by means of a fund that had been set up during the year called 'The Harp Fund'. The cash in the Society's bank account at the end of 1922 amounted to £64. 1s. 5d and forty pounds of this had been transferred to this special account. Donations amounting to £5. 1s. 0d were contributed by Rev. Humphreys, Mrs J. T. Bolitho, Mr T. F. Michell and J. A. Hawke Esq., making a total of £45. 1s. 0d. A trumpet had been purchased from La Fleur & Son for £23. 17s. 6d and in 1924 a trombone was bought for £9. 19s. 6d and other sundry items paid for, but the fund disappears from the financial records by 1927. Why it was called a 'Harp' Fund is not at all clear!

As well as the Society's annual accounts, each concert had its own statement of income and expenditure which provide information helping to create a picture of the organisation of the concerts. As well as professional fees to the soloists and extra players who may have been needed, from the Royal Marines in Plymouth, for example, there was the hire of St John's Hall and its caretakers, printing of posters, programmes and tickets, and advertisements in the local press. But there were other, less obvious expenses, such as the installation of electric lighting over the platform in the hall (costing 5s. 0d in 1923), and entertainment tax amounting to £10. 12s. 0d. Also the conveyance of the drums and music stands from the practice room to St John's Hall had to be arranged and paid for (5s. 0d) and "the writing in of brass parts in the score of the Symphony" (7s. 6d). And, in these days of bottles of wine or flowers presented to soloists, it is amusing to find that one of the concert expenses was "Cost of Pipe presented to Mr Cresser 13s. 6d", Mr A. Victor Cresser (principal bass, St Asaph) being the soloist in December 1923. The total expenditure for this concert was £43. 10s. 7d. and with an income from the sale of tickets and programmes of £50. 1s. 10d. a profit of £6. 11s. 3d. was achieved.

In January 1924 Walter Barnes was to be found not, as might be expected, contributing to the musical life of Cornwall, but in Ascot, Berkshire, as one of the artistes in a concert arranged by Her Highness, Margaret, Dowager Ranee of Sarawak. The concert took place in her house, 'Greyfriars', on Monday 21st January at 3 p.m. Apart from Walter and the Ranee who was a pianist, the other performer was a Miss Dora Labbette. Accompanied by the Ranee, Walter played a Grieg violin sonata and other violin solos. Miss Labbette, then twenty six years old, was already an established and well known English soprano who had studied with Liza Lehmann. She had a long career, and for her operatic performances she took the name Lisa Perli.

The reason for this concert in Ascot was explained in the programme:

"Cornwall. Our Lady of the Lizard. We live in an island, and are dependant on the sailor men whose lives are spent for our comfort in bringing us the supplies needed for our daily existence... "The concert was held.... "in order that the proceeds should be given towards the erection of a small shrine on one of the cliffs of Cornwall overlooking the sea, known as the Lizard, the Cape of Storms, and the chapel is to be dedicated to Our Lady". The Ranee felt that it need not cause controversy because as well as ships from Catholic countries crossing the waters, "others there are, who, although not belonging to the same religion, might find comfort from the fact that nearby, prayers were being sent up on behalf of 'all in peril on the sea'".

Nothing more is known about this concert, nor the outcome of the Ranee's scheme. However, she herself, entering the pages of Walter Barnes' programme books at this point was one of the more exotic characters in the history of the Orchestral Society.

H.H. Margaret, Dowager Ranee of Sarawak

Margaret Jennings was born in 1849, her mother having to leave a performance of Rossini's 'William Tell' at the Paris Opera to rush home for her birth! To please her maternal grand-mother Margaret's parents took the family surname, de Windt. Her father, Clayton Jennings, introduced Margaret to the piano and by the age of seven she was playing the easier Mozart Trios, and "Poverty stricken violinists were bidden to Epinay" (the family home) to play music

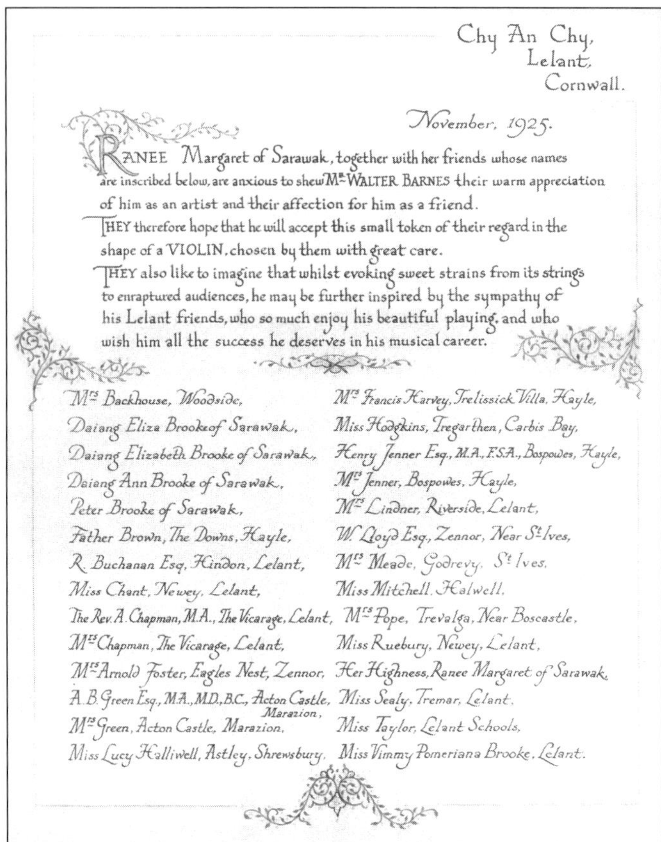

Chy An Chy,
Lelant,
Cornwall.

November, 1925.

RANEE Margaret of Sarawak, together with her friends whose names are inscribed below, are anxious to shew Mr WALTER BARNES their warm appreciation of him as an artist and their affection for him as a friend.

THEY therefore hope that he will accept this small token of their regard in the shape of a VIOLIN, chosen by them with great care.

THEY also like to imagine that whilst evoking sweet strains from its strings to enraptured audiences, he may be further inspired by the sympathy of his Lelant friends, who so much enjoy his beautiful playing, and who wish him all the success he deserves in his musical career.

Mrs Backhouse, Woodside,
Daiang Eliza Brooke of Sarawak,
Daiang Elizabeth Brooke of Sarawak,
Daiang Ann Brooke of Sarawak,
Peter Brooke of Sarawak,
Father Brown, The Downs, Hayle,
R. Buchanan Esq, Hindon, Lelant,
Miss Chant, Newey, Lelant,
The Rev. A. Chapman, M.A., The Vicarage, Lelant,
Mrs Chapman, The Vicarage, Lelant,
Mrs Arnold Foster, Eagles Nest, Zennor,
A. B. Green Esq., M.A., M.D., B.C., Acton Castle, Marazion,
Mrs Green, Acton Castle, Marazion,
Miss Lucy Halliwell, Astley, Shrewsbury,
Mrs Francis Harvey, Trelissick Villa, Hayle,
Miss Hodgkins, Tregarthen, Carbis Bay,
Henry Jenner Esq., M.A., F.S.A., Bospowes, Hayle,
Mrs Jenner, Bospowes, Hayle,
Mrs Lindner, Riverside, Lelant,
W. Lloyd Esq., Zennor, Near St Ives,
Mrs Meade, Godrevy, St Ives,
Miss Mitchell, Halwell,
Mrs Pope, Trevalga, Near Boscastle,
Miss Ruebury, Newey, Lelant,
Her Highness, Ranee Margaret of Sarawak,
Miss Sealy, Tremar, Lelant,
Miss Taylor, Lelant Schools,
Miss Vimmy Pomeriana Brooke, Lelant.

The decorative list of subscribers who bought Walter Barnes a violin in 1925.

with her and her two brothers. In 1869 she married her cousin, Charles Brooke, nephew of the first white Rajah of Sarawak who had inherited this title in 1868. Her life in Sarawak is recorded in her autobiography, *Good Morning and Good Night*, published in 1934. Charles Brooke died in 1917, but before this he had bought a house in Lelant for Margaret who had been visiting West Cornwall for many years, and she spent the winters there.

Her love of music and talent as a pianist fostered her friendships and one of her neighbours, a Mrs Pennell, who had been a violin pupil of Joachim, and the Ranee "spun out Bach, Mozart and Beethoven" to their hearts' content. Walter Barnes was engaged to go to her home for her to accompany him on the violin, and this became a regular Thursday afternoon commitment when her friends would be invited to listen to them. They decided that the violin Walter was playing was not good enough for him, so the Ranee organised a collection among her friends and bought him another, in November 1925, accompanied by an inscribed list of the subscribers. The violin, by A Chappuy, Paris, made in 1756, is to be seen in the portrait of Walter Barnes painted by Stanhope Forbes. Walter's hand apparently shrank a little as he grew older, and in 1939 he sold it to his protégé and pupil, Morgan Hosking, for £50.

The Ranee was invited by Walter to play a concerto with the Orchestral Society which she did at their concert on 27th April 1927, playing Beethoven's Third Piano Concerto in C Minor, Op. 37. She was asked to perform a second concerto but during rehearsals she and Walter had a row and she refused to continue with her engagement. The late George Lloyd recalled that "The real reason was that the old lady was not up to playing the programmed concerto... I think it was the Schumann... and it was she who picked a quarrel with Walter as an excuse to get out and not admit the work was too much for her. I was around at the time and I got all this from my father." Walter Barnes had an autocratic attitude to his music-making, and a short fuse, so if there were problems during rehearsals it is not difficult to imagine a point of dispute leading to fireworks! If he did show any rudeness or lack of courtesy towards the Ranee it was more than their friendship could stand. Whatever the cause and effect their relationship was ruined and, sadly, Walter's friendship with this remarkable lady came to an end. It was one of the rare occasions when the maestro's temperamental outbursts could not be forgiven and forgotten.

This remarkable and well-connected lady is vividly portrayed in a book written by her daughter-in-law, Sylvia, Lady Brooke called *Queen of the Head-hunters*, another autobiography of a Ranee of Sarawak published in the 1970s. "I shall never forget our entry into 'Greyfriars'" wrote Lady Brooke, "The Ranee Margaret was seated regally in a high-backed chair....There was nothing very feminine about her, either in her manner, or in the way she decorated her ordinary and rather ugly home; but she could dominate a room with her personality and her magnetic eyes, and enchanted everyone in it...When this strange woman was not seated at her piano she would recline in a blue armchair with the green parrot perched upon her wrist".

The Dowager Ranee Margaret of Sarawak in 1934. By permission of Llyfrgell Genedlaethol Cymru / The National Library of Wales

Penzance Orchestral Society gave its usual two concerts during 1924, and it is from newspaper reports that we learn that one of Walter Barnes's sons was among the second violins in the spring concert, and that the soloist in this concert, Miss Marian Carfax, was the daughter-in-law of Rev C. F. Rogers, a former vicar of St Mary's Church, Penzance. The concert on Wednesday 26th November 1924 was fulsomely reported by 'H.T.' under the heading "Musical Penzance". Dvorak's Symphony No 5 in E Minor Op 95 'From the New World' was the chief work on this occasion, its first performance by the orchestra. The orchestra by now had increased to fifty-six players and three of the instrumentalists, playing for the first time in this concert were to secure places in the orchestra's history; Mrs Crosbie Garstin, first violin, Mr William Lloyd, flute and Mr M. A. Cardew, clarinet. Two movements from Gustav Holst's

'St Paul's Suite' were noted as "the first performance in Cornwall of any of this famous composer's works".

The Society's concerts in March and December 1925 were, as usual, interspersed with performances by the Cornwall Symphony Orchestra, and in June a Chamber Concert was held in St John's Hall at 3 p.m. under the patronage of "Her Highness Margaret of Sarawak, who is as devoted to music as she is attracted to animals and beat (sic) on increasing pleasure and decreasing pain by precept and example". The chief participants in this concert were the Penwith String Quartette (Walter Barnes, May Stewart, violins, Barrie Bennetts, viola and May Bartlett, 'cello), who played the Schumann Piano Quintet (Op 44) with Miss Kathleen Frazer at the piano. Dvorak's Quartet in F Major Op 96, the 'Nigger' (now known more acceptably as 'The American') was the other major work.

The advertisements on this programme and those for the two orchestral concerts reveal some changes in Walter Barnes' life at this time. Mr A.Victor Cressor (bass soloist in December 1923) was advertising his music shop in the March 1925 orchestral concert programmes as "Late H. J. Watkins & Co., 29 Clarence Street, Penzance". In the June Chamber Concert programme is an advert for "West Penwith School of Music. Subjects – violin, viola, 'cello, pianoforte, singing, orchestral and ensemble playing. Trios and small orchestras supplied for homes, receptions etc. Terms on application to Walter Barnes, 22, St Mary's Terrace, Penzance".

By December of 1925 the orchestra programme is advertising "The Upright Grand Pianoforte by Adam used at this concert is supplied by the Penwith House of Music, sole concessionaires for all the great British pianoforte makers, and for the celebrated 'HMV' Gramophones and Records. Expert tuners visit all parts of the Duchy. The Penwith House of Music (Mr Walter Barnes, Mr G. H. Shakerley and Miss May Stewart) 29, Clarence Street, Penzance. Telephone 29. Advice by Mr Walter Barnes on stringed instruments gratis".

Aware that his income from the Savoy Cinema orchestra would be drawing to a close with the onset of the 'talkie' films it seems that this was the year in which Walter decided to form a new business. Did Mr Cresser temporarily run H. J. Watkins' shop knowing that Walter would be taking it over, or did Walter Barnes buy the business from him to set up his own establishment? We do not know but it must have been both a demanding and exciting year for Walter.

This did not, however, result in any lessening in his development of the Orchestral Society, because the orchestra had again increased to sixty-eight players by December, and was also the possessor of its own set of cymbals given to them by F. R. King, Esq. Most innovatively of all, two performances were given on Wednesday 2nd December 1925, one at 3 p.m. and the evening one at 8 p.m. The afternoon concert, reported in *The Cornishman* the following Wednesday, consisted of an almost entirely different programme, with the violin soloist, Margaret Fairless, playing the Beethoven 'Romance in F' instead of the Mendelssohn Violin Concerto. The only item played in both concerts was the Overture to 'Mignon' by Ambroise Thomas.

Perhaps a less substantial programme was chosen for the afternoon concert to avoid over-running their time and allow enough of a break for the performers before the evening concert. But so many works to be rehearsed indicates that the confidence of both conductor and orchestra had grown sufficiently to 'bring it off'. Apparently the afternoon was a frosty one but this was compensated for by the interior, decorated "with flowery azaleas and graceful palms and lit by many lamps which almost created the illusion of summer".

The Birth of Penzance Operatic Society

Walter Barnes was more than once described as "indomitable" and this is borne out by his taking on another huge commitment in 1926, when he founded the Penzance Amateur Operatic Society. From its beginnings the Operatic Society orchestra was made up of the most able members of the Orchestral Society. The two organisations became inextricably linked and, apart from a few years, they had the same conductor until 1966. It was always deemed an honour to be regarded as good enough to play for the Operatic Society productions.

In early February 1926 the Pavilion Theatre on the promenade had re-opened under new management, that of Mr Robert Thomas, and he installed new lighting, scenery and curtains and improved the seating and stage. A full orchestra was to be available and at the opening event, a 'Bouquet' revue, reported in *The Cornishman* on Wednesday 24th February, the music was provided by Walter Barnes and his cinema orchestra. This was to be the venue for the Operatic Society's performances until 1975.

The Operatic Society chose Gilbert and Sullivan's 'Iolanthe' for its first production, and there were six performances during the week spanning the end of February and early March 1926. The Operatic Society appears to have been well organised from its beginnings with an extensive programme containing photographs of the cast, the Musical Director (Walter Barnes playing his violin) and the Producer, Mr John C. Holliday. The list of patrons was lengthy and included many of the artistic, musical, professional and 'gentry' people of the area.

There were seventeen full or half page advertisements for trades people and events in Penzance – fascinating in themselves – with the Penwith House of Music advertising the opportunity to purchase "the complete records of 'Iolanthe' recorded under the supervision of Rupert D'Oyly Carte. A charming souvenir of the First Performance by the Penzance Amateur Operatic Society". Also the twenty-first Anniversary Concert of the Penzance Orchestral Society in April 1927 was announced.

Thanks were accorded to the Orchestral Society for the use of their rehearsal room and musical instruments and to the members who played, and Robert Thomas is thanked for much valuable assistance and advice. No Cornishman report has been found following this important musical development in the town, but it must have been a success, because the Society flourished and went on to become an eagerly anticipated annual event.

With little time to recover from this arduous week the Orchestral Society gave its thirty-second concert on Wednesday 19th March 1926 in which the soloist for the Schumann Piano Concerto in A was Miss Kathleen Frazier, who appears from the concert account not to have charged for her services. But Miss Marjorie Hallward, a mezzo-soprano from London concerts (via Lelant) and known in private life as Mrs Buchanan, charged £7. 7s. 0d

Kathleen Frazier

Kathleen Frazier was a young local musician, born in St Ives, who joined the Orchestral Society in 1924 as a violinist. But her great accomplishment was as a pianist, and for many years she accompanied soloists at the concerts. She made a second concerto appearance with the orchestra in 1949. Her story is told in her short autobiography *My Story* which is an interesting and entertaining picture of her successful career culminating in her appointment, in 1945, as staff accompanist for the BBC in Bristol. She also provides vivid and tantalising glimpses into the musical life of West Cornwall between the wars: playing chamber music at the Bernard Leach pottery where little mementos were made and fired in the kiln for the performers; playing instrumental trios with Walter Barnes, and 'Jerry' Baker, "a wizard with the Bassoon", at the Porthminster Hotel in St Ives after dinner on Sunday evenings; accompanying Heddle Nash at a Mousehole Male Voice Choir concert.

She was, according to Walter's daughter, Enid, a very fine pianist, but when Enid's 'cello teacher, Cedric Sharpe, came to play with the orchestra in 1931 Walter wanted his daughter, who was also an excellent and trained pianist, to accompany him in his 'cello solos. Miss Frazier was, not unnaturally, rather upset about this and although she carried on as a violinist in the orchestra for a short while, her happy association with it during this period gradually came to an end.

Though not of direct relevance to the history of the Orchestral Society it is of interest in any study of the culture of Cornwall to record that, "A Great Public Meeting" took place in St John's Hall on Monday 10th May 1926. Held under the auspices of the University College of the South West of England, Exeter, the meeting was to "explain the aim and object of establishing a University College in the west of England." The Mayor of Penzance, Councillor W. H. Lane presided over the proceedings which consisted of speeches by various people and musical entertainment. Among the local artistes was Walter Barnes as violin soloist, accompanied by E. Fugler Thomas. Many decades were to pass before this dream would be realised.

An afternoon concert was again given, on Wednesday 17th November 1926, in addition to the evening one and this was thought a very good idea by 'H.T.' in his concert report the following Wednesday, especially for "those travelling from a long distance". He also reported that a member of the audience had asked him to thank the Conductor "for ensuring the full and dignified rendering of the National Anthem at the close of the concert – some concert givers being content to scamper through a few bars of the anthem as if it were a tag with no value or significance". The soloist was the eminent baritone, Mr Herbert Heyner, who sang different selections of songs in each concert.

The evening concert might have been entitled "Tchaikovsky and Cornwall" because with minor exceptions, they were the themes of the evening. As well as the Symphony No. 6, 'Pathetic' (sic) and 'Marche Slave' by Tchaikovsky his 'Variations on a Rococo Theme' was performed with Miss May Bartlett as the 'cello soloist. The Cornish part of the programme was mostly contributed by John C. Holliday, whom we first met as the producer of 'Iolanthe'. He not only conducted his own composition 'Two Folk Tunes, Skipton Rig, and The Geeze Dance' (an old Cornish custom) but also two of the songs sung by Herbert Heyner. These were Holliday's settings of words by the well known local author, Crosbie Garstin, 'Sea Lights' and 'The Privateersman'; the author's photograph was included in the concert programme. John Holliday, according to 'H.T.' was "a member of the St Ives Arts Club....and is an entertaining actor and lecturer". He accompanied Herbert Heyner for his song settings and the performers were joined on stage by Crosbie Garstin at the end of their performance. *The Cornishman* report stated that these were the first verses by Crosbie Garstin to be set to music and "recalled the stirring life and adventures of Otto Penhale", who was a chief character in the author's novels "that have won the admiration of book lovers throughout the world".

The other, seemingly unimportant, item of information in this concert programme was the fact that among the list of scores donated to the orchestra's library was a 'Concertante Quartette' by Mozart, given by M. A. Cardew, Esq., more of which will be told later.

A Twenty-First Birthday

And so to 1927 and the Orchestral Society's Twenty-First Anniversary concerts, its "coming of age". These were held on Wednesday 27th April, with two concerts in St John's Hall, at 2.45 p.m. and 8p.m. A sixteen-page programme was produced for this special occasion "In Celebration of the 21st Year of Existence of the Society". Its Frontispiece was a photograph of Mr Frank Latham (in military uniform) with the caption "President of the Society since its foundation in 1907". The orchestra members are listed, totalling sixty-six in number with Miss May Stewart as Principal Violin. Walter Barnes in 'A Retrospect' points out that seven members of the original 1907 Orchestra were still playing. A photograph of "The Clefs" in 1907 was included where it is interesting to note that Osbert Howarth is ccredited as "Founder of the Orchestral Society", and Walter Barnes is pictured as a very young man. Also listed are all the gifts to the Society and their donors, where two French horns have been added to the orchestra's assets, given by Rev and Mrs Bloomfield, while the donated scores numbered sixteen.

The soloist was "Her Highness, the Ranee Margaret of Sarawak", who played Beethoven's Piano Concerto No. 3 in C Minor Op 37, and songs were sung by Mr J. C. Truscott, (who was one of the soloists in the foundation concert in 1907), and Miss Clarice Edwards, a local soprano, and a medallist of the Royal Academy of Music. The concert opened with Beethoven's Fifth Symphony, and in the second half of the concert Brahms' 'Academic Festival Overture' was conducted by Dr Charles Rivers "Hon. Conductor of the Cornwall Symphony Orchestra, the value of whose work for music in Cornwall cannot be over-estimated." Johann Strauss's Viennese Waltz 'On the Beautiful Blue Danube' was played and the concert finale was the Prelude to Act II of Wagner's 'Lohengrin'. The concert ended, as usual, with God Save the King.

Many column inches were devoted to this concert in *The Cornishman* for Wednesday 4th May 1927, the occasion described as a "Brilliant Festival of Music" and performances were congratulated. Walter Barnes' 'A Retrospect' was also printed in the paper, and a further article called 'Musical Musings' by The Man in the Street describes wandering from the Morrab Gardens, the "Garden of Palms", to St John's Hall on "a night of stars, not in the sky, but under a roof made by man's hand." Margaret of Sarawak is described as having a "Great Philosophy of Life and many devoted admirers, not only of her musical gifts but of her splendid womanhood and unique personality." Ivan James' particular memory of this concert was of the brilliant, sparkling red light reflected from the massive ruby stones in a brooch worn by the Ranee!

In fact, this must have been a very difficult occasion for Margaret, because the previous November her much beloved youngest son, Captain Harry Brooke, had died suddenly in London following an emergency operation. The Ranee writes movingly of this in her autobiography, speaking of the kindness of her friends in Cornwall at this time, but added that she found it very hard to pick up her life. She returned from London to Lelant and worked hard on the Beethoven Concerto she had promised to play. "I played the concerts, not caring much what people thought; it had given me some work to do and something to think about." Despite these emotions, her performance was described as a "brilliant effort" which received a tremendous ovation. Unknowingly, the Society had provided the means of helping the Ranee Margaret through her sadness.

The Society's celebrations continued after the concert with a supper and dance two evenings later. This event was by invitation only and a dance band, stewards, waiters and a lanternist were engaged. The whole evening incurred expenses of £58. 16s. 5d which was mostly paid for by the £51. 16s. 5d profit made on the concert. This was a rare example of the Penzance Orchestral Society spending money on indulging themselves, but for their coming of age party it seems wholly justified.

The opening concert of the 1927-28 season on the 7th December 1927 could, understandably, have been something of an anti-climax both for the players and audience alike. But the orchestra's committee and Walter Barnes had the foresight to choose both a soloist and a programme which would maintain the spirit of optimism and enthusiasm kindled by the 21st Anniversary celebrations.

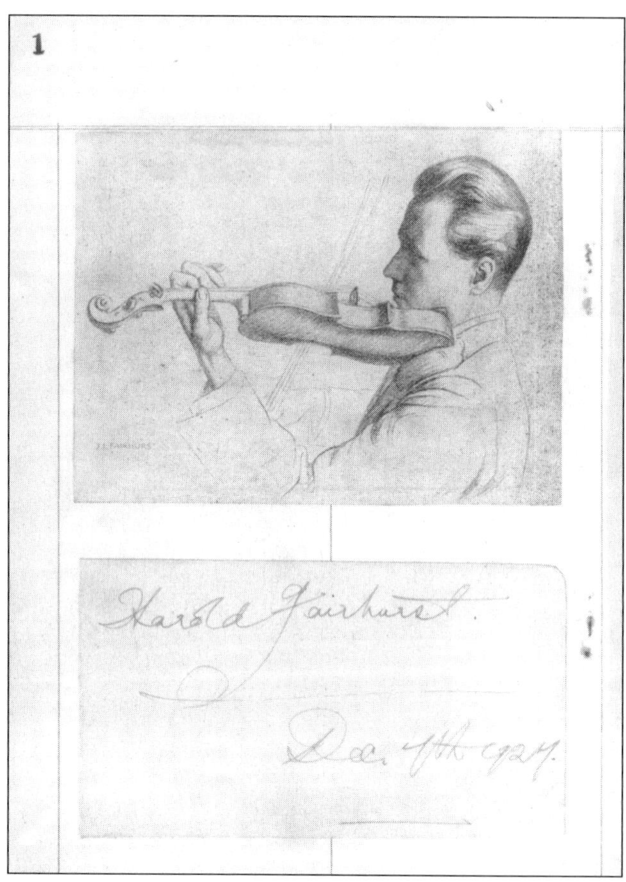

Sketch and autograph of Harold Fairhurst. Morrab Library, Penzance

The soloist chosen was Harold Fairhurst, a young man regarded as one of the "coming violinists of the day" in an unidentified newspaper preview. He was also very good looking and in Walter's cuttings book there is a beautiful pencil drawing of him playing the violin, with his autograph. Such a performer playing the Brahms Violin Concerto in D Op. 77 was a potent combination!

The programme began with a performance of Mozart's Symphony in E Flat Op. 39 and the other orchestral items were works of which the full orchestral parts and conductor's score had been donated to the orchestra: The Overture to 'Euryanthe' by Weber, donated by T. C. Beadsworth, Esq.; the Second L'Arlésienne Suite by Bizet, donated by Mrs Crosbie Garstin and Handel's Water Music Suite (arranged by Hamilton-Harty) donated by Frank G. Heath, Esq. Also, the sum of £5 had been donated to the Society by Mrs Reginald Rogers of Carwinion, Falmouth, in memory of her son, Mr E. A. Gordon Rogers, the first Hon. Secretary of the Society.

Mrs Crosbie Garstin was, for the first time, Principal Violin, a position she was to hold, with the exception of the years during and following the Second World War, until her death in 1972. The newspaper preview also revealed that the violin used by Harold Fairhurst was made by the same maker as one of those used by Walter Barnes, telling us that "The Zanoli in the possession of Mr Barnes has an interesting history. It originally belonged to William Light, leader of the private band of King George IV. It was used at the dancing lessons of Queen Victoria, and was left by Madame Bourdin, dancing mistress to her Majesty, to Mr Latham, President of the Penzance Orchestral Society, by whom it was presented to Mr Barnes."

That the concert was a success was borne out by the report in *The Cornishman* on Thursday 15th December – "Fine music at Penzance...sparkling orchestration and solo technique". A. W. Robinson on the harp and Major William Lloyd playing the flute were selected for special praise. The accounts reveal that ticket prices at this time ranged from 5s. 0d to 6d , and that 736 tickets were sold for the two concerts, producing a profit of £44. 12s. 7d which was given to the West Cornwall Infirmary.

During 1928 two concerts were given by the Orchestral Society, on Wednesday 18th April and Wednesday 21st November both of which were well received and made small profits. Orchestral members took their usual places in the orchestra of the Operatic Society's production of 'The Mikado' in early February and at Choral Society concerts as well as the Cornwall Symphony Orchestra's concerts on 4-5th November, in Camborne and Truro. Walter Barnes was invited to conduct Mozart's 'Magic Flute' Overture in the C.S.O. concerts and the short

programme notes for this item included a tribute to him. Forty concerts had now been undertaken by the Society and life was continuing to get even more challenging and interesting for Walter and the players as 1929 breasted the horizon.

A Remarkable Year

Nineteen twenty-nine – an unremarkable sounding year, but not for the Penzance Orchestral Society! It began in the normal way, with the players providing the orchestra for the Operatic Society's production of 'The Pirates of Penzance' from 4-9th February, and contributing to the Cornwall Symphony Orchestra's Eleventh series of concerts in Camborne and Truro in March, Walter Barnes remaining their leader.

The forty-first concert of the Orchestral Society took place on Wednesday, 17th April in which the main item of interest was their first performance of Beethoven's great Symphony No. 3 in E Flat, the 'Eroica'. Newspaper reviews reported "a crispness about the playing which told of a meticulous attention to detail by the conductor....Such uniformity of bowing, by the way, is seldom found in a combination of their description." They also revealed that the tenor soloist, George Garner, an American who had recently sung with the Helston Choral Society, had a gleaming golden tooth and that the concentration of the audience during the Society's concerts was encouraged by lowering the house lights during each orchestral piece.

But it was the light of a summer's evening which illuminated the music of nine members of the Orchestral Society at the end of August 1929 when they provided the musical background for a performance of Shakespeare's 'A Midsummer Night's Dream' in a meadow by a stream in the hamlet of Crean, near St Buryan. This event was to take on an unexpected historic importance in the cultural life of West Cornwall. It heralded the creation of the Minack Open Air Theatre on the cliffs at Porthcurno, the history of which has been well documented by Sir Darrell Bates, Avril Demuth, Denys Val Baker and others.

Memories of this 1929 production on Friday, Monday and Tuesday 23rd, 26th and 27th August have been recorded in recent years with Mrs Edith Angove, who was one of the fairies, providing a first hand account of it. The orchestra was situated behind the stage, across the

A Midsummer Night's Dream, Crean, 1929. The Minack Theatre Trust, Porthcurno

stream beneath the trees. The music was, of course, Mendelssohn's Incidental Music to 'A Midsummer Night's Dream' performed by Mrs Crosbie Garstin and Mrs Beckett, first violins, Miss Hilda M. Quick, second violin, Mr Barrie Bennetts, viola, Mr William Lloyd, flute, Mr W. Clay, clarinet, Mr C Baker, bassoon, and Miss Enid Barnes, piano. The performance was advertised in the press and tickets were sold at Bridger's Library at 3s. 6d, 2s. 6d, and 1s. 0d. A Motor Bus Service was scheduled to leave Penzance Station at 3.30 p.m., the return fare costing 1s. 6d. Teas were available between 4 and 5 p.m. at 1s. 0d, and the performance began at 5 p.m. The proceeds were in aid of the West Cornwall Hospital.

The cast was made up of amateurs, organised and produced by Dorothea Valentine. Both she and Miss Rowena Cade, who made the costumes and scenery, were well known in the local amateur theatrical community, but many of the players were ordinary people from the parishes of St Levan and St Buryan and the experience has never been forgotten by them. It was well reported and deemed a great success and the musical contribution was well praised with "nature's orchestra, the wind and the brook" providing additional accompaniment.

The winter concerts given by the Penzance Orchestral Society on Wednesday 20th November 1929 at 3 p.m. and 8 p.m. appear from the programme to have followed the usual pattern, but there was much about the day that was memorable and noteworthy. For the first time the printed programme had a 'logo' on its cover in the form of a woodcut designed by the artist Hilda Quick, a member of the orchestra. It represented a conductor with his arms outstretched in front of an orchestra, baton 'at the ready', and bears a striking resemblance to the stocky figure of Walter Barnes. It has been used on the Society's concert programmes ever since.

Hilda Quick

Hilda Quick was born in Penzance in 1895 and trained as an artist at the Central School of Art in London, later studying in Paris. She was a gifted artist specialising in wood engravings, and in 1930 she illustrated the complete works of Edmund Spenser for the Shakespeare Head Press. Her interest in the theatrical activity in West Cornwall led to her designing costumes, posters and programmes for many productions, including the Penzance Operatic Society and, in particular, the Minack Theatre. She also designed the costumes for the production of George Lloyd's opera, 'Iernin', which received its debut in Penzance in 1934.

In 1950 she moved to St Agnes, in the Isles of Scilly, to pursue her love of birds and flowers. She continued to produce wood engravings and in 1964 her illustrated edition of *Birds of the Scilly Isles* was published. She was always an active and popular member of any community in which she lived and remained productive as an artist until her death in 1978.

The soloist at the November 1929 concert was Miss Margaret Severn, contralto, and the orchestral work of especial interest was a 'Concertante Quartette' by Mozart for four wind instruments and orchestra. The soloists were Mr Alfred Brien, hautboy, (or oboe as we now know it), Mr Michael Cardew, clarinet, Mr Charles Baker, bassoon and Royal Marine bandsman, Mr William Parsons, horn.

Michael Cardew, a potter who had worked with Bernard Leach in St Ives, had presented the music of this composition to the orchestra in 1926 after he had discovered it in a library in Oxford. How he obtained the score and orchestral parts has not been recorded, but it was he who suggested to Walter Barnes that the orchestra should play it.

In the concert programme Walter Barnes explained that he had approached musicologists Rosa Newmarch and Ernest Newman and the composer Hamilton Harty for information about the work, none of whom had any knowledge of the piece. Dr Cyril Rootham of Cambridge was contacted by Mrs Crosbie Garstin and he "rather thought he had heard it at Salzburg, but was not sure." Walter gathered from this that the work had not been played in England for a very long time. Two years later the work was performed by the Royal Philharmonic Society, and *The Times* and other newspaper reviews claimed this performance as the first in England of a rare Mozart work. Walter later commented, "I suppose they were being careful not to tread on the toes of the touchy Cornishmen by once more showing to the World that Cornwall is not England."

Morgan Hosking later tried to clarify this through a friend, Charles Gregory, who had been a horn player in the Royal Philharmonic Orchestra and a member of the Royal Philharmonic Society. He wrote to their secretary who verified that the RPS had claimed it as a first English performance, and their concert programme for 5th November 1931 seems to confirm this,

though not actually saying so! Their detailed account of the provenance of the manuscript and more recent research into this work casts doubt on whether or not Mozart composed it as we now know it, but whatever its authenticity as a Mozart composition the performance by the Penzance Orchestral Society can still be regarded as the first in England.

This, in itself, is a fascinating story, but the concert performance was not without incident. Morgan Hosking remembered it vividly, not only because it was his first one playing in the orchestra at the back of the second violins, but because of the drama over the broken oboe. During the playing of the first movement of the Concertante Quartette something went wrong with Mr Brien's oboe, preventing him from playing. With great presence of mind, Walter took the Leader's violin and played the oboe part on it until the end of that movement. The performance was then halted and Walter explained to the audience that the interval would be taken early while they tried to remedy the situation. The orchestra's other oboist, Mr G. L. Bradley, had a daughter who was an optician in the town (she may even have been in the audience) and the broken oboe was taken to her office where a repair was effected.

After the interval the performance of the work continued without further incident. But Walter Barnes was taking no chances and he took Morgan Hosking's violin and kept it with him on the rostrum 'just in case'. It is not too hard to imagine the young violinist's feelings of disappointment at not being able to play and the realization that his position in the orchestra could easily be dispensed with.

Three newspaper reports record a night of gales and rainstorms, but two of them were at odds over the audience support, one reporting a good audience, another castigating the "Penzance folk" for their apathy – "Larger support has come from outside than from within the borough." Everyone concerned in the performance was highly praised, "It has been said that this orchestra is one of the best amateur orchestras in England....". Walter Barnes was congratulated for introducing the public to the Mozart Concertante Quartette and the information about it being rarely performed was emphasised. None of the newspaper accounts mention the disaster with the oboe, because, according to Morgan Hosking, this incident took place during the afternoon performance, thereby allowing the sixteen year old violinist his full part in the evening concert!

So as the nineteen twenties drew to a close the Penzance Orchestral Society had reached adulthood and had become a highly regarded and vital force in the cultural life of Cornwall, not only with its own concert performances, but providing a source of able musicians for other musical and dramatic groups in the area. Walter Barnes, now aged forty-five, was in his prime and, as "veritably the father of music in Penzance", on hand to guide them forward to even greater things.

Penzance Orchestral Society, St John's Hall c.1930. A view from the balcony of the auditorium showing how it embraced the orchestra. Note the specially installed overhead lighting.

4

Years of Development and Drama 1930-1936

Introduction

The years between nineteen thirty and nineteen thirty-six were especially significant for the Penzance Orchestral Society, musically and administratively. To provide a proper context for the Society's public performances during these years this chapter is devoted to important developments within its administration. It also reveals some of the problems which were encountered and resolved. Then, following diversions into both the artistic and broadcasting studio, the orchestra's involvement in the theatrical and operatic world of West Cornwall is detailed, culminating in the collaboration with George Lloyd and the birth of his opera, 'Iernin'. A separate chapter will provide the information about the Society's concerts during the same period.

The Junior Orchestra

The Junior Orchestra came into existence during the early months of 1930, though the only evidence for this is found in the annual accounts for the year ending May 1930, with the entry "Members contributions Junior Orchestra £7. 10s. 0d". There are no further details of its activities except similar entries in the next three years' accounts. In his 1937 history of the orchestra Walter Barnes simply says "In 1933 a Junior Section of the Orchestra was formed and has since been conducted by Morgan Hosking with great ability and enthusiasm, giving their own Annual Concerts". From this it seems that the Junior Orchestra met and rehearsed for the first three years with very few public performances, but was deemed ready by Sunday 25th May 1933 to give a concert in St John's Hall at 8 p.m. *The Cornishman* report says that the idea for the concert came from Walter Barnes and the Junior Orchestra itself and was arranged by the Mayoress, Mrs J. W. Meek, to raise funds for the West Cornwall Hospital.

The concert programme describes the orchestra as "Penzance Orchestral Society (Junior Section)", naming both J. Morgan Hosking and Walter Barnes as conductors. The soloists were local musicians, with Mrs Crosbie Garstin and Walter Barnes among them. The Secretary of the Junior Section was Lillian Tonkin who also played in the main orchestra from 1931. Along with songs, violin and cornet solos the orchestra played two overtures, Gluck's 'Iphigenie in Aulis' and 'Raymond' by Ambroise Thomas, the 'Intermezzo' from Mascagni's 'Cavalleria Rusticana', Schubert's 'Moments Musicals' and three movements from Mozart's Symphony No. 39. Mrs Garstin and Walter Barnes were the soloists in Vivaldi's 'Concerto in A Minor for two violins', making up a substantial programme. *The Cornishman* reported that St John's Hall was "comfortably crowded" despite it being a lovely evening of weather, and gave praise to all concerned, concluding that it was "An evening of beauty, yes, naturally and musically."

Contrary to what the name suggests, the Junior Orchestra was not intended only for instrumentalists of tender years. Its 'raison d'être' was to provide training and opportunities in ensemble playing for any inexperienced players, for those who wanted to learn a second instrument, or for players who wanted to improve their performance within the main orchestra. These ideals were expressed in an article entitled "The orchestra with a 'Reserve' Team" printed in *The Western Independent* for 6th June 1954. Morgan Hosking (by this time the conductor of the Orchestral Society) told the interviewer that: "There can be seen the spectacle of a senior and responsible member of the 'chiefs' experimentally plucking the comparatively rope-like strings of the double-bass in the reserves"

Walter Barnes asked other members of the senior orchestra to act as deputy conductors for him in the Junior Section, among them his daughter Enid. But the main burden fell onto the shoulders of the young Morgan Hosking and during the nineteen thirties Walter saw in him a musician whom he could encourage and nurture as a conductor with the aim of providing the orchestra with his successor when he felt ready to hand over the baton.

The Junior Orchestra continued to flourish and give annual concerts for charity in various towns such as St Buryan and Porthleven as well as Penzance, and provided a valuable 'pool' of improving players to sustain the senior orchestra. No one, now, remembers when the Junior Orchestra ceased to exist and its demise is not recorded in the Society's minutes. It was probably in the early nineteen sixties when the musical scene in Cornwall was expanding, providing more opportunities, through the developing county music service and the Cornwall Rural Music School, for instrumentalists to acquire greater expertise and experience.

Problems of Pitch

In the 1931 Penzance Orchestral Society Annual Accounts there is a puzzling entry – "Special Donation Fund £91. 0s. 0d" – which was a lot of money at that time! What was this all about? All is revealed in 1932 when a separate "Low Pitch Fund" account appears which includes the sum of £91. 0s. 0d as being "Donations to 14th May 1931" and the additional figure of £36. 11s. 0d being "Donations to May 14th 1932" producing a total of £127. 11s. 0d. More light is shed on the subject from a note in the concert programme for November 1931:

> *At this concert the orchestra are for the first time performing at low pitch, and so coming into line with the standard pitch used by the great orchestras of the world. The Society offers its sincere thanks to all those ladies and gentlemen who have so kindly contributed to the great cost of the change from high to low pitch.*

The problems of pitch had been hotly debated for many years coming to a head in the late nineteenth century. The complexities of the subject are discussed at length in Groves Dictionary of Music and Musicians, but Percy Young's book *The Concert Tradition* provides a concise résumé of the argument which centred around the pre-eminence of the organ, with its high pitch, and woodwind instrument makers insisting that a high pitch ensured better tone. The gradual rise in pitch over the centuries resulted in not only some chaotic results with orchestral performances but also in great discomfort for singers in works such as Beethoven's 'Choral Symphony', "where the sopranos have rows of high A's to sing, which with the high pitch of the orchestral instruments, were strained into painful A-sharp yelps". On the continent a lower pitch had been established known as the 'diapason normal' and the Royal Philharmonic Society had adopted this in 1895.

So Penzance were at last facing the challenge and appealing for help to defray the costs of making the change from high to low pitch, though the entries under expenditure from this fund do not always seem to reflect its purpose. Can "Installation of Gas Fires £6. 7s. 6d", or "Conductor's Music Desk £1. 2s. 6d", or "Librarian's Shelves 18s. 6d" really be connected with the pitch problem? Let us assume that the music lovers of Penzance were over-generous with their donations allowing a few less essential items to be purchased by the Society. The fund gradually diminished and faded from sight within a very few years.

Discordant Notes

The generally harmonious co-operation between the various musical groups in and around Penzance suffered a setback during 1930 and 1931. Walter Barnes usually led an orchestra, when one was required, for the Penzance Choral Society, but a series of letters which have been preserved reveal a severe breakdown in relations between the Orchestral and Choral Societies at this time.

Even with the balm of passing decades it would be unwise to introduce names into the story, but it seems that a clash of personalities between the conductors of the Societies and some of the leading members resulted in formal but increasingly acrimonious letters being exchanged, chiefly between the two Secretaries, over whether or not Walter Barnes should lead an orchestra for the Choral Society's performance of 'Hiawatha' on 5th December 1930. He was named as leader in a newspaper advertisement for which the Choral Society denied all responsibility.

The true facts of this sad episode will never be discovered but *The Cornishman* report of the concert reveals that the orchestra was led by Mrs May Hocking, the former May Stewart, leader of the Orchestral Society until 1927. The disputatious correspondence continued through December and on into February 1931. It seems that two members from the Societies who met in the street one day nearly had a public fight over the issues involved, and even as late as 1933 things were still unresolved, with the possibility of solicitors being brought in by the Orchestral Society.

This was, thankfully, a very rare occurrence and it is to be hoped of short duration. Certainly in years to come relations between the two Societies resumed their normal harmonious state.

Within the Orchestral Society itself all was not always sweetness and light as even among amateur musicians 'professional' jealousies can erupt and cause difficulties. One such problem occurred in the 1938-39 season when the minutes record that Mr Freddie Hodson volunteered to interview the second trumpeter to try and persuade him to end the disagreement between him and the first trumpet. As no further reference is made to this, we can assume Mr Hodson was successful. He was the Chairman at another committee meeting when the problem of a bassoon player was discussed. The bassoonist, who played an instrument belonging to the Society, had not attended any practices and it fell to Mr Hodson to call on him and reclaim the bassoon. Freddie Hodson taught English at the Penzance County School for Boys from 1910 until his retirement in 1949, and is always referred to warmly. In his history of the school *Three Score Years and Ten* published in 1980 Ben Batten refers to him as "genial, inventive and witty", so perhaps his experience of handling schoolboys well equipped him for dealing with troublesome musicians!

The Bandroom

It seems fairly likely that from 1922 onwards, rehearsals of the Penzance Orchestral Society were held in the building in Chapel Street, known as the Mounts Bay Academy. The earliest known Minutes of the Society are from Friday 29th September 1933 when a Special Meeting of the General Committee was held. It appears that a property had become available in Queen Street, Penzance which had been the Conservative Club Room, "now known as 'The Sunrise Cafe'", and a Sub-Committee had been set up by the Society to look into the posssibility of buying or leasing it from the owner, Mr Ellis Slack, a town Councillor and local businessmen.

The Sub-Committee reported that the purchase price was £450 with immediate possession, and after some discussion on details the General Committee voted unanimously that the Society should go ahead with the purchase. Five Trustees were appointed to be responsible for the new acquisition, Mr Frank Latham (President of the Society), Miss W. Beadsworth, Mr A. W. Robinson, Mr William Lloyd and Mr Barrie Bennetts. The Operatic Society was represented at this meeting and re-assured that if they continued to share the use of the Orchestra's practice room the rent would continue to be "about the same as at present".

A mortgage had to be arranged to facilitate the purchase and from the "Sunrise Café Building Account" forming part of the Annual Accounts for the year ending May 1934, a loan of £450 was made by Mrs W. Barnes, Walter's wife. Morgan Hosking thought that it was through Alfred Robinson that the loan was arranged and not to be repaid until he died. Whatever the arrangements were, the purchase was made possible and the Accounts and Minutes do, from time to time, refer to sums of money being used to pay off the mortgage.

A number of improvements were made to the new rehearsal room: heating pipes were installed and various other repairs were effected amounting to about £60 but offset by the sale of fixtures and fittings in the old venue to its owner. The first rehearsal in the new Bandroom took place on Friday 8th November 1933 and there was a formal opening ceremony during which the President, Frank Latham, made a speech and the Leader, Mrs Crosbie Garstin, was invited to officially declare the room open, perhaps as an acknowledgement of her recent gift of new oak music stands to the orchestra. Walter Barnes thanked both Mr Latham and Mrs Garstin for their kind remarks about him and "made us get on with the rehearsal immediately"!

Over the ensuing years the Bandroom became a real 'home' for the orchestra, as well as a welcome source of additional income from rents for its use by other musical groups such as the Operatic Society and Newlyn Male Choir to name but two. Its walls were, and remain today, lined with photographs, and the Society's music is stored in cupboards, as well as bulky instruments housed there.

The Orchestral Society at rehearsal in their bandroom in the 1930s.

Of course, the ownership of a property was not without its problems. Not long after they had bought it the Society received a complaint from the person living next door to the Band Room that they had taken away her chimney-pot without asking her permission and she now wished it to be reinstated. The pot had been considered dangerous and removed by the Society who thought it was part of their new property. The neighbour's claim to the chimney pot resulted in the floor boards of the Band Room being removed to "ascertain if there was once a fireplace underneath, in which case it would seem that the chimney was ours". The Treasurer, Mr A. W. Firth, was left to deal with this and "investigated the question of the chimney and had found that (the neighbour) was quite in order in asking to have it restored. This had been done at a cost of 25s".

Over the years the minutes of the Society include many references to work needing to be carried out on the Band Room. This was sometimes carried out by professional tradesmen after getting estimates and on other occasions a working party from the Society would be organised to do the work. But these occasional problems and their resolution in no way detracted from the tremendous benefits which owning their own practice room has conferred on the Society, and, in no small measure, contributed to its stability and longevity.

Subscribers and Friends Scheme

The earliest indication that the Orchestral Society had any sort of mailing list of its supporters comes in the concert programme in March 1936, where at the end of the programme a note is added: "Do you Receive Our Preliminary Circular? If not and you wish to be informed of forthcoming concerts, please send name and address to the Hon. Secretary, H. D. Morris, Polwithen, Penzance." This was a form of extra publicity for the orchestra and not a money-raising exercise. Later in the year it occurred to the Committee that regular supporters should be invited to join a Subscription Scheme, which was agreed at a Committee Meeting in September 1936. The subscription was to be 10s. 6d or 7s. 6d for the year, entitling ticket holders to one ticket of either 5s. 0d or 3s. 6d at the Spring and Autumn concerts: subscribers would receive a seating plan and "the usual seats would be permanently reserved on payment of a subscription."

During the 1936-1937 and 1937-1938 seasons twenty-two subscribers are recorded producing modest guaranteed ticket income, but at the beginning of the 1938-39 season out of the 168 people appealed to, over 100 had responded, producing over £60 for the season ahead and this support continued. It was not until 1938 that details of the scheme were included in the concert programme when in December a whole page was devoted to it. By this time it had developed to annual subscriptions of £1. 1s. 0d (two tickets per annum); 10s. 6d (one ticket per annum) or 5s. 0d for "Friends of the Society", with all categories entitled to priority booking.

At the Annual General Meeting in June 1948 an effort to increase the number of subscribers was announced and Morgan Hosking suggested that, in view of the large amount of work this would generate for the Treasurer, a new post of Subscribers' Secretary should be created, and Miss Winifrede Beadsworth was elected. This post occasionally reverted back to the Treasurer for short periods, but generally the Scheme and its Secretary has continued, with minor modifications, through to the present day.

National Federation of Music Societies

The National Federation of Music Societies had been set up in 1935 with the intention of improving education by promoting and assisting public performances. It was not until 1939 that their representative, a Mr Weaver, was invited to a committee meeting to explain the advantages of becoming affiliated to the Federation. The Society applied for affiliation for a fee of two guineas. Mr Weaver was made an honorary member of the Society and was asked to represent them on the regional committee. He often attended committee meetings over ensuing years to advise and guide the Society through the complexities of grant funding from the Carnegie Trust via the N.F.M.S.

"I was there..."

Despite his incredibly busy musical life Walter Barnes found time, in 1933, to commit himself to involvement in another sphere of the creative arts. It would result in an enduring memorial to him and through him to the Penzance Orchestral Society.

The artist and doyen of the Newlyn School of Artists, Stanhope Forbes, had been a member of Walter's orchestra in its early formative years, from 1909 to 1911. He had learned to play the 'cello during the time he was working on his painting 'The Village Philharmonic', completed in 1888. He told his wife-to-be, Elizabeth Armstrong, that "I did something on Monday I ought not to have done. I had my first lesson on the 'cello. You won't be enlightened by the result I fear, I am put back to making all kinds of... sounds, shakes, tremors, arpeggios etc". How diligent a pupil he was is not recorded, but by 1909 he was at least capable of being a member of the 'cello section of the orchestra.

Stanhope Forbes and Walter Barnes were friends, and each was intrigued by the other's artistic capabilities. This resulted in Stanhope Forbes inviting Walter to sit for him to paint his portrait in 1933. Apparently the artist insisted on Walter wearing the same clothes at each sitting and if he wore a white instead of a blue shirt would send him back home to change, much to his annoyance. "Walter Barnes almost exploded when he saw the minimal amount of shirt exposed in the painting". But he was forgiving because he appreciated Forbes' attention to detail.

There are two contemporary accounts of this artistic undertaking. One is from *The Cornishman* entitled "A Cornish Musician's Portrait: Walter Barnes as Stanhope Forbes, R.A. sees him: a Penzance celebrity at the Newlyn Gallery". This is a long and detailed account of the artist's work, and the painting of Walter Barnes in particular. The writer, 'H. T.', the memorable Herbert Thomas, tells us that the portrait is "Impressive and satisfying, both as a picture and as a portrait. Mr Barnes is seated, and in the act of playing his favourite violin. The lighting of the strong features, and the light on the instrument and bow hand, is achieved with masterly touch, and one is struck with the contrast between the powerful build of the violinist and the light and delicate movement of the hand as it manipulates the bow. How was this caught so happily? Well, during the sitting in the Forbes' studio at Higher Faugan, Mr Barnes beguiled the artist and himself by playing each and every favourite air that Mr Forbes named, and it is difficult to imagine anything more conducive to real inspiration and naturalness, for it made painting doubly a labour of love, while posing as a model ceased to be a tiresome ordeal to the sitter".

The other, much more personal account of the painting of the portrait is from the memory of Stanhope Forbes' butler at the time, Lambert Ivey, recorded before his death in 1996. Lambert was born in 1903 and lived in the village of Townshend from a very young age. He was taught to play the piano and had a life-long love affair with the instrument, becoming a talented pianist and teacher. He had many friends in Newlyn, among them the family of the young Morgan Hosking and his sister, Dora, and took part in the many concert parties in which those two young musicians were involved during the 1920s. In 1926 Lambert worked as a gardener but was looking for a change of employment and experience so when he saw an advertisement in the local paper for a position in the household of Stanhope Forbes at Higher Faugan in Newlyn he eagerly applied for, and was offered, the post.

Lambert Ivey's relationship with Stanhope Forbes and his second wife, Maudie, flourished through their mutual love of music. She was an able pianist and she and Lambert played duets

together and he also accompanied Stanhope on the 'cello. Musical entertainment was a frequent after dinner diversion at Higher Faugan, when many local artists would be among the guests. Lambert would be asked to play and as the musical part of the evening rarely began before 9 p.m. he would resign himself to another "of these all night jobs", for he described the family and their guests as "night crows"!

Painting was, of course, the prime activity at Higher Faugan and Lambert would have seen the master at work on many paintings. Stanhope Forbes occasionally worked on portraiture and had painted pictures of Madame Gilardoni, the famous singer, and portraits of local people such as Edward Bolitho, Alderman R. G. Rowe of Helston and others. And in 1933 he carried out a long cherished desire by painting Walter Barnes.

When reminded of this, Lambert Ivey responded eagerly, "Yes, and I was there". Usually Mr Forbes worked in the studio, his favourite room in the house. Here there was a large table at which the family often ate, and a large open fire which burnt peat especially brought down from Scotland and, as 'HT' has written, some of the work on the painting was carried out there. But on other occasions sittings took place in the drawing room because Lambert would be told by Stanhope Forbes that, "Mr Barnes is coming on Sunday and I want you to play the piano for him while I work".

The music that Lambert played would include such items as the 'Rondo Capriccioso' by Mendelssohn, or other favourite pieces requested by Walter Barnes or Stanhope Forbes. Sometimes Mrs Forbes would also be present at these sittings and afterwards Walter would stay to lunch. Lambert Ivey got to know Walter Barnes well and was always a regular member of the audience at the Penzance Orchestral concerts during the years of Walter Barnes' conductorship and later when Lambert's old friend, Morgan Hosking, became the conductor. He regarded his years at Higher Faugan as some of the happiest of his life.

The finished portrait was first hung in the Opie Memorial Gallery in Newlyn and 'HT's article concludes "Those who wend their way to the Newlyn gallery can decide whether they share my belief that the men and the moment have met and produced harmony in colour as well as harmony of sound in the studio".

In the spring of 1934 it was hung in the Royal Academy, but prior to this, on Tuesday 6th March, the Orchestral Society Committee held a special meeting after the rehearsal to discuss a proposal put forward by Frank Latham, President of the Society. He suggested that the Mayor should make an appeal at the concert the following day to patrons of the Society for contributions to a fund for the purpose of purchasing the painting. This would result in the portrait being the property of the public, but would be hung in the Society's Bandroom for the time being.

Walter Barnes was not present at this meeting but the Secretary reported that he "did not approve at all of this suggestion" though his Leader, Mrs Garstin, did. She "thought it would be a great pity to miss such an opportunity", and after much discussion it was decided that the matter be "got on with". Printed slips were to be produced for insertion in the following day's concert programme with the name and address of Councillor H. D. Morris as Hon. Treasurer of the Barnes Portrait Fund. The portrait was also referred to in an article in the *Western Morning News* for Thursday 19 April 1934 entitled "Cornwall at the Academy" which said "Cousin Jacks who visit the Royal Academy this year will be pleased to see two old friends represented on the walls – one by his work and the other by his portrait".

The whereabouts of the portrait between 1934 and 1937 is not recorded but at the Society's Thirtieth Anniversary Concert on the evening of Tuesday 16th March 1937 the picture was presented to the President of the Orchestral Society, Frank Latham, by the Mayor of Penzance, Alderman Robert Thomas. The Mayor, in his speech, regarded the presentation as a dual tribute, "it not only shows the appreciation of the public to the Society, but also conveys in no uncertain way how much they want to retain a permanent memorial to this brilliant son of Penzance." He also told the audience that Stanhope Forbes had accepted a lower than normal price for the picture and that he had donated £20 of the sum to the Extension Fund of West Cornwall Hospital, which was a generous gesture.

At an orchestral committee meeting on 1st May 1937 it was recorded that the portrait would be hung over the conductor's rostrum in the Band Room and "suitably enclosed". It remained there for many years, only being removed to St John's Hall for special commemorative concerts. More recently it has been given, on permanent loan, to the Penlee House Gallery and Museum in Penzance where it can be seen as part of the Newlyn School collection of paintings.

BBC Broadcasts

In July 1934 the Director of the Western Region of The British Broadcasting Corporation, Reginald Redman, wrote to the Penzance Orchestral Society inviting them to broadcast their next concert on Wednesday 28th November, and asking for details of programme and soloists. The Secretary was asked to forward the information as soon as possible, and the Committee members decided to engage the famous violinist, Albert Sammons, for this concert.

A programme was discussed including an offer received from a harpsichord player, Miss Eleanor Wilkinson. She was willing to travel from London to play in the Respighi 'Ancient Dances and Airs' for £3. 0s. 0d plus her expenses, and the committee agreed to engage her. A local soloist, Miss Clarice Edwards, was asked to sing and Reginald Redman was invited to conduct his own composition, a suite called 'From a Moorish Village'. An overture was chosen and, at this point in the proceedings, Strauss's 'Blue Danube' waltz was programmed, with a male chorus, but this did not appear in the concert, when Smetana's 'Vltava' was played instead. In the minutes a programme plan with timings of each item was given with three minutes being allocated after each item for the applause!

Advertisements for this concert on Wednesday 28th November 1934 included the following: "For the first time in Penzance the first part of the concert will be broadcast by the British Broadcasting Corporation on the Western Region from St John's Hall. Patrons are kindly requested to be in their seats by 7.25, the broadcast commences punctually at 7.30". It is not hard to imagine the excitement this concert engendered among the members of the orchestra and its supporters, as well as a feeling of pride and responsibility at having been chosen for a live broadcast.

The *Western Morning News* music critic wrote a long report of the occasion the following day giving due weight to its importance, "....the broadcast of the Society's concert marked a step forward in the recognition of musical and orchestral talent in the West." Apparently there was not a vacant seat in St John's Hall and the audience came from "all parts of Central and West Cornwall." Albert Sammons' performance of the 'Concerto No. 1 in G Minor' by Max Bruch was complimented as were the songs sung by Miss Clarice Edwards, but much more was written about Respighi's 'Ancient Dances and Airs'.

According to the programme this was a first performance in the West of England and as well as Eleanor Wilkinson playing the harpsichord, Mrs Crosbie Garstin and Miss Enid Barnes were violin and 'cello soloists. Reginald Redman's 'From a Moorish Village' produced the interesting fact that "in Penzance Museum a Moorish drum was found to fit in exactly with the theme of Mr Redman's score. The drum, which is about 4 ft long, is played horizontally by tapping it with the fingers."

The reception on the radio was "almost ideal, there was a complete absence of fading or distortion, and the instrumental tone came through with admirable clarity." This first recording of the orchestra was regarded as successful and Walter Barnes received several letters of appreciation, including one from the Penzance Chamber of Commerce, and the BBC broadcast the Society's orchestral concerts on six further occasions. In his 1937 retrospect of the orchestra Walter Barnes was proud to point out that the concert was "broadcast on the Empire wavelength and was heard by Cornishmen all over the world."

Coverage of this concert in *The Cornishman* was extensive and informative. The writer had interviewed Albert Sammons who described Walter Barnes as a conductor, "who knows how to handle the instrumentalists... that is the great secret and he gets the best out of them".

An accompanying article reported that Albert Sammons had been taken by his host, Alfred Robinson, to meet Albert Coad, the Penzance violin maker, and the famous violinist had been impressed and delighted by Mr Coad's fiddles. Albert Coad was a well known and distinguished violin maker who had been awarded gold and silver medals in London and was described in the 'Strad' magazine as one of the finest makers at this time.

With the compliments of
THE BRITISH BROADCASTING CORPORATION

WEDNESDAY
977 kc/s 307.1 m.
West Regional

WALTER BARNES conducts the concert to be given by the Penzance Orchestral Society, with Albert Sammons and Eleanor Wilkinson as soloists, this evening at 7.30.

10.15 THE DAILY SERVICE

Time Signal, Greenwich, at 10.30

10.30 Weather Forecast for Farmers and Shipping

10.45 *Regional Programme*

(*See page 675*)

5.15 The Children's Hour
'The Island in the Mist', by Franklyn Kelsey
8—'The Blockade'

6.0 *Time Signal, Greenwich*
'The First News'

CHOIR
The Wanderer .... *Elgar*
Ar hyd y nos (All through the night); Rhyfelgyrch Gwyr Harlech (March of the Men of Harlech) — *arr. Harry Evans*

This Party was founded by the present conductor in 1909, and seventy-seven prizes have been won at Eisteddfodau.

ORCHESTRA
Concert Waltz, Dancing Nights — *Eric Coates*

CHOIR
Three Negro Spirituals: Go down, Moses; Peter, go ring dem bells; Were you there? — *arr. Bantock*

ORCHESTRA
Malaguena .... *Moszkowski*

7.30 An Orchestral Concert
Relayed from St. John's Hall, Penzance
ALBERT SAMMONS (violin)
ELEANOR WILKINSON (harpsichord)
THE PENZANCE ORCHESTRAL SOCIETY
(Leader, Lilian Garstin)
Conducted by WALTER BARNES

ORCHESTRA
Overture, Iphigenia in Aulis ... *Gluck*

This Society was formed in 1906 and still has the same President and Hon. Conductor. Three of the original members are still with the Society which is now giving its sixty-fifth concert; the members come from all parts of Cornwall to rehearse.

ELEANOR WILKINSON AND ORCHESTRA
Ancient Dances and Airs for the Lute *trans. Respighi (Sixteenth Century)*
1. Ballet, Il Conto Orlando (Simone Molinari, 1599); 2. Gagliarde (Vincenzo Galilei, 155?); 3. Villanella (Anon., end of the Sixteenth Century); 4. Passo mezzo e Mascherada (Anon., end of the Sixteenth Century)

ALBERT SAMMONS AND ORCHESTRA
Concerto in G minor ...... *Max Bruch*

The Radio Times *entry for the first BBC broadcast in November 1934.* Morrab Library, Penzance

All the World's a Stage...

Following the successful performances of 'A Midsummer Night's Dream' in the meadow at Crean during August 1929 this production was repeated in July 1930 with a slightly altered cast and with Enid Barnes' place at the keyboard taken by Mr E. Fuglar Thomas, FRCO "at the Organ". More of Mendelssohn's music was played by a larger orchestra of fourteen instrumentalists and songs were included sung by Miss Annie Jefferey, Miss Eileen Ash and Miss Edith Trenary (the future Mrs Edith Angove).

This time *The Cornishman* report was more fulsome in its praise of the orchestra saying "If it were only to listen to Mendelssohn's Incidental Music played by an orchestra, under Mr Walter Barnes' able leadership, the evening would have been a thoroughly enjoyable one". The proceeds were, once again, donated to the West Cornwall Hospital and also the Y.M.C.A.

The first production at the Minack Theatre. Shakespeare's 'The Tempest', 1932. Walter Barnes and a small orchestra can be seen to the left of the stage. Note the variety of the seating in foreground.

Two years later, during the week of 16th – 20th August 1932, Walter Barnes and fifteen members of his orchestra were to be found on the cliffs near Porthcurno. After the success of the production of 'A Midsummer Nights Dream' during the previous two summers the company of drama enthusiasts, led by Dorothea Valentine and Rowena Cade, had decided to move their activities to an area of cliff in Rowena Cade's garden. During the spring of 1932, she had created a natural amphitheatre to accommodate an outdoor stage and auditorium for a performance of 'The Tempest'. This was the first production at the now world-famous Minack Theatre. Once again, Walter Barnes was asked to organise the orchestra, and they played Sir Arthur Sullivan's 'Incidental Music to the Tempest'. The performances attracted attention from national newspapers, with a report in *The Times* and the *Daily Mail* as well as the local newspapers. The *Daily Mail* report is well worth noting for the fact that it said that the music "was rendered by an orchestra of 12, conducted by Mr Wagner Barne". One wonders what Walter's reaction to that would have been!!

In November 1932, the Falmouth Opera Singers performed Mozart's 'Il Seraglio' in which Penzance players were involved.

The Falmouth Opera Singers

The Falmouth Opera Singers was created in 1923 by two remarkable sisters, the Misses Evelyn and Maisie Radford and it became known as an important force for pioneering operatic productions of national importance. Their work has been vividly portrayed in their delightful book *Musical Adventures in Cornwall*, and also given an excellent summary by Geoffrey Self in his *Music in West Cornwall*. The sisters were involved, in some way or another, with most of the musical institutions in the County, and they made an enormous contribution to Cornish music-making at all levels, from Women's Institutes to the County Music Competitions. They were wonderful, eccentric ladies, fine scholars and musicians, and loved by everyone, so that members of the Penzance orchestra were part of their annual operatic productions for many years, both before and after the Second World War.

During August 1933 Walter Barnes was again at the Minack Theatre, conducting an orchestra of sixteen players from his orchestra for a production of 'Twelfth Night'. The music chosen was all by Mozart, the Overture to 'Il Seraglio', the Allegro-Minuet Movement from Symphony No. 39 in E Flat and the 'Eine Kleine Nacht musik' Serenade. The producer of this production, Ernest Pierce, had written a moving tribute to this production which was printed on the title page of the programme. "In the Autumn days of my life I shall ever remember the golden hours spent rehearsing Shakespeare's 'Twelfth Night' on the sun bathed cliffs, and recall with a sensitive gratefulness the whole-hearted cooperation of the splendid company to whom I owe the success of this production".

Cornwall Shakespeare Festival

Ernest Pierce had had a distinguished career as an actor, theatre manager and producer, and he came to Cornwall in 1928 to devote himself to painting and etching. He had become involved

Cornish Shakespeare Festival Group, including Walter Barnes, Enid Barnes and Morgan Hosking.

with the Minack Theatre production of 'The Tempest' in 1932 as a makeup supervisor! He was very impressed with the dramatic talent he found in Cornwall and this, combined with his passion and enthusiasm for the works of The Bard inspired him to create a Cornwall Shakespearian Festival in 1934. It was an ambitious venture with a company made up of drama students, professionals and talented locals. They had their own bus and travelled throughout the county presenting half a dozen plays for four days a week, sometimes giving two performances a day, for the months of July and August.

Walter Barnes was the Musical Director for these Festivals, which continued throughout the nineteen thirties. It was a huge commitment for all those involved, but especially for musicians who gave their time and talent to so many organisations during the rest of the year and could reasonably have expected a break during the summer. The Festivals ceased during the War, but were revived afterwards with amateur productions, and Ernest Pierce was the moving spirit behind the Penzance Town Council's decision to build an open air theatre in Penlee Park where the plays were presented for some years. Ernest Pierce also produced some of the shows for Penzance and St Ives Operatic Societies before he left the area in 1951.

Back in Penzance in early January 1934 the Orchestral Society provided the musical accompaniments for 'A Mixed Grill' at the Pavilion Theatre. This was presented by the St Levan Players and Singers. It was advertised to include "The First Stage Performance in the West of Ravel's 'Bolero', the Sensation of the Continent", (following the ballet's first performance at the Paris Opera in 1928). The proceeds from this "merry, bright, non-stop" event were to go to local charities and the Penzance Orchestral Society. The programme is a delightful creation in itself, with decorations in the form of an attractive woodcut on the cover by Hilda Quick, and a small design on the back page depicting the initials of the four main people responsible for the show, Dorothea Valentine, Dorothy Cade, Hilda Quick and Walter Barnes.

The content of the programme comprised sketches, songs and dances, and the orchestra, led by Mrs Crosbie Garstin, contributed the opening and closing items, a march 'By Imperial Command' by Safroni, and Franz Lehar's 'Gold and Silver' Waltz, as well as a performance of Strauss's 'Blue Danube' Waltz with the male chorus of the Operatic Society. The personnel involved were mostly those involved in the Minack Theatre productions and it was, perhaps, a jolly way of acknowledging the Society's help at the theatre in previous years. The Society's account for May 1934 includes a donation of £22.0s.0d given by Miss Valentine, which was, presumably, a share of the proceeds of 'A Mixed Grill'.

In May 1934 Gladys Tranter and her pupils at the County Grammar School for Girls in Penzance put on a production of 'Dido and Aeneas' in the Pavilion Theatre, as part of the 'coming of age' celebrations of the School. This was the first time an opera had been attempted by the County School and Walter Barnes conducted the performance, with a string orchestra of sixteen players led, as usual, by Mrs Garstin. The music mistress, Miss Dorothy Lake, trained the singers and Miss Marjorie Nash the dancers, "few of whom had any previous notion how to get arms and legs to obey the music!"

The first rehearsal with the orchestra took place in the orchestra's Bandroom and Gladys Tranter recalled that there were 67 children and the orchestra. The heat generated by all these bodies caused water to run freely down the windows! When the children became noisy, Walter would shout, "Now then!" and peace would be restored, but he was fond of children and was especially pleased with Nancy Bateman who sang the role of Dido. Miss Tranter also remembered Nancy's pure, lovely voice on this her only known public performance as a singer. The details of the production are vividly portrayed by Gladys in her history of the school, 'The Human Spring', and the local paper called the three or four performances "much above the average standard of school entertainment."

Walter Barnes, writing afterwards to Dorothy Lake, obviously enjoyed the whole thing, calling it "a joy from beginning to end. It was a good show". His work, along with that of the orchestra, was greatly appreciated and was warmly acknowledged in the programme. Walter was given a gift in the form of a cigarette box accompanied by a note saying "wishing you a 'bowsey farewell' but hoping to meet you again someday" – a reference to words in the opera, and written by the producer of the opera, Gladys Tranter.

Walter and the orchestra's participation in local drama continued, both at the Minack Theatre, the Cornwall Shakespeare Festivals and with groups such as the Penzance Players. In 1935 a triple bill of plays was produced at the Minack Theatre one of which was called 'The Play of the Weather' by John Heywood. It was presented by a local company, but a staff photographer from *The Times* went to see it. This resulted in a large half page photograph in *The Times* for Wednesday 14th August 1935, in which Walter Barnes and the orchestra can be seen on the left hand side.

AN IMPRESSION OF THE MUSICAL REHEARSAL
AT THE MINACK THEATRE AUG. 9TH 1935
by one of the élite.

In pious anger with lifted hand,
He solemnly cursed that rascally band.
He cursed the 'cello, he cursed the horn,
He damned the day that each was born;
He cursed the oboe, he cursed the flute
From the crown of his cap to the sole of his boot;
He cursed them in breathing, he cursed them in blowing,
He cursed them in stopping, in fing'ring, in bowing,
He cursed the harp, he cursed the bassoon,
But what gave rise
To no little surprise.
NONE OF THEM PLAYED ANY BETTER IN TUNE.

George Lloyd and the Creation of 'Iernin'

In the autumn of 1934 a remarkable event took place in Penzance, one which caught the attention of the operatic cognoscenti of England and focused their cosmopolitan eyes and ears on a small seaside town in West Cornwall.

During the week of the 5th to the 10th November an opera was performed at the Pavilion Theatre on the promenade in Penzance. Its title was 'Iernin' and the composer was a handsome twenty-one year old Cornishman called George Lloyd. Just under a year later, in June 1935, the opera was produced professionally at the Lyceum Theatre in London and received favourable notices in most of the national papers.

These are the basic facts of a memorable and unique event in the annals of the Penzance Orchestral Society. But before putting the flesh on these bare bones of the story one or two questions need to be answered. Who was George Lloyd? What was his connection with the Penzance orchestra?

George Lloyd was born in St Ives on 28th June, 1913, the son of Primrose and William Lloyd, two able amateur musicians. Primrose was a violin and viola player and William a talented flautist and all three were members of the orchestra. They divided their time between London and St Ives, but it was the latter that the family regarded as 'home'. The house, St Iaia, overlooked St Ives' bay and had a large studio which had been built for one of the local artists. It was big enough to accommodate a small orchestra and the Lloyds gathered other local musicians here to play chamber music whenever they were in Cornwall.

Ill health prevented George from regular attendance at school, but he began playing the violin at the age of five and was writing music by the age of ten. Mrs Loveday (Paddy) Pinchen remembered playing violin duets with him and it is likely, as she had been taught by Walter Barnes, that George also received lessons from him. Later he studied in London with the great violinist, Albert Sammons, and had lessons in counterpoint with C. H. Kitson, a member of staff at the Royal College of Music. After studying composition under Harry Farjeon at the Royal Academy of Music, George Lloyd wrote his first symphony in 1932, aged nineteen, and conducted its first performance at the Penzance Orchestral Society's concert on 23rd November 1932.

Despite this early symphonic achievement George was captivated by opera. His father, who was born and brought up in Italy, was a lover of Italian opera and educated his son in the works of such Italian composers as Vivaldi, Pergolesi, Bellini and Puccini. George was often teased by

'Iernin', 1934. Left to right: *Sydney Russell (Producer), William Lloyd (Librettist), Walter Barnes (Leader of Orchestra), Gaby Vallé (Soprano), Mrs William Lloyd (at the piano) and George Lloyd (Composer and Conductor) during rehearsal.* The George Lloyd Music Library, Kendal

his family for his devotion to the score of Verdi's 'Othello', calling it his bible! He had been seduced by the soprano and tenor voices combined with the colour and drama of operatic orchestration.

William and Primrose Lloyd became great friends with Walter Barnes and regularly invited him to their home in London to enjoy the season of Italian opera at Covent Garden. On one of these visits, probably in 1933, over breakfast after a performance, the two men were grumbling about the lack of an English opera school such as those in Italy, France and Germany. Walter said, "Well, if they cannot produce English opera, what about having Cornish opera? If you two get together to write it, I will get together the people to perform it in Penzance". "Are you serious?", asked William. "Yes, I am", replied Walter, and so work began. Within a few days, William Lloyd had produced the libretto for 'Iernin', and George began to compose the music.

The family house in Cornwall was, by this time, Bridge Cottage in Zennor, and it was on the moors and cliffs around there that George gathered his inspiration for the music of 'Iernin'. The story is based on the Cornish legend of the fairy maidens turned to stone by the curse of a Christian priest, for tempting mortals by bewitching them with their singing and dancing to become their lovers. George "had feelings for the stones", sensing that they had a mysterious life of their own and the opera is set at 'The Nine Maidens (a stone circle on the moor)', as it is described in the libretto.

One year later Walter Barnes again visited the Lloyds in London; George had worked late into the night before his arrival to complete the score. From then on the venture was under way and William Lloyd engaged a professional producer, Sydney Russell, to manage the production. The four leading roles were sung by professionals, Gaby Vallé, Bruce Flegg, Philip Bertram and Mona Thomas, but the rest of the cast and chorus were made up of good local amateurs, many being members of the Penzance Operatic Society.

An orchestra of forty, led by Walter, was chosen from the Orchestral Society, with George Lloyd as the conductor. (Morgan Hosking, leading the second violins in the orchestra, recalled frequent temperamental clashes between the young conductor and his experienced leader!) Behind the scenes were the Operatic Society's Stage Manager, Electrician, Wardrobe Mistress etc, and the costumes and scenery were designed by Hilda Quick, the well known local woodcut artist and designer.

The opening night was Guy Fawkes Night, 5th November 1934, and performances

'Iernin', 1934. The full cast. The George Lloyd Music Library, Kendal

continued throughout the week, with full houses each night. Apparently the lead tenor's daughter was born on the opening night and was, appropriately, named Iernin. Among the audience on the first night was the *Times* chief music critic, Frank Howes, who had a holiday home in the area. His review appeared in 'The Thunderer' on the 7th November, giving the performance unexpected prominence. He revealed that on the first night an illness "virtually robbed the last act of its chief figure" and that the performance "was presented under the difficulties inherent in amateur operatic productions", but that to anyone who knew the location for the setting of the opera "and has floundered through bogs and gorse to these unapproachable stone maidens it is as queer an experience to listen to the translation of their history into music in Cornwall itself as to hear 'The Meistersingers' in the city of Nuremburg".

Of the opera itself and its composer he was very complimentary and said that George Lloyd, "showed that rarest of all qualities in a British composer, an almost unerring perception of what the stage requires. He has written out of the blue a full-length opera in which the balance of interest is fairly held between the voices, the stage situations, and the orchestra. To have realised that greatest of all operatic problems is an extraordinary achievement". About the orchestra he thought that they had given "an account of a fairly complex score that was more taut than most amateurs can achieve". This long, detailed, and enthusiastic write up concludes,

'Iernin' at the Pavilion Theatre, Penzance, 1934. The George Lloyd Music Library, Kendal

"Who would have expected to find opera at Land's End, and, what is more, a good opera?"

The result of this influential music correspondent's support was that a decision was made to put 'Iernin' on to the London musical scene. George Lloyd regarded the review as the "introductory card" without which a move to London would not have been possible. His father, William, set up the New English Opera Company, gathered together people to provide the financial backing and waited for a theatre to become available. This proved to be the Lyceum Theatre and the company moved there in June 1935 with a double cast and three principal sopranos. The orchestra was made up of many of the best instrumentalists in London, eager for employment in those days of very little work; George Lloyd was again the Conductor and he paid Walter Barnes the compliment of inviting him to London to lead the orchestra.

George Lloyd conducting 'Iernin' at the Lyceum Theatre, London 1935. The George Lloyd Music Library, Kendal

The London opening took place on Wednesday 19th June, 1935 and the response of the public was extremely good. The review in *The Times* was, this time, more critical of the production, especially the first act, but none of the deficiencies in performance could "obscure the dramatic power of his music, the excellence of the construction of the opera, and its resourcefulness." The composer himself remembered that the scenery was very simple, which nowadays would be acceptable, but a backcloth, two or three stones and a clump of gorse was not grand enough for some at the time.

All went well and 'Iernin' proved to be among the record breaking productions of English opera, along with Sullivan's 'Ivanhoe' and Rutland Boughton's 'The Immortal Hour'. George was irritated by those who compared it to the latter because he disliked 'The Immortal Hour' with its mystical Celtic twilight atmosphere. In fact Frank Howes endorses this in his review by saying that "Mr Lloyd's fairy is less fairylike than Mr Boughton's; but his mortals are more full-blooded, and his music is more frankly romantic".

Many other national newspapers, the *Telegraph*, *The Star*, the *Evening Standard*, and the *Morning Post* all reviewed the London production of 'Iernin', and frequently criticised it, especially the clarity of the words, one going so far as to say that "only about one word in ten was distinguishable". But Spike Hughes, writing in the *Daily Herald* for 20th June was enthusiastic about the work regarding 'Iernin' as genuine opera, "not music-drama" and said, as did other reviewers, that above all George Lloyd was a good conductor and that "this young man has an undoubted talent."

'Iernin' was very well received by its audiences, and many prominent musicians of the day came to see it. George, who knew none of these people, remembered that Thomas Beecham came, "stroking his little beard" saying "Very good, my boy, very good, you keep the interest going throughout the whole opera," which was a "terrific compliment" to him. Vaughan Williams "in his black farmer's boots" also came and said after the performance "Isn't fair I've been trying all my life to write opera." John Ireland was another well known composer to meet George Lloyd as a result of this production telling him that there were "bits of Stravinsky in that". Their friendship developed and George learnt a lot from him, but remained unconvinced that Stravinsky's influence could be seen in the opera.

George Lloyd. The George Lloyd Music Library, Kendal

The successful run of 'Iernin' was brought to an end by the unlikely cause of the onset of a heat wave in London! People stopped going to the theatre in the evenings, and without today's mass of tourists to sustain an audience there was not enough funding available to continue the performances.

George Lloyd died, aged eighty-five, in 1998. A valuable account of his life by Jane Lofthouse was printed in *Cowethas Ylow Kernowak*, the Cornish Music Guild Journal, to mark George's eightieth birthday in 1993. Another by Geoffrey Self in his *Music in West Cornwall* and obituaries following George's death provide much of his life story. They record the ups and downs of his life: the early successes with opera and symphonies; severe mental and physical health problems as a result of shell shock after his ship was blown up on an Arctic convoy during the war; discouragement when his works were neglected or poorly produced during the nineteen fifties; his gradual return to health and composing vigour and return to public appreciation with the support of musicians such as John Ogdon, the pianist, and the conductor Edward Downes, and the growth of recordings of his work in the United States.

The final years of his life were very active, both as a conductor of his own works world wide, alongside a continuing output of music, both orchestral and choral. Described by Edward Greenfield as "the most amiable of composers", George Lloyd's close involvement with the Penzance Orchestral Society can be regarded as one of the "jewels in the crown" of the orchestra's history.

5

Concerts and Music-making 1930-1936

The events and developments highlighted in the previous chapter were played out against the backcloth of the Orchestral Society continuing with its seasons of rehearsals and twice yearly concert days. In addition Walter Barnes continued to conduct or lead groups of instrumentalists from the orchestra in other musical events, some of which are relevant to this history.

The new decade began for the Penzance Orchestral Society on Wednesday 2nd April 1930 with its spring concerts. The orchestra comprised 58 players and the major work in the programme was Mozart's 'Symphony No. 40 in G Minor'. This was regarded by one of the reviewers as among the most ambitious tasks they had ever taken on by virtue of the need for meticulous treatment. They were congratulated on the result and *The Cornishman* report refers to the orchestra as, "second to none in the West".

The November concerts for that year featured the celebrated violinist Harold Fairhurst as soloist, playing Beethoven's Concerto in D Major, as well as local singer Eric Thomas, who was a substitute for Edward Lancaster who had been taken ill. Eric Thomas sang one of local composer John Holliday's songs 'Hinton, Dinton and Mere'. What *The Cornishman* report did not reveal about the evening concert on Wednesday 26th November is recounted by Kathleen Frazier in 'My Story', where she tells of the pleasure she found in accompanying Harold Fairhurst – "one of the greatest joys of my life....his lovely playing had that elusive quality which I sometimes felt was not quite of this earth." She goes on to say that at this November concert, where she had accompanied him in his group of solos in the second half of the programme, "at the end of the concert when the audience were leaving, a considerable number stayed behind and asked us to play yet some more! So Harold and I played on for nearly another hour I should think, to a most thrilled and enraptured audience." The soloist gave more than his 15 guineas worth on that occasion!

Following the performances of 'HMS Pinafore' and 'Trial by Jury' in February 1931 by the Penzance Operatic Society, the forty-eighth and forty-ninth concerts by the Orchestral Society took place on Wednesday 18th March. The most notable thing about these concerts was that during the afternoon concert, "Mr Walter Barnes broke his baton in 'Finlandia' and the wisp of timber flew back into the audience, where there blossomed forth a second conductor, who proceeded to follow the music with it according to her own taste. But Mr Walter Barnes had a spare...."

Two extra concerts, the fiftieth and fifty-first, followed quickly after those in March. These had been loudly proclaimed in the March programmes of both the Penzance orchestra and the Cornwall Symphony Orchestra concerts the following week as "the first visit to Cornwall of Mr Cedric Sharpe... Come and hear our greatest 'cellist and give him a real Cornish reception"! With only a month between concerts the orchestra must have had to work very hard with a new programme to rehearse. How this had come about is not known but the fact that Cedric Sharpe was Enid Barnes' teacher at the Royal Academy may have been a factor. Perhaps it was the only time he could visit Penzance, for he was the principal 'cello with the London Symphony Orchestra. However it happened the concerts took place on Friday 24th April 1931 and Cedric Sharpe played Boellman's 'Symphonic Variations for Violoncello and Orchestra Op. 23'. He also played three 'cello solos in the second half of the programme and the accompanist for these and for three songs sung by Miss Peggy Bazeley was Miss Enid Barnes. It was quite natural as Cedric Sharpe's pupil that she should have been asked to accompany the

Penzance Orchestral Society, April 1931. The soloists were Cedric Sharpe, 'cello, Peggy Bazeley, soprano with Enid Barnes as accompanist.

soloists on this occasion, as Enid was by now an accomplished pianist. When she returned to Penzance on completion of her studies at the Academy, Walter continued to use her as the soloists' accompanist.

In November 1931 Walter Barnes and Mrs Crosbie Garstin were violin soloists in a performance of Bach's 'Concerto No. 3 in D Minor' with the Cornwall Symphony Orchestra at concerts in Camborne and Truro. Just over two weeks later the Penzance Orchestral Society gave their autumn concert on Friday, 27th November. A new post of 'Hon. Concert Director' appeared in the programme but was short lived.

These concerts are notable for the opportunity the programmes provided for individual members of the orchestra to display their talents. An unusual work opened the programme – Beethoven's 'Three Equali for Trombones' performed by Messrs W. B. Prowse, Herbert Kessell and J. H. Gillis on tenor trombones and Mr Charles H. Roach on bass trombone. A trio for two flutes and harp from Berlioz' ' Childhood of Christ' was played with Messrs. William Lloyd and F. N. Hodson as flautists and Mr Alfred Robinson on the harp. Mr Barrie Bennets also took the viola solo in Jacob Arcadelt's popular 'Ave Maria'. Even the audience was "Cordially invited" to join in by singing 'God Save the King' at the end of the concert.

The concert was well praised in the local press, though the orchestra was criticised for its accompaniment of the tenor soloist in an aria 'Cujus Animam' from Rossini's 'Stabat Mater', "the orchestra, as too frequently happens, overweighting him", but whether the words in parenthesis referred to orchestras in general or Penzance in particular is not clear!

The year ended on a nostalgic note for Walter Barnes when he directed 'The Old-Time Cinema Orchestra' in a concert at the Pavilion on Boxing Day. Other participants in this event were Miss Ursula Boase, soprano, Mr George Lloyd, solo violin and Miss Enid Barnes, Med. RAM, LRAM, pianoforte. The programme was made up of light orchestral items, songs and violin solos, and *The Cornishman* reported that "encores were frequent" with the violin playing of Mr George Lloyd, a 17 year old youth, "a highly appreciated feature of the programme."

1932 appears, from the programmes preserved by Walter Barnes, to have been an incredibly busy year, with barely a month passing without him and members of his orchestra being involved in major musical events in Cornwall and even across the Tamar. In January, Walter was leader and soloist in the Redruth Choral Society concert. February took members of the orchestra to the Pavilion Theatre for the Operatic Society's production of 'The Yeoman of the Guard'.

In March, Walter was invited to lead the orchestra of the Plymouth Orpheus Society who gave a performance of Elgar's 'Dream of Gerontius' in Plymouth Guildhall and several Penzance Orchestral Society members are listed in the orchestra of 76 players. There were some problems to be overcome on this occasion because the organ in the Guildhall had not been brought to low pitch, and it was difficult to get perfect tuning and intonation, but with "Walter Barnes as principal first violin, there was marked steadiness in even the most difficult passages and the confidence which comes with a first rate leader was noticeable throughout the orchestra".

Later in March Walter was leading "a large orchestra" for Dvorak's 'Stabat Mater' given at the annual Good Friday concert in Camborne Wesley Chapel, and in April he was both leader of the orchestra and soloist at the Mousehole Male Voice Choir Annual concert. This was in addition to his own Society's concert on 15th April and to directing a small group for the Penzance Players production of a comedy 'Damsel in Distress' by Ian Hay at the Pavilion at the end of the month.

An Invitation to Truro Cathedral

In June 1932 an important Choral Festival took place in Truro Cathedral, the annual festival of the Diocesan Choral Union of Canterbury, Bath and Wells and Truro. The Penzance Orchestral Society were invited to take part and contributed five items to the programme – Beethoven's Fifth Symphony, Handel's 'Organ Concerto No. 2' in which the soloist was the cathedral organist, Guillaume Ormond, the Beethoven 'Equali' for trombones, the Finale from Handel's 'Water Music', and Elgar's 'Imperial March'. Also, one of the anthems was opened by a few bars of triumphant music scored for horns, trumpets, trombones, tuba and tympani which had been composed by Walter Barnes.

This was a major event for the cathedral and city of Truro and was the inspiration of a Major Gill who had always wanted to hold a Choral Festival in the Cathedral. It had now become possible because "in the Penzance Orchestra we had one which was worthy of playing in the Cathedral". The music was relayed by loud speakers to the people in the streets around the Cathedral watching the pageantry of the occasion. This included the participating choirs with their banners processing around the building singing hymns.

"That day the cathedral had had the thrill of its life" according to Major Gill in the extensive newspaper reports. At a supper in the evening not only did Frank Latham, on behalf of the Orchestral Society, speak of their appreciation for the invitation but also for the way they had been entertained. Major Gill, in reply, said the Society had "carried out the trust we put in you and your conductor to keep up the standard of the Church of God in Truro".

A Young Conductor's Debut Appearance

A concert which has some significance in the history of the orchestra took place in Newlyn on Friday 22nd July 1932. This was a performance at the Newlyn Wesleyan Methodist Church Centenary celebrations of Mendelssohn's 'Hymn of Praise', a symphonic cantata for choir, soloists and orchestra. The organist at the chapel was Morgan Hosking, and before committing himself to putting on this performance Morgan consulted Walter Barnes as to whether he thought him capable of conducting it. Walter did, and gave him opportunities to conduct the Junior Orchestra promising his full support. The chapel choir was augmented to about eighty singers by inviting members of the Camborne Wesley choir to take part, and the orchestra numbered twenty five players with Walter as leader and Morgan Hosking's other musical mentor, Hugh Branwell, at the organ.

A *Cornish Evening Telegraph* report for 23rd June gives a detailed account of the performance praising the soloists, Kathleen Coombs, soprano, from Plymouth and Teify Bonner, tenor, who had come from London, as well as the chorus and orchestra who were "a large measure of the success of the performance". Of the young conductor (Morgan Hosking was eighteen years old) the reporter said that one would have expected such a performance to be in the hands of an experienced musician, "such was not the case... but he has musical ability. He must be heartily congratulated on the way in which he trained such a large choir, as well as the orchestra". This was Morgan Hosking's first public appearance as the conductor of an important musical event and he must have been very much encouraged by these remarks and by the support afforded him by everyone involved.

Local Composers

The Orchestral Society's concerts in April and November 1932 both involved compositions by local composers. The spring concert featured a work by Ernest Henry Oates from Blackwater, near Truro, who was a French horn player in the orchestra. He had written an opera 'Andromeda', to a libretto from a poem by Charles Kingsley. The second half of the concert opened with the Introduction to Scene 3, 'Perseus at the Rock' from this one-act opera. The programme notes informed the audience that the work was to be conducted by the composer, and that the Society was giving the first performance in Cornwall. The *Western Morning News* music critic regarded it as a "brilliant work" and E. H. Oates a "master of orchestration", describing the vivid musical colours of the piece, concluding, "Altogether it is a most interesting work on which Mr Oates is to be congratulated".

In November 1932 the Penzance Orchestral Society played the 'Symphony in A' by George Lloyd. This was his first symphony and was conducted by him. The performance was fully reported in the *Western Morning News* the following day saying that the composer, "reveals a keen feeling for effective orchestration, ability to move freely from key to key, ability to write a vigorous brass part and marked contrapuntal skill...Thus to maintain interest for nearly half an hour is a big achievement for a musician of 19....Hats off, therefore, to Mr Lloyd, who bids fair to do big things in the future."

The guest artiste at this concert was Miss Betty Bannerman, a soprano well known for appearances at the Queen's Hall and other major venues. In Scenes 1 and 2 of the Dream Pantomime from Humperdinck's 'Hansel and Gretel' she sang the part of the sandman, and Hansel and Gretel were sung by Miss Kitty Rogers and Miss Isabel Elford who were both pupils at the Penzance County School for Girls. Miss Bannerman also sang an aria from Gluck's 'Orfeo' and a group of solos, accompanied by Enid Barnes. Bizet's 'Suite 'L'Arlésienne' was played and the *Western Morning News* reviewer complimented "Dainty solos" by William Lloyd, flautist, A. W. Robinson, harp and Mr Kenneth Woolcock, saxophone. Of the latter he wrote "the last showed that the saxophone can be respectable and well-behaved, though its tone colour is surely too characterless and flabby to entitle it to full orchestral honours"!

From *The Cornishman* report we learn that there was a capacity audience for this concert, with hundreds unable to obtain admission, and "many people standing and sitting in inconceivable spots". George Lloyd's symphony received an enthusiastic reception and the composer conducted "like a veteran... modern youth is not so decadent as some would have us believe".

George, this time as a solo violinist, was involved along with Walter Barnes, Mrs Crosbie Garstin, Enid Barnes as the solo 'cellist and other members of the orchestra in another concert in St John's Hall on the Wednesday after Christmas 1932. This was a concert given by Miss Molly Mitchell, "the Penzance contralto of London, Paris and Broadcasting Concerts", and the programme was made up of songs, instrumental solos, orchestral pieces and Vivaldi's 'Concerto for Two Violins' in A Minor performed by Walter Barnes and George Lloyd. Enid Barnes, "with Academy honours fresh upon her "performed Max Bruch's 'Kol Nidrei' on the 'cello and "held her audience enraptured".

At the end of such a busy and eventful year Walter Barnes had good cause to wear a satisfied smile, but there was another reason for him to chuckle, in early December. *The Western Independent* newspaper featured a cartoon entitled "Some Well Known Sports" by Shaw Baker, one of whom was Walter Barnes. The caption reads, "Mr Walter Barnes, a keen Patron of Sport as well as a Musical Genius"! Viola player, Barrie Bennetts, was also featured in golfing gear as "County Coroner who shines in all sports," as was "Mr Ernest White of St Ives, a well known Cornish singer and rabid "Argyle Fan". The other characters depicted were all well known

personalities in West Cornwall society with differing areas of responsibility as well as being keen supporters of various sports.

Falmouth Concerts

At this period in his life Walter Barnes went to Falmouth to give violin lessons on a weekly basis, so it was not too difficult for him to accept an invitation to conduct an orchestra in the town. There had been no amateur orchestra in Falmouth since the disbandment of the Falmouth Philharmonic Society in 1921, and in 1933 the feeling grew that there was a need for one. The Reverend C. Daly Atkinson, vicar of Mabe, was a keen amateur musician and composer and it was he who appears to have organised others to form a committee and assemble an orchestra. They rehearsed on Monday evenings at 6 p.m., which was probably the day on which Walter visited the town to teach, and gave their first concert on Wednesday 17th March. Many column inches in the *Falmouth Packet* and *Cornish Echo* newspapers were devoted to reporting this concert and the members of the orchestra are listed. The leader was Mrs L. M. Twite, who also played Mozart's Violin Concerto in E Flat, and the other soloist was the well known local baritone, Bernard Fishwick. There were about fifty players of whom nearly a half were members of the Penzance Orchestral Society. Their support and the loan of music by the Penzance Society was acknowledged in the concert programme.

It seems to have been a great success and much appreciated by the audience in the Princess Pavilion, though one writer bemoans the fact that the hall was not full. Another concedes that "unfavourable weather" may have kept some people at home. A second concert was given in December 1933, by an orchestra of only 34 players when Walter Barnes and Mrs Crosbie Garstin were the soloists in Vivaldi's 'Concerto in A Minor for Two Violins'. In both concerts Arcadelt's 'Ave Maria' was performed, the viola solo being played in March by Mr Barrie Bennetts and in December by Mrs Dudley Harris. The programme for the latter concert announced that the next one would take place in March 1934 and would include Beethoven's First Symphony.

'Some Well Known Sports', by Shaw Baker. Sunday Independent Ltd

Walter Barnes' programme books did not include any programmes for the Falmouth concerts, and press reports which have been kept provide a sporadic picture. Another concert was held in March 1937, this time held in the Drill Hall, which was very cold, and again the weather was bad, but it has yet to be discovered for how long the Falmouth Orchestral Society existed and how regular their concerts.

The 1933 spring concert by Penzance Orchestral Society was given on Wednesday 26th April when Sonia Moldawsky played the 'Concerto No. 1 in G Minor' by Max Bruch – a first complete performance of this work by the Society. Wagner's 'Siegfried Idyll' was also played by them for the first time as the score and orchestral parts had been given to the orchestra by "our esteemed honorary member Ernest Oates and Miss Oates". It was to become a firm favourite in the orchestra's repertoire, particularly under the baton of Morgan Hosking.

This concert was attended by W. H. "Willie" Reed, the Leader of the London Symphony Orchestra and a friend of Margaret, Ranee of Sarawak. *The Cornishman* report opened with the following words: "A high tribute to the orchestra and its conductor was paid by Mr W. H. Reed... " and his words were quoted: "Down here in Penzance you have an orchestra that can play good music... Mr Barnes puts his last ounce into this orchestra, and you must see that (it) does not go under... ", which sounds as though W. H. Reed had been invited to speak to the audience from the stage. From such a distinguished and experienced musician these words must have been welcomed by the orchestra, and they received further encouragement in an article by the *Western Morning News* music critic reviewing the recent orchestral activity in the West of

England. After talking about orchestras in Torquay and Plymouth he continued, "Mr Walter Barnes has been a tower of strength, not only in Penzance, where the programmes of the Orchestral Society have been of first class musical interest, but also in Falmouth, where a new amateur orchestra has made a promising start under his conductorship".

The concerts on Friday 24th November 1933 maintained this "interest" by including Wagner's 'Faust' Overture and Bach's Suite No. 3 in D for oboes, trumpets, drums and strings. The latter piece was conducted by Guillaume Ormond, "our County Organist.... Master of the Music of Truro Cathedral" to whom thanks were extended for "consenting to conduct this important work". Also, at the evening concert only, Johann Strauss's Waltz, 'The Blue Danube, Op. 314' in its original version for Male Chorus and Orchestra was performed with the men's section of the Operatic Society providing the chorus. The soloist was Miss Vivien Worth, soprano, a native of Truro, who sang 'Vissi d'arte, vissi d'amore' from Puccini's 'Tosca' and a group of songs.

The newspaper report from the *Western Morning News* was lengthy, opening with an amusing sentence "Were it not that I fear his wrath too much, I should be inclined to refer to Mr Walter Barnes....as the grand old man of music in the West". (Walter was just forty-nine years old in 1933). It continued to praise him: "he led them through the subtleties of Wagner's syntax with a touch which was as sure as in the simple grace and liveliness of Haydn.... and he does not take refuge in the backwaters of hackneyed versions of the classics" going on to cite the Strauss and Wagner as innovative programming.

There were, unusually, criticisms of the performances, such as a tendency in the climaxes "for the weight of the brass and percussion to overwhelm the strings", and "some raggedness and hesitancy" showed itself among the woodwind, and in the 'Faust' Overture the woodwind and brass "seemed unable to fix themselves in with the scheme of things". The reviewer suggested that the faults could be partly overcome by "shifting the position a little of the brass players and curbing the otherwise quite worthy impetuosity of the timpanist"! But the great feature of the evening concert, "which was responsible for a packed house" was the Strauss 'Blue Danube' Waltz. "Mr Barnes is a showman as well as a musician, and he held his trump card until the end, so that the audience were thoroughly keyed up with anticipation", and high praise was given to all involved.

And so to the end of another year in which the conductor and members of the orchestra were found in concerts and performances here, there and everywhere!

Edward Elgar had died in February 1934 and this was acknowledged at the Spring concert of the Penzance Orchestral Society on Wednesday 7th March. The programme announced that "As a humble tribute to the late Sir Edward Elgar, the muted strings of the orchestra will play his beautiful 'Elegie'. The audience are respectfully invited to stand".

One of the soloists at this concert was the famous tenor, Trefor Jones, who sang 'The Flower Song' from Bizet's 'Carmen' and a group of songs in which the accompanist was E. Fugler Thomas, the well known and accomplished local organist and pianist. He also played the organ in Henry Wood's arrangement of the 'Purcell' Trumpet Voluntary in a performance by trumpets, trombones, drums and organ. The trumpeters were Victor Martin, Thomas McGuiness and William Moon, and the trombonists W. B. Prowse, Herbert Kessell and Charles H. Roach. Leonard Stewart played the tymps and Bernard Beardmore the side drum.

Enid Barnes in the Limelight

This programme is a good example of how the music for a concert may be built up after a soloist has been chosen. Walter Barnes' daughter, Enid, LRAM and double silver medallist at the Royal Academy had been invited to perform Rachmaninov's Second Piano Concerto in C Minor, Op. 18, so could not be expected to accompany the vocal soloist in his group of songs. Choosing another accompanist who was also an organist gave Walter the opportunity to select a work involving the organ in St John's Hall. The organ was given an overhaul for this concert and the concert programme included thanks to "Messrs Hele & Co. Ltd., the eminent organ builders of Plymouth and London, for their great kindness in attending to the organ free of cost so that it might be used at these concerts". Gratitude was also expressed to "The Public Buildings Co. Ltd., for the use of the organ" – an intriguing statement raising queries as to what or who the "Public Buildings Co. Ltd." was, but lack of space precludes further speculation here!

Schubert's 'Unfinished' Symphony and Wagner's 'Ride of the Valkyries' opened and closed the concert, but the other item of interest was the overture to Rossini's one-act opera 'La Scala di Seta' for which the programme notes were specially written by Mr Francis Toye, "the eminent critic and writer whose book on Rossini is about to be published. Our sincere thanks are

Enid Barnes at the piano in St John's Hall, 1934.

offered to him". An unidentified press report for this concert regarded this as probably the first provincial performance in England of this work, saying that "it was played by Sir Thomas Beecham last year, and the only other set of band parts in England were captured for yesterday's concert by Mr Barnes".

Of the concert itself the writer tells us that the proceeds were to go to "the Mayor's Fund for the distressed fishermen of Newlyn and Mousehole", and that one of the songs sung by Trefor Jones, 'Calleo' had words written by local author Crosbie Garstin to music by Mr G Graham, a schoolmaster at St Erbyn's School in Penzance.

Enid Barnes as solo pianist was reported as "having a light, clean touch and strict sense of time values". The reviewer obviously approved of her performance but it was rather sparsely expressed. He wrote at length, however, about his dislike of the choice of concerto. "If this concerto is a favourite of the pianist that explains why she played it otherwise the choice is rather puzzling. To begin with, the piano has to sustain a more than usually unequal duet with the orchestra. Rachmaninoff gives the impression of having written it with both eyes on the orchestra, and when he did turn his head now and again it was to give but a glance at the piano"! *The Cornishman* reviewer who signed himself "Lanyon Chronicler", surely one of the many pen-names of Herbert Thomas, reported that the piano (a Steinway grand) was "overpowered in the Rachmaninov Concerto, but when heard there was no question about Enid Barnes' brilliance and mastery of technique." She received two magnificent bouquets after her performance, which must have been a very proud moment for her father, Walter, on the rostrum.

Walter and Male Voice Choirs

The year 1934 provided another interlude in Walter Barnes' life worthy of record. The conductor of the Newlyn Male Choir, Irving Thomas, was unwell in the spring of 1934 and this, combined with extra responsibilities in his business, led to his resignation. The choir, keen to enter the County Music Festival, persuaded Walter Barnes to take over the choir for this period so that they could compete in the Festival in Bodmin. They were past winners of the Bullerhowell Shield and eager to repeat their success but on this occasion were beaten into second place by Marazion Apollo Choir. Walter continued to conduct them for some local

Newlyn Male Choir with their conductor, Morgan Hosking, 1936. Opie, Redruth

engagements, and restored their honour by taking them to the British Music Society's Festival in Plymouth where they won first place in their class, beating their 'rivals', Mousehole Male Voice Choir, by four points!

Walter's other commitments prevented him from taking on the position as their conductor on a permanent basis. Morgan Hosking accepted the post later in 1934 and, apart from during the war when the choir's activities were suspended, remained the conductor of Newlyn Male Choir until 1948. He continued as their President from 1948-50, resuming this position again for a year in 1987-1988.

An amusing postscript to Walter's involvement with male voice choirs comes in July 1938 in the form of a postcard, elaborately decorated with a Penzance Operatic Society emblem, sent to Morgan Hosking by Walter. It has a short newspaper cutting pasted to it headed "Why the hybrid attire?" which bemoans the fact that male choirs had a tendency to wear lounge suits with a "dress collar and tie", presumably meaning a bow tie – "a horrible combination... neither fish, flesh nor good red herring". The writer, rather patronisingly, understood that choir members often could not afford the "expensive rig out" of evening dress, but regarded this combination as "a sham which gives the choirs such a smug self-satisfied look which nearly always puts me off their music."

Walter added: "Hooray! I quite agree with all this... the height of this hybrid season is reached on Paul Feast when gents in this costume indicated hang around the outside of the Newlyn Prim. Chapel until the last minute and then make a grand entry into the choir seats feeling that the admiring eyes of the world are theirs." He exhorts Morgan to "hang this up for the choir to read". We can assume that Morgan Hosking did not heed this advice for he continued as the Newlyn Male Choir conductor for another ten years!

The achievements of Walter Barnes and the orchestra during the early years of the 1930's received acknowledgement by his being among those included in the series of articles printed in the *Western Morning News* entitled "Musicians in the West". This article, printed in June 1934, and already referred to in the section on Walter Barnes, provides a valuable and vivid portrayal of Walter when he was, perhaps, at the height of his musical achievements, written, as it was, only eight years before his early death at the age of fifty-eight.

The Operatic Society's programme for their 1935 production of 'Iolanthe' included an advertisement for the Orchestral Society's spring concert in late March which was unusually appealing, announcing the soprano soloist, Gaby Vallé as:

> *...the Great Operatic Soprano – who created the title role in the Cornish Opera 'Iernin' – with the male section of Penzance Amateur Operatic Society – Richard Tregoning, tenor, in the opening scene of Act IV of 'Il Trovatore' – Verdi. The Orchestra in an Entirely New Programme – 60 players. Book your seats now – and support the Society that has maintained a High Musical Standard, and placed Penzance on the Broadcasting map.*

As well as the 'Il Trovatore' extract Gaby Vallé also sang an aria from Verdi's 'Aida' and a group of songs at the evening concert. Apart from an arrangement of Schumann's 'Liebesgarten', arranged for string orchestra by Walter Barnes, and the 'Suite Espagnole for Orchestra' by the French composer Paul Lacome, the entire programme was an operatic feast. It opened with the Overture to 'Der Freischutz' by Weber and continued with excerpts from Massenet's 'Werther'. Ponchielli's 'Dance of the Hours' from the opera 'La Gioconda' and the Triumphal March from Mancinelli's opera 'Cleopatra' completed the programme.

The November 1935 concert also featured a vocal soloist, this time the bass, Malcolm McEachern, better known to the public as "Mr Jetsam of Flotsam and Jetsam", well known entertainers of the day. This concert was broadcast on the BBC West Regional network but, according to the *Western Morning News*, reception "was rather spoiled by atmospherics." The concert programme contained a special message of thanks to "The Worshipful The Mayor of Penzance (Alderman Robert Thomas, C. C.) for his kindness throughout many years in decorating the stage for these concerts at his own expense, and for many other kindly acts, and wishes him a successful and pleasant year of office." (This was the first of six periods of office as Mayor of Penzance for 'Bob' Thomas and he received the Freedom of the Borough in 1946 at the age of seventy-six which *The Cornishman* reported as "The Crown of a useful and unselfish career of service... a noble Record of Bold and Imaginative office as Alderman and Councillor.")

Nora Gruhn, soprano and Audrey Piggott, 'cello were the two soloists at the concert on Wednesday 18 March 1936, the first half of the programme being classical in nature. The concert opened with Mozart's Symphony No. 40 in G Minor, followed by Nora Gruhn singing the aria 'Non mi dir' from Mozart's opera 'Don Giovanni'. Bach's 'Air from the Suite in D' was performed, and the programme note reveals that "The noble air – one of the finest ever – is played at the request of a lady who has attended the concerts of the Society from its inception." Reward indeed for 37 years of loyalty! Haydn's "Cello Concerto in D' was played by Audrey Piggott to end the first half of the concert and the second half contained music by Bizet, Saint-Saëns, and Weber.

In November 1936 another extract from E. H. Oates opera 'Andromeda' was played, but the main work was Beethoven's 'Symphony No. 3 in E Flat', the 'Eroica'. The performance was regarded by the *Western Morning News* music critic as an appropriate choice for an orchestra approaching its 30th birthday, "a paean, as it were, for accomplishment after many years of work." The performance was "not without ragged patches" but "had the spirit of the work... best in the scherzo, which had a rhythmic grace and swing... " The celebrated English tenor, Heddle Nash, was to have been the soloist at this concert but was taken ill with influenza and his place was "pleasantly filled" by Leonard Gowings.

The *News Chronicle* for the day of the concert, 18th November, contained a picture of the Orchestral Society, wonderfully portraying Walter Barnes in action at a rehearsal, and announcing that the concert was being broadcast from St John's Hall, Penzance.

Walter Barnes in action at a rehearsal with Penzance Orchestral Society and soloist, Leonard Gowings, November 1936.

Celebrations and Concerns 1937-1939

Plans to commemorate the thirtieth anniversary of the Penzance Orchestral Society were first mentioned in the minutes of the Annual General Meeting in May 1936. Walter Barnes, in his report, referred to the first concert given in April 1907 and suggested that "a special effort be made to mark the thirty years existence of the Society in April of next year".

Discussions continued in committee meetings for the rest of the year and by December 1936 it was confirmed that Mr Reginald Redman, Director of the West Region of the BBC, would be invited to conduct a piece of his own composition. Mrs Garstin suggested that Mr Barnes should play the violin and this received "general and loud applause", Mr Barnes finally consenting to play a short concerto. He also suggested that the Male Chorus of the Operatic Society should sing the 'Blue Danube' by Strauss and that this should be conducted by Morgan Hosking, which was agreed.

The Thirtieth Anniversary

Most of these ideas were put into practice at the two concerts held on Tuesday 16th March 1937. The Souvenir Programme with a special version of their regular logo, probably designed by Miss Hilda Quick, comprised twenty-two pages, and is a valuable record of the Society at this time. Patrons, Vice Presidents and officers were listed, and a statement of the orchestra's aims provided, stating that it "exists for the fostering of orchestral music in South Cornwall." Three pages of photographs included pictures of the chief officers and Walter Barnes with the orchestra rehearsing in the Bandroom. Walter's "few notes of happenings" ended with his distinctive signature.

One page listed all the instruments presented to the Society with the names of the donors. As well as a complete set of oak orchestral stands given by Mrs Crosbie Garstin the gifts included a set of Tubular Bells donated by the Corporation of the Borough of Penzance. The list of instruments comprised a Triple Tone Premier Snare Drum; a pair of Orchestral Turkish Cymbals; two French Horns; a Chromatic Glockenspiel; a Buffet Low Pitch Bassoon; Percussion Accessories and Drum Case; a Chinese Gong; a Tenor Trombone, and a Tenor Side Drum and Stand.

At the end of these lists was an appeal to the effect that "Any Patron who would like to present a set of orchestral covers for use of the orchestra would confer a great benefit on the Society". Also included were the names of all those who had given their services or talent to the Society over the years, and there is a whole page advertisement for "His Master's Voice" records, with details of the recordings available for the orchestral works being played at the concert.

The soloist chosen for this important occasion was Helen Sandow, described as "the Cornish Contralto", whose photograph was included in the programme. The full programme was as follows: Elgar's 'Pomp and Circumstance March No. 4 in G', Op. 39; Dvorak's 'Symphony No. 5 in E Minor', Op. 95 'From the New World' and the Cavatina and Aria 'O Priests of Baal' from Meyerbeer's 'The Prophet' sung by Helen Sandow. Reginald Redman conducted his composition 'Pan's Garden' to complete the first half of the concert. Part II, which was broadcast, opened with 'Finlandia' by Sibelius followed by Walter Barnes as the solo violinist in the Beethoven 'Romance in F', Op. 50. Helen Sandow then sang a group of three songs accompanied by Enid Barnes, after which Hamilton Harty's arrangement of a Suite from Handel's 'Water Music' was played, "By desire of a patron". The programme ended "By general desire"

with Johann Strauss's Waltz 'On the Beautiful Blue Danube', Op. 314 sung by the male choristers of Penzance Operatic Society with the orchestra, (which does not appear to have been conducted by Morgan Hosking as originally planned). The student song 'Gaudeamus Igitur' and the National Anthem ended the concert .

At the afternoon concert Lady Vyvyan of Trelowarren was invited to give a short speech before the start of the concert. At the end of the evening concert the Mayor, Alderman Robert Thomas, made a presentation to the Society of the portrait of Walter Barnes by Stanhope Forbes, which had been purchased by public subscription.

This celebration concert was written up at length in the local press with headlines such as "A Proved Record" and "Birthday Concerts", and while the performances of the orchestra and soloists were given some attention, many column inches concerned themselves with paying tribute to the orchestra and to Walter Barnes in particular. Praise was heaped upon his head by the writers, and his playing in the Beethoven 'Romance' was "finished in style and with a remarkable breadth and beauty of tone." The speeches by Lady Vyvyan, the Mayor, and Frank Latham, President, who accepted the Forbes portrait on behalf of the Society, were reported in detail and Mrs Garstin, as Leader, and Enid Barnes, received gifts. Walter Barnes was presented with a cheque for £30 representing £1 for every year he had been conductor.

There were three of the original founder members still playing in the orchestra, Barrie Bennetts, viola, Frank Latham, bassoon, and Alfred Robinson, harp. In the programme Walter paid tribute to their friendship and loyalty over the thirty years, but he also made an appeal to any young men who would consider taking up a wind instrument, adding that "Some of us are getting on in years, and cannot hope to go on indefinitely."

The evening of congratulations and appreciations drew to a close with everyone linking hands and singing 'Auld Lang Syne', and what a hearty rendering it must have been. But before another decade passed and another anniversary commemorated, the orchestra would see great changes and pass through sad and troubled times. They would lose their founding conductor and, as one newspaper wrote "an orchestra without a conductor is akin to a ship without a captain; almost, one might say, without a rudder." Who would be found to take over the helm in stormy waters? And would the brave ship that was the Penzance Orchestral Society continue to steer a steady course?

The Coronation of King George VI

Celebrations were in the air, generally, during the Spring of 1937 with preparations for the Coronation of King George VI and Queen Elizabeth taking place in communities throughout the country. Penzance produced an official souvenir and programme for the great day, Wednesday 12th May, and events which lasted for the rest of the week. Coronation Day saw a Civic Procession, special services in churches and chapels; a Royal Salute in the morning; a children's sports and tea held in St Clare Cricket Field in the afternoon; an Invitation Ball held at the Winter Gardens in the evening with a Cabaret Show by the pupil's of Gays Academy and a Public Dance held in St John's Hall.

Cricket matches, motor gymkhanas, concerts on the Promenade Bandstand, a Coronation Carnival, Firework Displays, distribution of souvenir canisters of tea and biscuits to senior citizens, and mugs to children, and "Burning the boats off the Promenade" all took place from Thursday to Saturday. On Sunday 16th May the Penzance Orchestral Society gave two concerts of patriotic music in the Morrab Gardens at 2.45 p.m. and 7.45 p.m. The programmes included works by Elgar, Edward German, Binding, the local composer John Holliday and others, and local singers sang popular ballads as well as 'Land of Hope and Glory'.

The entrances to the Morrab Gardens were decorated with flags and bunting as were the main streets of the town and the promenade. An arch "suitably decorated and inscribed" was erected at the eastern entrance to Penzance, near the railway station. In addition the Coronation Committee had arranged for the Penzance Gas Company to floodlight St John's Hall, the Market House, the Bathing Pool, St Anthony Gardens and the Morrab Gardens. The town was 'en fête' and the mood of excitement and jubilation must have seemed to the Orchestral Society like a continuation of their own celebrations.

The Calm Before the Storm

In November 1937 a young Australian pianist, John Simons, was engaged as soloist to play the Liszt Piano Concerto No. 1 in E flat. This concert included a Suite from the film music of

The Emergence of Morgan Hosking

This concert report provides some interesting but disturbing news, for we are told that "The programme concluded on a stimulating note with the suite from Luigini's 'Ballet Russe' in which Mr Barnes handed the baton to Mr J. Morgan Hosking, one of the orchestra's first violins, who made his first appearance at the Society's concerts as a conductor....and during Mr Barnes' illness he deputised at the Orchestral Society's rehearsals. He handled the 'Ballet Russe' Suite skilfully". In *The Cornishman* Morgan's conducting was described as "superlative... an interesting display which greatly impressed us". Walter had conducted, however, with "his accustomed vigour and command".

Two conductors in action. Walter Barnes and Morgan Hosking, March 1939. *Western Morning News*, Plymouth

Morgan himself recalled being very concerned about Walter at this time, but he remained as active and enthusiastic as ever in the committee meetings held during the spring and early summer, and at the AGM in May he "thanked the Leader and all members of the Society for their whole hearted support during the year and expressed his grateful thanks to all during his recent indisposition." Morgan's growing reputation as a conductor was acknowledged by the *Western Morning News* which carried a report of the March concert alongside three photographs – one of Walter Barnes conducting, one of the orchestra in rehearsal and one of Morgan conducting. The pictures of the two conductors are interesting in that they depict the distinctive hand formations they both used when conducting.

Despite the "in house" worry over their conductor's health and the encircling atmosphere of political instability with the prospect of war in Europe, the Society went ahead with ambitious plans for their autumn concert. Walter was collaborating with the Plymouth orchestra over soloists, and while it is not clear whether their plans worked out Penzance decided to engage the well known violinist, Alfredo Campoli, for the November concert. The programme chosen was to include Beethoven's Symphony No.7, the ballet music from Coleridge–Taylor's 'Hiawatha' and the 'Entry of the Gods into Valhalla' by Wagner. A concerto and a piece for strings was to be decided at a later date. Plans for the spring concert in 1940 were already under discussion, but a date was left until the schools Easter holidays were known. Public support was felt to be dropping and so a meeting was planned to discuss ticket prices and methods of selling them. And it was agreed that on Sunday 3rd September 1939 Messrs Hosken, Graham White, Morgan Hosking, Jerry Baker, Alan Wood and one of the two Thomases in the orchestra would gather to distemper the walls of the Bandroom, in readiness for the coming rehearsal season.

But that was not to be because on that Sunday morning came the broadcast to the nation by the Prime Minister, Mr Neville Chamberlain, to the effect that following Hitler's invasion of Poland two days earlier and his negative response to the British Government's ultimatum, war had been declared with Germany.

Penzance Orchestral Society had survived one war and grown to maturity since 1918, but with their conductor suffering bouts of ill health and his young protégé, Morgan Hosking, rushing off to enlist in the Royal Navy the very morning that war was declared how would the Society cope with this second threat to its continuity?

Penzance Orchestral Society. Rehearsal, St John's Hall, March 1939. *Western Morning News*, Plymouth

Years of "Sturm und Drang" 1939-1945

The Early War Years, 1939-1941

The first committee meeting of the Penzance Orchestral Society following the declaration of war with Germany took place on Monday 11 September in the Bandroom. The Secretary reported that the re-decoration of the Bandroom had not taken place owing to the National Emergency. A long discussion resulted in agreement that the Society should be kept going, giving concerts at intervals, and devoting profits to any war charities which the Mayor might name. The concerts planned for November would go ahead but the soloist, Alfredo Campoli, should be asked to release the Society from his engagement. Rehearsals would begin on Sunday 24th September when members' opinions on the best day and time for future rehearsals would be sought. A letter was to be printed in the local press drawing attention to the continuing existence of the orchestra and inviting "any musicians who may be around for the war period to come and play".

At the rehearsal members agreed that practices, for the time being, should be on Sundays at 2.30 p.m. and a brief committee meeting held after a rehearsal revealed that Campoli was willing to end his engagement, but it was resolved that he be considered for an early engagement "when happier times prevailed". Two local singers, Mr Eric Thomas and Miss Kitty Hall, had accepted an invitation to sing on 27th November.

Discussions continued over problems which had arisen, such as the Hon. Secretary Mr H. D. Morris leaving because he had volunteered for war service. It was agreed that his wife should be asked to take on the post, and she is listed as Hon. Secretary at the committee meeting on 15th October. The blackout of St John's Hall had to be arranged satisfactorily otherwise the evening concert could not take place there and adequate lighting at the entrance of the Hall arranged. The Secretary was to ask whether a reduced fee for St John's Hall could be levied and a third of the fee was donated by the Borough Council. It was also decided that as the concert was in aid of charity, ticket prices should be reduced to 2/6, 1/6, and 1/- and Walter Barnes suggested that the French 'Marche Lorraine' should be played instead of one by Elgar.

Walter also proposed that the usual invitation should be sent to the Education Authority for school children to attend the afternoon concert at 6d. each. This would mean that an application could be made to the Commissioner of Customs and Excise for an exemption from the Entertainments Tax levied at that time. Much debate took place over application for grants against loss from the Carnegie Trust via the National Federation of Music Societies. Eventually it was pointed out by Mr Weaver, the NFMS representative, that "no grant could be expected or given, unless the Society was working entirely for itself and not for Charities". The question of renewing the subscription to the NFMS then arose, and it was decided that the subscription should be suspended for the duration of the war.

The first war-time concert took place on Monday 27th November 1939 at 3 p.m. and 7.15 p.m. in St John's Hall and the charity to which the profits would be given was the Central Hospital Supply Service (West Penwith Depot.). The 'Marche Lorraine' by Louis Ganne opened the concert, followed by Gluck's Overture to 'Iphigenie en Aulide', and one of the orchestra's favourites, the 'Ave Maria' by Arcadelt, was played with Mrs Gwyneth Andrewartha taking the solo viola part. The *Western Morning News* found that it was "interesting to compare how the lighter feminine touch brought out the same sweetness in the music". The second half of the concert, as well as an aria by Kitty Hall, in which Kendall Baic (later to become Leader of the orchestra) played a violin obbligato, included excerpts from 'Yeoman of the Guard' by Sullivan and a Johann Strauss waltz 'Roses from the South', and the Finale from Beethoven's Fifth Symphony.

The final item should have been a rendition of Elgar's 'Land of Hope and Glory' sung by Mr Eric L.V. Thomas, but newspaper reports reveal that he was unable to sing having fallen ill. His place was taken by Mr George Cook who was a customs officer in Newlyn, and his songs had a suitably 'national' flavour, being 'Sea Fever' and 'Fishermen of England'. The Society later received a letter from Mr Cook in appreciation of the "splendid backing he had been given by Leader J. Morgan Hosking and all the orchestra". Morgan, who had not yet received a posting, was Acting Principal Violin in place of Mrs Crosbie Garstin who was on active service and the *West Briton* thought him "a clever young violinist". The broad appeal of the music had resulted in good audiences with over £30 raised for the nominated charity.

The mood of national crisis is amusingly captured in an advertisement, which appeared in the concert programme, for a performance of 'The Band Box' by Ellis Slack's Company at the Pavilion Theatre. It makes a special appeal for public support by saying, "Remember – The Company is living in the town, purchasing its food in the town. It does not arrive in a tin box on Monday and depart again on Thursday or Saturday. And they in common with all of us have the right to live – so Please Support Them."

In March 1940 the spring concerts ended the first wartime season by the Orchestral Society and this time proceeds were given to the Mayor's Fund for the Poor. The borough council again reimbursed the Society for the hire of St John's Hall and caretakers, amounting to £7. 1s. 6d. The soloist was Miss Juliette Alvin, the celebrated French 'cellist and student of Pablo Casals. The engagement of such an internationally famous artiste seems surprising, but a letter from her to Enid Truman regarding the music for her solo group of pieces, reveals her address as Kilmarth, Par, Cornwall. It looks as if she must have had a home there, so her visit to Penzance for a fee of only £5. 14s. 0d is explained. She played the ''Cello Concerto in B Flat Major' by Boccherini and her performance was warmly praised in *The Cornishman* review of the concert, one of her encores being 'The Swan' by Saint-Saëns which would "linger long in the memory".

This reporter was writing about his first visit to a concert by the orchestra and was "agreeably surprised at the quality of the performance which, for a town the size of Penzance, must be accounted first rate." He congratulated the Society for "keeping the flag of music flying so efficiently under the present trying conditions". Walter Barnes, he felt, "would continue to rouse enthusiasm for the Society if an earthquake was to visit the district". He congratulated all involved in the concert and commented movingly on the performance of Sibelius's 'Finlandia'.

This had, without doubt, been chosen as a tribute to the people of Finland who fought so bravely against the Soviet Russian invasion of their country during the early months of 1940. "I wonder if it was just mere sentiment... or did 'Finlandia' sound even more wonderful than usual?" Also the orchestra's performance of 'A Life on the Ocean Wave' by E. Binding was regarded as very appropriate since two members of the orchestra were in uniform, one being Morgan Hosking who was in the Royal Navy, and the other in the Merchant Navy. The audience stood and joined in the final part of this work, 'Rule Britannia'. Walter Barnes had arranged a Schumann melody, 'Love's Garden', for strings which "provided one of the loveliest pieces", according to another reviewer, and his conducting was commended: he "held his orchestra in a grip of steel", but tempered by sensitivity and musicianship. At the end of the concert, 'God Save the King', was "sung, as it nearly always is in these days, with unwonted fervour".

In the spring of 1940 the committee of the Orchestral Society discussed a request from the town council asking for concerts to be run monthly for the troops in the area. A decision was deferred until the autumn because it was felt that the troops would not need entertainments in the summer months and the matter does not appear to have arisen again. At the AGM in September 1940 it is recorded that the Junior Orchestra would cease to function during the war, "its Hon. Conductor, Mr J. Morgan Hosking, being on active service". In October, Walter reported to the Committee that "Poushinov was staying at Carbis Bay and would play at the two concerts on 2nd December for a very reduced fee of £40". This was presumably the Russian pianist, Pouishnov, and the committee thought this was a splendid opportunity but that he should be asked if he would reduce the fee even more. If he was engaged to play, ticket prices would be raised to their pre-war prices of 5/-, 3/6, 2/6 and 1/6. As nothing more is heard of this it must be assumed that Pouishnov could not comply with the request.

The soloist at the autumn concert in 1940 was a local soprano, Frida Morton, who sang

Tosca's Prayer from Act 2 of Puccini's opera. Four lady violinists from the orchestra performed the 'Concerto in B Minor for Four Solo Violins and String Orchestra, Op. 3, No. 10' by Vivaldi. Two of them were regular members of the orchestra, the acting leader Miss Winifrede Beadsworth and Miss Marjory Fry, but the other two, Miss Raymonde Jeltes and Miss Winifred Kent, only made a brief appearance among the ranks of the violins for a year or two during the war. Miss Kent was specially mentioned as being the Principal Violin of the Maidstone Orchestral Society. The orchestra was maintaining a reasonable number of players, numbering fifty for this concert, but four of them were from the Junior Orchestra.

This time the proceeds went to the Penzance St John Ambulance Brigade and Penzance St John Nursing Division. The orchestra is described in *The Cornishman* report as "a somewhat reconstructed combination... musicians seeking succour in Penzance and district have joined the Society.... it is a tribute that they wish to". In fact the bulk of the instrumentalists were regular players, who were overcoming problems of getting to rehearsals by sharing transport wherever possible.

Walter Barnes, "with a sprig of white heather in his buttonhole", the performers and soloists received high praise, the writer wishing that "perhaps oftener an afternoon performance could be held....especially in wartime when cultural entertainment is hard to come by." There was a 'casualty' at this concert, however, for the minutes tell that Mr Howard White's double-bass was damaged while being moved from the Bandroom to St John's Hall, and he was given two guineas for the repair.

Howard White also accepted a fee of £5 per annum as caretaker of the Bandroom during the war period, and the insurance cover on the property was increased from £400 to £800. The contents cover remained the same, but at least Mr Howard White would be 'on hand' to keep an eye on his double bass in future! The Operatic Society, who had disbanded for the war period, were querying whether or not they should continue to pay a share of the maintenance of the Bandroom during the war years. It was left to the Treasurer to point out to them that it was a great advantage to both Societies to have such a practice room, and their contributions did continue.

At the end of 1940 Miss Beadsworth and Miss Atkinson took on the task of sorting out the Society's music library which was kept in the Bandroom and they were helped in this work by Walter's wife, Chrissy. The post of Hon. Secretary was again cause for concern early in 1941 as Mrs Morris had now left the area. A non-member of the society, Mr R. H. Pezzack, filled the post for few months, but Miss Lilian Tonkin was appointed Acting Hon. Secretary at the AGM in June 1941.

Walter Barnes' Increasing Ill Health

Two more successful concerts were held on Wednesday 26th March 1941 when Harold Fairhurst was once again the violin soloist playing the Mendelssohn Concerto. *The Cornishman* write up for this concert was very unusual because it took the form of a letter. It was headed "Letter to Tommy, Orchestral music in Penzance" and begins "Dear Tommy, Writing to me recently from a small town in Loamshire...". It is a detailed and complimentary account of the concerts but written in this original format provides a poignant reminder of the times. Morgan Hosking had been able to get home on leave to play in this concert, and it is likely that his concern for Walter Barnes would have prompted him to make every effort to be there. The two men were close and Morgan knew that his being on active service was a source of anxiety to Walter.

That Morgan's concern was justified is borne out by the fact that Walter Barnes was unable to attend a committee meeting on 5th June 1941. He had sent a letter explaining his absence and included a list of the Conductor's duties prior to a concert, showing how much work had to be done so a small sub-committee was formed to deal with many of these duties. It was also decided that the Society should give a concert in the late autumn, which would be recommended to the Annual General Meeting of the Society on 26th June. This meeting ended with a unanimous decision to make an honorarium of £25 to Walter Barnes – "a small token of our appreciation of all he does for the Society" and the Secretary was to write to him "conveying the Committee's warmest thanks for all his services and wishing him a speedy recovery from his illness".

Walter Barnes had recovered enough to be present at the AGM three weeks later, and the minutes record his usual involvement in the proceedings. It was more interesting than previous Annual General Meetings and some of its decisions are worth noting at this stressful time in the orchestra's history.

Mr Frank Latham, the Society's President since its beginning, was made a Life President which would relieve him of his duties as he was very busy with war work. Mr A. W. Robinson was unanimously elected President in his place and Mr G. L. Bradley was made a Vice President to fill the vacancy created by A. W. Robinson's new position. The other officers were re-elected, thanks were accorded to both the Librarian, Miss Atkinson, for her work and to Miss Beadsworth for filling the position of Principal Violin so well.

When the meeting was told of the Committee's decision that the Society should continue its activities as usual and give a concert in the autumn Walter Barnes endorsed this but proposed that one concert only be given in the afternoon. He knew that several more members would be called up by November but felt that there would still be enough players to give a good concert. He also told the members that the Plymouth Orchestral Society had lost everything, rehearsal building, instruments and music library in a blitz on the city, and suggested that a letter should be written to them expressing the Society's concern and offering the use of their library. The subject of insurance cover was discussed as to whether or not a War Risks Policy for damage to contents of the Bandroom should be taken out. To avoid costly premiums Mr Graham White offered to store and be responsible for the drums and double basses through the summer months when the matter would again be discussed.

Walter remained anxious as to how many players would be available for the autumn session of rehearsals. Many of those who lived outside the town were finding that they could only attend rehearsals every other week due to shortages of petrol. An orchestra of about 40 instrumentalists looked possible, but with few rehearsals and irregular attendance it was felt that engaging an artiste was something of a gamble. Nevertheless,they decided to go ahead and engaged the singer Kenneth Ellis at an inclusive fee of ten guineas. Walter Barnes suggested that any profits from the concert should be given to the Madron Boy Scouts whose Scout Hall in Heamoor had been recently wrecked by a bomb, and this was agreed.

In the programme for the concert on Friday 7th November 1941, an afternoon concert starting at 3 p.m. in St John's Hall, all those members of the Society serving in the armed forces were listed. There were seventeen names in all, five in the RAF, two in the Navy, seven in the army, one in the National Fire Service, one in the Ambulance Casualty Service and Mrs Garstin in the ATS. Two of them must have been based locally in their war work because they were also listed among the fifty-two strong orchestra.

The 'Toy' Symphony

Among the works performed were two of contrasting character. 'A Lament from the Keltic Suite' was an affecting piece for solo 'cello, strings and harp by J. H. Foulds, a composer who had died in 1939. Enid Truman was the solo 'cellist and she was "deservedly applauded for her sensitive treatment of the beautiful melody" according to one newspaper report.

Other members of the orchestra were also in the spotlight for their performances in Haydn's 'Toy' Symphony. The audience must have smiled to see Freddie Hodson as the cuckoo, Mr G. L. Bradley (Headmaster of the Boys' County School) as the quail, Alan Wood, viola, as the nightingale, horn player J. Turnbull on the drum, Charlie Roach the trombonist wielding the rattle, the two trumpeters on toy trumpets, and two young ladies, Miss Marie Brown and Miss Barbara Stewart, performing on the bells and tambourine.

However, Mr Hodson, flute, and Mr Ernest Thomas, trumpet, also had the opportunity to show off their usual talents as soloists, the former in the accompaniment to Kenneth Ellis's singing of the aria 'O Ruddier than the Cherry', from Handel's 'Acis and Galatea', and Ernest Thomas performing 'The Willow Song', one of the movements in the 'Othello' Suite by Coleridge-Taylor.

The Cornishman reported a crowded hall for this concert and congratulated the orchestra for "carrying on during these war years... come wind, come weather; come battle or blitz, almost with the regularity of seed time and harvest come the concerts of the Penzance Orchestral Society". The writer was also encouraged to see many schoolchildren in the audience. In the interval the local Scoutmaster, Mr C. E. Venning thanked the Society for donating the profits of the concert to the restoration fund for the bombed Scouts' Hall. He described graphically the scene of destruction after the bombing, but said that the reaction had been, "to hell with Hitler; he might destroy our Scout Hall, but he is not going to destroy the Madron Troop". (An article in *The Cornishman* in February 1961 marking the Madron Troop's Golden Jubilee recounted this disaster but also the fact that after using temporary accommodation a new hut, the Venning Hall, was built in Heamoor and opened by Sir Edward Bolitho, the then Lord Lieutenant of Cornwall, in December 1950.)

Although not realised at the time this was Walter Barnes' last concert as Conductor of the Penzance Orchestral Society. His daughter Enid recalled that he was so weakened at the end of this concert that during the applause he had to remain seated on the chair which he had on the rostrum. He was present, however, for the last Committee Meeting of 1941, held on 7th December, when plans were made to hold the next concert, again in the afternoon only, on Friday 20th March 1942. They decided to invite the 'cellist, Madame Juliette Alvin, to return as soloist and rehearsals would recommence on Sunday 11th January 1942.

This was the last Committee meeting which Walter Barnes attended and it is clear that from then on he became seriously ill. Morgan Hosking remembered that Walter was constantly worried and depressed by the war. This sturdily built, vigorous and, seemingly, indomitable character was more fragile than he looked. At a rehearsal one Sunday in early February 1942 the President, A. W. Robinson, made the members of the Society aware as to how ill Walter was, and the hopes of all present were that he would make a good recovery. Mr Robinson also reported that for the time being Mr Maddern Williams had agreed to act as Deputy Conductor, this arrangement having been made after consultation with Walter Barnes.

It was decided that the plans for the March concert should be altered and a concert held in May which would be for the benefit of Mr Barnes "to whom we owed so much and who had never spared himself in his duties as Conductor". Maddern Williams became involved with concert arrangements from March onwards and suggested two pianists who might be engaged as soloists, Eileen Joyce (fee 30 guineas) and Phyllis Sellick (fee approximately 20 guineas) and the latter was chosen for the afternoon and evening concerts on Friday 22nd May.

The minutes do not reveal what an anxious and problematic time these weeks must have been for the orchestra committee. Most of them would have been very aware that in Walter Barnes' mind there was only one possible candidate to inherit his position, Morgan Hosking, and that he had intended to hand over the baton to him on his return from war service.

Morgan's eagerness to join the Royal Navy on the outbreak of war had caused consternation in many quarters. Firstly among his family where he was the 'apple of their eye' and involved in the family business, B. J. Ridge, with its harbour side offices at Newlyn, and whose proprietor, Benjamin Ridge, Morgan's uncle, was unwell at the time. Secondly, at the Newlyn Trinity Methodist Chapel where Morgan was organist. They were very upset at the loss of this talented young musician, though it has to be said that some disenchantment with this position was one of the reasons Morgan was eager to join the Navy and have a break from Newlyn. Lastly, and by no means least, Walter Barnes was heartbroken, but even his closeness to Walter did not make Morgan hesitate. Perhaps at the age of twenty-six Morgan felt that this was his only chance to go away and experience life outside the confines of his beloved Cornwall and he did not anticipate any immediate crisis occurring within the orchestra.

Crises, by their very nature, often come when least expected, and with the onset of Walter's serious health problems the orchestra was presented with a dilemma. Their effective deputy conductor was on war service and there would have been few other musicians available to stand in for Walter Barnes. It must have seemed like an answer to a prayer that Maddern Williams was on hand and willing to step into the breach during Walter's illness.

R. J. Maddern Williams FRCO, FTCL.

A Wartime Saviour – R. J. Maddern Williams

Richard John Maddern Williams was born in Pendeen where his father and two uncles had been church organists. He learned to play the cornet and was one of the instrumentalists who supplemented the music of the organ in the Parish Church. He became a student at the Royal College of Music, and was a pupil of Sir Walter Alcock, the distinguished organist famous for having played in Westminster Abbey at the coronations of Kings Edward VII, George V and George VI. (Sir Walter Alcock was, also, the grandfather of Rosemary Tunstall-Behrens, one of the longest serving violinists who is still a member of the Penzance Orchestral Society). Maddern Williams, as he was always known, became a Fellow of the Royal College of Organists and later a Fellow of Trinity College of Music. After a period as assistant organist at Wells Cathedral he was appointed, in 1906, aged twenty, as deputy organist at Norwich Cathedral, and in 1908 also became the organist at St Peter Mancroft Parish Church.

In 1923 he was appointed Director of Music for the Norwich City Corporation and in this capacity formed a municipal orchestra, military band, choral society and male voice choir and also conducted the Norfolk and Norwich Amateur Operatic Society. One of his most notable achievements was when he conducted, for two years running, the choir and orchestra of the London and North Eastern Railways, totalling 400 performers, in the Queen's Hall in London.

Maddern Williams had retired back to his native Cornwall in 1941 and with a wealth of musical expertise and experience behind him was, indeed, the 'right person in the right place' in early 1942 to solve the orchestra's problems.

The Death of Walter Barnes

On 11th March 1942 a small entry in *The Cornishman* newspaper reads: "It is with deep regret that we report the serious illness of Mr Walter Barnes. We are sure that all his numerous friends will join us in extending sympathy and good wishes for his quick recovery". But all the good wishes were to no avail and Walter died in West Cornwall Hospital on Saturday 4th April 1942, when, as his daughter Enid put it, "his heart gave out", just three weeks after his fifty-eighth birthday.

Looking back over more than sixty years it is almost impossible to imagine the effect that the news of Walter's death must have had on the musical community. *The Cornishman* for the following Thursday included a long tribute to him as well as a full report of the funeral at the Penzance Crematorium on Tuesday 7th April. The service was led by Canon C. H. S. Buckley, Vicar of Gulval, where, according to the funeral report, Walter had sung in the choir as a boy. It seems to have been a simple funeral service with no special music; in fact there is no mention of any music at all, apart from the singing of the 'Doxology'. There were no ladies at the funeral and Walter's family was represented by his brother-in-law, Mr T. J. Simons, his son-in-law, Norman Truman, some cousins and a nephew. Walter's sons were both on war service overseas, but were represented by Corporal Jack Allen, a family friend.

The respect and high regard which Walter had commanded in the community is reflected by those who attended the funeral. As well as the Mayor, Alderman E. C. Harvey, his Deputy, Alderman Robert Thomas and other Aldermen and Councillors, all the musical organisations were represented, with a large number of gentlemen, naturally, from the Orchestral Society. Many other local organisations, including the Penzance Cricket Club and *The Cornishman* newspaper, were represented as well as a large number of people from all over Cornwall.

The following week in *The Cornishman*, under the correspondence column, was a letter from Mr John R. Bazeley. He paid tribute to Walter by saying that the area had gained from Walter never having had the opportunity to exploit his musical talents in wider spheres, but that it was perhaps a tragedy for him that he had never been able to conduct a great symphony orchestra through which he could have expressed the music that was in him.

Mr Bazeley goes on to reminisce about times in the Operatic Society chorus where Walter's patience was so evident, but also the loss of it when the singers would be:

> *...treated to a magnificent flow of withering comment... usually it ended with Walter talking himself – and everybody else – into good humour... And on 'the night' ...whatever grimaces he might make at the orchestra or singer, his back to the audience remained imperturbable and unruffled until the moment when he turned to acknowledge the applause that was his very just due... Time and the endeavours of those who follow in Walter Barnes' footsteps will put his position in its deserved and proper perspective... His is the best and most enduring epitaph of all... happy memories written in the hearts and minds of the many people who have worked with him or heard him.*

A. W. Robinson, President of the Orchestral Society, responded to this with another letter printed in the same paper on 16th April 1942 saying that Mr Bazeley's letter "has given unbounded pleasure, particularly to the few whose unbroken connection with Walter covers over forty years". He then goes on to say that during Walter's illness the orchestra was "ever in his mind" and that it was a source of consolation to him, "when his old friend, Mr J. Maddern Williams consented to conduct". A. W. Robinson was also a friend of Maddern Williams and announced the date for the Walter Barnes Benefit Concert on the 22nd May when "in spite of existing difficult conditions, no effort will be spared in upholding the standards of performance which Walter always required... It may be noted that I do not use the word 'late' in connection with Walter Barnes. This is intentional, for he will remain a living and vital memory to those of us who enjoyed his long and unbroken friendship, and benefited from the reflection of his genius."

Mrs Crosbie Garstin also wrote a short letter which concluded:

> *The orchestra has been sadly depleted in numbers in this time of national emergency, and we heartily applaud those who are 'carrying on'. When we, who are serving away from home can again take up our instruments the Penzance Orchestral Society will continue in strength. This must be our tribute to Mr Walter Barnes.*

Morgan Hosking was on his day off from his ship, berthed at Avonmouth, when he received the news of Walter Barnes' death via a telegram from his uncle, Benjamin Ridge. Shocked and deeply saddened at the loss of his close friend and musical mentor, he was unable to get leave to attend the funeral. Surprisingly, the funeral report does not even include his name among those being represented at the service.

Morgan clearly recalled that with the death of Walter Barnes he knew that the long term future of the orchestra lay in his hands. He also knew that there was nothing that he could do about it until the war came to an end, but the commitment to carry on Walter's work was strong and unhesitating. It was, in his mind and many of those concerned with the orchestra, a natural inheritance to which he would, eventually, succeed. In the meantime, amid the sadness and grief, everyone was thankful that Maddern Williams was on hand taking the helm to steer a stricken vessel on its wartime course.

It was not until June 1945 that a poem about Walter Barnes was written by Mr W.V. Poole, a violinist in the orchestra. He lived in the village of Breage, and following his death in 1948 his widow left his violin to the orchestra. The poem provides an affectionate and poignant 'farewell' to Walter Barnes who has, in truth, never been forgotten throughout the ensuing years of the orchestra's history.

Walter

We know of Toscanini
Of Boult and Sargent too,
Stokowski, Coates and Cameron,
To mention but a few.

Yet here in rugged Cornwall,
That part known as "The West"
For many years reigned Walter –
His orchestra – the Best.

Beethoven, Bach and Mozart,
Composers new and old,
Our Walter mastered all of them
With the players in his fold.

Many miles those players came
To practice in Penzance –
And any slackness on their part
Well! Remember Walter's Glance?

As a humble fiddler midst them all
I scraped and practised hard,
Old Walter's eyes were everywhere,
You had to be on Guard!

Walter Barnes ne'er spared himself
And from that portly frame,
Perspiration poured for hours,
Perfection was his aim.

Rehearsals done, St John's Hall saw
His orchestra arrayed –
And oh! That back with outstretched arms
What power it thus portrayed.

Genius is very rare,
Except that found in 'yarns' –
But Morrab Road did harbour one
In Brilliant Walter Barnes.

His life was shortened there's no doubt
By efforts on his part,
Great in music, great in deeds
And truly great in heart.

The spirit of that mighty man
His orchestra still keeps,
May Cornwall always honour him
As thro' the years he sleeps.

God rest your soul dear Walter
And when the Maidens Nine
Desire to hear sweet music
The baton shall be thine.

WVP
Tremarvi,Breage
June 1945

Carrying on

In *The Cornishman* for Thursday 7th May 1942 an article appeared announcing "Penzance Orchestra's New Conductor". It gave an account of Maddern Williams' distinguished career and said that he "should prove a worthy successor to the late Mr Walter Barnes, under whom the orchestra has flourished since its foundation". Someone must have authorised this announcement but in view of the fact that the appointment of a conductor following Walter's death was not officially discussed by the Orchestral Society's Committee until 5th July, it seems a little previous!

It must have been something of a 'foregone conclusion', however, because the following week the newspaper contained not only an advertisement for the Society's forthcoming concert on 22nd

May but also a letter from Maddern Williams taking the form of a preview of the concert. This informed readers that "As a paper restriction prevents the usual programme notes, a lecture on the music will be given in the orchestral rehearsal room at the bottom of Queen Street, on Saturday afternoon next, May 16th at 3 p.m." to which admission was free. He ended the letter, "On a personal note if I may? I consider it a great privilege to be allowed to conduct such an excellent band of amateurs, and will do my best to sustain the high standard set by Walter Barnes".

The day before the concert, further news appeared in *The Cornishman* to the effect that an additional attraction at the two concerts would be "the painting of Walter Barnes by Stanhope Forbes R.A. which will be on view in the vestibule of St John's Hall on Friday, and prints of the picture will be on sale at 1s. 0d each. These prints are also on sale at Messrs. Robinson and Son's premises, Causewayhead, Penzance, from today, and no doubt there will be a large demand for this most attractive picture of two great artists". The same paper also contained an article about the soloist at the concert, Phyllis Sellick, who had married the well known pianist, Cyril Smith, in 1937. They had made their two-piano debut playing at the opening night of the 1941 Henry Wood Promenade Concerts.

The Orchestral Society's first concert under their new conductor took place on Friday 22nd May 1942, their ninety-third and ninety-fourth concerts at 3 p.m. and 7.30 p.m. This was to have been a benefit concert for Walter Barnes and the programme states that "Profits of the Concerts will be handed to Mrs Walter Barnes in appreciation of the valuable services rendered to the Society by Walter Barnes." The annual accounts for the year record a profit of £39. 14s. 8d, but donations to the Benefit Fund amounted to £81. 19s. 0d making a total of £121. 13s. 0d which was given to Mrs Barnes.

The concert opened with Mendelssohn's overture, 'Ruy Blas' which was followed by Tchaikovsky's 'Andante Cantabile' played by the strings of the orchestra, and Phyllis Sellick then performed the Grieg Piano Concerto in A Minor. The second half of the concert began with Schubert's 'Unfinished' Symphony, after which the soloist played a group of piano solos and the concert ended with the 'Dance of the Tumblers' by Rimsky-Korsakov.

Everyone present, players and audience alike, must have been very conscious of the significance of these concerts – the first occasion when someone other than their 'founding father' was in charge. Any stranger in their midst would have been made aware of it by a note, surrounded by a black border, in the programme announcing that "As a tribute to the memory of Walter Barnes (Hon. Conductor of the Orchestra since its foundation) Walford Davies' 'Solemn Melody' with be played before the commencement of each concert".

Despite there being now nineteen members of the orchestra serving in His Majesty's Forces, some of them were able to play in this concert, including Morgan Hosking who is listed among the first violins. The orchestra totalled fifty-six players, and their performances were praised in the concert report printed in *The Cornishman* for 28th May 1942.

This report was headed "Vale" and opened with words from W. J. Cory's poem 'Heraclitus' – "Still are thy pleasant voices, thy nightingales awake; For Death, he taketh all away, But them he cannot take." It is a moving account of the concert stressing the strangeness of not seeing "Walter Barnes' broad back, with arms outstretched... that imperious pose as he waited for some inconsiderate late-comer to scurry to his seat, or while the shuffling and coughing died down". But the writer congratulated Maddern Williams who had "picked up the fallen baton... to lead this orchestra on," and thought that, "under him all sections of the orchestra seemed perfectly happy" and that "they well upheld the traditions of this Society". Phyllis Sellick had given, "a performance to be counted with" and her piano solos were "things of unforgettable loveliness."

After "due consideration" the Committee resolved to recommend Maddern Williams' appointment as conductor "for the ensuing year". This was carried unanimously at the General Members Meeting on Sunday 5th July 1942 and Mr Williams was thanked for "bringing us through the concert so successfully under abnormal difficulties and distressing circumstances." In reply Maddern Williams said that he had never expected to find such a vigorous orchestra in Cornwall especially under war conditions. He thought it was "a wonderful organisation and hoped they would resume practices immediately in preparation for a concert before the long blackout evenings arrived."

Morgan Hosking was paid a tribute, in his absence, for his keenness and enthusiasm as conductor of the Junior Orchestra and re-elected to the post on the nomination of the President A. W. Robinson, seconded by Mr Maddern Williams. The position of Hon. Secretary was left unfilled at this meeting following the resignation of Miss Ethel Tonkin, due to ill health,

and as no one volunteered to take on the post the Hon.Treasurer, A.W. Firth, said he would do the best he could to carry on as Deputy. (He did so for another twelve months until the Rev. H. Gardner, the Priest in charge of St Paul's Church, was asked to take up the office which, as a non-playing member, he did for the next two years.) Financially, the Society was in a fairly healthy state with over £200 in the bank after all expenses had been paid.

Innovations, 1942-1945

Rehearsals were resumed immediately, from 12th July, preparing for concerts in the autumn. These concerts would inaugurate some of the changes in style that would occur during the period of Maddern Williams' conductorship. Firstly, local male voice choirs would be invited to take part in orchestral concerts, and secondly, there would be annual concerts in association with the local branch of the Toc H.

According to *The Cornishman* report these concerts, the first of which was held on Friday 2nd October 1942, overcame "almost insurmountable difficulties" during the weeks of preparation. Whereas before the war players used their cars to travel from all over the county to rehearsals this was now increasingly difficult with petrol restrictions and other transport problems. It seems that Maddern Williams would rehearse with such small groups of players as could be gathered, somehow managing to weld them together with very few rehearsals of the full orchestra. Perhaps it was to help with this problem that he incorporated the Pendeen Male Voice Choir, of which he was the conductor, into the programming of the concerts, though they only performed two part songs in the Friday concert, but contributed much more to the second concert on Sunday 4th October.

The instrumental soloist in the Orchestral Society's 95th concert on the Friday was an Armenian violinist, Olive Zorian, who played the Max Bruch Concerto in G Minor "with consummate skill and understanding", and a group of solos, accompanied by Mrs Enid Truman. As well as Elgar's 'Pomp and Circumstance March No. 4 in G', Mozart's 'Eine Kleine Nachtmusik' and 'The Geeze Dance' by John Holliday, the orchestra also performed Beethoven's 5th Symphony, a substantial programme for such a hard-pressed orchestra.

The Sunday afternoon concert was held under the auspices of the Penzance Branch of Toc H, and all profits from this concert were given to their War Services Club Appeal. With the exception of the concerto the orchestra played all the works from the Friday concert plus Edward German's Suite, 'Three Dances from Henry VIII', and the guest performers were the Massed Male Voice Choirs of the villages of Mousehole, Pendeen and St Just. The choirs sang two groups of part songs, one group conducted by John Potter, conductor of the Mousehole Male Voice Choir, and were joined by the orchestra for a performance of Grieg's 'Landerkennung', in which the soloist was William Harvey. Nothing more is known about this concert nor the amount of money it raised, the only reference in the press being a letter from a Mr W. H. Pengelly, Chairman of the local branch of Toc H thanking everyone for their support. The Orchestral Society made a loss of £3 on their own concert which was considered to be quite "satisfactory under the circumstances".

Members of the Orchestral Society joined forces again with the Pendeen Choir on a Sunday afternoon in February 1943 to give a concert in aid of the West Cornwall Hospital which was trying to raise £1,000 in a week of fundraising events. The rest of the year followed a similar pattern to 1943 with concerts in the Spring and Autumn including an extra one for the Toc H. The Spring concerts on Friday 28th May at 3 and 7.30 p.m. were well reviewed and the soloist, Miss Linda Parker, a well known soprano from the Sadler's Wells Opera Company, was highly regarded. The profit from these concerts, £15. 9s. 6d, was given to the Red Cross and St John Prisoners of War Fund.

An interesting development never referred to in the minutes of the Society is that Sir Henry Wood had consented to become a patron of the Society. This had, perhaps, been the work of the conductor, Maddern Williams, because a week or two previously the local paper had announced that Sir Henry had become the patron of Pendeen Male Voice Choir.

The first weekend in October saw the Orchestra giving three concerts. On Friday 1st they held their own 98th and 99th concerts in St John's Hall with the pianist, Freda Caplan, playing Beethoven's Piano Concerto in G. Haydn's 'Oxford' Symphony was the other major work performed and Bach's 'Ave Maria', styled 'Prelude', had been orchestrated for the strings by Maddern Williams. *The Cornishman* report of this concert was written by 'J.T.W.' and entitled 'The Charms of Music'. His review of the concert follows a long rumination on the dark days of war bringing out a greater appreciation of the arts, and music in particular: "a nation that can make music in adversity cannot suffer defeat at the hands of a nation that tells its people what it shall look at and what it shall play". He then goes on to praise the orchestra and regarded the soloist's performance as "excellent and charming, and she well captured the grandeur of the Concerto".

On Sunday 3rd October, in a concert organised by Toc H, the Orchestra was again joined by four male voice choirs, this time from Heamoor, Ludgvan, Marazion and Pendeen. The orchestra repeated its programme, including the first movement of the Beethoven Piano Concerto performed by Miss Camilla Lyster, and the Grieg 'Landerkennung' for choirs and orchestra was sung once again.

The Cornishman provided a lengthy and fulsome report of the Toc H concert headed "Music and Song: how do they manage to do it?", referring to its coming only two days after the Orchestral Society's Concerts, attended "by all who liked this sort of thing", yet the Toc H managed to fill St John's Hall all over again. The reasons given for their success were thought to be two-fold, firstly, the real need for Sunday entertainment in Penzance. There was "nothing more depressing than seeing people in the services... wandering the streets with nothing to do. No wonder there is increased drinking and immorality". Secondly, there was nothing Cornishmen like more than massed male voice choirs, and their fans came to hear them in St John's Hall, "which to many down here is equivalent to the Albert Hall or Queen's Hall". The report then praises all the performers, thanks all and sundry, including the Savoy, Gaiety and Ritz cinemas for exhibiting slides – which makes one curious as to what these portrayed. 'J.W.T.' concludes his eulogy by saying that the Toc H War Services Club was doing great work "and music is the finest way of helping it".

On the 14th October 1943 *The Cornishman* printed two letters, the first from 'Pythagoras' who, in paying a tribute to the late Walter Barnes, bemoans the fact that the people of Penzance had not honoured his memory in some permanent form. He thought that "some form of artistic memorial wouldn't exactly cost a fortune". One wonders who 'Pythagoras' may have been as he must have been unaware, as the Society's President, A. W. Robinson, pointed out in his reply, of "the fine portrait by our great West country artist, Stanhope Forbes, R.A." Mr Robinson wrote that "At present this hangs over the conductor's stand in our practice room, but after the war we hope to arrange for a more suitable place for this fine memorial. Meanwhile, I shall be only too delighted to show it to 'Pythagoras' or any other admirers who have not yet seen it". He went on to say that "every letter, circular, poster and programme bears the name of our founder, and on the cover of every programme an etching of him in characteristic pose from a block designed by another well-known local artist and admirer".

The One Hundredth Concert

The war dragged on through the short days of another Cornish winter, with the Orchestral Society approaching the next landmark in their history – their hundredth concert. This was planned for Friday 19th May at 3 p.m. with the one hundred and first concert the following Sunday 21st May 1944. The Conductor suggested using massed male voice choirs again, thereby incurring only travel expenses. Rehearsals for these special concerts began on Sunday 6th February 1944 at 2 p.m.

Detailed advertisements and a preview article appeared in *The Cornishman* during the two weeks prior to the celebration concerts. The printed programmes were still subject to paper restrictions and remained at a folded 'A4' size but listed Subscribers and Friends, and members of the orchestra who numbered forty-four players. Among the first violinists there appears a Madame Olga Lukashevitch which was the married name of Miss Olga Bennett. She had originally joined the orchestra in 1927 playing in three concerts, and one in 1932. She was professionally trained and had married a Russian violinist and made fleeting appearances in the Penzance orchestra.

The one hundredth concert began with an arrangement by Elgar of the National Anthem in which the soloist was Edward Tregarthen. Glinka's Overture 'Ruslan and Ludmilla' was followed by Mozart's Symphony No. 39 in E Flat. The second half of the concert comprised a group of songs sung by the male voice choirs. Two of these, Bach's 'Jesu, Joy of Man's Desiring' and 'The Blue Danube' by Strauss were accompanied by the orchestra which also played Moussorgsky's 'Gopak'. The choirs, orchestra and three soloists then combined for the final work, a 'Fantasia on Nautical Airs' arranged by Maddern Williams. The soloists were Morley Curnow, Abraham George and Silas Glasson – names which might well have derived from a Thomas Hardy novel, but the gentlemen were probably members of the various male choirs.

The concert was repeated at 3.30 p.m. on Sunday 21st May with a slightly shortened orchestral programme and more songs from the choirs.

The Cornishman report written following the Friday concert was generous and appreciative, paying tribute to the orchestra saying that "How much, spiritually, the orchestra has done since it came into existence... can never be measured... as a cultural combination (it) must not be allowed to go under, even in the very harrowing days which we are now passing". The writer also points out that when the orchestra assembled on Friday afternoon it was the first time they had met as a body as they had been rehearsing "in bits and pieces. It is, therefore, excusable if at times there was a certain raggedness in the performances."

In 1994, *The Cornishman*, in its 'Yesteryear' column selected the 100th concert as one of the items of news under "50 Years Ago" quoting briefly from the concert report, "For the past five years now, despite all the odds of war, this society has managed to produce two concerts a year. This is a proud record. Profits from the concerts were, as usual, given to charity, in this case the West Cornwall Hospital Appeal."

There were no further concerts under their own auspices given by the Orchestral Society during 1944 but neither conductor nor players were idle. They were involved in a concert at St John's Hall on Sunday 23rd July as a Grand Finale to a "Salute the Soldier Week", an orchestral and choral concert involving a total of 120 performers. Mendelssohn's 'Hymn of Praise' was performed with soloists Elise Harvey, Sheila Lawrey and the Rev C. H. S. Buckley. Part 2 of the concert consisted of orchestral items including Beethoven's 'Romance in F' in which the soloist was Madame Olga Lukashevitch, and Handel's 'Hallelujah Chorus'. This concert was repeated in St Just on the following Friday in aid of the St Just Forces Fund. At the end of the year the Orchestral Society and Male Voice Choirs joined together in the annual Toc H concert on Sunday 10th December.

Solomon at Porthcurno

The Cornishman newspaper revealed, in a fairly brief article, that at the end of July 1944 an unlikely and surprising event had taken place in Porthcurno. The world famous pianist, Solomon, had given a piano recital in the Cable and Wireless Station's theatre. The cable station at Porthcurno was, at this time, the largest in the world with the capacity to receive and transmit, via fourteen submarine cables coming into the bay at Porthcurno, up to 2,000,000 words a day. A vital centre for communications during the war it was heavily guarded by troops, and ENSA concerts were held in the theatre to entertain the soldiers and technicians in this remote valley. Whether the recital by Solomon was one of these is not known, but however it happened he had taken his own small Steinway grand piano there on which to perform. According to the paper it "was a rare treat... and his interpretation of music extremely beautiful. The dextrous way his fingers moved up and down the keyboard afforded the sight of a lifetime." Apparently the audience was "held spellbound for nearly two hours" and to be in the hall that night was "a never-to-be forgotten experience".

Death of a Patron

Sir Henry Wood had died on 19th August 1944, bringing his patronage of both the Orchestral Society and the Pendeen Male Voice Choir to an end. This sad event received a lengthy article in *The Cornishman* a few days later revealing Sir Henry Wood's associations with West Cornwall. In his autobiography *My life of Music* he recalled how he had been a private pupil of a gifted organist and violinist at the Royal Academy of Music called H. C. Tonking, who was then a sub-professor. Sir Henry described this man as "a raw Cornishman", whose father kept a chemist shop in Camborne. "One summer I spent a holiday there. Rather a busman's holiday I fear, for Tonking and I gave recitals in places such as Plymouth and Penzance, he playing the violin and I the organ or piano".

The Cornishman also confirmed that Maddern Williams had known the great man and received the benefit of his advice during his career in Norwich. Incidentally, Sir Henry Wood had been an advocate of introducing women players into orchestras during the early years of the century, but had not succeeded in this until 1913 when women had been allowed to play in the Queen's Hall Orchestra. So Walter Barnes had beaten him to it in 1911!

The Orchestral Society held their Annual General Meeting on Friday 8th September 1944. The main point of interest was the election to the post of Hon. Treasurer of Mr G. L. Bradley who had recently retired as Headmaster of Penzance County School for Boys after 33 years in the post. He was taking on this post following the retirement of Mr A.W. Firth, now aged seventy-six and who, by a numerical coincidence, had held the position for 33 years. At the meeting the President spoke with feeling of Mr Firth's many years of faithful and devoted service to the Society and he was elected as a Life Member.

When the Orchestral Society's Committee met in January 1945 they chose a provisional date for their next concert, 11th May. No one could have seen how fortuitous this choice of date would be and that the concert would take place at the end of the Victory in Europe week. As the end of the war approached feelings of relief and anticipation must have built up among members of the Society. Those who had kept the orchestra going through the war years would welcome back colleagues to provide greater musical support, and those on active service would look forward to returning to the more enjoyable ranks of the orchestra. Mrs Crosbie Garstin, the official leader of the orchestra, was restored to them in time for the Spring concert, but did not assume her position as Leader for some time to come.

The End of the War

Victory in Europe was announced to the nation in a radio broadcast at 3 p.m. on Tuesday 8th May 1945. Anticipating this moment the people of Penzance lost no time in getting out flags and bunting, decorating the streets and themselves. *The Cornishman* for that week in an article headed "Round About on VE Day" reported that "red white and blue adornments decorated button holes and clothes." The children of the Treneere Estate even made time to organise a fancy dress parade followed by a tea and sports. Church bells in and around the town "could be heard far across the meadows", and the ships and boats in the harbours of Penzance, Newlyn and Mousehole were dressed overall and they sounded their sirens in a victory salute. The Penzance promenade quickly became "gay with a colourful crowd". But there were some feelings of bewilderment – "All these decorations, for example, were being displayed before the actual official announcement. And was the black-out still to be kept up?" The atmosphere, as well as joyous, was one of a public "not quite knowing where they were".

In the evening events went ahead with confidence. Churches and chapels held services of thanksgiving and in lighter vein hotels and pubs were granted an extra hour of opening time and were filled with "cheery laughing crowds". Dances, too, were hastily organised, one at the Winter Gardens on the promenade to raise money for the local hospital, and another in St John's Hall.

This mood of celebration must have permeated St John's Hall on Friday 11th May when the Orchestral Society gave its two Spring concerts. The programme, having been chosen and rehearsed during the previous months, does not especially reflect the mood of the moment but was cheerful enough in itself. Opening with Smetana's Overture to 'The Bartered Bride' the first half of the concert comprised Elgar's 'Serenade for Strings' and Mozart's 'Piano Concerto No. 1 in A (K488)' performed by Michal Hambourg, daughter of the well known pianist and composer, Mark Hambourg. After the interval, Beethoven's Second Symphony was followed by a group of Chopin piano solos played by the soloist, and the concert ended with Tchaikovsky's 'Valse' from 'The Sleeping Beauty' ballet.

The newspaper reviewer paid tribute to the orchestra for its war time survival despite difficulties and the death of Walter Barnes. He was not very enthusiastic about Miss Hambourg's performance of the concerto but her Chopin pieces were "some of the most charming things of the evening". The orchestra's playing was generally praised, especially the 'Larghetto' movement of the Elgar 'Serenade' which was played with "exceptional delicacy". The report concluded that the orchestra could now look forward to a brighter future to "make the air laugh with their music in a world purged of many evil things".

Committee meetings during the summer months reveal that it was only now, ten years after its acquisition, that the portrait of Walter Barnes by Stanhope Forbes was to be insured, but no details are recorded. Rehearsals for the first post-war concert season would begin on Friday 14th September, and repairs to the Bandroom were to be put in hand. It is assumed that these were necessary only because of wear and tear or wartime neglect because there was no suggestion that the property had received bomb damage. With a balance in hand of over £173 and the estimate for repairs being about £14 there was no problem, and a decision was also made to reduce the mortgage on the Bandroom by a further £100. This all implies a mood of confidence and optimism among those responsible for the Orchestral Society. Having come through the ravages of war and internal trauma the feeling must have been that "normal service will be resumed" and not "as soon as possible", but with their next concert on Friday 7th December 1945.

8

Post War Problems 1945-1946

With the trials and tribulations of six years of war behind them one might have expected the Penzance Orchestral Society to have produced performances which reflected the joy and relief of victory. But the evidence does not provide such a picture, though one must assume that these feelings were present among the individual players. The concerts on Friday 7th December 1945 were previewed in *The Cornishman* with a tribute to the orchestra's survival during the war when their concerts provided "attractive programmes of first class music and, on many occasions, soloists of national merit". This first peace-time concert was to feature an old and greatly admired friend as the soloist, Harold Fairhurst, playing the Brahms Violin Concerto, as well as music by Weber, Haydn and Smetana.

It seems that despite players returning from war service, the preparation for the concert had been beset by problems, mainly due to illness among the instrumentalists. Then, at the very last minute, Harold Fairhurst was taken ill with pleurisy and one can imagine the frantic activity needed to find a replacement who could perform the Brahms Concerto.

This turned out to be a young Scottish lady, Miss Elizabeth Lockhart, unknown to the orchestra. She had not played the concerto for six months, but *The Cornishman* reviewer regarded her performance as one of "superb artistry" and "worthy of her glorious 'Strad'", referring to the fact that her violin was a Stradivarius worth £2,000. Her ability to deputise at 24 hours notice in such a major work and the information that she was leaving for a series of recitals in Hamburg, Brussels and Paris indicates that she was a violinist of some repute. Her solo items were Spanish dances by Sarasate and De Falla, accompanied on the piano by Mrs Enid Truman, who also showed her true ability by bringing new accompaniments up to performance standard in such a short time.

Despite the success of the soloist the concert itself received only modest acclaim, the orchestra coming through "a trying time with commendable success" but only playing "competently". To add to this rather muted reaction the applause came from "a not too crowded house", resulting in a financial loss on the two concerts of £32. 9s. 1d. On a more positive note the orchestra had increased to fifty-one players, including a new member, Mrs N. Horsfall, among the second violins who would later learn to play the double-bass and become one of the most memorable characters in the post-war orchestra.

Among the members who had returned from war service was Arthur Miners. Though they may not have been unique, his experiences during the war serve as a reminder of what some of those coming back into the orchestra had endured.

Arthur Miners

Arthur had attended Penzance Grammar School for Boys where he was taught to play the flute by Freddie Hodson and joined the Orchestral Society in 1932. He also learned a great deal from another of the Society's regular flautists at this time, William Lloyd, a very talented amateur musician.

Arthur was apprenticed as a pharmacist and when war was declared he quickly joined the army and went into the Medical Corps. While serving in Crete, where he worked in the army hospital pharmacy, the Germans invaded and Arthur was sent to a prisoner of war camp in southern Poland. During this time the Red Cross provided Arthur with a silver flute which became a 'life-saver' for him and with time to practice he increased his accomplishment on the instrument.

At the end of the war Arthur faced a traumatic and circuitous journey home during which he was again taken prisoner by the Russians who mistook him and his fellow survivors for Germans. He was eventually released, discharged from the army and returned to Cornwall where he resumed his career as a pharmacist and re-joined the Orchestral Society in the autumn of 1945. Living in various parts of the South-West and north Cornwall he showed his commitment to the Society by travelling thousands of miles to rehearsals and concerts in Penzance during his many years as a member of the Society.

In late December 1945 *The Cornishman* published an article looking back at the musical and dramatic events of the year, and talked about the work of CEMA (the wartime Council for the Encouragement of Music and the Arts which later became the Arts Council of Great Britain) in West Cornwall, and the recently formed Penzance Society of Arts. This organisation had been officially inaugurated in February 1945 when the Boyd Neel String Orchestra had given a concert in St John's Hall.

Its second concert, in March 1945, was a recital by the young British pianist, Colin Horsley, and reaction to these concerts was that people were "apt to say that Penzance was being put on the map" as far as music and drama were concerned. The writer went on to point out that the Penzance Orchestral Society had existed long before CEMA and the new Society of Arts, and had "done much to keep the town in its place on the musical map...by bringing to Penzance such musicians...as Phyllis Sellick and Elizabeth Lockhart, the latter unknown here until her recent triumph with the orchestra." This was a much more encouraging statement on which to end the year rather than one which showed a concert deficit! Plans had already been made for the Spring concert in 1946 for which a concert sub-committee had been appointed in the form of Messrs Morgan Hosking and Kendall Baic, both of whom were emerging as prominent personalities from the ranks of the orchestra.

The minutes for the early months of 1946 are brief and give the impression that they were entered up 'en bloc', possibly at a later stage. This may have been because at a meeting in January the resignation of the secretary, Mrs Yeadon, was announced to members. A Miss Green was elected to replace her, but she does not seem to have held the position for very long. At the Annual General Meeting in July the problem of obtaining the services of a Hon. Secretary was acknowledged and Morgan Hosking, who had been writing the minutes, promised to continue dealing with secretarial work with the help of the Treasurer, Mr G. L. Bradley.

At the rehearsal on 1st February 1946 the President, Mr A. W. Robinson, announced the death of Captain Frank Latham. Despite being ill for some time his death on 29th January was unexpected and tributes were paid to his memory as a man who had been a "generous supporter of the Society from its earliest days" as well as "a great gentleman and keen musician". Members stood in silence as a token of respect and regret.

Frank Latham. President of Penzance Orchestral Society, 1907–1941.

Captain Frank Latham, M. Inst. C.E. (I); F.S.E.

The many and frequent references to Frank Latham in the minutes, and in the history so far, bear witness to his importance and value to the Orchestral Society over the years. He joined as a clarinettist in 1907, became a bassoonist in 1909 and was even to be found among the violinists in 1940. He had been President of the Society since its formation, remaining so until June 1941 when he was made a Life President. This title seems to have been altered to Life Patron by the time of his death, perhaps to avoid any confusion with the position of the succeeding President Mr A. W. Robinson.

The Cornishman for Thursday 31st January 1946 devoted many column inches to his obituary. Not only was Frank Latham a leading member of the Orchestral Society but he was someone who had played a vital and memorable part in the history of Penzance itself, as the former Borough Engineer and Surveyor, during formative years of the town's development. He was appointed to this post, aged only twenty-five, in 1899 and carried out his duties with distinction until his retirement in 1933.

We learn from the obituary that during his period of office:

> *...many of the present amenities of Penzance owe their presence to his skill and imagination....the Alexandra Gardens, with their tennis courts and bowling greens, the Bedford Bolitho Gardens, with their picturesque exterior in the form of a Norman castle with rounded bastions and their interior containing that 'Italian' suggestiveness..., the Jubilee Bathing Pool, one of the finest of such constructions in the West of England, the delightful little St Anthony Gardens linked up with the bathing pool, and the Penrose Gardens at Lescudjack.*

He was also responsible for the housing estates at Parc Wartha, Penalverne, and the Gwavas Estate at Newlyn. For research that he did on the effect of erosion on sea walls he was awarded the gold medal of the Royal Society of Engineers and elected to its Council and in 1912 became the President of the Institute of Municipal Engineers. He also wrote books and articles on his subject and gave lectures to various societies and was, generally, a man devoted to public service. On his retirement he received the Freedom of the Borough of Penzance, an honour which deeply gratified him.

In addition to his love of music, Latham was also very interested in sport and, though he did not take part, was a keen supporter of both football and cricket. This remarkable and talented man was also known to have been a skilled performer on the bagpipes, and this, along with his many other attributes and "a somewhat old world charm... endeared him to a wide circle of friends... Penzance is the poorer for his passing." The funeral was attended by a large number of borough officials including the Mayor, Alderman Robert Thomas, the current Borough Surveyor, Mr J. H. Blight, Alfred Robinson, President of the Orchestral Society and other prominent men of the town and district. Sadly, some of the attractive assets of Penzance which he created no longer remain, but one of his greatest, the Jubilee Bathing Pool, is still in use.

Other sad losses for the Orchestral Society occurred with the death of Mrs Walter Barnes on 21st March, and that of Mr A. W. Firth on 25th April 1946. The deaths of Frank Latham and Mrs Barnes were noted in the programme of the concert in April 1946, where she was described as "a Great Friend and supporter". The death of A. W. Firth coming so soon after that of Frank Latham must have caused feelings of deep sadness among the orchestral members and, combined with the death of Mrs Barnes, underlined the fact that this was, indeed, the end of an era. But none of these grand old folk of the Society would have regarded themselves as indispensable and would have been the first to insist that things carried on as usual.

The spring concert took place on Friday 12th April 1946 and at some point a decision had been made that Morgan Hosking should conduct one of the items in the programme, Rossini's Ballet Music 'La Boutique Fantasque'. The soloist was a tenor called Edward Reach who sang an aria from Handel's 'Jeptha' and the symphony was Dvorak's 'New World'. Concert reports all say that the orchestra lacked much of its pre-war brilliance. *The Cornishman* even headed its article, "Orchestra Loses Its Sparkle" saying that, "It was like meeting an old friend, but one felt that that friend, having withstood the ravages of time, and the stress and strain of war, had lost much of its zest and verve". The soloist was a "highlight in an otherwise rather disappointing afternoon", and with the symphony, "One felt that in tackling this long, but beautiful piece, the orchestra had undertaken too much".

The Rossini ballet suite, conducted by Morgan Hosking, was very well written about. *The Cornishman* thought that it was "the orchestra's best rendering for the afternoon" and that they seemed to capture their "pre-1939 spirit" in it, and the *Western Morning News* felt that it showed "something of their old form". This must have been encouraging for Morgan Hosking, but it is fair to say that the nature of the work probably added to its success, as a "pleasing and lively" work.

Handing on the Baton

At a committee meeting in June 1946 a letter from the conductor of the orchestra, Maddern Williams, was read. He regretted his inability to attend the meeting and stated that he did not seek re-election as the Society's conductor at the Annual General Meeting because he understood that Walter Barnes had intended Mr Morgan Hosking to succeed him. He now felt that his work with the orchestra was done but, was prepared at any time to assist the orchestra in any way as he had not lost interest in the Society. After other committee business had been dealt with this letter was discussed, and the President expressed the gratitude of the Society for what Mr Williams had done to keep them going during the war years following Walter Barnes' death, remarks with which the committee agreed. It was decided that a presentation should be made to Maddern Williams, the form and timing of which should be decided by members at the A.G.M.

This took place on 12th July 1946 at 7 p.m. and due to the late arrival of the President, who had mistakenly thought the meeting started at 8 p.m., the chair was taken by L. Graham White. Following routine business the election of officers took place. When the question of Maddern Williams' letter of resignation came up there was some anxiety on the part of one member that this may have been connected with the newspaper reports following the April concert. On an assurance from the chairman that this was not so, the letter of resignation was accepted and Maddern Williams was unanimously elected a Life Vice-President of the Society. It was decided that the sum of £21 should be presented to him and the President was asked to find out how the cheque should be presented. The Chairman, Graham White, then proposed that Morgan Hosking be made the Hon. Conductor. This was seconded by Mr Roach and the motion carried.

These are the recorded facts of the handing over of the conductorship from Maddern Williams to Morgan Hosking. It is from reading between the lines and the memories of those closely involved that an impression is gained that it was not quite as straightforward as the minutes indicate. Firstly, Maddern Williams' letter of resignation did not say that he "knew" Walter Barnes had intended Morgan Hosking to succeed him, but that he "understood" that this was so, implying that he had been made aware of the fact. Secondly, the fact that the President, A.W. Robinson, had arrived late for the meeting is surprising given his position. He was known to be a close friend of Maddern Williams and was one of the small group believed to have wanted Maddern Williams to continue as conductor. Perhaps he engineered a late arrival so as to avoid an awkward situation, because he, apparently, felt very strongly about this.

The only evidence in support of this idea is that he is not recorded as having attended any committee meetings for the ensuing year and at a committee meeting on 24th July 1946 it was decided at the beginning of the meeting that Mr L. Graham White should be elected the permanent Chairman of the Committee. However, by the next Annual General Meeting any difficulties had been overcome for Alfred Robinson was present and re-elected to the position of President.

L. Graham White

L. Graham White. Committee Chairman, 1946–1979.

Graham White joined the orchestral society in the autumn of 1935 as a double-bass player and became a very familiar presence in the orchestra during his forty-four years membership.

Born in 1895 Graham attended the Penzance County School for Boys during its early years, and then emigrated to America as a young man. He quickly returned at the outbreak of World War I, joined the Irish Guards and served with the army in France. Later, he transferred to the newly formed Royal Air Force and became a fighter pilot. After flying in India and Afghanistan he was finally demobilized at the end of 1919.

After his marriage in 1923, to Winifred Bird, a young woman whose family had moved to West Cornwall, they began farming at Croft Hooper alongside the A30 at Crowlas. Both Graham and Winifred were committed to public service, Graham once saying that, "My belief is that people should not live for themselves".

This credo was exemplified by his life's work in horticulture, education and local government, where he made an important contribution in the many responsible positions he held. Winifred became a magistrate, founder member of West Cornwall Footpaths Preservation Society and supported many other causes. She was also a member of the orchestra and played the viola for a number of years before and during the Second World War.

Graham White was a vital and authoritative member of the Society throughout the middle years of its existence. He was the Committee Chairman for many years and valued for his experienced judgement and ability to make things work. He is remembered as "a gentleman to his fingertips". Graham and Winifred also frequently provided hospitality for visiting soloists.

Morgan Hosking greatly appreciated his Chairman's support and recalled the amusing occasion when, during a rehearsal, he became aware that something was amiss in the double-bass section. "Was that you, Graham?", he asked and back came the reply "You know d*** well it was, Morgan"! Graham White retired from the orchestra in 1979 and died in July 1980, a great loss to both the Orchestral Society and the wider community.

Another situation that arose at the 1946 A.G.M. was that the acting leader, Winifrede Beadsworth, wished to be relieved of the position. Ken Baic was elected as the new Principal Violin having been proposed by Morgan Hosking and seconded by Mr Freddie Hodson. Mr Baic proposed a hearty vote of thanks to Miss Beadsworth for her splendid services to the orchestra which was endorsed by all at the meeting. So Morgan Hosking faced his first season with the orchestra not only having to blend together a group of musicians who may have had cause to disagree among themselves, but with a new, untried leader.

Kendall Baic

Kendall Baic had a romantic background. According to Enid Truman his father was from Serbia where he had been "a prince or something very high up". He came to Cornwall to study at the Camborne School of Mines but his accommodation, or lodgings, were in Clarence Street in Penzance. It seems that the daughter of the house was very beautiful and Mr Baic senior fell in love with her, their relationship resulting in a baby boy who was called Dick. Mr Baic returned to Serbia but came back to Penzance with the intention of taking the young lady back to Serbia as his wife. When she discovered that she would only be one of his wives she refused to marry him and he went away again, but she gave birth to Ken after his departure. Both boys remained in Penzance and Ken's full surname was Baic de Brenovich, but he only ever used the first part. He was, apparently, endowed with continental good looks. It is probable that he was taught the violin by Walter Barnes and he became a very good violinist joining the orchestra in 1932, and was its Principal Violin from 1946 to 1948.

The appointment of Morgan Hosking as the new conductor of the Penzance Orchestral Society received attention in many of the local papers where reports of the Annual General Meeting appeared. Photographs of Morgan and brief accounts of his musical activities were included. He was, of course, already a familiar figure on the rostrum to the members of the orchestra and they would have been fairly confident of his capabilities. But still the future would be challenging in the post war days, with a thirty-three year old, musically self-educated and relatively inexperienced conductor to take them forward.

Penzance Orchestral Society circa 1947. Conductor J. Morgan Hosking, Principal Violin Kendall Baic, Co-Principal Violin Winifrede Beadsworth and President A. W. Robinson. Richards Bros., Penzance

Under New Management 1946-1949

During the summer of 1946 there were signs of musical and cultural life in West Cornwall returning to normal. The Penzance Pavilion, on the promenade, re-opened after a closure of six years, having been used by American troops for a period during the war. A performance of John Gay's 'The Beggar's Opera' was produced in St Ives during the week of 13th -17th August under the auspices of the St Ives Society for the Advancement of Music and the Arts which had been formed in 1944. In Penzance the restarting of the Operatic Society was announced at the AGM of the Orchestral Society. It was decided to fully support their production of Gilbert and Sullivan's 'The Gondoliers' in the spring of 1947, to be conducted by Mr J. Maddern Williams.

The Orchestral Society began planning for the forthcoming season. One of the committee members was a cousin of the trumpeter, George Eskdale, who was invited as the soloist for the concert in December 1946. Alan Loveday was eventually chosen as soloist for the fortieth birthday concert in April 1947 to play the Beethoven Violin Concerto for a fee of £35.

Prior to their autumn concert in December, members of the orchestra joined with other performers for a Remembrance Day Concert in St John's Hall on Sunday 10th November 1946. This was organised by the Penzance and Newlyn branches of the British Legion, and involved the orchestra, soloists and the Newlyn Male Choir, which had re-started in January 1946, Morgan Hosking remaining its conductor. The *West Briton* regarded the evening as "One of the finest concerts heard in Penzance for some years" and "a personal triumph for Mr J. Morgan Hosking who trained the choir and also a fine orchestra".

Morgan's First Concert

Morgan Hosking's first concert as conductor of the Orchestral Society was previewed in *The Cornishman*, again including a photograph of him, this time holding his violin. It also announced that it would be the first time in its forty-year history that the Society would have a trumpeter as soloist, and that George Eskdale was the principal trumpet of the London Symphony Orchestra and a noted broadcaster.

For the two concerts on Friday 6th December 1946 the printed programme took on a style and format that was to continue for many years. Inside the cover the first page listed all officers and committee members of the Society. The orchestra members and their instruments were listed, along with the names of Subscribers and Friends and any remaining pages included information about some aspect of the orchestra's activities, or advertisements for forthcoming concerts.

The centre pages revealed the music to be played at the concerts. Programme notes were only included if deemed necessary and helpful and, for special concerts, photographs and a short 'curriculum vitae' of soloists was included. On this occasion a page was devoted to the orchestra itself stating that rehearsals were held on Friday evenings at 6.30 p.m. and that there were vacancies for new players. Also, the Junior Orchestra was to resume its activities in the New Year, meeting on Tuesday evenings at 6.30 p.m. The back page of the programme drew attention to the fact that the spring 1947 concerts would be in celebration of the Society's Fortieth Anniversary.

The music performed at the autumn concerts provided something for most people's taste. The programme opened with Rossini's overture, 'Semiramide', which was followed by the

soloist, George Eskdale, playing Haydn's Trumpet concerto in E flat, and concluded with the 'Symphony No. 40 in G' by Mozart. George Eskdale appeared again in the second part of the concert as the trumpet soloist in Bach's Brandenburg Concerto No. 2 in F Major – some of the most difficult music ever written for the trumpet, according to the newspaper reports. The other soloists, taken from the ranks of the orchestra, were Arthur Miners, flute, Mr A Brien, oboe, Kendall Baic, violin, Ethel McCreery, 'cello and Enid Truman, continuo. The strings of the orchestra then performed a Purcell Suite arranged by John Barbirolli, after which a local singer, Jack Dunn, sang a group of songs accompanied by Enid Truman. The concert ended with Elgar's 'Wand of Youth' Suite No. 2 (Music to a Child's Play).

This programme placed many demands on the orchestra (which totalled fifty-nine players) but they obviously rose to the occasion and received good write-ups in the local press, the orchestra showing "considerable improvement on the last two concerts". The reports also revealed that at the afternoon concert the audience included many schoolchildren, who had the music introduced to them by the conductor.

Musical activities in West Cornwall were given publicity in *The Cornishman* for Thursday 19th December 1946, but the Penzance Orchestral Society received the greatest notice as the article was entitled "'Cello, Fiddle, Big Bass Drum, a Cornish Orchestra" (the quotation is from the words of the Helston Flora Dance) beneath which was a photograph of the orchestra taken at the recent concert. This was a welcome tribute to the orchestra at the close of the year.

January to March 1947 – the months of "The Great Blizzard", when the country, including Cornwall, was in the frozen grip of snow and ice. Orchestral rehearsals began on Friday 17th January and one can only surmise that some members may have had problems getting to them all. Snow was a rarity in West Cornwall, and heavy snow with freezing conditions for weeks on end merited much coverage in the press, but no problems are evident as far as the orchestra was concerned. The Operatic Society, too, went ahead with its first post-war production of 'The Gondoliers' in mid-March.

The Fortieth Anniversary Concert

By Friday 25th April spring would have been in the air in Penzance and celebration, too, when the Fortieth Anniversary concerts took place in St John's Hall in the afternoon and evening. A special commemorative programme was produced with double the usual number of pages. It included photographs of the founder conductor, Walter Barnes, J. Morgan Hosking and the soloist, Alan Loveday, a young nineteen year old New Zealand born violinist. He came to England aged only eleven to study with Albert Sammons before going to the Royal College of Music. Having played with the London Symphony Orchestra during the 1946 Promenade Concert Season he was at the beginning of a distinguished career. A brief history of the Penzance Orchestral Society had been written by F. N. (Freddie) Hodson which began with the words, "Forty years old and still flourishing, with a great future before it".

The programme reflected something of the musical tastes and enthusiasms of its new Conductor, each half of the concert beginning with a work by Wagner! His overture 'Rienzi' was played in the first half and the Prelude to Act III of 'Lohengrin' in the second. Alan Loveday played Beethoven's 'Violin concerto in D Major, Op. 61' as well as a group of solo pieces in the second part of the programme accompanied, as usual, by Enid Truman. The other orchestral items were the 'St Paul's Suite' for String Orchestra by Gustav Holst, and Bizet's 'L'Arlésienne Suite No. 2.' Programme notes were provided for the Wagner items and the concerto, written by the conductor. The orchestra numbered sixty-two players with a full wind and brass section, including a tuba and saxophone.

The concert was well received by the local press, Alan Loveday being regarded as someone with a great career ahead of him. The orchestra was generally congratulated, but one or two reports thought that the brass section was "over-exuberant" at times! Its long history was acknowledged, players of many years mentioned and it was "a night of music which endorses the pride of Penzance in its splendid orchestra".

The summer of 1947 saw an innovation in the orchestra's activities which had first been brought forward at a committee meeting in February. Morgan Hosking had received enquiries from many people who wanted the orchestra to give a strings only performance between the spring and autumn concerts. The string players agreed to this so the arrangements were made and a local professional pianist, Berkeley Mason, was engaged as soloist. St John's Hall was available at a reduced cost of five guineas because the concert would provide entertainment for summer visitors to the town.

This concert, which took place on Friday 20th June, 1947 was previewed in *The Cornishman* the day before, the article concentrating on a new work which was to receive its first performance at the concert. 'The Newlyn Suite' had been written by a percussionist in the orchestra, Tom Paynter.

Tom Paynter

Tom Paynter was born in 1901, the youngest of three children born to Hugh Paynter, brother of Colonel Camborne Haweis Paynter of Boskenna, an estate west of Penzance which incorporated the beautiful valley of Lamorna. Colonel Paynter had only one child, a daughter, Betty. A legal entailment stating that the estate must pass to a male heir meant that it was Tom, not Betty, who would inherit Boskenna. Colonel Paynter naturally wanted his daughter to receive the inheritance and he managed to buy Tom out of the entailment ensuring that Tom became a gentleman of independent means. But he was far from idle, for after receiving his education at the prestigious Repton public school he went on to become an expert skier, as well as a qualified architect.

During World War II Tom was a Commando Major training with the Lovat Scouts in Canada. Towards the end of the war he sustained injuries to both his ankles while instructing Commandos in cliff-climbing and it was during his enforced period of inactivity that he returned to a life-long interest, that of composing music. He wrote a movement of a string quartet and it was from this that his first important work, 'The Newlyn Suite' was born.

The three-movement work was well received by the audience, according to press reports, the work having "a charming, lyrical quality rather reminiscent of Grieg", drawing its inspiration from the sea and its moods. The orchestra's "extremely fine playing of this delightful composition" was applauded warmly.

Berkeley Mason played Schumann's 'Carnaval' and a group of piano solos.

Berkeley Mason, F.R.C.O., L.R.A.M.

Berkeley Mason was well known in Cornwall as an excellent organist and pianist. *The Cornishman* regarded him as one of the finest organists in England and he had been something of a child prodigy in his native Bradford. In 1918 he moved to London and was employed by the BBC as a staff pianist and organist from 1927-1945 during which time he accompanied Kathleen Ferrier in her first radio broadcast. He retired to live in Newlyn in 1945 but was recalled to London in 1946 to make his last appearance at the 'Proms'.

During his retirement in Newlyn he became active in Cornish and West Country musical life, giving piano and organ recitals as well as being called upon as accompanist. He was made President of the Cornwall Organists Association and was "a trusty tower of strength for all concerned" at many oratorio performances throughout the county. Following a minor operation at West Cornwall Hospital in 1950, which had nothing to do with his hands, he suffered a temporary paralysis in some of his fingers but recovered to continue playing and one of his last appearances was in June 1954 at Richmond Church.

Berkeley Mason died in May 1955 aged 72, and the following May the BBC presented a tribute programme on the West of England Home Service entitled "A Musician is remembered". One of the participants in this recorded programme was his piano pupil, Ronald Paul from Penzance, who played excerpts from 'Carnaval' and Debussy's 'La Fille aux cheveux de lin' which were among his favourite works, and the Head of West Region Music, Mr Norman Fulton, presented an appreciation.

In addition to 'The Newlyn Suite' the orchestra performed works by Handel, Boyce, Grieg, and Purcell, and their efforts were rewarded, not only by the applause of the audience, but by Tom Paynter when he treated orchestra members and friends to a party after the concert at Chirgwin's restaurant.

In the audience at this concert was a Mr Herbert Ware, a man with local connections but who lived in Cardiff and was well known as a conductor in South Wales. He was both delighted and amazed at the standard of the performance, and offered to come as guest

conductor in a future concert. This successful summer concert by the strings of the orchestra set the precedent for another annual event in their musical calendar, and they continued for many years.

During 1947, minutes of the Society record administrative matters being dealt with alongside planning and discussions for future concerts. The Newlyn Male Choir, in need of a new rehearsal room, was given permission to use the Bandroom on a Monday evening for an annual rental of fifteen guineas; the Bandroom chimney was cracked and needed repairs and the room was redecorated by volunteers; the Society bank accounts were transferred from the Midland Bank to Lloyds; a pair of unused cymbals were to be sold to raise money for the Instrument Fund so that clarinets could be bought for a clarinettist who wanted to return to the orchestra but had no instruments; dates, programmes and soloists for the 1947-48 concert season were discussed. The subject of whether Tchaikovsky's 4th Symphony should be performed involved not only the warning that full attendance at rehearsals would be required, but also the anxiety that the current petrol crisis might prevent this. So music for both Tchaikovsky's 4th Symphony and Schubert's 5th was ordered and a decision deferred as to which would be played.

Penzance Orchestral Society seemed to have had, on a number of occasions, a happy 'knack' of choosing concert dates which coincided with a national event of importance or celebration. This time their autumn concert in 1947, on Friday 21st November, took place on the day following the wedding of Princess Elizabeth to Prince Philip Mountbatten. Post-war patriotism had led to enormous enthusiasm and excitement for this royal wedding. The music chosen for the orchestral concert, by a happy coincidence, was suitably popular and tuneful.

It was, as *The Cornishman* review said, "a concert which danced", containing two ballet suites, Tchaikovsky's 'Swan Lake' and Massenet's 'El Cid', and another dance 'La Calinda' from Delius's opera 'Koanga'. The concert began with Mendelssohn's Overture 'The Hebrides' Op. 26 and the symphony finally chosen was Schubert's 5th in B Flat Major. The soloist, soprano Muriel Peters, sang the aria 'One Fine Day' from Puccini's 'Madame Butterfly' and a group of songs by British composers. Miss Peters was a local singer from Falmouth who generously made no charge for her performances, which was just as well because a professional harpist had been engaged for these concerts at a fee of £21. 18s. 10d and the concert made a loss of £8. 5s. 5d.

Favourable reviews provide extra snippets of information. We are told that 'La Calinda' had never before been played in Penzance and at the afternoon concert Morgan Hosking, in his explanatory words to the schoolchildren in the audience, alerted them to its exciting rhythms but asked them to resist the urge to stamp their feet during the music! He prefaced each piece with a few words in this concert which "helped to create an unusual intimacy between orchestra and audience".

Morgan became well-known for his talks to the schoolchildren, but he often spoke to the audience at the evening concert as well and his speeches were keenly anticipated and hugely enjoyed. He was a good communicator and often very humorous, making the audience feel a special and personal involvement with the Society.

The performance of 'La Calinda' prompted one loyal supporter and friend of Enid and Norman Truman to write a letter of appreciation to them as he regarded himself as "a bit of a fanatic over Delius". He felt that there were few people who could conduct his music "for all that he is and has to say, and not so many who can play him either. I think your conductor understands his Delius,....last Friday's performance had a something that one would travel far to try to find". What more could a conductor of an amateur orchestra wish to hear!

The spring concert on Friday 19th March 1948 is of interest for two main reasons. Firstly, the programme included three works being performed for the first time in Penzance – the Elgar 'Cello Concerto, performed by Juliette Alvin, Saint-Saëns', 'The Carnival of the Animals' and the 'Second Suite of Ancient Airs and Dances for the Lute' orchestrated by Respighi, the latter two works requiring two pianos which were played by Enid Truman and her old college friend, Louise Sumner. Secondly, the newspaper reports of the concert were at great variance with one another, heralding a period of more critical newspaper reviewing of the Society's concerts, with the *Western Morning News* reports written, from this time onwards, "By our Music Critic".

The concerts, in the afternoon at 3 p.m. and in the evening at the earlier time of 7.30 p.m., began with the overture to 'A Roman Carnival', Op. 9, based on music from Berlioz' opera 'Benvenuto Cellini', and in addition to the works already mentioned, included a group of 'cello solos in the second half of the programme.

Faith Harris

During the evening concert Morgan Hosking made a presentation to one of his players, Mrs Dudley Harris, who had been a member of the viola section for twenty-five years. She was given a silver brooch to mark her silver jubilee with the orchestra. Morgan pointed out that her two daughters, Mrs Oliver Price and Mrs George Carn, playing 'cello and violin, were also regular members of the orchestra. Faith Harris was the wife of a Falmouth doctor and the family lived in a house overlooking Falmouth harbour. By way of contrast to her great involvement in the musical events of West Cornwall, Faith could often be found "messing about in boats" and was, at one time, Commodore of the Falmouth Yacht Club. She was a staunch and loyal member of the Orchestral Society and became its President in 1968.

A Clash with the Critics

The local newspapers were mostly very approving and congratulatory about the concert. *The Cornishman* reporter attended the afternoon concert where he was pleased to see a large number of schoolchildren in the audience, remarking that "If the programme had been intended especially for them it could scarcely have been better arranged". He found it interesting how "between laughs, the schoolchildren....realised that they were listening to passages of great beauty" one of which was 'cellist Ethel McCreery's solo performance of 'The Swan' which was "loudly applauded." Juliette Alvin, returning to play with the orchestra after an eight-year break, played the Elgar Concerto with "brilliant ease... the programme was a further triumph for Mr Morgan Hosking, who handled the orchestra of over 60 members with great ability." The pianists in both the Saint-Saëns and the Respighi played with "skill and sensitivity".

The *Western Morning News* music critic, however, was less enthusiastic, though the article was headed "Masterly Playing at Penzance", referring to Miss Alvin's performance. He devoted much of his report to her playing and also thought that there had been some excellent solo work by Ethel McCreery and the two pianists in the Saint-Saëns. But the short article opened and closed with rather discouraging words "The programme was not a particularly interesting one from a musical point of view" and he concluded that, "All this music produced plenty of noise but very little lyrical beauty. The orchestral playing, if competent, was lacking in variety and was at times overpowering in its volume".

This criticism was reinforced in reviews following the concert by the strings of the orchestra on Friday 21st May when the soloist was Miss Diana Ford, a nineteen year old local girl who was still studying at the Royal College of Music. Her performance of Bach's Piano Concerto, No.1 was greatly praised showing her to be an "accomplished pianist with a delightful touch" according to the report in the *Western Morning News* the following day. *The Cornishman* devoted most of its report to her local connection and developing talent while at Penzance Girls' County Grammar School. But both reports complained that the orchestra "drowned her" in parts of the concerto, still not having "overcome its tendency to excessive loudness."

The *Western Morning News* felt that it was in pieces from Bach's Suite, No. 3 in D that the orchestra showed how well it could play. The concert had opened with Grieg's 'Holberg' Suite, but "the orchestra was not at its best" until the second half of the programme. Miss Ford's solo pieces by Debussy and Chopin were followed by two encores from "an insistent audience", who had filled St John's Hall despite a beautiful evening of weather with "Mount's Bay like a blue lake – a deep sunlit peace enfolding the countryside".

However peaceful his surroundings, Morgan Hosking could not let these criticisms of his orchestra go without a vigorous response. He wrote a long letter to *The Cornishman* saying that the remarks by the paper's representative were so "inaccurate and misleading that I am compelled, not only for the honour of the orchestra, but in the interests of the music itself, to write this letter". He then went on to suggest that the critic "can know very little about the construction and style of a Bach Concerto" and proceeds to explain, quoting at length from a scholarly work on the concerto in question. This points out that the piano was "a glorified obbligato to the whole" and not a display of instrumental prowess more familiar in modern concertos, and that the score is often marked 'tutti' in passages where the piano is also participating.

Morgan then turned to the matter of loudness of the orchestra pointing out that the orchestra was a large one playing in a small hall, "the acoustics of which have been completely ruined by the removal, since the war, of the organ, leaving an alcove to amplify every sound and throw it to the audience". He felt that the music critics would have shown generosity had they taken these facts into account and that "generosity would seem to me to be an essential feature of

amateur music-making". Until the time that Penzance had a concert hall worthy of its many musical activities "occasional blasts from brass and drums must be endured, or else there will be no Orchestral Society in Penzance. What shall it be? We will let our audience answer that question, and feel confident of their reply".

This brave and forthright or, alternatively, rash public reaction to press criticism received the support of the Society's members at their AGM later in the year, but was not to be Morgan Hosking's, or the Society's, only brush with the music critics.

In the autumn of 1948 Morgan reported to the committee that he had resigned as conductor of the Newlyn Male Choir. As well as conducting the Orchestral Society and its Junior Orchestra he was involved in many other musical events and organizations in the area. He frequently led orchestras for both the Operatic Society and the Choral Society and took part in chamber music concerts. Also, he was, for a period, Vice Chairman of the Penzance Society of Arts, and accepted invitations to talk about music. These commitments involved rehearsals and preparation in addition to the heavy workload which his role as conductor of the Orchestral Society demanded.

Herbert Ware's offer to come as a guest conductor had been accepted and his forthcoming visit in December 1948 created a great deal of interest, along with that of the soloist, John Moores, who was a protégé of the conductor. Preview articles appeared in the press in which the promising career of the twenty-year old pianist was revealed – he had already achieved distinction in the First International Pianoforte Competition in Genoa and would be giving a recital in London a few days prior to coming to Penzance. The fact that Herbert Ware had been born locally was made much of, for although he lived and worked in South Wales he regularly returned to Cornwall to visit his many relations.

Herbert Ware

Born in Newlyn in 1895 Herbert, with his parents moved to Tonypandy in South Wales while he was still very young. His early career bears comparison with that of Walter Barnes for he became a talented violinist, worked in a cinema orchestra and set up his own teaching studio in Cardiff. From this developed an amateur orchestra which for more than twenty years achieved repeated success both in Wales at the National Eisteddfod and in English music festivals. This group eventually developed into the Cardiff Philharmonic Orchestra. Many pupils benefited from Herbert Ware's expertise and experience and it was said that in his later years he had at least one former student in all the professional orchestras in Britain. He constantly fostered the idea of a national orchestra for Wales and that this had not been established by the time of his death in 1955 was a great disappointment to him. How delighted and proud he would have been had he lived to hear the internationally acclaimed BBC National Orchestra of Wales today.

Herbert Ware as a young man.

In 1931 Herbert Ware wrote an article on 'The Amateur Orchestra in South Wales' printed in the journal 'Y Cerddor' in which he puts forward the idea that a successful orchestral conductor should have a "first rate knowledge of the technique of stringed instruments, and should be able to mark the parts by way of fingering and bowing, so that the best possible results may be obtained from the material at his disposal", because "the string section is the foundation of the orchestra". This theory had been put to the test with commendable results not only by himself, but by both Walter Barnes and, later, Morgan Hosking and may have been an important contributory factor in the success of the Penzance Orchestral Society.

This, then, was the man who came as guest conductor for the Society's two concerts on Thursday 9th December 1948. He also brought the score and parts for Mozart's Symphony No. 34 in C, K338. Apart from the opening and closing overtures, he conducted the whole programme. In addition to Beethoven's Piano Concerto No. 5 in E flat 'Emperor' and a group of Chopin piano solos the programme included two Hungarian Dances, No. 5 in G minor and No. 6 in D Major by Brahms.

The orchestra was under a new leader at this concert due to Kendall Baic receiving promotion and, presumably, leaving the area. Mrs Iola Coleman, a long standing member of the orchestra, was elected in his place. She had first joined the orchestra as Miss Iola Keskeys and was, according to those who remember her, a fine violinist. Also, the orchestra's principal flautist, Freddie Hodson, had been ill (though he was among the audience) so two Royal Marine musicians formed the flute section, and others played second bassoon and second horn. Among the 'cellists was Herbert Ware's wife, a talented performer and teacher.

company and lived in Plymouth at the time. Refusing to change his attitude to please his employers he resigned from the company and set up his own business in Newlyn. Among the rioters was a young, nineteen-year old fisherman, Nicholas Paul Hosking. Though by nature a gentle person, he was among those committed for trial at the County Assize Court in Bodmin. The rioters were treated leniently and returned to Newlyn where Nicholas Hosking also set up a business, as a fish buyer and merchant.

Nicholas married one of the five daughters of Benjamin Ridge and they, in turn, had five children four of whom survived into adulthood, Morgan being the youngest son, born on 1st October, 1913. When he was six the family bought a substantial, granite terraced house,'Lagos', overlooking Newlyn harbour and Mount's Bay, Morgan's much loved and life-long home.

So the sea and fishing were in Morgan's blood, but also intermingled with music, for his grandfather, B. J. Ridge, was a music-lover and encouraged his daughters to play an instrument. One of them, Bella, became especially proficient as a pianist having been taught by two eminent musicians in Plymouth, travelling there to continue lessons after moving to Newlyn. She suffered from delicate health but became a piano teacher in Newlyn and Morgan remembered sitting beside her during her lessons, after which she would play Beethoven and Mozart sonatas to him. She taught Morgan's older siblings and he, too, soon learned to play simple tunes by ear. Bella died young, so at the age of about ten Morgan began his piano lessons with Mr Hugh Branwell in Penzance.

Morgan Hosking aged sixteen.

Hugh Branwell, who had trained at the Royal Academy and was a Fellow of the Royal College of Organists, became a well known music teacher in the town. He was up to date in his teaching methods and as well as teaching Morgan to play the piano gave him a thorough grounding in musical theory, harmony, counterpoint etc, as well as extensive ear tests. He also introduced Morgan to a method of attaining perfect rhythm, known as French time names, whereby notes were given names which, when spoken aloud, reproduced the rhythmic effects required within a given tempo. For example a crochet was 'taa-aa', a quaver 'taa' and a semi quaver 'taatai'. Morgan found this method invaluable in his later conducting career and regarded his tuition under Hugh Branwell as both formative and vitally important in his development as a musician.

At Hugh Branwell's suggestion Morgan later had lessons from him on the organ, playing on the three-manual Walker organ in Chapel Street Methodist Chapel in Penzance where Hugh was organist for over forty years. Morgan admitted that though organ playing ruined his technique as a pianist, he loved the sense of power and big sound provided by the organ!

Shortly after beginning his music lessons Morgan became intrigued by the sight of a girl regularly passing his home carrying a violin case. This was the young Rowenna Maddern who was having violin lessons with Miss Violet Nunn. Rowenna joined the orchestra in 1925 and became one of its longest serving violinists by the time she retired in 1991. Morgan asked to have a violin and his mother bought one for ten shillings from a neighbour whose daughter had lost interest in it. It came with a tutor from which Morgan learned to tune the instrument and he was soon playing simple melodies from a monthly music magazine regularly bought for him and his sister, Dora, also a pupil of Hugh Branwell.

This magazine included easy versions of music from operatic and orchestral works, including the music of Richard Wagner. The essence of the music contained in the Wagnerian excerpts made an impact on Morgan to which he ascribed his interest in Wagner which developed into an on-going study of the man and his music. Morgan's family were rather impressed by his ability to teach himself to play the violin and decided that he should receive violin lessons.

When Morgan was twelve his father, Nicholas, died suddenly and much of the family responsibilities were assumed by his uncle and aunt, Benjamin and Margaret Ridge. It was with their encouragement that violin lessons were arranged with Walter Barnes who said that a smaller, three quarter-size violin was needed, so this was bought by Morgan's grandfather, Benjamin Ridge senior. Morgan's account of his 'audition' with Walter Barnes indicated an amusing precociousness in the budding violinist, as he offered to play the 'Intermezzo' from Mascagni's 'Cavaleria Rusticana' which rather surprised Mr Barnes! This was the start of a very fruitful musical relationship leading not only to Morgan joining the orchestra as a second violinist in 1929 but to his entrée into the musical society of the area.

After meeting Walter Barnes he immediately demanded to go to the orchestral concerts, attending his first one in December 1925. He also insisted on sitting in the side gallery from

where he could look down on the orchestra to watch all that was happening, and recalled the thrill as the green shaded electric lighting (especially installed in St John's Hall for the orchestral concerts) came on, and the smile he received from Walter Barnes as he came onto the platform.

From the age of four Morgan attended the local village schools in Newlyn but failed to pass a scholarship examination for secondary education. However, money was found to send him to the Penzance County School for Boys as a fee-paying student. He was the first to admit that, apart from music, he was a 'duffer' at school and enjoyed telling the tale that in a geography lesson, when asked to name the chief minerals of Cornwall, started listing ginger beer, vimto...! But his musical talent was fostered and encouraged as many of the staff were musicians and there was a flourishing school orchestra. He was even excused Wednesday afternoon detentions when they were imposed because he had his violin lesson that afternoon and that was considered more important. Sport, especially cricket, was out, too, in case he should damage his fingers, and as Morgan disliked participation in any sport this suited him very well. Later on, of course, these same considerate schoolmasters, including the Headmaster, Mr G. L. Bradley, would all submit to Morgan's authority as members of his orchestra.

On leaving school Morgan attended Miss Olive Wesley's commercial school and learned shorthand, typing, book-keeping and business methods. An idea that he should then go to Plymouth to train with an insurance company was abandoned when, at the age of sixteen, he was offered the post of organist at Newlyn Trinity Methodist Church – his family thought that this was much more important. So he remained in Newlyn and joined the family business of B. J. Ridge.

During the war Morgan was a signalman in the Royal Navy and though he never achieved a senior rank he had many valuable and memorable experiences. Whenever and wherever possible he pursued his love of music despite his violin being left at home in the care of his family, and his letters from this period include his instructions as to how to look after it. He attended a series of concerts in Liverpool conducted by Malcolm Sargent, became involved with the Portland Youth Symphony Orchestra while in America, requested music from home to enable him to play the organ while on a course at Lancing College near Brighton, and went to concerts in most of the major ports around the United Kingdom, all of which broadened his musical and social horizons.

John Morgan Hosking, circa 1946.

It was in the role as Hon. Conductor of the Penzance Orchestral Society from November 1946 that Morgan Hosking's greatest talents were revealed. These were evident to the public in the successful concerts where his conducting was confident and pleasurable to watch. But it was in rehearsals that he was most impressive, moulding a disparate group of people, some skilled professionals and some still inexperienced amateurs, into a harmonious whole.

Over the years he achieved a technical mastery in his conducting, giving much credit for this to Hermann Scherchen's *Handbook of Conducting*. This had been published in its English translation in 1933 and Walter Barnes had given Morgan a copy for his twenty-first birthday in 1934. Scherchen was a distinguished German conductor regarded as "one of the twentieth century's outstanding musical pioneers", whose conducting was "functional, clear and scholarly, but it combined knowledge of detail with vitality of spirit".

This statement contains three elements which Morgan applied to his work with the orchestra. Firstly, clarity of beat, something he was often congratulated on by orchestral players and soloists. Secondly, knowledge of detail, whether it was applied to the musical score, the instrumentation of the orchestra, the capabilities of his players or the history and background of the music being performed; all this Morgan would arm himself with before attempting any given work. Thirdly, vitality of spirit, a vague concept, maybe, but one that Morgan embodied, transmitted to his orchestra and, in turn, through them to the musical performances.

Rehearsals were hardworking sessions but full of pleasure and fun for the orchestra. Members attended regularly because they enjoyed them so much. Morgan's warm friendliness and sense of humour were always to the fore, and he had a way with words and a lack of pomposity which eased the players through the musical problems to be overcome. To achieve a particular effect he would produce similes which everyone could relate to – for example, he would say, "I want this passage to be as crisp as one of Honor Price's lettuces which she brings in for us", or "as soft as the fur on a cat's tummy" (he was a great lover of cats!). On another occasion he said that "This should sound like a lady in a long dress alighting from a sedan chair". Knowing his players well he could chastise them with a light-hearted touch which rarely upset them and would cajole them through a difficult section by saying with a chuckle, "You will try to play every note, won't you"?

One of the things that the members of the orchestra appreciated about Morgan's rehearsals was being allowed to play through a piece without unnecessary interruption before settling down to detailed analysis of the music. Also he began rehearsals promptly, often putting the Bandroom clock right before starting, and ended exactly at nine o'clock but still at an acceptable musical point. He needed the Bandroom clock because, for some reason, he found it impossible to listen to music or conduct it while wearing a wristwatch. By the time of the concert he always appeared immaculate and relaxed but imbued his orchestra with a sense of occasion and responsibility for a good performance. He knew that there was nothing more he could do to ensure this, trusting that thorough preparation and good luck would prevail – and they usually did.

Morgan remained an able violinist despite the time he devoted to his conducting. His name appears frequently in orchestras and string groups, often as their leader, and he occasionally performed as a soloist, in musical evenings at the Penzance Society of Arts, for instance. He also played in chamber music ensembles, both publicly and privately with friends, but this was not his natural 'forte', and he was most at home and at his best on the conductor's rostrum controlling larger musical forces.

When Morgan announced his retirement from the orchestra in 1981 most people were shocked and surprised, feeling that he still had much more to offer. He said that he wanted people to say, "Why did he go?" rather than, "When is he going?", but perhaps, too, he was conscious of not wanting to out-do his old friend, Walter Barnes, in his tenure of the position.

Morgan Hosking at rehearsal in the Bandroom, 1977.

Approaching the Half Century 1950-1956

During the late nineteen forties a former secretary of the Orchestral Society, Harold Morris, was living in the Hampstead area of London where he was a close neighbour of the conductor, Stanford Robinson. They became friends, Harold often talking about his days with the orchestra in Penzance and how he would love Stanford Robinson to conduct it, and eventually persuaded him to do so. It took many months to arrange a mutually agreeable date but finally Friday 31st March 1950 was chosen with Stanford Robinson's wife, the soprano Lorely Dyer, as soloist.

The Visit of Stanford Robinson

Stanford Robinson was, at this time, conductor of the BBC Theatre Orchestra and the new BBC Opera Orchestra. Having one of the most well-known conductors in the country as their guest must have generated great excitement among the players in Penzance. The programme selected was the 'Ruy Blas' overture by Mendelssohn, Beethoven's 5th Symphony, the overture, 'Nell Gwyn' by Edward German, Borodin's 'On the steppes of Central Asia' and Rossini's ballet music to 'William Tell', the final item being the only one conducted by Morgan Hosking. Lorely Dyer sang the 'Jewel Song' from Gounod's 'Faust' and a selection of songs.

Press reports regarded the concert as a success, with the performance of the Beethoven Symphony receiving a detailed analysis in *The Cornishman*. There were criticisms, but the *Western Morning News* wrote that under Mr Robinson's direction the orchestra showed that "the amateur orchestra... if given professional guidance, can achieve impressive results". Morgan Hosking may have read these words with mixed feelings, but the overall mood of approval in the reviews would have pleased him. He would certainly have used the day (a rehearsal with the guest conductor took place instead of an afternoon concert) to learn from a 'maestro' such as Stanford Robinson. Lorely Dyer had an "enchanting" voice, but was heard to best advantage in the songs. Stanford Robinson spoke to the audience and begged them and the people of the town and district to support the orchestra, "who were a fine company of players" and who had worked very hard in rehearsal.

Morgan Hosking was now approaching the peak of his musical activities. He had taken on the conductorship of the Penzance Choral Society in September 1949, succeeding Donald Behenna. He led the orchestra for the Penzance Operatic Society and was frequently invited to lead orchestras for the St Just and Redruth Amateur Operatic Societies. Despite these commitments, added to that of the Orchestral Society, he still found time to become the local Hon. Secretary of the Cornwall Music Competition to be held in Penzance from 10th – 14th May, and to pursue other interests such as the RSPCA, of which he was the local branch secretary, and an active membership of the Penzance Society of Arts.

An unusual event claimed one afternoon of some orchestral members' time on Monday 8th May, 1950. This was the occasion of a visit to West Cornwall by Her Royal Highness the Duchess of Kent. She received a Civic Welcome at St John's Hall where she had tea, after which "she smoked a cigarette from a medium length holder". During tea light music was played by a small orchestra, led by Morgan Hosking. The musicians were each given a letter from the Penzance Town Clerk stamped by the Penzance Police Inspector's Office admitting them to St John's Hall as "a Member of the Orchestra officially engaged to play at the Reception". Personal recollections of this event have, sadly, not been recorded but it provided variety and some 'cachet' to the musical year.

An ambitious and varied selection of music for string orchestra was presented by the Society on Sunday 21st May in which all the instrumental solo parts were taken by members of the orchestra. Among the works was Elgar's 'Introduction and Allegro for Quartet and Orchestra' Op. 47, described by Morgan Hosking as one of the most "fiendishly difficult" pieces attempted by the orchestra in recent years. The quartet was formed by Iola Coleman and Clarice Nicholls, violins, Gwyneth Andrewartha, viola, and Enid Truman, 'cello and they played with "an efficiency which startled the audience....a finale which should be long remembered".

Morgan Hosking also startled the audience by his remarks after thanking them for their attendance. He revealed that at the December 1949 concert a profit of only 2s. 5d was made, and the March concert had suffered a loss of over £4. (These came on top of other more serious losses on concerts during 1948 and 1949). He feared that unless support was greater, or costs could be reduced, the price of tickets would have to be raised.

This wake-up call was, as always on such occasions, directed at the wrong people for there was a loyal and substantial list of subscribers of the orchestra. But it was timely, for St John's Hall had a relatively small number of seats and, increasingly, there was competition from more frequent visits to the county of large professional orchestras, such as the Hallé concerts in Truro Cathedral. The May concert also lost money, so it was decided later in the year to go ahead with a rise in ticket prices from 5/-, 3/6, 2/6 and 1/6, to 7/6, 5/-, 3/6 and 2/6. A grant from the Carnegie Trust of £45 in June 1951 was of great help, too, because there were not only concert expenses to be met, but the costs and maintenance of the Society's invaluable Bandroom to cope with.

Another boost to the Society's income came at the end of the year when a local singer and teacher, Gladys Harris, put on a concert involving, as well as herself and other guest artistes, pupils of her Academy of Singing and Voice Production assisted by members of the Orchestral Society, the proceeds of which were in aid of the Society.

Financial anxieties apart, the Society was in good heart, and welcomed back into their midst Mrs Crosbie Garstin who had at last returned from her extended war service. Mrs Iola Coleman gracefully stood down as 'acting' leader in order that Mrs Crosbie Garstin could resume her place as Principal Violin, a position she retained until her death in 1972. Six concerts were planned for the 1950-51 season and one of the works chosen for the November 1950 concert was Mozart's Flute and Harp Concerto as the Society had been offered the loan of a concert harp.

Operatic Society Drama

During the latter part of the year something of a crisis arose in the Operatic Society which involved the Orchestral Society. It had been announced in June that the production chosen for 1951 would be Johann Strauss's 'Die Fledermaus' which was to be its first performance in Cornwall and, possibly, in the West of England. The conductor would, of course, be the Operatic Society's Musical Director, Maddern Williams.

The Orchestral Society expected to provide the orchestra for this production as was normally the case. However, Morgan Hosking reported to the orchestral committee in September that the intention on this occasion was for the Operatic Society to form their own string orchestra assisted by a Mustel organ. He considered that the Orchestral Society should have been consulted over this, and was supported by the committee chairman, Graham White, who said that the producer of 'Die Fledermaus', Thomas J. Bell, had stressed the importance of the orchestral contribution in the opera. (Morgan had doubts from the start as to whether the proposed orchestra would be able to cope with the music). Maddern Williams was unwell at this point, so it was decided that when the situation was clearer the two committees should arrange to meet and discuss the situation.

By early October Maddern Williams was a patient at the Royal Masonic Hospital in London, undergoing an operation to have one of his legs amputated. During this period operatic rehearsals were conducted by another local singer and conductor, Stephen Hichens, but when the severity of their Musical Director's illness became apparent, Morgan was asked to step in to take over his role. He was prepared to do so on condition that, where necessary, one or two professional singers were engaged, and that the first three rows of the stalls in the theatre were removed to make room for a substantial orchestra. It seems that only the score for a full orchestra was available and Morgan reckoned he would need about forty players. How things actually worked out will be revealed later.

Amidst all this drama and tension rehearsals for the Orchestral Society's concert on Friday 24th November continued. The soloist was the pianist, John Vallier, well known to local audiences because he had already given a number of recitals in the area, at the Penzance County Grammar School for Boys and other venues. This was due to a wartime friendship forged between him and Mr A. C. Todd, a member of the Cornwall branch of the Worker's Educational Association. John Vallier frequently came to stay with Mr Todd, and even kept one of his pianos at the house in Penzance.

As well as his playing of Tchaikovsky's 'Piano Concerto No. 1 in B Flat Minor' the programme included a second concerto, the already mentioned 'Concerto in C Major (K299) for Flute and Harp' by Mozart, performed by the Society's flautist, Arthur Miners and a guest harpist, Enid Quinney. The orchestra contributed a Wolf-Ferrari overture, Prokofiev's 'Classical Symphony' and the Suite No. 4 'Scènes Pittoresques' by Massenet. John Vallier also played at least four solo items, so with such a programme of music this concert was a major undertaking for both conductor and orchestra.

Another Battle with the Critics!

With the benefit of hindsight and in view of the aftermath, it could be said that Morgan Hosking and the committee were over-ambitious in choosing such a demanding programme. But as he had reminded members at the AGM in July 1949, the primary purpose of the Society was to meet together to study and perform orchestral music.

Press reports following the concert appeared from their headlines to be kindly, "Ambitious music at Penzance: Orchestral Society's enthusiasm", "Musical Treat", and from the *Western Morning News*' music critic "Bold venture by amateurs". Their content, however, was less favourable and while they all tried to find areas in the performance to praise, especially giving credit to the conductor, there was a great deal of criticism. The Steinway piano was "just not good enough", though the soloist's performance in the concerto was well regarded, and his solo pieces "confirmed the reputation which Mr Vallier has already earned".

It was the Mozart Flute and Harp Concerto which suffered most. Arthur Miners' playing was "academically correct without being inspired" and "unable to rise to the full demands of the music", while Enid Quinney, though "precise and agile" sometimes "could not be heard at all". It was in this work that "the limitations of the orchestra became woefully apparent. The playing was on the whole untidy and lacking in discipline. The true magic of Mozart was smothered by a lack of finesse and essential details were obscured".

Well! This was too much for some supporters of the orchestra to stomach! It was the *Western Morning News* music critic, Geoffrey Baggs, who provoked Mr Oliver Price, Chairman of the Falmouth 3 Arts Committee and husband, son-in-law and brother-in-law to three members of the Penzance Society, into writing a letter to the Editor of that paper, Noel A. T. Vinson. Between 29th November and 8th December 1950 six letters were exchanged, (reproduced in Appendix 8). Oliver Price asked whether the music critic could not be given space in the paper to "formulate his views on the future of orchestral music in Cornwall"? In his final letter the Editor replied that this might be possible.

On Monday 22nd January 1951 Geoffrey Baggs had an article printed, headed "Amateur orchestras in West Country are not giving value for money" which was over fifty column inches in length! He refers to other letters from "people who felt themselves aggrieved" following his concert review, and his substantial article left the amateur musicians of Devon and Cornwall in no doubt about his many reservations over their attitudes to music-making and reactions to his criticisms. Throughout January and into February the battle waged with many musical personalities and musicians, as well as audience members, contributing to the debate. *The Cornishman* resisted the urge to get involved, merely reporting the ongoing correspondence and referring to it, briefly, in its report of two concerts given by the strings of the orchestra in February 1951.

Geoffrey Baggs

Geoffrey Baggs had come to Plymouth as a music critic for the *Western Morning News* in 1947, having started his career in London. Twenty-five years later he reviewed his work in the West Country and the article was published as a memorial to him when he died in 1972. He admitted that the distinguished performances and up and coming artists he heard in London were "criticised with acid in my pen and conceit in my head", and that he had no knowledge of what went on, musically, in the provinces.

It was as the years passed that he began to "appreciate the sharp distinction which must be drawn between the amateur and the professional", and that "the critic should become critical of his own work". His memoir implied that he had grown to much enjoy his years in the West, making many friends and accepted as a critic "whether people like me or not". He continued to take an interest in, and write about, the Orchestral Society and while they may have been wounded by his scathing remarks in 1950 they were a healthy body and the scars soon healed.

1951 – Festival of Britain Year

Concerts by the strings of the Society on Friday 23rd February 1951 were fairly well treated by both the *Western Morning News* and *The Cornishman*, the former pointing out that the greater part of the programme was devoted to British music. This was, of course, Festival of Britain year, so a conscious decision was made by the committee to embrace the mood of the country by drawing attention to British composers. A rarely heard work by Gerald Finzi, 'Dies Natalis', was the most notable work performed on this occasion. It is scored for tenor soloist and string orchestra, and is a cantata-like setting of words by the mystic poet, Thomas Traherne. It has been described as "a minor masterpiece of English music". The soloist was George Chitty.

The performance demanded much from all concerned, which was acknowledged by Geoffrey Baggs in his review, but his words were still chosen to "damn with faint praise". A member of the audience, the Reverend Richard Rutter, Superintendent of the Penzance Methodist Circuit, wrote to *The Cornishman* saying that he had been attracted to the concert by the Finzi work alone and its setting of Traherne's poems. He had lived in Manchester for many years, accustomed to hearing "the best" in music and felt that Penzance had "no need to apologise for its orchestral society". Both he and *The Cornishman* bemoaned the fact that St John's Hall was only half-full but neither stated whether this was at the afternoon or evening concert, or both.

Two weeks later the Operatic Society's production of 'Die Fledermaus' opened at the Pavilion Theatre on Monday 5th March, running until the following Saturday. Morgan Hosking's 'conditions' had been met, with two professional singers, Terence Conoley and Gladys Lewis, engaged to play the leading roles. An orchestra of thirty was provided by Orchestral Society members and a Corps de Ballet by the May Nicholson School of Dancing. This operetta by Johann Strauss demands a great deal from both singers and instrumentalists and there were those who felt that the Penzance Company could not 'bring it off'. But they did and with every appearance of success from the press reviews. The *Western Morning News* found fault with the scenery and lighting but gave credit to the singers and chorus. The orchestra came in for criticism but "on the whole, the production is one of which the Society can congratulate itself".

Penzance Operatic Society's production of Johann Strauss's 'Die Fledermaus' in 1951. Dress rehearsal at the Pavilion Theatre with Morgan Hosking, conductor, and members of the Orchestral Society.

The Cornishman gave a fuller and more interesting account written by Spencer Waters and especially praised the way in which the two professionals blended with the local singers, the amateurs "holding their own with the 'stars' and the 'stars' obviously enjoying every minute." This was confirmed a few weeks later in a letter, received by one of the local cast members in 'Die Fledermaus', from Gladys Lewis who wrote that "I did enjoy being with you all for two weeks. It is one of the periods of my career that I shall always remember." Maddern Williams was in the first night audience, now at home recovering from his operation, but by the next year his position as Musical Director of the Operatic Society was handed over to Morgan Hosking.

After such a busy start to the year and following the Choral Society performance of 'The Creation' on Friday 20th April which was deemed a success, Morgan must have been glad of the month of May, relatively free of public performances. But he would have attended the concert given by the BBC West of England Light Orchestra in Penzance on Sunday 13th May, conducted by an old friend of the Orchestral Society, Reginald Redman. This was part of a Festival Tour and the programme included Maddern Williams' Suite 'Three Cornish Impressions', the movements entitled 'Land's End', 'Mounts Bay' and 'Helston'.

This concert tour was one of many events which described themselves as 'Festival' occasions. Even such disparate organisations as the Cornwall Lawn Tennis Association Championships, the Penzance Mayoral Dance, and handicraft exhibitions used the Festival of Britain in their advertising, as the government of the day hoped would be the case. This was, after all, not just an echo of the Great Exhibition of 1851 but an attempt by the Labour government to promote post-war Britain's technical, scientific and artistic achievements and provide the nation with some relief from the years of austerity.

The Orchestral Society did not jump on the band-wagon and advertise its concerts in June as Festival inspired, but the second half of their programme was devoted to music by British composers. The concerts, held on Friday 1st June were, as usual, subject to criticism in the press reports, but generally received sympathetic treatment by *The Cornishman* and the *Western Morning News*. Both agreed that the soloist, Alan Loveday, playing the Max Bruch Violin Concerto in G Minor, lived up to his reputation as one of the most popular young violinists in the country. He played Vaughan Williams' Romance for Violin and Orchestra, 'The Lark Ascending', in the second half of the concert, and for an encore an unaccompanied Gavotte from Bach's 'Suite in A Minor' which showed off his "brilliant technique... combined with a deep insight into the nature of the music".

As well as Delius's 'On Hearing the First Cuckoo in Spring' and 'Summer Night on the River', the British theme was upheld by the final item, Elgar's 'Imperial March', Op. 32. Adding a Cornish flavour to this programme was a performance of the 'Introduction to Act III' and 'Perseus at the Rock' from the opera 'Andromeda' by Ernest H. Oates – the composer himself playing French horn at the concert – which had received its first performance by the Society back in 1932.

The choice of music being selected by the Society for their concerts was coming under scrutiny at this time, though no real debate in committee on the subject is recorded. In April 1951 violinist, Mr S. Costello, handed in his resignation expressing his opinion that the music attempted recently by the orchestra was beyond the capabilities of the average member. Then at the end of the June concert Morgan Hosking asked the audience for comments on the choice and arrangement of concert programmes.

The Cornishman immediately responded to this, at some length, by saying that "general opinion" seemed to say that the music chosen was "far too weighty", and that by giving concerts of the "Grand Hotel" type the orchestra might raise money to afford two concerts a year, at least, of the more difficult works". The music at the June concert was regarded as "far too unvaried: as the ordinary music-lover might say, 'with no tune to it'". It is hard to think of a more tuneful programme than that played in June 1951 (which had opened with Brahms' Variations on a Theme of Haydn, 'St Anthony') but it had to be faced that the concerts had made a loss of over £43.

The idea of audience participation in selecting programmes was raised again in August, following a concert by the Western Philharmonic Orchestra in Truro Cathedral. This organisation had printed a form in their programme asking for the audiences' preference in music. The reviewer suggested this as a method which should be employed by the Penzance Orchestra. It was "not a suggestion that a society should be completely ruled by its supporters...merely a desire that the audiences who pay....should at least be granted some proportion of the music they want to hear." So it was after "lengthy discussion", and a suggestion by the conductor that works already in the Society's music library should be played, that the programme for the 1951-52 season was chosen, to include works by Gluck, Schubert, Mendelssohn, Berlioz, Rossini, Smetana, Wagner, Barber and Sibelius.

Changes in the officers of the Society were recorded in the minutes of the July AGM for 1951. The Hon. Librarian, Helen Atkinson, had resigned in January after many years service and was now seventy-seven years old, and Mr J. Treglown was appointed in her place. But by July he, too, had to resign and Enid Truman became the new Librarian. The Hon. Treasurer, G. L. Bradley also tendered his resignation and was replaced by Norman Truman, and both Enid and Norman held these positions for many years to come. The Society's President, A. W. Robinson offered to resign on grounds of failing health but it was unanimously decided that he should be asked to continue.

Helen Atkinson

Helen Atkinson is a good example of the many members of the Orchestral Society who, over the years, came to Cornwall to live, bringing with them a rich and cultured background. Born in 1874 she was sent, along with her sister, to 'finish' her education at the Dresden Conservatoire. Home was in a Yorkshire rectory, but the family visited London and went to concerts, listening to great performers such as Joachim. She returned to Germany in 1897 to continue studying the piano, and also attended classes in music theory and history and ensemble playing. She was highly regarded by her teachers and on her return to England in 1901 became a music teacher. One of her headmistresses referred to her as "a distinguished musician and teacher of music". In addition to the piano she learned to play the violin, viola, 'cello and flute and also conducted an orchestra in one of the various educational establishments in which she worked.

Helen retired to Penzance and joined the orchestra in 1937 as a viola player, but transferred to the violin in 1943 and remained a member until 1952. She had a working knowledge of a number of languages, including Icelandic and Hebrew, and pursued many hobbies as well as travelling. Her contribution to the Orchestral Society would have been manifested in a number of ways, quite apart from her playing, and on her retirement from the post of Hon. Librarian she was made a Life Member and a Vice-President of the Society. She died in late 1952 or early 1953 and this sad event was noted in the concert programme in March 1953.

With the Festival of Britain fading from prominence the Penzance Orchestral Society provided their audience with some summer magic on Wednesday 28th November 1951, with a performance of Mendelssohn's Incidental Music to 'A Midsummer Night's Dream'. The vocal elements of the music were provided by Gladys Lewis, who had been invited back to Cornwall to sing the part of the First Fairy. Second Fairy was sung by local soprano, Elise Harvey, and the Chorus of Fairies was provided by the Penzance Girls' Grammar School Madrigal Group which had been trained by Mrs Mary Williams. In Mendelssohn's score, Puck's words at the end of Shakespeare's ("If we shadows have offended..."), play are spoken above the final bars of the music, and these lines were spoken at the Orchestral Society's performance by Sheila Barefoot. A more apt name would be difficult to find for a fairy!

The Cornishman reporter was very pleased with the music chosen for this concert. Schubert's 7th Symphony was the other major work and after three paragraphs of introduction about the rebuffs the orchestra had been receiving, he felt that this programme "approached nearer to the ideal than has any other for at least two years". The *Western Morning News* reviewer also seemed much happier, the Symphony being given "A surprisingly good interpretation". *The Cornishman* report of the afternoon concert also revealed that the schoolchildren present showed "delightful appreciation".

The Society's concert account actually records the details of the schools which supported this concert, and they sent a total of 236 children. The Penzance Girls' Grammar School provided, not surprisingly, the largest contingent of 97, but their neighbours, the Boys' Grammar School only managed 5. St Ives Grammar School sent 38 pupils and Lescudjack (Penzance) Secondary School 50. The School of St Clare sent 22 children and West Cornwall College 8 (both were Penzance Secondary fee-paying schools). Even the Tolcarne Primary School in Newlyn sent 16 little ones to hear this concert. This was a remarkable, but not by any means unique, attendance and even though they would have paid a minimal amount for their tickets, contributed to a profit made at the concert of £3. 13s. 1d.

This was a cheering start to the 1951-52 concert season for the Society, and their conductor received further publicity during December when *The Cornishman* printed a full page feature on his home village of Newlyn. It focused mainly on working life, but under a sub-heading of "Sport and Musical Distinctions" included Morgan among the "well-known men who have made names for themselves". For social historians this page provides fascinating information from the many advertisements for shops and businesses in Newlyn in the early 1950s.

A 'Near Calamity' in Truro!

To round off the musical story of 1951 it is impossible to resist a newspaper account of a concert in Truro Cathedral on 5th December of Bach's 'Christmas Oratorio', performed by combined Cornish choirs and conducted by Sir Adrian Boult. The following day *The Cornishman* provided a short and factual account of the occasion, commenting that "seeing this world-famous conductor in action was a treat to be long remembered". The following week in its "Around West Cornwall" column the paper revealed a "Near Calamity" at this prestigious concert in which Penzance choirs took part.

Apparently a box had been placed on the rostrum for Sir Adrian to stand on, which sounds like a last minute 'make do and mend' solution to a problem. Soon after the performance began the box splintered and continued to buckle every time the great man raised his arms for a crescendo. "It was almost with relief that one welcomed the end of the Oratorio without the world-famous conductor toppling from his rostrum." The report concluded with high flown phrases about a "momentary perfection of mood and music" and suggested that the occasion was one of them, but how very different it might have been!

For Morgan Hosking the New Year, 1952, began before the old one had ended. Early in the previous December he had been asked to take over as Musical Director for a pantomime, 'Babes in the Wood', being put on by the Redruth Amateur Operatic Society. Their own conductor, Captain Charles Nicholas, had been taken ill and had to go to hospital, so from 31st December 1951 to 5th January 1952 Morgan travelled to and from Redruth for the eight performances of this show. The music consisted mostly of popular songs, and he conducted an orchestra of 16 players including three saxophonists. It was hailed as a great success with over 8000 people going to see it at the 1000-seater Regal Theatre.

Following this hectic start, 1952 carried on in much the same way, with Morgan and many of his orchestra participating in most of the musical events in West Cornwall. The combined Grammar Schools production of Britten's 'Let's Make an Opera' in January; the Penzance Borough Procession on the occasion of the civic memorial service following the death of King George VI on 6th February; St Just Operatic Society in March; Camborne Wesley Chapel's Good Friday performance of Judas Maccabeus in April; Penzance Playgoers in May and so on... when did these people ever take a break! Committee meetings, too, had to be fitted in between practices and performances and the Orchestral Society managed only four throughout the year, including the Annual General Meeting.

At the end of February the Operatic Society celebrated their Silver Jubilee with a production of Gilbert and Sullivan's 'Mikado', which received plenty of press coverage all of which was favourable. Acknowledgement of Queen Elizabeth II's accession to the throne was made by a full page photograph of her in the 'Mikado' programme with the caption "God Bless Our Queen".

Diana Ford returned to her home town once again as soloist with the orchestra for their two concerts on Friday 28th March. She played the Beethoven Piano Concerto No. 4, Op. 58 in the first half of the programme as well as a group of solos in Part II. Weber's Overture 'Oberon' opened the concerts after the playing of the National Anthem, now God Save The Queen of course. These concerts, again attended by about 200 schoolchildren in the afternoon, received very good reviews in all the papers with Miss Ford's performance given much attention and Morgan Hosking was quoted as considering her "a very sensitive and able artiste, who deserved to go a long way".

This refreshing mood of approbation from the press continued in their reports of the autumn concert on Friday 21st November 1952. The soloist was the young Vienna born violinist, Erich Gruenberg. Aged just twenty-eight he had become a British citizen in 1950 after studying in Vienna and Jerusalem. He was at the start of a distinguished career, and the beauty of tone and phrasing for which he became noted was apparent in Penzance. The Vivaldi Concerto in A Major for violin and string orchestra was regarded as the most satisfying experience of the concert, and in Saint-Saëns' 'Introduction and Cappriccioso', which he played with the orchestra at the opening of the second part of the programme, his playing left "no doubt of this soloist's artistry." The orchestra's performance of Tchaikovsky's 5th Symphony was "very impressive... highly creditable to all concerned". According to *The Cornishman* reviewer this was "the best concert given by the orchestra... since 1949", causing local music-lovers to "think of the comparative shallowness, musically, of West Cornwall without the Society and its hard work."

The programme printed for these concerts appeared as usual from its cover but was more substantial than hitherto and included detailed programme notes for each work. These had not been a regular feature of the programme for many years and their inclusion had been suggested by violinist, Derek Tamblyn, during the 1951 Annual General Meeting. Who wrote them is not recorded but it was very likely the conductor himself. As well as noting the deaths of two long standing members of the orchestra, Mr Len Stewart, timpanist and Mr George Cave-Day, violin, the programme also acknowledged the support of the Arts Council of Great Britain for the first time.

In November 1952 *The Cornishman* announced Penzance town council's "Ambitious Coronation Programme" for the coming year, which was to include two performances of Edward German's 'Merrie England' by the Operatic Society. These would be in addition to their usual production in the early spring of 'The Song of Norway', an operetta based on the life and music of Edvard Grieg.

Looking ahead at his musical commitments during Coronation Year, 1953, Morgan Hosking would have been aware of a great deal of hard work to be done, though he had handed over conductorship of the Choral Society to Leslie Jacobs in September 1952. There was the week of opera, three concert dates and two separate performances of 'Merrie England' to cope with, disregarding the other musical events in which he was asked to participate or lead an orchestra. He would have looked forward to visits during the year by large professional orchestras such as the London Philharmonic, the Hallé and the Bournemouth Symphony Orchestra. The latter's visits to Cornwall, usually in Truro Cathedral, were organised by the Western Symphony Concerts Committee of which Morgan was a member. So – a lot to achieve and a lot to be done in a year, and it is as well that he could not foresee the personal trials and tribulations that would affect him and his family during the early months of 1953.

1953 – Coronation Year

Preparations and rehearsals for the 'Song of Norway' were well under way by mid-February when an interesting preview article appeared in *The Cornishman*. Morgan, during his research into Grieg's life, was fascinated by the striking resemblance between Nina, wife of Edvard Grieg, and one of the Operatic Society's cast, Joy Moorley, who was to take the role of Nina. It was "identical and uncanny" he commented on a photograph of Nina, "you would really think it was Joy."

The problems to be overcome were numerous. For some reason there were only 15 scores available to the chorus and there were disparities between American and English settings of the libretto. The producer had to contend with a very small stage at the Pavilion Theatre and a special set to cope with this was being built by a firm from Weston-super-Mare. Last, but by no means least, a grand piano had to be stored off-stage for its appearance in the final scene where Grieg, played by Stephen Hichens, is to be found playing his Piano Concerto. For such a small theatre this was a major obstacle!

A later article also points out that in the final scene there would be no hidden pianist or gramophone recordings involved because Stephen Hichens, an able pianist, was teaching himself to play, in condensed form, the required ten minutes of Grieg's Concerto and would do so without music. It was thought that this was the first time, in England at least, that a singer had done this. The production was to take place, over eight days from Friday 20th to Saturday 28th February.

A Sad 'Song of Norway'

This detailed background is provided to emphasise the complexities of the show in order to fully appreciate the daunting situation the company had to face following the previews. On Thursday 12th February a tragic accident took place in Newlyn when Cecil Gilbert, a chief engineer with W. S. Stevenson & Sons, fell from a harbour wall ladder onto the deck of a trawler below, and died in hospital next day. He left a widow and two daughters, as well as the local

Cecil Gilbert.

community, in shock and deep distress for he was a popular and respected man. Cecil was well-known in the district as a singer and actor and had taken the role of the Mikado in the Operatic Society's production twelve months previously. He was to have played a major part in the 'Song of Norway' and his daughter, Cynthia, also had a named role. In addition, he was Morgan's first cousin to whose personal grief was added concern for 'The Song of Norway', opening the following week, during which Cecil's funeral was to take place.

Of course, the show had to go on. Understudies, Edgar Roberts and May Robinson, were brought forward and given the training and help required to prepare them in the few remaining days. This would have been quite enough for any company to cope with but on the day before the opening night Morgan's uncle, Benjamin Ridge junior, died. He had been unwell and it is thought that the shock of his nephew being killed hastened his death. He was the head of the family firm, B. J. Ridge, the running of which now fell totally onto the shoulders of Morgan and his brother. How he coped during this traumatic period is hard to imagine but cope he did.

'The Song of Norway' played to over 4,500 people during its nine performances. It received good press coverage including a report in *The Cornishman* about yet another drama which occurred behind the scenes. One of the company, George North, a member of the chorus who had a minor role in the second act, had to be rushed to hospital on the Monday evening for treatment after nearly collapsing due to a painful boil. This was all dealt with during the first act and although an understudy was placed on alert George was back in time to sing his part in the second act!

The Operatic Society's annual ball on 5th March must have provided much needed light relief and cheer for members and friends, but for Morgan another bereavement two weeks later had to be endured, that of a close family friend who lived with them. Though an old lady, her passing would have involved Morgan in yet more funeral arrangements because he was the head of the household and depended upon by the rest of the family to 'see to things'.

The Orchestral Society, too, was encountering problems as it prepared for the concerts on Friday 27th March. Thea King, principal clarinettist with the Sadler's Wells orchestra, had been engaged to play the Mozart Clarinet Concerto, (a first performance for the orchestra), but had to break the engagement having to leave the country for the sake of her health. Fortunately her replacement, Stephen Waters, had experience with many major orchestras and had both played and broadcast the Mozart Concerto on frequent occasions. His performance and the orchestra's accompaniment of it was warmly praised in the press reports as was a performance of Manuel de Falla's Suite from the ballet 'Love the Magician'. Despite the dreadful stresses and strains through which he had passed during February and March Morgan Hosking "showed, as usual, decision and vigour in his conducting."

A Financial Crisis

Vigorous, too, was his speech to the concert audience when he announced that, financially, the Orchestral Society was "on the rocks"! Concerts were still playing at a loss and unless things improved the Society might have to stop giving public performances if not disperse altogether. The press rallied to the cause by reporting this situation and pointing out the merits of the Society's concerts to the county, and its approaching Golden Jubilee. It castigated the music-loving public for supporting large professional orchestras but neglecting their own. Local authorities were criticised for taking "the unrealistic view that, while Shakespeare, literature and art deserve to be subsidised from the rates, and, indeed are, Mozart, Beethoven and Haydn do not". *The Cornishman*, in its leader article on 16th April, made an emotional appeal, "Where there is no vision, the people perish... there can be no hope in these anxious days of rising rates from civic authority, but some effort should be made to prevent the dissolution of this band of cultured players."

What was to be done? The orchestra's committee met on 24th April to discuss the financial position of the Society taking decisions to try and reduce costs on a number of fronts, mostly of a relatively minor nature. But enough money was available to go ahead with the next concert, by the strings of the orchestra, on 15th May when the soloist was their own pianist, Enid Truman.

While the newspaper writers may have shown concern and support over the financial crisis they did not allow this to influence their reviews of this concert which were very discouraging. *The Cornishman* reviewer even went so far as to say that in the Bach 'Piano Concerto No. 14 in

F Minor', the second movement (Largo) effect was "as though Mrs Truman was being accompanied by a quartet of banjos"! There was the odd positive remark, but it must have been painful for players and conductor to face such public criticisms.

It was at this concert that Morgan Hosking revealed that the members of the orchestra had contributed £15 to the Society's funds from their own pockets and the concert account included a figure of £4. 18s. 6d taken at the door in the afternoon. This is rather puzzling in view of the fact that there was only one concert given in the evening! It is possible that schoolchildren were admitted to the final rehearsal in the afternoon, but however it happened the concert day made a welcome profit of £31.16s. 7d.

Despite everything, the Society made plans for the future and the 1953-54 season was discussed at a committee meeting shortly after the May concert. In the meantime Coronation week was upon the town and among its celebratory events was a concert version of Edward German's 'Merrie England' presented by the combined Operatic and Orchestral Societies. This was part of the town's official Coronation programme and took place in St John's Hall on Friday 5th June at 2.30 and 7.30 p.m.

'Merrie England' was being performed up and down the country at this time and in West Cornwall there was another performance by the St Ives Choral Society in August with Heddle Nash among the soloists. The concert version in Penzance involved local soloists, Elise Harvey, Betty Lawrey, Hilda Hunkin, Edgar Roberts and Stephen Hichens, all regular singers with the Operatic Society. The role of Sir Walter Raleigh was sung by the young Douglas Williams who was making his first appearance with the Operatic Society. His singing received great acclamation, his voice being confident "and of a very pure quality".

A. W. Robinson. President 1941–1953.

This information was provided in a long report in *The Cornishman* for Thursday 11th June, 1953 and the town was regarded as "lucky that such a range of talent can be called upon for these roles". For the orchestra there was "a special word for their ability to make the most of their powers and abilities without exceeding them", and for the conductor, "guiding and controlling the whole performance was a task Mr Morgan Hosking showed to be well within his powers". The afternoon performance was poorly attended, apparently, but in the evening there was "a packed house."

The writer of the report admitted that he was "an unexpectedly enthusiastic critic" and regretted that there was only one day's presentation of 'Merrie England'. This was rectified by another performance later in the year, on Sunday 4th October, which was just as warmly reviewed, and accompanied by a picture of the performance. The Town Council officially acknowledged the June performances by sending the orchestra committee a "Memorial of thanks" for the support the Society had given to the Coronation festivities in the town.

At the Orchestral Society's A.G.M. on 10th July 1953, the recent death of their President, Mr A.W. Robinson, was acknowledged. The Chairman, Graham White, spoke of the many years of invaluable service Alf Robinson had given and members stood in silent tribute to his memory.

Alfred W. Robinson

Born in 1876, Alf Robinson had been one of the original members of the orchestra in 1907 as their keyboard player, on piano or organ as required. He taught himself to play the harp and from the nineteen twenties onwards this was the instrument he played in the orchestra. Harp players were not easily found in West Cornwall and Alf Robinson's ability made it possible for the orchestra to perform works for which a harp was scored. Otherwise they would have had to engage a harpist and this became necessary for a few years following his death. As the official harpist to the Cornish Gorsedd, he was admitted as Telenner Kernow (Harpist of Cornwall) at the 1929 Gorsedd.

He was a first class rifle shot and as a young man had been a member of the lst Volunteer Battalion of the Devon and Cornwall Light Infantry, but served with the R.A.F. during the First World War. Between 1939 and 1945 he was the local emergency information officer. His family business was Robinson and Son, house furnishers, auctioneers and valuers located at St George's Hall, Causewayhead, Penzance, where the Society's concert bookings were handled by the firm for many years.

Alf Robinson had been a vital member of the Orchestral Society's management team, and their President for twelve years. He had played an active role in the Operatic Society and was their President, too, for a time. He was also a well-known Freemason and in whatever organi-

sation he was involved his impressive stature marked him out as someone in authority. At a memorial service, for men only, at St Paul's Church, all the spheres of activity in his life were represented. Many members of the Orchestral Society were present, and their wreath was among the floral tributes.

The Society decided that Mrs Charles Williams should be invited to become the next President and the Secretary, Frank Hartley, wrote to her. In a letter to Morgan Hosking dated 24th July she expresses doubts about her suitability for two reasons. Firstly she admitted to being more ignorant of music than she wished to be and, secondly, she was so busy that she feared not being able to attend concerts. Morgan replied reassuring her that he realised how very busy she was but the Society felt that by accepting the office she could benefit the orchestra and stimulate interest in it through her connections and influence throughout the County.

Mrs Charles Williams

Mary Williams was a member of the well known Bolitho family, being the daughter of Thomas Bedford Bolitho, and she had married Charles Williams who was for many years the M.P. for Torquay. He was also Deputy Speaker of the House of Commons for a period. Mrs Williams' interests were many and varied and the positions of authority which she achieved in them resulted in there being very few areas of county affairs in which she did not play a part. She was a member of the Newlyn Pier and Harbour Commissioners, so was well known to Morgan Hosking through this connection, and they also shared a mutual love of Scotland where the Williams family were landowners and had a home. Her Presidency of the Orchestral Society only covered the 1953-54 season but she remained a supporter of the Society until her death in 1977.

It was at this same AGM in July 1953 that the Society named two new Vice Presidents, Mrs Carter and Mr Harrison. Mrs Carter, who lived at Trannack near Heamoor, was a great supporter of the orchestra. She played the harp and loaned her concert harp to the orchestra when one was needed. More will be told of her and the harp later on.

'Fluffie' Harrison

Arthur Ganderton Harrison, whose childhood name, 'Fluffie', remained into adulthood, was born in Hayle where his father was a chemist, and also the organist at Phillack Church. Mr Harrison senior was a friend of Walter Barnes and after moving to the Liskeard area his family became friendly with Enid and Norman Truman who lived there for some years after their marriage. 'Fluffie', born in 1895, inherited a love of music but his chosen career was the RAF. He was a pilot in the Royal Flying Corps during the First World War and also in the RAF during 1939-45 reaching the rank of Squadron Leader. He was a bee-keeper and after leaving the RAF he pursued a second career as the Cornwall County Bee-keeping Officer for the Ministry of Agriculture and Fisheries. He lectured on this subject all over the county and made a series of broadcasts on this and other topics for the BBC. He and his wife, Jane, maintained their friendship with the Trumans all their lives and frequently holidayed in a caravan at Hayle. They became loyal 'fans' of the Orchestral Society, and through his connections at the BBC 'Fluffie' was able to re-awaken their interest in the orchestra's activities, which was acknowledged by his being invited to become a Vice President. Letters written by Fluffie Harrison reveal a man of great courtesy and charm; in response to this invitation he was, "thrilled to my marrow to be asked and even though it is an honour out of all proportion to any little boosting I may have been able to give the Society I am not going to be diffident about it but I will say at once that I am accepting with the most enormous pleasure... I look forward to each concert with increasing happy anticipation."

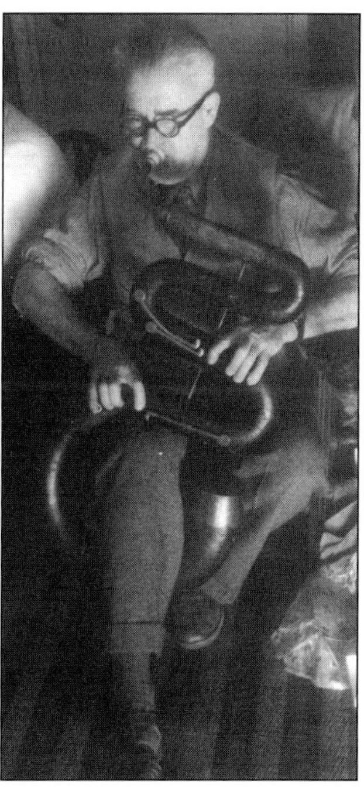

Vice-President, A. G. 'Fluffie' Harrison, playing the Serpent.

The finances of the Society had improved by the end of the 1952-53 financial year with a balance of £97. 5s. 4d, but this was still an increase of only £7 over the year so there were no grounds for complacency. The "deplorable state of the Bandroom" was raised by Mrs Nora Horsfall but action was deferred, though Mrs Garstin undertook to get an estimate for window cleaning. Later, in September, a Jumble Sale was held at the Penzance Y.M.C.A. with the aim of raising money to redecorate the Bandroom.

There is no recorded committee discussion on letters which passed between Mr John Edwards, chairman of the Welsh Orchestral Development Guild and Morgan Hosking during

September 1953, regarding an invitation to the Orchestral Society to go to South Wales to take part in the National Eisteddfod of Wales competitions in 1954. Despite Morgan having discussed this possibility with Herbert Ware, and his obvious interest in the idea, nothing more is heard about it. Did the committee members ever consider that it might be a viable proposition? The problems to be overcome would have been many and costly but the evidence available merely poses questions and answers none.

Another minor spat with the press took place in early September following a preview article in *The Cornishman* about a visit to Truro Cathedral by Sir John Barbirolli and the Hallé Orchestra on 4th September. The writer made the following rather unkind remarks: "A reflection of the reasons for the present mood of cynicism adopted towards Cornwall by the organisers of musical and dramatic tours by first class artists is found in the fact that the Penzance Orchestral Society has been unable to organise motor-bus transport to and from the concert because of 'lack of enthusiasm'". What prompted this comment is unclear, but the Penzance orchestra's leader, Mrs Crosbie Garstin, was stung to retaliate with a letter which was published the following week: "Sir, in reply to your criticism of the Penzance Orchestral Society and arrangements for attendance at the Hallé concert at Truro, over 50 programmes were sold in Penzance and all who previously have been transported by motor-bus were either away or were taken by private car. There is also a convenient train service. Lilian Garstin, September 8th". Good for her!

Better publicity came in mid-September when a BBC broadcast in the arts series, "Apollo in the West," featured Penzance and its orchestra. *The Cornishman* reported this event on 24th September referring to the involvement in the programme of "the eminent critic", Colin McInnes. He described the orchestra as being "one of the greatest amateur orchestras in the country". This was praise indeed! The programme appears to have featured Morgan Hosking, but its style and format was not revealed. With regard to local support, or rather the lack of it, Colin McInnes found it, "amazing that so many people...did not know that Penzance had an orchestra of its own". 'Fluffie' Harrison thought that it was "a lovely recording and it has opened the eyes of many people" and it must surely have boosted the morale of Society members so often bruised by criticisms.

Cornwall was treated to another visit by a professional orchestra during October 1953 when the Bournemouth Municipal Orchestra, under conductor Charles Groves, gave a concert in Truro Cathedral. The soloist was the renowned violinist, Alfredo Campoli whose engagement with the Orchestral Society had to be given up at the outbreak of the Second World War. No doubt many of the Penzance musicians took this opportunity to hear him and Morgan Hosking preserved his programme which had been autographed by the great man himself.

Back in Penzance the soloist at the Orchestral Society's 142nd and 143rd concerts on Thursday 26th November 1953 was Victoria Elliott, principal soprano with Sadler's Wells Opera. A Thursday was chosen to accommodate Miss Elliott, and *The Cornishman* reporter thought that this may have been one of the reasons for a "much larger audience than of late" at the evening concert, because many people were already in the town on a Thursday, it being market day. Victoria Elliott sang 'The Letter Scene' from Tchaikovsky's 'Eugene Onegin' and "thrilled (there really is no other word) the audience by the power of her rich soprano voice".

Beethoven's Symphony No. 6 in F (the 'Pastoral') was the major orchestral work and both *The Cornishman* writer and the *Western Morning News* music critic were complimentary, the latter devoting most of his review to its performance. He felt that the work had "been very carefully rehearsed and scrupulous attention was paid to detail". He regarded it as a severe test for any orchestra, relying on individual sections of the orchestra for many effects. Especially selecting the bassoons for their "extremely polished and fluent playing" he concluded that the playing of the symphony was "one of the best efforts this orchestra has done for a long time". The rest of the programme was equally well treated and he ended his article by saying that "This orchestra deserves all the public support that Cornwall can give it". Could this really be Geoffrey Baggs writing? Assuming that it was, it was a refreshing change from his previous reviews.

BBC Broadcast

In view of the traumatic and busy year which Morgan Hosking had endured he must have been delighted with players, soloist and reviews at the start of another orchestral season. More cheering news came on Christmas Eve when *The Cornishman* announced that the Orchestral Society would be making another BBC broadcast in late January 1954. This was as a result of recordings made by the orchestra for inclusion in the "Apollo in the West" programme which had been heard by Mr Norman Fulton, successor to Reginald Redman as West of England Director of Music for the BBC. The invitation to give a 45 minute programme on the radio was a "high compliment" in view of the fact that the BBC had established regional orchestras. Only one or two other amateur orchestras were known to have been similarly honoured in recent years. This was to be a 'live' broadcast with an audience, and an eagerly anticipated event in the New Year.

When the time came a 'live' recording was not possible because St John's Hall was unavailable on the evening of 22nd January 1954, the date scheduled for the broadcast by the BBC. A recording was organised for the evening before and the event portrayed vividly in the press. The audience was a "private" one, presumably drawn from the Society's subscribers, of about 100 people described as "sound ballast." They were first asked to be seated in the gallery, then asked to move from the side to the centre, and then to the floor of St John's Hall so it was as well that they were "patient and compliant" during the hour and half of preparations and sound tests. These necessitated the frequent shifting of microphones, pulling down of blinds, and blankets being suspended from the balconies, all of which point to the notorious over-resonant acoustic being as much a problem for the BBC sound engineers as for the orchestra in its normal concerts! The control panel and recording equipment was accommodated in a room behind the platform and the recording transmitted by land lines to the BBC West Regional Studios in Bristol.

The works performed were Weber's Overture to 'Euryanthe' and the Handel 'Overture in D Minor' arranged for full orchestra by Sir Edward Elgar, both of which had been played at the previous November concert. In addition, an old favourite of the orchestra, Schubert's 'Unfinished' Symphony completed the selection. Despite having to sit through the long build-up to the recording the orchestra, far from suffering as a result, "seemed to be put at their ease" and gave "one of their best performances". According to *The Cornishman* report the reception was "loud and clear" and although the players were able to listen to their own performance the writer felt that it was a shame that the area was still without the joys of television. It would have been, "so thrilling to see, if only for a few minutes, so many familiar local figures playing carefully and enthusiastically for our pleasure".

Yet more media coverage, to use a modern phrase, came in the June of 1954 with the *Western Independent* article "The Orchestra with a 'Reserve Team'" already referred to. Although mainly devoted to the work and activities of the Junior Orchestra it did, nevertheless, pay tribute to the longevity of the Orchestral Society and its achievements.

Years of Stability – 1954-1956

In the years approaching its half-century of existence the Society enjoyed a period of great popularity and stability. The former could be attributed to fresh awareness created by the 'Apollo in the West' and other broadcasts, but also more kindly newspaper reports and reviews must have helped, reflecting a cohesion which the Society had achieved during the first ten years of Morgan Hosking's conductorship, both musically and as an organisation. Stability came from an improved financial situation during these years with a substantial increase in the 'Friends' of the Society who contributed an annual fee on top of their regular ticket subscription. The BBC also paid the orchestra for the broadcasts, concerts made more profits than losses for a change and jumble sales were held from time to time. These factors all combined to present a much healthier bank balance as the 1950s progressed.

The pattern of concerts became firmly established during this period with two concert days, in May and November, each with an afternoon and evening performance. Concerts by the string section were abandoned but a work for strings was often included and programming appeared to settle down to a happy combination of reliable favourites interspersed with less familiar works. For example, Gabriel Fauré's Suite 'Pelleas et Melisande' Op.80, Rimsky-Korsakov's Introduction and March from 'Le Coq d'Or' in 1955, and 'Pineapple Poll', the ballet music based on Sir Arthur Sullivan's music, arranged by Sir Charles Mackerras, in 1956, just five years after its creation for Sadler's Wells in 1951.

These were years, too, of exceptional soloists, musicians of international repute who provided memorable performances. Maurice Cole playing Saint-Saëns' 4th Piano Concerto, Op. 44 in the spring of 1954 gave the orchestra its first opportunity to enjoy this lovely work.

Penzance Orchestral Society. Afternoon concert, March 1954. The Penhaul Collection, Penlee House Gallery and Museum, Penzance

He was regarded as "a pianist of stature and at times of nobility" in a review headed "Brilliant solo pianist at Penzance", which included a picture of the orchestra. In November of the same year Anna Pollack sang two arias from Bizet's 'Carmen' and was warmly praised, though in her solo group of songs a stormy night "nearly drowned Enid Truman's delicate and well-controlled accompaniment".

Hopefully the weather was more clement in May 1955 for a visit by the violinist, Tom Jenkins, well known through the radio 'Grand Hotel' programmes. He played the Mendelssohn Concerto in E Minor to great acclaim on a £4,000 Stradivarius instrument, showing "superb musicianship which was deeply appreciated by a critical audience." Tom Jenkins also gave an interview to *The Cornishman* reporter in which he made complimentary remarks about the orchestra. He confessed to feeling the strain of playing the concerto twice in one day but was impressed to notice, during the afternoon performance, some of the schoolchildren following the concerto, "apparently quite intelligently" from a score.

The Dvorak 'Cello Concerto in B Minor, Op. 104 was attempted for the first time by the orchestra in November 1955 when Anthony Pini, recognised as the country's finest 'cellist at the time, was the soloist. The orchestra "played confidently" and the soloist gave "a most eloquent interpretation", according to the *Western Morning News* music critic. Mr Pini obviously enjoyed working with the orchestra because, in Morgan Hosking's words, "he was so chuffed with the Dvorak that he asked if he could bring his son back with him on another occasion to play the Brahms Double", which he did in November 1957.

Problems at the Pavilion theatre

In the meantime the Operatic Society was also achieving popular success with its productions of 'The Pirates of Penzance' and 'Trial by Jury' in 1954 and 'Night in Venice', a new version of the Johann Strauss operetta, in 1955. Their success did not come easily, however, because of the uncertainty surrounding the future of the Pavilion Theatre. It was put into the hands of the receivers, and the secretary of the Operatic Society went to London to discuss the situation regarding its use by the Society. Permission was finally granted with only three weeks left before the opening night in 1954. With no resident theatre management the Operatic Society had to organise everything themselves, including sale of tickets, but having had to do this for the production of 'Die Fledermaus' they were old hands!

The problem over the Pavilion continued for the next two years, and a sale of fixtures arranged in February 1956 prompted another crisis prior to the production of 'Yeoman of the Guard'. After negotiation it was agreed that vital equipment would be kept in the theatre after

the sale for use by the Operatic Society. *The Cornishman* reported that a good deal of equipment would still have to be found by the Society, "and work will go on in the Pavilion night and day" after the sale until the opening night. However, the sale was cancelled at the last minute and following the production it was announced in *The Cornishman* that the Pavilion Theatre and the Palm Court Restaurant were to come under the control of Mr Rowland T. Davies of the Kenegie Hotel and Country Club. He had bought the unexpired lease on the building (the land being owned by the Penzance Corporation) and was making plans for its future.

Despite these ongoing worries the Operatic Society under its Musical Director, Morgan Hosking, continued to present shows which maintained high standards and attracted an enthusiastic audience. Indeed, the Operatic Society productions became such an eagerly anticipated event that from the mid-fifties onwards, on the day that the booking office opened to sell tickets for the forthcoming production, queues would form in the early hours of the morning with families sharing the hours of waiting between them.

Fond Farewells

Between late 1954 and the early months of 1956 a number of musical personalities died, some of whom had played a significant role in the Orchestral Society's history.

Albert Brien

Albert Brien had joined the Society in 1922 and for over thirty years had played the oboe, and cor anglais when required, alongside another stalwart member, G. L. Bradley. This oboe duo had seemed a permanent fixture in the orchestra! Mr Brien had come to Falmouth during the First World War as bandmaster to the Royal Fusiliers, married a local girl and settled in the town. Whenever an orchestra existed in Falmouth he was part of it, and most of the operatic societies and musical organisations in West Cornwall depended on his contribution. He made many solo appearances with the Penzance orchestra, most memorably as one of the four wind soloists in the Mozart Concertante in 1929 when his instrument broke during the afternoon performance.

Illness had prevented him from playing the well known and loved cor anglais solo in the second movement of Dvorak's 'New World' Symphony at the November 1954 concert when an oboe was substituted in his place. *The Cornishman* reviewer thought the oboe had been "unable to do complete justice to this noble conception", so his presence was sorely missed. He had recovered to play in a chamber music recital in Falmouth with Miss Maisie Radford on 29th November but collapsed next day and died on Wednesday 1st December 1954.

The death of Herbert Ware in March 1955 was marked by a long tribute to him in *The Cornishman* which included his appearance with the Orchestral Society in 1948. It was felt that but for this appearance in his home town his "abilities which marked him out in Cardiff went almost unrecognised in his native village", and the article was headed "Noted Newlyn Musician". Two months later and within a week of one another, Maddern Williams and Berkeley Mason both died. The passing of such a well-known musician as Maddern Williams prompted an obituary in *The Cornishman* of one and a half columns. On the Sunday following his death, at a concert given by his former choir, the Mousehole Male Voice, all stood in tribute to his memory, and his arrangement of the Nunc Dimittis was sung by the choir.

C. L. Taylor

More significant, historically, to the Orchestral Society was the death in London on 19th December 1955 of Charles Lawrence Taylor, at the age of 80. He had been one of the founding members of the Orchestral Society, playing the oboe in the first two decades of its existence. He was the eldest brother of Mr J. L. Taylor, proprietor of Taylor's Garage in Penzance and had been a well known sportsman. As well as having been a champion cyclist in the 1890's he had become a prize-winning billiard player in the South-West and county champion of Cornwall. For many years he had been the organist of both Madron and Gulval Churches.

Charles Taylor was made a bard of the Cornish Gorsedd in 1936, taking the name Lorgh Vras, meaning Strong Staff. This was the name given to a cup awarded by the Cornwall Music Festival to the winner of the competition for a choral setting of words with a Cornish theme. The cup was donated by Charles Taylor and although it is not known why he made this gesture his wife was a singer, and was a soloist with the Orchestral Society in 1908, so music was important in their lives. Although he had moved to London, Charles Taylor's family connections with Penzance and the high regard in which he was held during his years in Cornwall prompted an obituary in *The Cornishman*.

Of even greater sadness to the Society was the death of 'Jerry' Baker on 29th January 1956, aged 77 years.

Charles Jasper 'Jerry' Baker

Jerry Baker was born in 1879 but his place of birth and upbringing are unknown. He was a founder member of the Orchestral Society and would have been in his late twenties in 1907. Apart from some years during the 1930s he was the orchestra's principal bassoonist until his death, but he played other instruments, most notably the saxophone. In March 1948 he was even to be found playing the xylophone in addition to the bassoon when the orchestra performed Saint-Saëns' 'The Carnival of the Animals'.

He was a member of Walter Barnes' Savoy Cinema Orchestra, but also played with the Royal Marines Band in Plymouth for many years. Where he received his professional training and how he organised his life to cope with these two commitments was not revealed in his obituary in *The Cornishman* on 2nd February 1956. It is possible that he was a Penzance boy who joined the Royal Marines, was musically educated by them, and then 'commuted' between Penzance and Plymouth as his jobs demanded, maintaining a family home in Penzance. This is merely conjecture, but the obituary did provide a brief pen portrait of a man devoted to music, making himself available in many ways to the musical life of West Cornwall.

He retired from the Royal Marines, probably after the Second World War, because in 1945 he was appointed as clerk-in-charge of the Penzance Information Bureau and for a time was also Clerk of the Weather for the town. He retired from these duties in 1954, but continued his musical activities, performing with many amateur groups, arranging music for them, and organising musical programmes for various municipal functions. At some point in his life he founded the Savona Dance Orchestra and often played the saxophone in the Norris Williams Concert Orchestra.

At the Annual General Meeting of the Orchestral Society in September 1955 Jerry Baker was made a Vice-President "in recognition of his long service to the Society". In the November 1955 concert he had played at both concerts as its sole surviving founder member. He could be justifiably proud of his many years' service, and on the eve of the Golden Jubilee celebrations it seems unkind of the fates to have deprived him of participating in them.

12

Golden Days 1956-1957

Although the Orchestral Society's Golden Jubilee season did not officially begin until the November 1956 concert the celebrations were heralded by the visit of the world-famous pianist, Harriet Cohen, in May 1956. Among the famous musicians who had performed with the orchestra in previous concerts her star shone very brightly, and has continued to sparkle through the ensuing decades of memory.

Harriet Cohen

Pre-eminent among English pianists of her era Harriet Cohen, born in 1895, had achieved renown as a Bach player and a champion of contemporary British composers. By the time she came to Penzance she had survived tuberculosis and had made a recovery from a serious accident in 1948, when a glass she was holding in her right hand shattered. She played one-handed for a few years, and also underwent eye-operations in the early 1950's. That she survived these disasters and continued to perform is a measure of her remarkable perseverance and courage. Her beauty, charm and vitality drew people to her and throughout her life and career she formed close friendships with musicians, artists, writers, and politicians. Though music was at the centre of her being her enthusiasm for life embraced many areas of interest, including a love of cricket and football!

Among the artists Harriet got to know were Harold and Gertrude Harvey from Newlyn and she became aware of the problems many artists encountered in trying to get galleries to show their work, and the often high prices asked for their paintings. In league with George Bernard Shaw, she presented an exhibition of Gertrude's paintings in her home in London where any picture could be bought for five pounds, leading to its title as a "Woolworth" exhibition! It may have been through these artist friends that she first visited Cornwall; she grew to love the county and by 1956 had a cottage in Cadgwith on the Lizard peninsula.

Harriet Cohen. National Portrait Gallery, London

Two regular supporters of the Orchestral Society at this time were the artists Charles Breaker and Eric Hiller who lived in Newlyn and had an outdoor painting school, the Newlyn Holiday Sketching Group, which they ran from their Gurnick Field Studio. One day Charles Breaker asked Morgan Hosking how he would like it if Harriet Cohen came to play for him. Morgan replied that he would like it very much but wondered why such an eminent lady should wish to do so. Charles Breaker explained that he knew her very well and would invite her to come and play with the Penzance Orchestra.

She accepted the invitation and the decision was made to play Mozart's Piano Concerto in A Major, K414, a popular concerto and one often performed by Miss Cohen. Before the concert Morgan and Graham White visited her at the cottage in Cadgwith where she gave them lunch. Afterwards Harriet Cohen told Graham White to go for a walk while she and Morgan worked on the concerto. He remembered this experience as being "a revelation" as they went through the music, note by note, and she revealed how she wanted to play the work. He recalled her beauty and elegance, but also her intense personality and the tiredness he felt at the end of, for him, a thrilling afternoon.

The concert on Friday 4th May 1956 was a huge success, with the newspaper reports paying tribute to Harriet Cohen's "exceptional gifts". *The Cornishman* especially noted her care and interest in the whole work, at no point attempting to outshine the orchestra. Her performance, "showed not only Miss Cohen's ability, but also her interest in the orchestra and integrity as an artist". Her solo pieces reflected the composers with whom she was most closely associated, Bach, Sibelius and Manuel de Falla. Between three and four hundred schoolchildren were present for the afternoon concert, taking up the whole of the ground floor of St John's Hall. Miss Cohen's pleasure in the concerts is shown by the message she wrote on Morgan's programme: "For Morgan Hosking, exquisite accompanist in a concerto and generous and great colleague, Harriet Cohen". She also asked him if she could return to play de Falla's 'Nights in the Gardens of Spain', a work she knew intimately from her friendship with de Falla who had personally taken her around the places which had inspired him to write the work. Sadly, this was not to be because before anything could be arranged Harriet Cohen retired from public performances, a few years before her unexpected death in 1967.

Morgan, whose recollections of such memorable occasions with his orchestra were frequently interspersed with amusing stories, often told against himself, remembered the wonderful party which followed this concert at the home of Charles Breaker and Eric Hiller. Here he tasted Wiener Schnitzel for the first time, and fell in a patch of stinging nettles as he left the house and "got stung to death"! Back in London, Harriet Cohen wrote to Morgan saying that the concerts "were a wonderful experience: it is rare to have such a sympathetic conductor, especially about the Tempi!.... I shall indeed look forward to coming again: please convey to the orchestra and their charming leader my heartfelt appreciation...." Eric Hiller also heard from her and wrote to Morgan saying that she "seems to have enjoyed every moment including our little party to finish up the day".

The Golden Jubilee Season

Many more committee meetings than usual were held during 1956 as plans for the Golden Jubilee season got underway. Sir John Barbirolli had been invited to come as guest conductor and had agreed. But when approached for confirmation Sir John had to decline, due to his doctor's advice that the journey and whole experience would be too much for him following a period of ill health. This was disappointing news, but instead the committee decided to engage two soloists for the major concert in November 1956.

Alan Loveday, violin, and Victoria Elliott, soprano, were chosen as being two of the most popular young musicians in recent years, and by May 1956 the Jubilee programme had been chosen. Victoria Elliott would sing two arias in the first half of the concert and Alan Loveday perform Beethoven's Violin Concerto in D, Op. 61 at the opening of the second half of the concert. It was also agreed that the concert should be scheduled for a quarter of an hour more than the usual two hours to accommodate the two soloists and anticipated speeches etc.

The persons chosen to make the speeches during the evening concert were the Mayor of Penzance, Councillor J. F. W. Bennett, and Mr Barrie Bennetts, a founder member of the Society. In the event Barrie Bennetts was ill and unable to attend the concert so the committee chairman, Graham White, read a letter to the audience which Mr Bennetts had written for the occasion.

It was at the 1956 A.G.M. that two members suggested that the orchestra should adopt procedures at the start of their concerts similar to those taken for granted by concert-goers nowadays. These were that after the entrance of the leader, the oboe should sound an 'A' to introduce the period for orchestral tuning, and that the orchestra members should stand to greet the appearance of the conductor. It was also felt that someone should be given the responsibility of over-seeing the seating of the orchestra and looking after the soloists, and Gerry Barton agreed to do this.

Gerry Barton was not a playing member of the orchestra but his wife, Helen, was a second violinist and, later, Hon. Librarian. For many years Gerry took on the duties of Front of House Manager and his handsome and commanding presence suited the role to perfection. The Bartons and their close friend, Robin Whitehead, percussionist, were among those members who devoted themselves whole-heartedly to the Society and were an integral part of its unique character during the fifties, sixties and seventies.

Helen Barton was one of those selected, along with Mr M. Whitt, Mr S. Costello, Mr J. H. Woolfrey and Miss Cora James, to form a sub-committee to make the arrangements for a 50th Anniversary Dinner. Cora James was an invaluable behind-the-scenes supporter of the orchestra, and though not playing an instrument, became a vital cog in the society machine. She organised Jumble Sales, arranged refreshments after concerts, and for those and many other services she was greatly appreciated. There was a 'secret' committee meeting held at Enid and Norman Truman's house in late September 1956 to discuss a presentation to Morgan Hosking at the November celebration concert to mark his own 10th Anniversary, and "the esteem in which he was held by all members, and his long membership of the Society".

The build up in the press to the Society's Jubilee concerts began over a month in advance with *The Cornishman* printing preview articles from 18th October onwards. The concerts would be "a gala performance... St John's Hall would be decorated for the occasion", in the first week, followed by the announcement that the Mayor would make a speech. By 15th November there had been "an unprecedented demand for tickets... people waiting outside 'White's' at Alverton, the booking office, before it opened on the past two successive Monday mornings. Now there were only a few balcony seats left." By 22nd November it was "a complete sell-out for the evening concert", and readers were told that two harps, played by Miss Ann Ross and Miss Ann Harvey, were to be used during the concerts.

The stage and foyer of St John's Hall were to be specially decorated for the occasion with flowers, and the minutes record that the Borough Park Keeper, Mr Haynes, was to be asked to supply these for this special concert. As no costs to the Society are recorded it must be assumed that the Borough donated the flowers as a gesture of goodwill, though they are not named in the programme among those receiving the thanks of the Society. Walter Barnes' portrait by Stanhope Forbes was also put on display in the foyer.

So the scene was set for the Golden Jubilee concerts on Wednesday 28th November. They were the one hundred and fifty-fourth and one hundred and fifty-fifth to be presented by the Society – in itself an impressive record. Their fifty-year history was written by Mr W. E. Williams, taking up seven pages of the special twenty-two page commemorative programme. Morgan Hosking also contributed a three-page article, "The Orchestra Today and Tomorrow".

The printed programme included, in addition to the music being played and programme notes, photographs of Walter Barnes, Morgan Hosking and the full orchestra with its President, Miss Winifrede Beadsworth. Miss Beadsworth had ended her time as a violinist with the orchestra in 1952 but remained a committee member and was elected as President of the Society at the AGM in 1954. All the officials of the Society were listed, and it is interesting to note that among the ten Vice-Presidents four were still playing in the orchestra. Four more were former members of the orchestra, and these eight along with the President had, collectively and amazingly, given a total of 291 years of service to the Society! Friends and Subscribers were listed and numbered 158 with a great many of them named in both categories.

The music chosen for this concert was representative of the orchestra's varied repertoire, as well as including a work by one of the conductor's most revered composers, Richard Wagner.

Penzance Orchestral Society. Golden Jubilee, November 1956. Richards Bros., Penzance

But this was, of itself, a most apt choice, the Prelude to the opera 'The Mastersingers of Nuremberg', because, as the programme notes pointed out, the opera is a glorification of the Art of Music, and as Wagner himself stated, "in the C Major of Life". What better work could have been found to open the celebrations of fifty glorious years of music-making!

Victoria Elliott sang two arias, the 'Song to the Moon' from Dvorak's 'Rusalka' and the 'Ritorna Vincitor' from 'Aida' by Verdi. Although not programmed, *The Cornishman* report of the evening concert revealed that she returned later in the concert to sing again, this time accompanied by Ann Ross on the harp. Her choice of songs was 'O, My beloved Father' and a setting of The Lord's Prayer. Part 1 of the concert ended with Debussy's 'Petite Suite', a four movement piano work which had been orchestrated by Henri Büsser in 1907.

After the ten-minute interval the Mayor made a lengthy speech in which he paid tribute to the Society on behalf of the town. He outlined the help which the orchestra had given on various civic and notable occasions over the years and especially praised the way in which the Society had encouraged a love of music among schoolchildren, resulting in some of them now being members of both the junior and senior sections of the orchestra. Barrie Bennetts' letter was read by Graham White, which emphasised that the Society was a friendly one, epitomised by the word, 'loyalty' – to one another, to the Society and to the present conductor.

It was the Principal Violin, Mrs Crosbie Garstin, who paid tribute to that conductor, Morgan Hosking. "We were founded", she said, "by a genius! – how fortunate we are to have another genius to carry on the good work." She presented a portable typewriter to Morgan as a gesture of the Society's admiration to which he "gratefully replied", according to *The Cornishman*. Although his comments are not recorded he would have been unable to resist making something of a speech of his response which, no doubt, included a quip of humour so beloved by his audiences!

After all these spoken words the music continued with Alan Loveday's performance of the Beethoven Violin Concerto, and the concert concluded with the Fantasy-Overture 'Romeo and Juliet' by Tchaikovsky, and God Save the Queen.

The next day's *Cornishman* printed an impressive full page feature of the occasion with many photographs. These included one of the full orchestra, as well as pictures of the three conductors of the Society and its leader. This was not a review of the performance but simply reported the events of the concerts and announced the celebration dinner at the Queen's Hotel that evening. It devoted its many column inches to the speeches, and gave an account of the two articles in the programme by Billy Williams and Morgan Hosking. All officials and members of the orchestra were listed and the coverage was, generally, a true acknowledgement of the importance of the Society in the community.

Reviews of the performances appeared in The *Western Morning News* on the same day and in *The Cornishman* the following week, one of which included another photograph, this time of Morgan Hosking receiving his gift from Mrs Garstin. They were unanimous in their praise of the concerts with the performances by both soloists receiving warm words. The Debussy work was selected by *The Cornishman* critic as the work in which "the orchestra began clearly to show the extent of its improvements over the past 10 years in a performance of high merit". The *Western Morning News* also pointed out that the orchestra was at its maximum strength, "I imagine there are not many amateur orchestras that can boast of two harps, three trombones, and three double-basses, which were included in the 60-string ensemble." When considering the 'ups' and 'downs' of the Society during the post war years it was commendable, as well as fortuitous, that the orchestra had, by the time of its Golden Jubilee, attained a level of performance that, by amateur standards, found favour with all the commentators. They had, indeed, been fifty years of great achievement and the Society deserved the many tributes and congratulations.

Penzance Orchestral Society

1906 — 1956

FIFTIETH ANNIVERSARY DINNER

at

Queen's Hotel, Penzance

on

Thursday, November 29th, 1956

Chairman: Mr L. Graham White, C.C.

The Golden Jubilee Dinner menu card, November 1956.

The Fiftieth Anniversary Dinner was held in the Queen's Hotel, on the Penzance promenade, on Thursday 29th November. It must have been a convivial and joyous scene with members past and present coming together as friends and musical colleagues to recall the Society's history and toast its future. Special guests at the dinner were Major Simon Bolitho, the Mayor and Mayoress of Penzance, the Town Clerk, Mr E. O. Wheale, Mrs N. Bennett, Mr Arthur Robinson (President of the Operatic Society), Miss Ann Ross and Miss Victoria Elliott, the Vice-Presidents of the Society, the 'backroom boys and girls', and the Press.

In responding to Major Bolitho's toast to the Society, Morgan Hosking said that they could not afford to relax in their music-making in the face of rival attractions. He especially stressed the coming of television where people could see as well as hear great orchestras, making local

audiences more critical of amateur performances. The Society would have to rehearse harder to improve standards, and also tackle new and more modern music, much of which was too difficult for amateur musicians. He made an appeal to composers to produce music which amateurs could play. But he paid tribute to his own players, and to the officials and committee, saying that the success of the Society was due to their loyalty and devotion over the fifty years. As an example of loyalty he spoke of Mrs Faith Harris from Falmouth, who had been a member of the Society for 33 years. In that time she had played in hundreds of concerts and rehearsals, and travelled 27,000 miles, in total, to do so! As the assembled guests and friends raised their glasses that evening there must have been many whose private toast would have been, "Here's to the next fifty years"!

As might be expected the costs of the special concerts were higher than usual. The two soloists' fees amounted to almost £100 and Miss Ann Ross, a professional harpist, who had occasionally been engaged following the death of A.W. Robinson, was paid a fee of 14 guineas. (Miss Ann Harvey was to become the orchestra's regular harpist from this time onwards). Also, an oboist had resigned during the autumn and had to be replaced by a professional, along with two bassoonists and a horn player. The printed programme, too, had been much more expensive to produce, so despite capacity audiences the two concerts incurred a loss of over £70. However, the Society's finances were so much improved that money was available to cover this and to make a contribution of over £18 to the costs of the Anniversary dinner.

There were still the spring 1957 concerts to look forward to during the Jubilee season, but in the meantime Morgan and the orchestra had to turn their thoughts to rehearsals for the Operatic Society's production of 'The Vagabond King' at the beginning of March. This was, once more, a time of petrol rationing due to the economic 'belt-tightening' in the aftermath of the Suez crisis which had come to a bitter conclusion at the end of 1956. Car mileage was limited to 200 miles a month, which must have caused problems for musicians travelling to rehearsals from all over Cornwall.

The St Ives Operatic Society was forced to cancel its planned production of 'No, No Nanette', but the Penzance society managed to keep going. This was, however, something of an achievement when one considers that during the month of February itself rehearsals were being held on most nights of the week, with the orchestra also being called in on many of these during the last two weeks. For those not within walking distance of the Bandroom and Pavilion Theatre car-sharing was probably arranged to help with any transport difficulties. The production went ahead with every success from 28th February – 9th March 1957.

On the BBC again

The orchestra received nation-wide publicity in February 1957 from an unlikely source, the BBC 'Woman's Hour' programme! On 12th February this was broadcast 'live' from the home in Penzance of the historian, A. C. Todd (already mentioned as a friend of the pianist, John Vallier). Many aspects of the town were covered in the forty-five minute programme, with local personalities speaking on their particular subjects, among them Morgan Hosking on the Orchestral Society. His five minute slot included much of the information about the Society contained in the Golden Jubilee coverage. *The Cornishman* printed a long article about the broadcast and photographs of the participants. This was exciting for all the town's inhabitants and members of the Society would have been delighted with this unexpected attention during the Golden Jubilee season.

Later in the same month the well-known violinist, Tom Jenkins, who had been the Society's soloist in May 1955, died suddenly. Articles in both *The Cornishman* and the *Western Independent* included the news of his death and the interview he had given following his performance in Penzance, and information about the Society's celebratory season. The *Western Independent* also referred to the forthcoming visit of the celebrated Maori bass, Inia Te Wiata, at the Orchestral Society's spring concert.

Inia Te Wiata

This distinguished young singer joined the Orchestral Society for their concerts on Friday 10th May 1957. He had come to England from New Zealand in 1947 for training at Trinity College of Music and the Joan Cross Opera School. By 1957 he had many opera successes behind him as well as radio broadcasts. Recent television and film appearances had made him more widely-

known to the general musical public and his striking good looks, combined with a friendly and likeable attitude to audiences and music alike, made him a popular performer.

This proved to be the case in Penzance where he sang the comic 'Catalogue' aria from Mozart's 'Don Giovanni', and a selection of songs accompanied by Enid Truman at the piano. Newspaper reviewers were enthusiastic about his performances and the concerts generally. Rossini's overture, 'The Barber of Seville', received some mild criticisms but was regarded as one of the pieces of music responsible for bringing many young people to an enjoyment of orchestral and operatic music. For the usual large contingent of schoolchildren present in the afternoon it would have provided the musical 'fireworks'.

Mozart's 'Symphony No. 36 in C', K425, 'the Linz', was "a polished piece of orchestral playing"and in the Delius Intermezzo and Serenade from 'Hassan', solos by Mrs Crosbie Garstin, violin and Miss Ann Harvey, harp, were played with "sensitivity" in "a finished rendering". Slavonic Dances Nos. 2 and 4 from Dvorak's Opus 46 and the Ballet Suite from Tchaikovsky's 'The Sleeping Beauty' completed the programme. The *Western Morning News* critic wrote that "in the Ballet Suite and at the end of an exacting day of two concerts, the playing had a freshness and vitality which one expects from a professional orchestra, but often looks for in vain among amateurs". This was a positive note, indeed, with which to close the Golden Jubilee season, and with potential audience members having to be turned away at the evening concert because it had sold out, the Penzance Orchestral Society could enter its middle-age not with a crisis but full of cheerful confidence.

Inia Te Wiata, bass soloist, May 1957, in Maori costume.

Continuing Success 1957-1959

The success and stability achieved by the Penzance Orchestral Society, recognised during its Golden Jubilee season, continued for the remaining years of the 1950s. Some criticism did creep into the press reviews, with the brass section once again being accused of loudness and the opening overtures often regarded as being hesitant. Morgan Hosking admitted, during his report to the Annual General Meeting in September 1961, that "we are not at our best when playing an overture"! But there were usually enough words of praise and congratulation to soften the pill.

More Notable Soloists

Soloists continued to be of the highest calibre and cooperated with the Society to present demanding and rare performances. In November 1957 Anthony Pini and his son, Carl, performed Brahms' Concerto for violin, 'cello and orchestra in A Minor, Op.102. This was a challenge for all concerned but *The Cornishman* reported that the performance, "served to show the stature to which the orchestra has developed". The father and son's playing was warmly praised, with both instrumentalists, "delicately attuned to a partnership which found them in ideal spiritual communion".

In 1958 the famous oboist, Evelyn Rothwell, wife of Sir John Barbirolli, performed two works with the orchestra, Haydn's Concerto in C and the Concerto for oboe and strings, which was a composition of themes from the music of Corelli, arranged by Sir John Barbirolli and dedicated to his wife. The latter work had to be re-scheduled to an earlier place in the programme in order that the soloist could catch the overnight train from Penzance to London in time to fly to Holland next morning for a concert in the afternoon! Evelyn Rothwell impressed the reviewers by her faultless technique and impeccable and virtuosic musicianship. In November of that year the Sadler's Wells soprano, Marion Lowe, was the guest artiste, her "lovely singing" and the "polished playing of the orchestra" contributing to concerts which the *Western Morning News* music critic thought "were among the most successful... in recent years".

John Vallier, well known to Penzance and playing to capacity audiences in May 1959, brought the Grieg Piano Concerto vividly to life by revealing that the score he had used in preparing the concerto had Grieg's own directions written in it. The score had come from a pupil of Liszt who had himself studied the work with Grieg. John Vallier's interpretation was, to the ears of the *Western Morning News* writer, a "somewhat over-dramatisation... unnecessarily dynamic.... storms which Grieg can hardly have envisaged", all of which he attributed to the link with Liszt! The soloist played different solo items at the afternoon and evening concerts which displayed greater "versatility of style". Among these pieces was one of the pianist's own compositions entitled "Witches Ride" which had been inspired by a visit to Zennor.

The guest artist with the orchestra in November 1959, violinist, David Martin, took on the dual role of soloist in the Max Bruch Violin Concerto No. 1 in G Minor, and leader of the orchestra for a performance of Rimsky-Korsakov's Symphonic Suite 'Scheherazade'. His playing of the concerto was "superbly fluent and flexible ...notable for its finish, its supple technique and scrupulous attention to details". The Rimsky-Korsakov work took up the whole of the second half of the programme in which Leader, Lilian Garstin, gave up her seat to David Martin. This dramatic work placed many demands on an amateur orchestra, but *The Cornishman* reviewer felt that the Penzance Society's reputation "had been enhanced", and the solo passages for some of the woodwind and brass were of "exceptional quality".

This concert was notable for another dual role, with Morgan Hosking welcoming Mrs Lilian Garstin to the stage both as Deputy Mayor and the orchestra's Principal Violin. He also offered the Society's thanks to the Mayor and Corporation of Penzance for providing a new stage which had been built during the summer. This had been part of improvements to St John's Hall to create more dance floor space thereby permitting an increase in dancing and seating capacity. The alterations also involved a new maple wood floor and a lower platform which provided more space for the orchestra.

This had been achieved with full consultation and cooperation between the Society and the Council. But the *Western Morning News* thought having more elbow room had not made any difference to the orchestra's "untameable propensity to play at a double forte strength when the music demands a more gentle approach". This does not quite stand up to the writer's later remark that in the 'adagio' of the violin concerto, "the strings achieved an admirable smooth and sustained softness"!

During these years the choice of music offered by the Orchestral Society continued to introduce unusual and more contemporary works to their audience. In addition to the Brahms Double Concerto and 'Scheherazade', Ponchielli's 'Dance of the Hours' from 'La Gioconda' and a 'Pastorale Suite' by the Danish composer Lars-Erik Larsson, written in 1938, were played. British music, too, received attention with Benjamin Britten's 'Simple Symphony', Butterworth's Rhapsody for full orchestra, 'A Shropshire Lad', and Vaughan Williams' 'Five Variants of Dives and Lazarus', scored for string orchestra and harp, getting their first performances by the Society.

Mrs Carter and Her Harp

The last mentioned piece was included in the November 1958 concert and it is probable that it was chosen as a suitable work with which to highlight two of the Society's recent acquisitions, a concert harp and a harpist. For several years whenever the orchestra needed a harp they had borrowed one from Mrs M. H. L. Carter of Trannack House, near Heamoor, and this help had been acknowledged by her becoming a Vice-President of the Society. Prior to this the orchestra had relied on Alf Robinson both to play and provide the harp, and a hiatus had occurred in the late 1940's and early 1950's when he was no longer available. Mrs Carter's harp had been played by a professional harpist, Miss Ann Ross, engaged whenever a harp was needed, but the situation improved for the Society when a string player in the orchestra, Miss Ann Harvey, learned to play the harp.

Although no record of it appears in the minutes Mrs Carter gave her harp to the orchestra because, according to Enid Truman, as she grew older she put on weight and "grew a bit away from the harp" and no longer played it. A generous-hearted lady, indeed, to make this substantial donation to the Society and to admit the reason for doing so! This gift was acknowledged by the Society in the November 1957 concert programme where the instrument is revealed as being made by Erard, "and Mrs Carter's action now ensures the permanent use of this most valuable instrument in the Orchestra".

A Permanent Harpist Once Again

Ann Harvey received some tuition on the harp from Ann Ross, whom she describes as a very sweet person and a close friend of Lilian Garstin. Something akin to a correspondence course developed between them with Ann Ross recommending or providing her protégée with suitable music to study and practice. Later, Ann met the distinguished harpist, Susan Drake, at a recital, who gave her some advice on modern techniques. But apart from this help Ann acknowledges that she is largely self-taught.

Her first concert as the orchestra's harpist was in 1956, and she continued in her dual role as harpist and viola player and for many years was the Principal of the viola section. Ann, who became Mrs Beric Tempest during 1969, has also made a valuable contribution to the Society as a committee member and chairman.

In 1979 she was received into the Cornish Gorsedd of Bards as Telynores am Howlsedhas, meaning Harpist of the West, and has been the official harpist at Gorsedd ceremonies from time to time. Her devotion to the harp and the expertise she has developed has provided the Orchestral Society with the rare combination in an amateur orchestra of a harp and a harpist all their own for the last fifty years of its existence.

Although a very welcome addition to the orchestra's assets the ownership of the harp incurred extra expense over the years. In 1958 Miss Ann Ross had used it for a recital and suggested that it should be overhauled in London at a cost of about ten guineas, including transport, and Ann Harvey was asked to make all the arrangements. Greater expense was necessary twenty years later when extensive repairs were needed.

The late 1950's found the Orchestral Society maintaining its support of other organisations, musical or otherwise, in the area. In May 1957 the strings of the orchestra joined with the Newlyn Male Choir for a concert in St John's Hall in aid of the Mayor's Welfare Fund. Both choir and orchestra gave their time for this concert to raise money for food and treats for the old, the needy and the hospitalised at Christmastime. During August of the same year Morgan Hosking was to be found conducting some of the items in a programme of music by the Camborne Town Band performing on the Bandstand in Morrab Gardens.

In December 1958 members of the Orchestral Society formed a small orchestra to accompany the Penzance Choral Society at their centenary performance of Handel's 'Messiah'. This concert took place in Richmond Methodist Chapel on the 18th December and the four professional soloists included the bass Gordon Clinton, who had sung the 'Messiah' on the radio only the night before the concert. The orchestra, led by Lilian Garstin, comprised four first violins, four second violins, which included Morgan Hosking, two violas, two 'cellos, two double basses and trumpet. This was a great occasion for the Choral Society, formed in 1858 and believed to be among the oldest choral societies in the country, and it is to be hoped that a night of dreadful weather did not mar their celebrations too much.

As usual, the orchestra would have taken part in the Operatic Society productions of Gilbert and Sullivan's 'Ruddigore' and Franz Lehar's 'The Merry Widow', keeping them busy in the early months of 1958 and 1959. 'Ruddigore', in particular, created a lot of interest for a number of reasons. Firstly, it had never been performed by the Society before due to the complications of staging the dramatic "portraits" scene in Act II, in overcoming this they achieved a long standing ambition. Secondly, W. S. Gilbert is believed to have conceived the ideas and setting for 'Ruddigore' when on holiday in St Ives, and the action takes place in the Cornish village of 'Rederring". Heavy snowfalls did not deter audiences, and both productions attracted all night queuing for tickets.

Appreciation and support, in whatever form, is always welcome to those involved in an amateur group activity, and the Orchestral Society's finances received a boost during 1957 in the form of a £50 legacy from the estate of the late Miss A. M. Cumberland. Apart from the fact that she had been a regular patron of the Society for some years nothing more is known about this lady, but the Treasurer reported to the 1957 A.G.M. that the gift had helped offset the overall loss of over £75 incurred during the Golden Jubilee` season.

Morale would have been boosted in April 1958 when an article about the orchestra appeared in that month's issue of the musical magazine, 'The Strad'. This magazine described itself as "A Monthly Journal for Professionals and Amateurs of all Stringed Instruments Played with the Bow". The two-page article, with a photograph of Morgan Hosking, outlines the history and activities of the Society.

How its publication in such a prestigious and internationally distributed journal came about is a mystery, but it produced a response from a reader in Spain, who wrote to Morgan Hosking with words of congratulation and asked to be sent a Golden Jubilee programme. He wanted to know the names of all the orchestral members and how the string section was made up. Apparently he had been a student at Plymouth College and was fond of Cornwall. He was also an amateur 'cellist in the "Corunna Municipal Simphonic (sic) Orchestra, at this town, not far geographically from you, where a small group greatly enjoy these good things". It was signed José Llorens Ebrat.

There were, inevitably, Society members who died during these years. The death of the Society's Sub-Principal Violin, Mrs Clarice Nicholls, was acknowledged in the November 1959 concert programme, her place being taken by Mr Jack Glasson. The previous year, in July, the last surviving member of Walter Barnes' original orchestra died, his old friend, Barrie Bennetts.

Barrie Bennetts

This man of Penzance had packed so much into his seventy-five years that he was something of a legend during his own lifetime. His death on 26th July 1958 called for a long and detailed obituary in *The Cornishman* along with his photograph. He was renowned in his younger days as a sportsman, "one of the finest...Penzance and Cornwall have ever produced", having played football for the town from 1902 and been a member of the rugby fifteen which won the county championship in 1907. He then went on to play rugby for England in 1909. In addition he had represented Cornwall in cricket, hockey and golf, as well as playing tennis and billiards. In retirement he was President of the Cornwall Rugby Football Union from 1945-1950.

Barrie Bennetts became a solicitor by profession with the Penzance firm of Boase and

Bennetts and from 1920-1946 was the County Coroner, as well as being the registrar at both the Penzance and Helson county courts. During the First World War he had served with the Argyll and Sutherland Highlanders and was mentioned in despatches, and during World War II was one of the first people to join the Local Defence Volunteers, later to become the Home Guard. Another of his life interests was the Royal National Lifeboat Institution with which he was associated from 1913. After 35 years of service on their behalf he was awarded their Gold Badge and received an M.B.E for his work in the 1951 New Years Honours List. He was the Hon. Secretary of the Penlee Lifeboat for many years and in 1957 was given the highest honour the R.N.L.I. could offer, that of becoming a Life Governor of the Institution.

When he reached the age of seventy in 1953, his friends arranged a birthday dinner for him. In a speech of tribute, Judge Scobell Armstrong said, "Into every activity in which he had been engaged, Barrie Bennetts has imparted an atmosphere of joy and good fellowship". One of his cherished leisure activities was playing the viola and he had been a member of that small group of friends, 'The Clefs', who went on to form the Penzance Orchestral Society. He became the orchestra's principal viola player, and, according to Ivan James, produced a powerful tone on his instrument.

Barrie Bennetts.

It is not surprising, given all his other areas of responsibility that he never held a major office in the Society. But during his thirty-eight years as a playing member and afterwards as a Vice-President and committee member to the time of his death he would have made an important and experienced contribution to the running of the Society. In 1948, after he gave up playing in the orchestra, he wrote a charming letter to Enid Truman accompanying the gift of his viola to her. This had been a long-standing arrangement with his old friend, Walter Barnes, and he hoped that Enid's husband, Norman, would "use it occasionally and I trust that he gets as much 'fun' out of its use as I have had". Enid and Norman obviously had a great affection for Barrie Bennetts, especially as he had been very supportive and helpful to Enid's mother, Chrissy, after Walter's death.

In December 1957 a letter was published in *The Cornishman* from Edward Collins of Newlyn, well known in West Cornwall as an organist and choral conductor. He congratulated the Orchestral Society on their recent concert and bemoaned the fact that they were only heard twice in a year. He went on to ask whether it would not be possible for the Town Council to make them a grant for an extra concert and suggested that a levy of a 1d. rate to facilitate this. He quoted the Bournemouth Corporation as an example of a town which financially supported its orchestra and thought that Penzance should do more to encourage those who made music, "thus helping to kill the apathy induced by the many very poor BBC broadcasts and TV shows".

This was a forlorn hope, and Penzance Council, along with other local councils were very reluctant to contribute to the Western Authorities Orchestral Association formed in 1958 "to preserve and foster an orchestra in the West" which would, in fact, be the Bournemouth Symphony Orchestra. In 1959 Mrs Crosbie Garstin spoke in favour of Penzance supporting the Association. The amount of money involved was £20 but the town voted against it, and the Bournemouth Orchestra visited Redruth instead where, in addition to the public evening concert, they advertised an afternoon concert when over 1,000 children were expected to attend the performance in the barn-like Flamingo Hall.

The approaching new decade would see a great development in the provision of music, especially for young people. A County Music Advisor had been appointed in Cornwall in 1947 in the person of William Pearson, and a Rural School of Music had been established, at long last, in 1956. Its first director was Jean Sadler, a man who went on to conduct a re-established Cornwall Symphony Orchestra from 1960.

The activities of the Cornwall Rural School of Music were mainly concerned with increasing the teaching of instruments and raising awareness of music in children by developing chamber ensembles and music appreciation classes. But its support group, the 'Friends' of CRMS, took on the task of bringing major orchestras to the County and organising large-scale choral performances. Also, courses for adult instrumentalists were becoming more common, and music festivals began to spring up in places such as Mylor and St Endellion.

So exciting times were coming for the music-lovers of West Cornwall, with more frequent opportunities to listen to professional performances and take part in an even greater variety of musical activities. But, hopefully, not to the detriment of their own lively and successful amateur orchestral society.

14

The Early Sixties 1960-1966

Noticeable among the musical activities in Cornwall during the 1960's was an increase in professional performances by visiting orchestras, opera groups, recitalists and chamber ensembles. Penzance Town Council eventually decided to support the Western Orchestral Association, bringing a section of the Bournemouth Symphony Orchestra or its Sinfonietta to the town on frequent occasions.

Porth-en-Alls Music

Another exciting development in West Cornwall was the emergence of the Porth-en-Alls Music Festival Group. This was the brainchild of the Tunstall-Behrens family who made their estate, Porth-en-Alls, near Penzance, available to musicians, professional and amateur, for a week of music-making at the end of which would be a public performance. Orchestral and choral concerts of the highest quality resulted from 1962 onwards. Who would have expected to be able to hear a UK premier concert performance of Monteverdi's "L'Incoronazione di Poppea" presented at Godolphin Manor, with the roles of Poppea and Nero sung by stars of the future such as Heather Harper and David Johnston, and with an orchestra led by the great Yfrah Neaman? Members of the Penzance Orchestral Society played in this and future Porth-en-Alls concerts. With the advent of the famous Hungarian violinist, Sandor Vegh, to Porth-en-Alls in 1972, he and Hilary Tunstall-Behrens transformed the festival into the now world-famous International Musicians' Seminar, of which Steven Isserlis is the Artistic Director

Back in the early sixties Morgan Hosking could have been justified in regarding these events as a threat to his own orchestra. But he took the opposite view, welcoming them and calling for more professional music in the area, believing that amateur musicians could only benefit from listening to or becoming involved with them. Whenever possible members of the Orchestral Society did involve themselves. They played in the re-formed Cornwall Symphony Orchestra and the Falmouth Opera Group, both of which had a professional input. Local musicians and singers took part in the performance of Elgar's 'The Dream of Gerontius', thought to be the first in Cornwall, in Truro Cathedral on 29th May 1962. Here, the Bournemouth Symphony Orchestra and choirs were conducted by Henry Mills, Cornwall's County Music Advisor at the time. Penzance orchestra members provided practical support, too, in the form of stewards and other front of house personnel for visits to Penzance by the Bournemouth orchestras.

Chamber music also played its part, with concerts by such eminent ensembles as the Amadeus String Quartet visiting Truro, and local musicians forming groups to play for their own pleasure. Sometimes surprisingly well known names would appear in these, such as Erich Gruenberg, the violinist, and Raymond Leppard, both of whom were stationed at RAF St Mawgan during their National Service days.

In the midst of this vibrant picture the Penzance Orchestral Society continued with its afternoon and evening concerts in the spring and autumn of the year, as well as providing orchestras for the Operatic Society and Choral Society when required. It was a memorable period for the orchestra with many notable soloists, as well as innovative and challenging music performed.

Royal Events

It all began rather disappointingly, however, due to the spring concerts in 1960 coinciding with the date of Princess Margaret's wedding to Antony Armstrong-Jones, on Friday 9th May. It had been announced a month earlier that all schoolchildren would be given a day off school for the Royal Wedding, thereby depriving the Orchestral Society of a large part of its audience in the afternoon.

The evening concert, too, was less well supported than usual and the press reports felt that people had missed a rare opportunity to hear, "really magnificent operatic singing" by the guest soloist, Charles Craig. He sang 'Nessun Dorma', from Puccini's opera, 'Turandot' accompanied by the orchestra as well as three other arias with Enid Truman at the piano. Four dances from William Walton's 'Facade', arranged by Walter Goehr, set the precedent for a number of unusual orchestral items to come.

Despite a loss of over £76 incurred at this concert, Morgan Hosking held no grudge against the Royal family because on the following Monday he was to be found, along with Mrs Garstin, at Buckingham Palace! They were among the guests at a Royal garden party representing the Royal Overseas League, of which they were both active members, in its Jubilee Year. Hopefully, the half-hour long rain storm which soaked the proceedings during the afternoon did not spoil their pleasure in the occasion.

More Memorable Soloists

The 1960-61 orchestral season presented two major string concertos to its Penzance audience. In November Florence Hooton, wife of pianist David Martin who was the orchestra's soloist twelve months earlier, performed Elgar's Cello Concerto to great acclaim. On 5th May 1961 Frederick Grinke returned to play the Concerto in D for violin and orchestra by Tchaikovsky. The afternoon concert provided some musical drama when, towards the end of the concerto, "Mr Grinke's instrument developed a technical hitch. He swung gracefully to the leader, Mrs Crosbie Garstin, changed instruments in a trice, and concluded the concerto with the brio it demands" The evening concert went smoothly when the soloist delighted a good audience with his concerto performance and four solo items, after which he was repeatedly encored.

Frederick Grinke was one of many soloists who appreciated Morgan Hosking's talent as a concerto conductor, and he was able to show this in a practical way. Morgan took his violin to London to be repaired at Hill's of Bond Street, but they were reluctant to do the work for, to them, an unknown musician from Cornwall. Frederick Grinke came into the shop and greeted Morgan with enthusiasm as an old friend, and, becoming aware of Morgan's problem, insisted that Hill's did the necessary work. He told them that Morgan was one of the most important musicians in the South West of England. Morgan, of course, was flattered and gratified and loved telling this story whenever the opportunity arose!

The orchestra received a supportive tribute in *The Cornishman* following this concert which said that, "Their policy of bringing noted soloists down to Penzance to perform with them, and to take a real financial gamble on the concerts paying off, shows their devotion to the cause of music". Its review of the orchestra's playing was not without criticism, and the Delius work, the Intermezzo from his opera, 'Fennimore and Gerda' was regarded as their best item. Here, "the exquisite playing and quality of Miss Mole, oboe", was beyond criticism, and "her phrasing and tone in the solo passages...was extremely beautiful, and stood out as an exceptional performance which helped to enhance the string playing".

Margaret Mole, who first played with the orchestra in May 1957, was, indeed, a real asset to the wind section. She had been introduced to the orchestra by their flautist, Charlie Jones, a former member of the BBC Concert Orchestra, and she came to play with the orchestra on a regular basis until, in the early 1970's, family demands brought her visits to an end.

Colin Horsley performed Rachmaninov's Second Piano concerto with the orchestra in November 1961 when a Steinway grand piano was hired from Moon's of Plymouth at a cost of £32. Bearing in mind that soloists' fees were, on average, about £40-50 at this time, this was a considerable added expense, and the lack of a good piano was a problem that would not be resolved for a few more years. On this occasion five anonymous donors covered the cost of hire, thereby ensuring a small profit overall.

Harold Rablen

The success of this concert must have been tinged with sadness among the orchestra because one of their viola players, Harold Rablen, had died suddenly the day before. Morgan Hosking wrote a moving and informative article about him, the essence of which was printed in the following week's *Cornishman*, paying tribute to Harold Rablen's life which had been devoted to music. "His musical experience was so wide," wrote Morgan, "that there were not many branches of the art with which he did not have an intimate knowledge."

Harold was a graduate of Exeter University, holder of a Royal College of Music Diploma,

organist, accompanist and teacher. He played the violin and viola, but was also able to play and teach the trumpet, trombone, guitar and piano accordion, as well as being qualified as a vocal coach. Morgan also admired his ability as a conductor who, in an emergency, "could take over command without turning a hair". In spite of this above-average contribution to the musical life of Penzance he never sought publicity, always remaining unobtrusive and self-effacing. The musical organisations of the town were well represented at his funeral, acknowledging the loss of this "gentle person who gave his life to music without demanding more than a simple living in return".

The start of the following year was also overshadowed by another loss to the Orchestral Society with the death of W. E. (Billy) Williams. He had joined the orchestra in 1924 playing the tubular bells but in the following year took his permanent place as principal double-bass player, a position he held until his death on 4th January 1962.

W. E. (Billy) Williams

Billy Williams was yet another of those remarkable band of schoolmasters who joined G. L. Bradley at the Penzance County School for Boys during the early decades of the twentieth century. He was a Cambridge trained classicist and historian and came to the County School in 1911. His forty-two years service there, thirty-seven of them as Senior Master, saw him teaching Latin to over 3000 boys through years of rapid growth and development at the school. Though slight of stature he was a considerable athlete and before the war was also a keen member of the school orchestra.

In his thirty-eight years as a member of the Penzance Orchestral Society he played under Walter Barnes, Maddern Williams, of whom he was a loyal supporter, and Morgan Hosking. Though he does not appear to have been active as an officer or committee member of the Society his many years membership would have provided a fund of knowledge and experience. He made a major contribution by recording the Society's history as the author of a lengthy account of its half-century of activities printed in the Golden Jubilee concert programme of November 1956.

Sadness, though of a less personal kind, was felt during the week of 26th February to 3rd March 1962, when the Operatic Society, so closely linked to the Orchestral Society at this time, gave its last performances in the Penzance Pavilion, or Grand Casino as it had been renamed. Its proprietor, Mr Rowland Davies, had announced in mid-February that the venue would close to theatrical performances due to lack of support, despite the popularity of the Operatic Society productions. It was a poignant coincidence that the opera that year was 'Iolanthe', the same with which the Society had started in 1927.

After the final show the Society's President, Arthur Robinson, Producer H. Powell Lloyd and Musical Director, J. Morgan Hosking, all made speeches regretting the loss of their venue but stressing that it would not mean the end of the Operatic Society. The press reviews of 'Iolanthe' all made a great deal of the closure of the theatre, suggesting that St John's Hall may become the Society's new home. Also, a town councillor asked that the Council should consider providing finance to make the necessary alterations to the St John's Hall stage for future productions.

Lack of space precludes the full story, but from 1963 onwards the Operatic society did move to St John's Hall, necessitating a huge amount of preparatory stage building and extra expense each year. This, in itself, generated letters to *The Cornishman* over the ensuing years bemoaning the lack of an adequate performance space in the town, but the Society's shows have continued in St John's Hall to the present day.

Penzance and Newlyn received an onslaught in early March of 1962 when their sea frontages suffered a terrible battering in what became known as "The Great Ash Wednesday Storm". Enormous damage was incurred throughout the district, and vast amounts of money and many man-hours were needed to rectify it. Closer to home for the orchestra was the worrying news of a fire in St John's Hall on 24th March, just two weeks before their spring concert. Despite considerable damage, a dance in aid of the Mayor's Disaster fund went ahead on the 27th March after temporary flooring was installed to cover a hole in the floor, and the hall remained available for the orchestral concerts on Friday 6th April.

All this doom and gloom was mitigated for the Orchestral Society by the keen anticipation for these concerts in which the soloist was to be Penzance's own rising star, the young soprano, Margaret Polkinghorne, singing under her professional name of Margaret Kingsley. She had not wanted to change her own name but was advised that it was too long, so chose Kingsley as "a kind of variation on Polkinghorne and because it has a West Country flavour".

Margaret Kingsley.

Margaret Kingsley

Margaret was on the threshold of what was to become a highly successful and distinguished operatic career. She was the first pupil from the Penzance Grammar School for Girls to pursue a professional singing career, having sung in the school concerts and carol services and in their production of Benjamin Britten's 'Let's Make an Opera' in 1952. She studied at the Royal College of Music from 1957, and by 1962 was singing in major oratorio performances in such prestigious venues as St Paul's Cathedral, Westminster Central Hall and Canterbury Cathedral. Her operatic career really began when she was offered a place on the Arts Council's 'Opera for All' tour of the United Kingdom in the autumn of 1961. They visited Cornwall in February 1962, where Margaret sang the roles of Violetta in Verdi's 'La Traviata' and Fiordiligi in Mozart's 'Cosi fan Tutte'. These performances in St Austell, Truro, Camborne and Falmouth were given publicity in local newspapers and no doubt paved the way for the warm welcome she received from capacity audiences on 6th April.

Her singing of two well known arias by Verdi and Weber accompanied by the orchestra, and five other songs were given detailed analysis in the press reviews. From them one gains the impression of a still youthful performer but with obvious talent and potential. *The Cornishman* spoke of, "a performance of high achievement" with her lower register having, "a richness of quality which is the pure operatic soprano's essential". This same report gave a harsh review of the orchestra's performance of Wagner's 'Siegfried Idyll', but the *Western Morning News* writer thought they had conveyed "insight and sensibility". Dvorak's 'New World Symphony' was approved of by both reviewers. But it was Margaret Kingsley's appearance which, quite rightly, captured all the headlines.

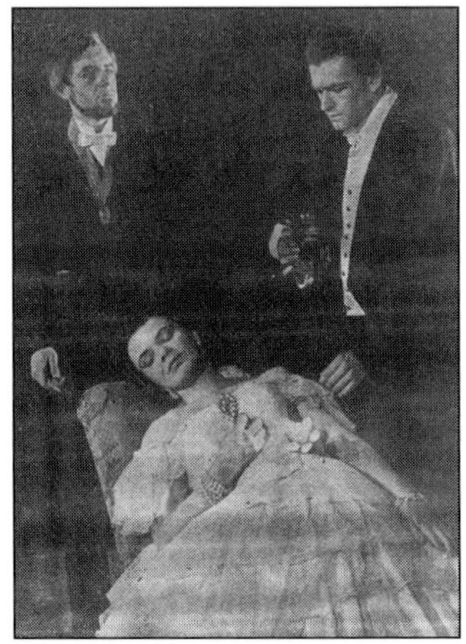

Margaret Kingsley as Violetta in Verdi's 'La Traviata', 1961–62.

The programming for the concerts on Friday 30th November 1962, opening their next season, is a good example of the Orchestral Society's willingness, during this period, to take on difficult and challenging music and to succeed in its performance. With the exception of Berlioz' overture, 'Le Carnaval Romain' all the works were being played for the first time in Penzance, and the concerto was distinguished by being "the first performance in the West", according to the *Western Morning News* music critic. *The Cornishman* went so far as to say that the Sibelius Violin Concerto was "the most complicated and technically difficult work ever to be performed in St John's Hall". It was played by a more mature Carl Pini returning to Penzance five years after his performance, with his father, of the Brahms Double Concerto.

In addition, the orchestra performed 'The Walk to the Paradise Garden' by Delius, Handel's Ballet Suite 'The Gods Go A-Begging' (both these works in arrangements by Sir Thomas Beecham) and Smetana's Symphonic Poem 'From the Woods and Fields of Bohemia'. With four solo violin pieces, accompanied at the piano by Enid Truman, this was a programme of variety, but *The Cornishman* reporter pointed out the one thing they had in common – all five composers had fought against their intended futures in other professions to make composition their life's work.

Carl Pini was given glowing reports for his confidence and control of his instrument and a "lustrous, sweet and firm tone", and the orchestra, too, was consistently praised in "an adventurous and triumphant programme". (Author's Note: many years later Carl Pini appeared in Aberystwyth at an orchestral concert as leader of the New Philarmonia Orchestra. I went to get his autograph and, tentatively, reminded him of his performance of the Sibelius Concerto with the Penzance Orchestra. He responded warmly, asking after Morgan Hosking and saying, "Do you know, I have played the Sibelius so many times, but I don't remember having enjoyed it more than when I played it in Penzance". – MW)

It is sad to relate that 1963 began with a serious loss for the Orchestral Society with the tragic death of Mrs Dora Reynolds. A harsh winter had resulted in icy road conditions and Mrs Reynolds was killed when her car skidded and crashed on the outskirts of Penzance. Although

she had only been in the orchestra for a year or two she was a great asset as an Associate of the Royal College of Music and a former member of the Sadlers' Wells Ballet Orchestra. She had become a peripatetic violin teacher in Cornwall and was Principal Second Violin in the Penzance orchestra. The shock and loss of her tragic death was felt keenly throughout the musical and educational community.

Another car accident, this time involving Mrs Crosbie Garstin, took place on 1st March. She was the current Mayor of Penzance and was a front seat passenger in a car being driven by her Town Clerk, Mr E. O. Wheale. Fortunately, no one was injured in the collision and in typical fashion Mrs Garstin was, a few minutes after the crash, "busy directing heavy traffic around the three cars that were badly damaged in the incident". After a delay she then went straight on to a council committee meeting and continued leading the Operatic Society Orchestra that evening and next day for their production of 'Trial by Jury' and 'HMS Pinafore'.

The 1962-63 season ended with two concerts on 3rd May when the well-known baritone, John Cameron, was the soloist. The orchestra tackled another major work, Beethoven's 3rd Symphony, the 'Eroica', which had not been played by them for thirty years, and their successful performance was regarded as, "a timely reward" for Morgan Hosking completing his fortieth concert as conductor. The playing of the Symphony prompted a letter of support to *The Cornishman* from John F. Gendall, emphasising the courage and capabilities of the Orchestral Society. This was followed later in May by another correspondent, this time a visitor to Penzance from Canterbury, writing in appreciation of the orchestra and its conductor.

There was intense musical activity in West Cornwall at this time with the Cornwall Music Festival taking place in Penzance during the week after the orchestral concert. The first week of June saw not only the Porth-en-Alls Festival Group giving concerts but there were also four exceptional concerts held in Truro, Falmouth, Newquay and St Austell, celebrating the seventh anniversary of the Cornwall Rural School of Music. These involved such fine artistes as David Galliver, tenor, and violinist, Alfredo Campoli, as well as local chamber ensembles and the Cornwall Symphony Orchestra. In late July the Mylor Festival presented three more concerts under the auspices of the Cornwall Rural School of Music. Members of the Orchestral Society participated in many of these concerts.

The Dream Becomes Reality

Morgan Hosking achieved a life-long dream during the late summer of 1963 when he, accompanied by Lilian Garstin, went to the world-famous Bayreuth Festival in Germany. Lilian, a fluent German speaker, was the ideal companion and they heard not only the four operas of Wagner's 'Der Ring des Nibelungen' but also 'Die Meistersinger von Nürnberg', 'Parsifal' and 'Tristan und Isolde'. Though they would not have been visible Morgan heard the results of conducting by Karl Böhm and Rudolph Kempe and, of course, the voices of numerous great Wagnerian singers. He often recalled how the memorable sounds from the orchestra in the unique acoustic of the Festspielhaus brought tears to his eyes and this was, undoubtedly, the greatest musical experience of his life.

In the three remaining orchestral seasons prior to the Diamond Jubilee celebrations in November 1966 the Penzance Orchestral Society presented twelve more exciting and successful concerts. The diversity of music was remarkable and the soloists continued to be of high quality. Of particular interest to audiences were those with local connections. The first of these was Una Hale, an Australian soprano who had made her name as a principal singer at the Royal Opera House, where she had met her husband Martin Carr. He was a stage manager there, specialising in its stage lighting and was the son of Mr and Mrs Rex Carr of St Erbyn's School in Penzance.

With even closer Cornish ties Benjamin Luxon continued the Society's tradition of inviting the finest of Cornish born artistes as their soloists, and he made a great impression with his rich tone and ability to entertain. In the afternoon concert, on 26th November 1965, he decided to sing Mussorgsky's song, 'The Flea', but not having the music for his accompanist, Enid Truman, he sat down at the piano and played it for himself without the music. The schoolchildren, as well as the adults present, were completely captivated by this impromptu performance.

Pianist Joseph Weingarten provided a 'double bill' at the evening concert in November 1964 when he played Mozart's Piano Concerto, No. 20 in D Minor in the first half of the concert and Cesar Franck's Symphonic Variations after the interval. The children, during the afternoon, were given lighter fare with the Mozart and some solo items. In the spring of 1965 an innovation was successfully carried out when the orchestra took advantage of the National Federation of Music Societies scheme which offered their young competition winner, violinist Frances Mason, as a soloist for a modest fee. Two other pianists, Iris Loveridge, playing Beethoven's 'Emperor' concerto, and David Wilde performing the Concerto No. 2 in F Minor by Chopin completed the line up of soloists to the end of the 1965-66 orchestral season.

Press reports in *The Cornishman* and *Western Morning News* during these years continued, as was often the case, to be at variance with one another. Generally, *The Cornishman* provided the more complimentary often glowing accounts, with the *Western Morning News* leavening the mood with more critical reviews. But credit, where it was due, was always given and the latter may well have provided the more objective and knowledgeable picture.

A Piano for the Society

The piano was always a very popular solo instrument and the problems involved in acquiring a decent one for soloists to play did not deter the Society from engaging pianists, as we have seen. Hiring an instrument was always an option, but costly, and in 1963 and 1964 they were fortunate in being given the use of a new Steinway grand piano recently bought by the owners of the Mount's Bay Hotel. This was a generous gesture and acknowledged in the concert programmes. However, in May 1965 Morgan Hosking was able to tell the orchestral committee that he had been offered a sum of money to buy a piano for the Society and that the gift was to remain anonymous.

This wonderful news was announced to the members at the September Annual General Meeting. By the end of the year John Vallier had been asked to help and advise on buying a piano and he had seen three reconditioned ones which he thought would be suitable. In January 1966 Enid Truman went to London to meet John Vallier and to see the pianos and a Steinway was chosen. The problem of housing the instrument was solved by Horace and Rose Tempest who offered to look after it at their home, Trevethoe, in Lelant.

By this time Morgan had been given permission to divulge to the committee the names of the generous donors, who turned out to be the Misses Dorothy and Pog Yglesias, owners of the Wild Bird Hospital at Mousehole. In January 1966 they wrote to Morgan enclosing a dedication for the piano to their brother's memory, which read: "The piano is given to the Penzance Orchestral Society In Memory of one whose love for music and Cornwall was very great." The accompanying letter repeats these sentiments in more general terms, adding, "Only one condition, not a word even to a bird!"

The new piano was used for the first time in the Society's concerts on Friday 6th May 1966 when David Wilde performed Chopin's Second Piano Concerto. An acknowledgement of the gift was made in the concert programme stating that it was a contribution, "not only to us, but to the musical enrichment of Penzance, we hope, for many years to come".

It was in the mid-sixties that the name of a young Cornish musician, already a prize-winner on frequent occasions at the Cornwall Music Festival Competitions, appears in the news. In November 1963 Morgan Hosking conducted a section of his string players at a concert for the Camborne Society of Arts. The programme advertised their forthcoming events one of which was a recital by Judith Bailey, clarinet and Mary Makinson, piano. More is learnt about Judith in April 1965 when she featured in *The Cornishman* column, "People in the News", after she had been presented to Queen Elizabeth the Queen Mother at the Albert Hall on being awarded her Bachelor of Music Degree. This was the young woman who would later return to her native Cornwall and become the conductor of Penzance Orchestral Society.

George Deason

During 1964 a violinist emerges from the orchestra's rank and file to temporary prominence in the person of George Deason. Their Principal Violin, Lilian Garstin, suffered a period of ill health during this year which affected her mayoral duties as well as her leadership of the orchestra. The lady mayoress, Mrs Mavis Lawrey, ably represented her on official engagements, and for the spring and autumn concerts of the Orchestral Society George Deason took over her position in the orchestra. The Sub-Principal violin at this time was Mrs Rowena Williams, an able violinist and one of the Society's longest standing members. Rowena, though, was of a shy and retiring disposition and would not have relished being in the limelight.

George Deason was an obvious choice to deputise as leader being a professional violinist who had been a member of the BBC Variety Orchestra between 1947 and 1956. Born in Australia, but with Cornish forbears, he was employed by the Australian Broadcasting Commission until 1959 when he came to Cornwall to join his cousin in a business in Penzance. "I was delighted to find music of such a standard as the Penzance Orchestral Society...and am thankful to have had the privilege of playing with them", he said. This was reported in an interview in *The Cornishman* when, at the end of 1964, he returned to Australia to resume his career with the ABC in Perth, having performed a final valuable service to the Orchestral Society for which he was thanked by Morgan Hosking at the November evening concert.

A very old friend and long-serving member of the Society died in October 1964, G. L. Bradley, best known in the town as the founding headmaster of the Penzance County School for Boys.

Gilbert Leslie Bradley

Born in Dudley in 1878, G. L. Bradley graduated with a First in Mathematics from Jesus College, Cambridge. After a period of teaching in Northampton and Worcester Grammar Schools he was appointed headmaster at Penzance County School which opened in January 1910. He remained the driving force behind the school's development and success until 1942. He played in the school orchestra which flourished before the war. Ivan James recalled, with obvious enjoyment, the times when Walter Barnes helped out and "dented the Headmaster's image by occasional deprecatory remarks about his not entirely satisfactory playing of the oboe". Whether Mr Bradley's lapses had anything to do with the fact that when practising the oboe he had difficulty in stopping his dog from joining in we shall never know!

G. L. Bradley. Hon. Treasurer, 1944–1950.

He joined the Orchestral Society in 1926 and was a member for nearly thirty years, his last concert being in May 1955. It is possible that his decision to stop playing was due to the death of his fellow oboist, Alfred Brien, during that year, as they had been the orchestra's oboe 'duo' for twenty-four years. In his many years membership of the Society, G. L. Bradley gave valuable service as Hon. Treasurer from 1944 to 1951.

Morgan Hosking remembered with affectionate amusement that towards the end of Mr Bradley's tenure as treasurer he had called for Morgan's help with the accounts. As an acknowledged dunce at school, Morgan thought his helping out a Cambridge 'First' in maths was quite an achievement, but no doubt it was his training as a book-keeper that was more helpful.

Joan Hancock, G. L. Bradley's daughter, had been a contralto soloist with the orchestra in the Coronation concert of May 1953, and she went on to take over her mother's optician's business in the town, the same business which came to the rescue of Mr Brien's faulty oboe in 1929. Mr Bradley had been made a Vice President of the Society in 1941 and retained this position as a non-playing member until his death in 1964. He was the last of those grand old gentlemen from the County School who had done so much, by nurturing music in their school and, more directly, as active members of the Orchestral Society, to foster its fortunes.

It was during 1964 that Morgan Hosking decided to retire from his position as Musical Director of the Penzance Operatic society, his last show being Sigmund Romberg's 'The Student Prince'. Although still relatively young at fifty-one Morgan had conducted the Society for fourteen years and taking musical responsibility for both societies was a demanding task. However, he continued to play in the orchestra for the Operatic productions, as principal violin in 1965 and then as sub-principal with Mrs Crosbie Garstin for many more years. His retirement as Musical Director was marked by his becoming a Vice-President of the Society.

Sixty Glorious Years 1966-1969

Celebrations were 'in the air' as the 1966-1967 concert season approached, for this would be the Penzance Orchestral Society's 60th Anniversary, their Diamond Jubilee. Plans were discussed in committee meetings nearly two years in advance, and *The Cornishman* announced in December 1965 that the normal booking rules for St John's Hall had been waived to allow the Society to book well ahead for its celebration concert in November 1966. Coffee mornings and sales of work were organised to raise money, and in his speech at the celebration concert Morgan Hosking said that he almost felt as if he had become a member of the Women's Institute. He also pointed out that while the audience would be aware that Robin Whitehead was "a damn good timpanist", they would not know that "he also makes the best pickled onions in West Cornwall"!

Returning to more musical matters, two soloists were invited for this concert, as for the Golden Jubilee. Pianist Peter Katin was engaged to play Beethoven's Piano Concerto No. 3, and Margaret Kingsley was invited to come and sing in her home town once more. Their fees alone amounted to over £200 but the feeling of the committee was that no expense should be spared on this great occasion. They also decided to invite past members of the Society to return and play with the orchestra as well as special guests such as Ian Graham-Jones, conductor of the Cornwall Symphony Orchestra who was among the 'cellists and Mr Siegfried de Chabot, a conductor of two London orchestras and a friend and admirer of the Penzance Society, among the violinists.

The music chosen was Mozart's overture 'The Impressario', to be followed by the piano concerto, after which the strings of the orchestra played the 'Good Friday Spell' from Wagner's opera, 'Parsifal'. Morgan had especially wanted to perform the latter work and the orchestra told him that they would perform it as a gift to him. The second half of the programme opened with Tchaikovsky's fantasy overture, 'Romeo and Juliet' after which Margaret Kingsley sang the 'Scene and Cavatina' from Act I of Verdi's 'Macbeth'. The evening concert concluded with a Cornish premier performance of 'A Festival Overture' by Shostakovich. There was, of course, an afternoon concert as well where Margaret chose to sing an aria from 'Cosi Fan Tutte' by Mozart as more suitable fare for the many schoolchildren present. Both concerts began with John Vallier's arrangement of 'God Save the Queen', with its flourish of trumpets to signal the mood of celebration.

A commemorative Diamond Jubilee concert programme was produced with illustrations of the chief protagonists including, of course, the orchestra itself, and an entertaining article on its history by Gladys M. Tranter entitled 'Journey to Jubilee...'. The officials of the Society were also listed. The President was still Miss Winifrede Beadsworth, now in frail health and in a nursing home but regarded with great affection and respect by the Society. Vice-Presidents were: Mrs Enid Truman, Mrs Lilian Garstin, Mrs Faith Harris, Mrs M. H. L. Carter, Squadron Leader A. G. 'Fluffie' Harrison, Mr L. Graham White and Mr Alan Wood. Enid Truman remained the Hon. Secretary and her husband, Norman was Hon. Treasurer, with Graham White the Committee Chairman.

In the month before the concert preview articles in *The Cornishman* and *Western Morning News* charted the sixty years of the Society's history. *The Cornishman* even posed the question as to where a natural successor to Morgan Hosking, as its conductor, would be found at a time when young musicians had to leave the area to train for a musical career. Fortunately this problem would not have to be faced for many years to come. Mrs Faith Harris's 'vital statistics', as Morgan called them, were updated from the 1956 Golden Jubilee – she had now, during her forty-three years membership, played in 148 concerts, attended 760 rehearsals and travelled a total of 47,000 miles to and from Falmouth to do so!

A Glittering Occasion

And so to Friday 25th November 1966 when all the planning, money raising and rehearsals would bear their fruit. We can safely assume that the afternoon concert enjoyed its usual success with the ground floor of St John's Hall filled with schoolchildren. Their awareness of the historical significance of the occasion may have been limited, though no doubt Morgan Hosking would have pointed it out to them and perhaps the presence of Walter Barnes gazing over the proceedings from his portrait provided a sense of occasion for them.

The evening concert needed no such reminders. All seats had been sold well in advance and as the audience settled down they could read a moving tribute to the orchestra printed in the programme and written by one of Walter Barnes' sons, Kenneth, who was living in Johannesburg. The Mayor of Penzance, Alderman Alfred Beckerleg, then made a speech of civic welcome to mark the Society's Diamond Jubilee and give the occasion a formal seal of approval. This and the other speeches, along with the music, have been preserved in a tape recording of the evening which, despite its quality and age, captures the atmosphere of celebration along with the appreciation of the audience. The dexterity and artistry of Peter Katin's playing is clearly heard and Margaret Kingsley's thrilling performance of the 'Macbeth' aria reminds one of her glorious voice.

Margaret's family, sitting in the audience, must have been very proud of this young singer, whose voice had now developed and strengthened to a complete instrument with which to perform the roles she was undertaking in Covent Garden and other major opera houses in Europe and America. The great ovation she received from the audience demanded an encore, but this was to be no dramatic showpiece. Instead Margaret sat down at the piano and accompanied herself in 'Home, Sweet Home', a poignant performance of beauty and simplicity which has remained long in the memory.

To the Penzance Orchestral Society on its Sixtieth Anniversary . . .

My Father, he who founded you, has gone
Long years ago, to well deserved rest;
But, in his day, a lonely star he shone,
As that bright star that glows when evening comes
To light the doors of countless simple homes,
A star that fostered music in the West.

And you go on, a shining galaxy
That stems from that one iridescent star,
A gifted, close-knit, happy company,
That loves the five-barred stave with all its pains,
Its joys and wonders, work, and binding chains,
That heaven-sent stave that made you what you are.

All Hail to you — devoted gallant band,
Who tread the path great predecessors trod,
Those men, who, somewhere, saw the promised land,
And music wrote that ne'er will pass away;
Great harmonies that hold us in their sway,
And point the pathway to the Throne of God.

KENNETH WALTER BARNES.
Johannesburg, 1966.

Poem by Kenneth Barnes.

Such a special occasion would not have been complete without a speech from Morgan Hosking. As well as the humour already mentioned this included many tributes to those to whom he and the Society were so indebted. Special praise was given to his leader, Mrs Garstin, Enid Truman, Helen Barton the Society's Librarian, and to their President, Mrs Faith Harris who received a huge bouquet of roses, one for every year of her long membership. He also thanked the press for their support over the years and, finally, his loyal audience. Listening to his words it is easy to understand why this man evoked such affection and respect, for it revealed

Penzance Orchestral Society, Diamond Jubilee, November 1966. Richards Bros., Penzance

his warmth, confidence and style as well as pride and pleasure in his orchestra. Graham White's response was equally relaxed and entertaining, culminating in a presentation to Morgan of a recording of Wagner's 'Ring' and an embroidered scroll, worked by Gladys Tranter and Enid Truman, depicting the signatures of all the members of the orchestra surrounded by an outline of the instruments.

This gala evening continued with a champagne buffet supper at the Queen's Hotel for the orchestra and their guests and friends, a well-earned indulgence for everyone concerned. *The Cornishman* reporter regarded the occasion as, "perhaps the most glittering day in the orchestra's history" and, while the headline was devoted to Margaret Kingsley's return home to sing in the Diamond Jubilee Concert, it was also a "Magnificent Day's Music at Penzance". It is true to say that there has not been such a lavish celebration by the Society since, either musically or socially, but it is equally true that there were to be many other memorable events ahead of the Penzance Orchestral Society as they embarked upon their years as a senior citizen among the Penzance musical organisations.

...And Still Going Strong

The Orchestra Society did not rest on its laurels following the excitements of the Diamond Jubilee celebrations. The sixtieth season ended with their concert on 5th May 1967, when violinist, Ronald Thomas, provided a 'double bill' at the evening concert. He played Mozart's Violin Concerto No. 4 and, instead of a group of solos, performed the Saint-Saëns 'Introduction and Rondo Capriccioso' with the orchestra.

It was fortuitous that the orchestra had chosen to include three works by German or Austrian composers in the programme because there were German guests among the civic party in the audience. Penzance was celebrating its official 'twinning' with the town of Cuxhaven and the Mayor and Mayoress of Penzance were accompanied by Cuxhaven's Oberburgmeister and his wife. To mark this event the concert opened with the orchestra playing the National Anthem of the German Federal Republic before God Save the Queen. The concert was well reviewed as "yet another exciting and rewarding evening's entertainment". Although the Diamond Jubilee concert season incurred an overall loss of over £170 the Society was still in good heart at the end of the financial year with a balance of over £400 in the bank.

Honoured by the Gorsedd of Bards

Morgan Hosking's work with the orchestra was recognised by his being awarded the Gorsedd shield for "Outstanding contributions to the musical life of Cornwall" at the yearly meeting of the Cornish Gorsedd in Saltash on Saturday 2nd September 1967. The award was timely in not only marking Morgan's twenty years as Conductor of the Orchestral Society but also its Diamond Jubilee. The shield was presented to him by the Grand Bard, Mr G. Pawley White, and it was hung in the orchestra's Bandroom for the year, acknowledging the fact the members of the orchestra had played a major part in his success and achievements.

The grand bard, G. Pawley White (Gunwyn), presenting Morgan Hosking with the Gorsedd Music Shield, September 1967.

The Society presented a wide range of music to its audiences during the latter half of the nineteen-sixties including some very demanding compositions. Vaughan Williams' 5th Symphony and Sibelius's Symphony No. 1 are two examples, along with Elgars' 'Enigma' Variations and the 'Royal Hunt and Storm' from Berlioz' opera 'The Trojans' – all works being played for the first time by the Penzance orchestra. The soloists, too, during this period gave memorable performances.

In November 1967 a brilliant young pianist, Marlene Fleet, came to play Manuel de Falla's colourful, impressionistic work 'Nights in the Gardens of Spain'. This performance could been seen as "In Memoriam" to the pianist Harriet Cohen, who had died just two weeks earlier. She had expressed the wish, in 1956, that should she return to perform with the orchestra, it was this work she would like to play. Her prophecy that the orchestra would meet the demands of the difficult score was borne out in their "inspiring performance" accompanying the pianist's greatly admired "sense of musicianship... and a glittering technique". Marlene Fleet became well known to the Society as this was the first of three visits she would make over the years.

Amongst the many musical events taking place in south-west Cornwall during the spring of 1968 was a prestigious and unusual concert in Truro Cathedral on 16th March. This was a "Tribute to Thomas Merritt", the Cornish composer born in Illogan, Redruth in 1863. This concert, under the auspices of the Cornwall Rural Music School, presented a programme which included

'A Tribute to Thomas Merritt' concert, Truro Cathedral, March 1968, with Malcolm Arnold conducting.

Merritt's anthems and a Coronation March as well as three of his best loved carols. There were also works by Malcolm Arnold, Sir Arthur Sullivan and Peter Warlock, all of which had some relevance either to Thomas Merritt or the county of Cornwall. Penzance Orchestral Society combined with the Cornwall Symphony Orchestra and the silver bands from St Dennis and St Agnes to accompany a choir of over two hundred voices from twelve West Cornwall choirs.

The composer, Malcolm Arnold, then living in St Merryn, was the inspiration behind this venture and also the conductor. It was a great occasion and a true celebration of Cornish sound and music, an excerpt of which was shown in a television 'South Bank Show' two-part documentary on the life of Sir Malcolm Arnold in 2005. His death at the age of eighty-four in September 2006 will have revived many memories of his involvement in the musical life of Cornwall and the works inspired by his love of the county and its brass bands. It was also fitting that the Penzance Orchestral Society had chosen to include his 'Four Cornish Dances' in the programme for their concert in November 2006.

By April 1968 the Orchestral Society had reached their 200th and 201st concerts. The soloist was Douglas Cummings who played the Schumann 'cello concerto. Michael Tunstall-Behrens recalled how delighted Douglas Cummings was, on arrival at Penzance railway station, to be introduced to the station-master, Welshman Harry Allen, and told that he would be one of the trombonists in the orchestral concerts. The soloist's excellent performance was rather overshadowed in the newspaper reports where much was made of the first performance in the west of England by an amateur orchestra of Vaughan Williams' 5th Symphony. Geoffrey Baggs, writing for the *Western Morning News,* regarded this as "a brave undertaking....an act of faith...." but that Morgan Hosking was to be congratulated "on his enterprise in leading his orchestra into such unfamiliar pastures, and securing such a resounding success."

This report devoted many words to the fact that over half the members of the orchestra were women, many of whom were section leaders, and that their part in a performance such as this symphony should receive its fair share of praise. He wrote of the final 'Passacaglia' movement as ending a "most moving and inspired performance".

There were, apparently, some empty seats in the hall for these concerts possibly due to the fact that the soloist was a 'cellist, an instrument which rarely drew a capacity audience. Also, the well known piano duo of Cyril Smith and Phyllis Sellick were playing in Truro on the same evening and there were many other attractive concerts and festivals on the near horizon, both professional and amateur. Potential audiences were, perhaps, being forced to select which, and how many, events they could attend.

Bearing this busy musical scene in mind it was not surprising that a shower of letters appeared in *The Cornishman* following an article printed in the *Guardian* in early May 1968. It was written by Judith Cook, a journalist who wrote regularly for the national paper. At the end of an interesting and pleasing report on the recent Porth-en-Alls Music Festival she referred to the area as "a cultural desert" and that, "the native Cornish, although they profess to be musical, seem to be satisfied with fisherman's choirs, a couple of amateur orchestras, and amateur productions of 'Goodnight, Vienna'." The indignation unleashed upon her head in the local press, in which members of the Orchestral Society contributed some salient points, lasted many weeks into early July when the editor brought the correspondence to a close.

The Society's President, Miss Winifrede Beadsworth, died in April 1968 and her funeral was attended by many members of the orchestra.

Winifrede Beadsworth

Winifrede and her brother, George, had joined the Orchestral Society in its early years, George in 1909 and his sister in 1913. They were both violinists, possibly pupils of Miss Violet Nunn, and became good friends with Walter Barnes. George was the Hon. Librarian of the Society for nearly ten years from 1924 and played in the orchestra until 1933, dying from cancer at a relatively young age. Little is known about their family background but George was a partner in a shoe shop in Penzance and Winifrede always seemed to be financially well-to-do.

She was an able violinist and took over the leadership of the orchestra in Mrs Garstin's absence during the war years and deputised as leader for Iola Coleman in December 1949. Happy to relinquish this position she continued as Sub-Principal Violin until she gave up playing in 1952. Miss Beadsworth also made a valuable contribution to the administration of the Society as a regular committee member. She was secretary of the subscribers scheme until ill-health forced her to resign in 1953 and was a long-serving Vice-President. Following the death of A. W. Robinson and the brief Presidency of Mrs Charles Williams, Winifrede Beadsworth was elected the Society's President at the A.G.M. in September 1954. In spite of ill-health necessitating her move to a nursing home for the last years of her life she was persuaded to retain this position until her death.

Winifrede's personality was much as one would expect of a well brought up maiden lady, rather reserved and timid in many ways. But her timorousness vanished when behind the wheel of a car when she was, according to Morgan Hosking, "a masterpiece". His friendship with her provided many amusing but affectionate anecdotes, one of which recalled the day in Torquay when she had an accident on the promenade, resulting in damage to her car. Her solution was to go to the nearest garage and buy another one! Although somewhat prudish and lacking in a sense of humour she inspired respect and affection among her friends in the orchestra. Never a lady to seek a starring role she deserves recognition as one of the longest serving as well as most loyal and devoted servants of the Orchestral Society.

The recurring idea, to perform a work for solo violin and viola, was finally achieved at the concert in November 1968. Mozart's 'Symphonie Concertante' for violin and viola was given a first performance by the Penzance Orchestral Society, with Penelope Howard and Joan Bucknall as the soloists, the former often to be heard as the leader of the Porth-en-Alls festival orchestra. In the soloists 'slot' in the second half of the programme the duo played 'Three Madrigals' for violin and viola by Martinů. Neither of the soloist's names was widely-known, to which *The Cornishman* attributed the smaller than usual audience, but also reported the high quality of their performance both in the concerto and the Martinů work.

Another 'first' for the orchestra was its playing of a Sibelius Symphony, No. 1 in E minor, which the audience, after some hesitancy, responded to with "stirring, enthusiastic applause". *The Cornishman* reviewer was very supportive of the orchestra for playing works not normally undertaken by amateurs, saying that it not only indicated the progress made by the orchestra in recent years but also gave Penzance audiences the chance to experience such works which "otherwise they would not hear short of a visit to London or one of the larger centres of music". Only the first and last movements were played at the afternoon concert, in themselves a challenge for a schoolchild's ear.

The early months of 1969 brought mixed fortunes for two members of the orchestra. Mrs Lilian Garstin was awarded an M.B.E. in the New Year Honours list, and in the press coverage she was described as, "musician and fighter for an unbelievable number of causes". Her visit to Buckingham Palace to receive the award caused her to be absent from her position as leader of

the orchestra for the first two performances of the Operatic Society's production of Sigmund Romberg's 'The New Moon' in mid-February.

Miss Gladys Tranter was much less fortunate in March when she was involved in a serious car accident. She was a passenger in a car being driven by the Borough Librarian, Mr John Cable, when the accident happened near Salisbury. All four passengers were injured and, tragically, Mr Cable died as a result. Miss Tranter suffered a fracture but recovered sufficiently to attend an orchestra committee meeting on 24th April when everyone expressed their pleasure at having her back amongst them.

John Vallier Brings Schumann to Penzance

John Vallier returned to Penzance for the third time in May 1969 to play the Schumann Piano Concerto. He had been corresponding with Morgan Hosking about his links with the Schumann family, a fascinating story briefly outlined here. John's mother was Adela Verne, in her time a world-renowned pianist, ranking alongside such great exponents of the instrument as Busoni and Rachmaninoff. Her older sister, Mathilde, was also a brilliant pianist and famous teacher and one of Clara Schumann's most gifted pupils. Mathilde was John's principal teacher and it was from her that he gained a special insight into the Schumann concerto. Clara Schumann had given its first performance at the Leipzig Gewandhaus on 1st January 1846, and John's study of Schumann's music was from scores annotated by her. So his interpretation was uniquely authentic and, as he told Morgan Hosking, "whatever else, I do know how it should **not** be played".

This alone would have made his performance of the Schumann Concerto special, but in addition he had brought a baton with him which had belonged to Schumann himself. He showed it to the audience, then placed it on the conductor's rostrum where it remained throughout the performance. Whether it inspired or intimidated Morgan the result was that, "Penzance audiences have not been rewarded by (a) more effective and moving piano performance – certainly for many years". John Vallier autographed Morgan's concert programme adding, "To my friend, Morgan, with happy memories of our Schumann association". As a gesture of welcome to an old friend the orchestra opened the concert with his arrangement of 'God Save the Queen'.

John Vallier's appearance, along with a popular programme made up of Sullivan's overture to 'The Yeoman of the Guard' and Beethoven's 5th Symphony, ensured a large audience. The concert ended with Malcolm Arnold's overture, 'Beckus the Dandipratt', written in 1942 whilst the composer was on holiday at Porthallow. It was a first Cornish performance, at which Malcolm Arnold had intended, but was unable, to be present.

A Dramatic End to the Decade

The final concert of the orchestra's sixth decade was held on 28th November 1969, and in typically courageous fashion they played themselves out with a flourish. The programme was designed to mark the centenary of the death of Hector Berlioz and included two of his major works. In his setting of six poems by Theophile Gautier entitled 'Les Nuits d'Été', the mezzo-soprano soloist was Oriel Sutherland. In this sensuous and elegiac work her voice reached "thrilling proportions with wonderful control and poise", the orchestra providing sympathetic accompaniment. The schoolchildren were treated to only three of the songs, including the more well-known, "Le Spectre de la Rose".

This was followed by the Symphonic Interlude, 'The Royal Hunt and Storm' from Berlioz' opera 'Les Troyens'. Regarded by some as one of the greatest pieces of musical nature painting it reflects an African forest scene with all the characters and creatures hurrying to take refuge from an approaching storm, which breaks and recedes allowing calm to return. It was a severe musical test for the Penzance orchestra but they coped well.

As if these two works were not enough of a challenge for the orchestra they also gave their first performance of Elgar's 'Variations on an Original Theme' (Enigma) Op. 36. Geoffrey Baggs, in the *Western Morning News*, recognised the orchestra's courage in tackling such a complex work and found, "moments when Elgar's intentions were impressively realised". Variation 13, depicts Lady Mary Trefusis from Flushing, near Falmouth, the former Lady Mary Lygon, and friend of Elgar. She had founded the Cornwall Music Competition, and her son, Henry Trefusis, was in the audience to mark his mother's connection with the work. The evening concert also included a work for string orchestra in the form of the 'Adagio for Strings' by Samuel Barber.

These November concerts had been in danger of not taking place at all due to the sudden illness of the orchestra's timpanist, Robin Whitehead. He had a heart attack and on the morning of the concert Morgan had to urgently find someone to deputise for him. John Weekes, chairman of Plymouth Orchestral Society and their timpanist, was able to come to the rescue. He managed to get to Penzance with his three drums by the start of the afternoon concert but had to perform, without rehearsal, these difficult and unfamiliar works. The storms and stresses of the music were exacerbated for Mr Weekes when he had to return to Plymouth after the concert in appalling weather conditions, with snowstorms and slippery roads. The orchestra acknowledged John Weekes' help by making a donation of ten guineas to the Plymouth Orchestral Society. This drama was recalled by John Weekes in 1988 following a reference in the *Western Morning News* to this first performance of the Elgar work in Cornwall. "It was the one and only time in my musical life I was the hero of the hour" he said!

Always supporting the thrills and excitements of concert days was the work of the orchestral committee. During these years they had diligently ensured that the day-to-day organisation of the society continued. The Bandroom was maintained and a new heating system installed; the tubular bells were repaired adding greatly to their value; new music stands were acquired, and 'tested' at concerts; schools attendance was monitored and controlled when problems such as over-large numbers or too young children created difficulties.

Members of the committee represented the Society at various other organisations, for example, the group which created the new West Cornwall Arts Centre housed in the old Parade Street Methodist Church in Penzance and officially opened by the Minister for the Arts, Jennie Lee, in October 1969. Financially, the Society had kept its head above water, supported in part by Arts Council grants obtained by their affiliation to the National Federation of Music Societies, but mostly by their own efforts. At the end of the 1968-1969 financial year they had in hand funds amounting to over £600. So all was well, but what adventures would befall this now middle-aged but flourishing and still enthusiastic band of players as they approached their three score years and ten?

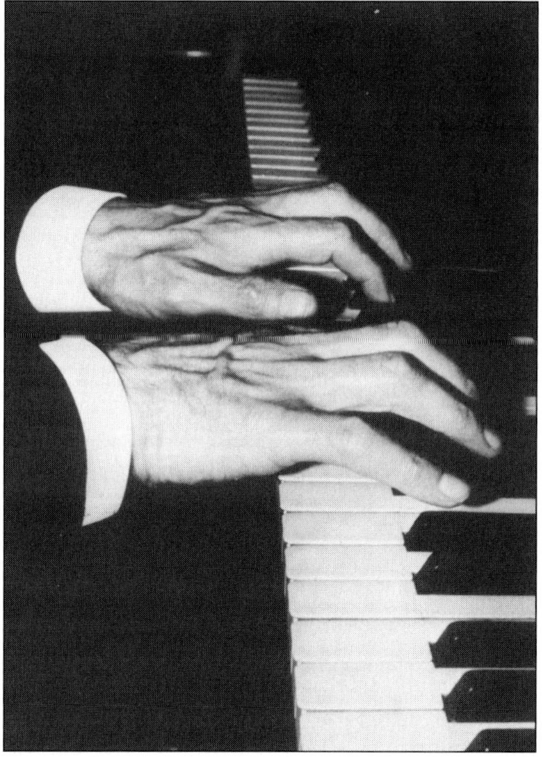

John Vallier, piano soloist with Penzance Orchestral Society, and his hands at the keyboard.

The Seventh Age 1970-1973

As the Penzance Orchestral Society entered its 'three score years and ten' members could be forgiven if they anticipated a period of continued hard work to maintain high standards but one of uninterrupted stability. This was not to be the case, however; and there would be many difficulties ahead, sad times to be endured and changing circumstances to adjust to. But there would also be memorable musical experiences and unique occasions to enjoy.

Securing the Bandroom

One of the first problems to overcome was brought to the committee's notice early in 1970. Following the death of Winifrede Beadsworth a situation had arisen whereby the Society realised that there were now no surviving trustees of their Bandroom and that, legally, it belonged to nobody! The legalities involved the need for registration of the Bandroom with the Land Registry, and a new Rule to be added to the Society's constitution. Eventually the matter was resolved, and the new trustees were Michael Tunstall-Behrens, Derek Tamblyn, Norman Truman and Paddy Pinchen. Later in 1971 the trustees received a valuation on the property of £3,000. Also during this time, in November 1970, the remaining two hundred and fifty pounds outstanding on the Bandroom mortgage was paid off.

The 1969-70 concert season ended on Friday 24th April 1970 when Barry Wilde was the violin soloist. He was a substitute soloist for Diana Cummings (sister of 'cellist Douglas Cummings) who had been taken ill. Barry Wilde was a former student of Alan Loveday and had recently accepted the position of Leader of the BBC Welsh Symphony Orchestra. The two major works in the programme were both first performances in Cornwall and rarely performed anywhere, although, by coincidence, they had both been heard shortly before the concert on the B.B.C. Barry Wilde was congratulated for his fine performance in the Paganini Violin concerto No. 1 and the orchestra "gave a good account of itself" in Franz Berwald's 'Sinfonie Singulière', the third of Berwald's four symphonic works. Morgan Hosking is recorded as saying that he thought, "it was a good thing we had played the Berwald symphony but he did not want to play any more Berwald".

St Mary's Church, Penzance, was arranging concerts during the summer of 1970 in aid of their restoration fund and the Orchestral Society provided a chamber orchestra for a concert on 1st July. The principals of the string sections, Lilian Garstin, Paddy Pinchen, Gwyneth Andrewartha and Enid Truman, were the soloists in a Corelli Concerto Grosso, and the church organist, Russell Jory, performed the Handel Organ concerto No. 2, Op. 4. The guest soloist was a soprano, Ann Murray, whose glorious voice was to become so well-known in future years.

The new season began, as usual, with an afternoon and evening concert in late November 1970 when Marlene Fleet returned to play the Brahms Piano Concerto No. 2 in B flat major. Marlene Fleet performed with "supreme confidence and artistry", and Enid Truman was praised for her performance on the 'cello in the third movement where she partnered the soloist "with such perception". The orchestra, congratulated for their "keen sense of responsibility" in the concerto, fared less well from Geoffrey Bagg's pen in his review of their playing of Tchaikovsky's Second Symphony, the 'Little Russian'. The symphony and Mendelssohn's 'Ruy Blas' Overture were harshly criticised, with only the strings achieving, "some refinement of utterance". But it was generally acknowledged that a performance of the mighty Brahms concerto would rarely, if ever, be heard in the area were it not for the efforts of the Penzance Orchestral Society.

Morgan Hosking was rather dismissive of the choice of solo instrument following the concert on 2nd April. *The Cornishman* reporter thought that the Society had shown "vision and no little originality in engaging a guitarist as soloist", and Charles Gregory had given an excellent performance of Vivaldi's Concerto for Guitar and Strings. But Morgan, though he had enjoyed the soloist, said afterwards that he did not want another guitarist for a long time. This ran true to his love of the more romantic large-scale repertoire and he was happier with the evening's symphony, Dvorak's No. 7 in D minor, as well as the other two more unusual items in the programme, Roger Quilter's 'A Children's Overture' and 'The Last Sleep of the Virgin', the only commonly played portion of Massenet's sacred work, 'La Vierge'.

Afternoon Concerts Come to an End

It was during 1971 that more problems arose which led, in one case, to a major change in the Society's routine. Firstly, although new members were still joining the Society a significant number of string players were unable to play in the forthcoming season. New members included young people who were benefiting from the increased provision of instrumental teaching in schools. Though they were an asset in many ways they often had to leave Cornwall to pursue their higher education so were not of long term service to the orchestra. An uneven balance in the orchestra could easily occur as it did in 1971, and concert programmes had to be chosen with care, for example, the music for the autumn 1971 concert excluded the involvement of trombones.

Secondly, age and infirmity were rearing their ugly heads at this time, with older members encountering health problems. Morgan Hosking himself suffered a period of ill health having developed a heart problem in the late sixties. At committee meetings during 1971 discussions about the viability of continuing the afternoon concerts took place, as it was generally felt that they were becoming too much of a strain on some members, and their conductor. At that year's annual general meeting the decision was taken to discontinue them.

This decision would not have been taken easily by the Society and the reason given in a preview article by Geoffrey Baggs in the *Western Morning News* in November was that it had been dictated by economics, though this factor was not recorded in the Society's minutes. He suggested that a drop in the attendance by schoolchildren at afternoon concerts was due to more opportunities for music-making in schools, citing the creation of a Cornwall Youth Orchestra as one example. "Whatever the reason", he wrote, "it will be a loss to the small but faithful band of adults who preferred the afternoon concert". For the music critics travelling to Penzance the afternoon concerts had sometimes been their preferred option, but however aggrieved he and others felt, the Society stuck to its decision and evening concerts only have been given ever since.

Soloists in the autumn and spring concerts of the 1971-72 season were Diana Cummings, violin, and Frank Wibaut, piano, a young pianist who had been heard at the Porth en Alls Music Festival. Miss Cummings played the Mozart Violin Concerto No. 3 in G and, instead of a solo group, Dvorak's charming 'Romance for violin and orchestra', Op. 11. Frank Wibaut impressed a large audience with his performance of the Concerto No. 1 in G minor by Mendelssohn and a generous solo contribution which included Debussy's Suite, 'Pour le Piano'. The major works played by the orchestra at these two concerts were Beethoven's Symphony No. 8, Schumann's Symphony No. 4, and the Intermezzo, 'The Walk to the Paradise Garden' by Delius.

Morgan Hosking, 1972.
Penwith District Council

A Tribute from the Town

In December 1971 an announcement appeared in the local press that Penzance Town Council were to admit seven people to the Roll of Honorary Freemen of the Borough. This was in anticipation of government proposals to rearrange the numbers, boundaries, titles and powers of Local Authorities in 1974, in which Penzance would lose its corporate identity and become part of a new Penwith District Council

The names of those to be honoured included Lilian Garstin and Morgan Hosking. The Roll of Freemen had been created in 1888 and only twenty-nine other persons had received the award, and none since 1958. It was also the first time that women had been elected as Freemen and there were three on this occasion. Only one other member of the Penzance Orchestral Society had received this honour, when Frank Latham's distinguished service as Borough Surveyor was recognised in 1938. So it was an historic occasion for the orchestra as well as the town when the ceremony took place on Wednesday 19th April 1972.

This was just two days before the spring concert and the warmth of the reception given to Lilian Garstin and Morgan Hosking that evening reflected the audience's appreciation of the

tribute paid by the town to them and through them "to all those whose love it is to make music". Morgan, as well as being deeply grateful for this recognition of his musical life, was almost as appreciative of the fact that his new status gave him the right to park in the forecourt of St John's Hall when shopping in Penzance!

The Freedom of the Borough Ceremony in St John's Hall, April 1972. Richards Bros., Penzance

Losing a Leader

Sadly, Lilian Garstin was only given a few months to take pleasure in the honour. At the annual general meeting of the Society in September 1972 Morgan told members that Mrs Garstin had fallen and cracked her shoulder but that she hoped to be back amongst them before too long. While this was an unfortunate enough occurrence for both the patient and the orchestra it did not seem especially alarming, and Miss Constance Bee deputised as Principal Violin during the autumn rehearsals. So it was a great shock to everyone when they learned of Lilian's death on 27th October.

Following a private cremation a memorial service was held on 14th November. Lilian Garstin's legacy to the orchestra included the proceeds from the sale of her Gragnani violin with its bows, and the arrangements for the sale involved a lot of work for Morgan Hosking who acted in this matter on behalf of the orchestral committee. After some months a sum of well over £2,000 was realised which boosted the finances of the Society considerably, providing stability for many years.

The concert on Friday 24th November 1972 must have been an emotional occasion for all concerned. Lilian Garstin had occupied the leader's position for as long as most people could remember. The programme included Brahms's Symphony No. 1 and, had it been chosen as a tribute to their late Principal Violin, no better choice could have been made because, as Morgan Hosking told the audience, this was, "the one symphony that Lilian loved above all others". According to the *Western Morning News*, "the splendid horizons revealed by this symphony were conveyed" by the orchestra. Connie Bee was a more than capable substitute for Mrs Garstin and Geoffrey Baggs felt that, "the violin playing was, in fact, the most successful and satisfying aspect of the concert". However, she did not want to remain leader and Jack Glasson became Principal Violin from the autumn of 1973.

The guest soloist at this 1972 concert was 'cellist, Keith Harvey, who played 'Variations on a Rococo Theme' Op. 33 by Tchaikovsky, giving a, "beautifully shaped rendering... tonality, phrasing and control were altogether excellent, and he was well supported by the orchestra".

Lilian Garstin, 1972. Penwith District Council

The Death of Geoffrey Baggs

These were the words of Geoffrey Baggs, music critic of the Plymouth based paper, the *Western Morning News*. The day after his concert review was printed he was taken ill with pneumonia and died, following a heart attack, two days later. He had been coming to Penzance to write about the Orchestral Society and its concerts since 1947. Geoffrey Baggs was a stern critic on occasions but his opinions were respected by players and readers alike, as he was known to be an accomplished organist and a devoted music-lover. One Plymouth organist said in response to his death, "He sometimes wrote things that were not entirely complimentary, but he always had good reason for doing so". Mr Baggs was replaced as the *Western Morning News* music critic by Robert Earl who also built up a lasting relationship with the Orchestral Society over the next twelve years.

The orchestra was in good form for its spring concert in April 1973, once more tackling a major work. Barry Wilde returned as soloist to play the Elgar Violin Concerto, a first performance for the Society. Though well-known to music lovers through the legendary 1932 recording by the youthful Yehudi Menuhin, with Elgar conducting, a 'live' performance in Penzance was a unique event and one to be relished. The orchestra and its soloist did not let the audience down, and Robert Earl opened his account with the Society by providing a good review. He pointed out that the orchestra benefited from its own reputation and the town's ability to attract retired professional musicians.

Presentation to the President

Robert Earl's report and the one in *The Cornishman* both made much of a presentation made, after the interval, to Mrs Faith Harris in recognition of her fifty years membership of the Society. She was given an embroidered tapestry, sewn by Gladys Tranter and Enid Truman, which carried the names of all members of the orchestra. Mrs Harris was now aged eighty-six and President of the Society. This was her final concert as a member of the viola section and Morgan Hosking told the audience that her journeys to and from Falmouth for rehearsals and concerts amounted to the equivalent distance of travelling twice around the world!

Morgan also referred to the news, reported in *The Cornishman,* that St John's Hall was to undergo major alteration and refurbishment during the following year. This meant that the orchestra would have to find another venue but he reassured the audience that concerts would continue whatever happened, and he hoped that the new St John's Hall would be, "a splendid place".

A Treasurer's Lot...

At the annual general meeting in 1972 Norman Truman, the Society's Hon. Treasurer, had been in this office for twenty-five years and he was made a Vice-President of the Society in recognition of his long service. He was always a diligent and prudent Treasurer but was especially busy during the early seventies. In 1971 he had the introduction of decimal currency to cope with, as well as the arrangements for new Bandroom trustees and the registration of the building with the Land Registry. Then early in 1973 a new Value Added Tax was announced. Norman studied the subject but told the committee that he felt that as the Society's income was less than £5,000 there was no need to worry about this for the time being.

In addition to these matters it had been brought to Norman Truman's notice by the National Federation of Music Societies that the Orchestral Society was eligible to apply to the Customs and Excise for registration as a charity. A new constitution was drawn up which was accepted by the Customs and Excise and a members meeting called to adopt this as part of the process of becoming a charity.

Preparing for a Move

The problem of finding a different venue for the concerts during 1974 was discussed at committee meetings during the spring and summer of 1973, and at the September annual general meeting members were informed that Truro Cathedral was to be the venue for the concert in April 1974. Meanwhile the programme was being chosen for the next concert, the last in St John's Hall as they had known it for sixty-six years.

A substantial part of the orchestra, led by Morgan Hosking, combined with the Penzance Choral Society for a concert in St John's Hall on 18th May 1973. Two choral works, Purcell's 'Te Deum Laudamus' in D and Haydn's 'Nelson' Mass were performed along with Telemann's 'Suite for Flute and Strings' played by the orchestra with Arthur Miners, the Society's flautist, as soloist. The concert was conducted by the Choral Society conductor, Dr Edward Weymouth, and Robert Earl, in an excellent review, pointed out that there were few other small towns in the West-Country which could successfully assemble the resources necessary to present such a concert.

Plans for the concert in Truro Cathedral went ahead alongside rehearsals for the concert on 30th November 1973. A twenty-seven year old pianist, Stephanie Bamford, who had studied in Paris with the great Vlado Perlemuter, had been engaged to play the Piano Concerto No. 21 in C (K467) by Mozart. Newspaper reports spoke of the rapport achieved by soloist and orchestra, giving credit to Morgan Hosking's ability when conducting concertos, and saying that Miss Bamford's playing had a "sureness of touch... without loss of clarity".

The second half of the concert was devoted to another 'first' performance for the orchestra, the Symphony No. 2 in D by Sibelius. Two extra horn players and two bassoonists had been brought in to swell the brass and wind sections which resulted in entries made "with firmness and brightness and the four horns sustained an enriching tone throughout the performance". This was gratifying for the brass section who often received unflattering words from music critics. Despite a change in rehearsal schedules – fewer Sunday afternoon practices and more sectional ones – both players and conductor worked hard to master this major work and the result was a performance of "emotional power and conviction".

Playing Away from Home 1974-1979

It must be left for others to place on record the full story of the conversion of St John's Hall during 1974, but there were many problems along the way. While both the Orchestral and Operatic Societies were consulted on their views and requirements the latter's performances were not affected. Their production of Offenbach's 'La Vie Parisienne' was held in St John's Hall as usual in February, before work began. The Orchestral Society was involved in many discussions and meetings, represented more often than not by Morgan Hosking.

Concerts in the Cathedral

The orchestral committee discussed an alternative venue for their 1974 spring concert over twelve months beforehand and Albert Sinfield, manager of the Cornwall Symphony Orchestra, offered to take on the organisation of a concert if they decided to apply for permission to use Truro Cathedral. This was granted by the Dean and Chapter and Albert, or 'Sin' as he was often known, attended a committee meeting to finalise the arrangements. Mr and Mrs Sinfield were a couple who made a remarkable contribution to the musical life of Cornwall in this period. Their work with the Cornwall Symphony Orchestra and the Friends of the Cornwall Rural Music School was prodigious and these were only two of many musical groups which benefited from their vision and commitment. As a facilitator Albert Sinfield was invaluable, but he was helped by others such as Horace Tempest, who offered both transport and manpower from his business to help with the preparations.

Morgan Hosking suggested a programme for this concert which would make the most of the opportunity, and this was agreed in May 1973. The major work was to be Saint-Saëns' Symphony No. 3 in C Minor, the 'Organ' Symphony, in which the Cathedral organist, John Winter, was invited to be the soloist. Wagner's Prelude to 'Parsifal' would be played and the first half of the programme would feature mezzo-soprano, Sylvia Rowlands, as the soloist in Elgar's Song Cycle 'Sea Pictures' Op. 37. The symphony would be the only work played after the interval, a fitting climax for this very special concert.

Penzance Orchestral Society had not played, in their own right, in Truro Cathedral since the occasion of the diocesan Music Festival in 1932, but during the spring of 1974 they appeared there twice within one month. On Sunday 31st March a Service of Thanksgiving and Dedication was held in Truro attended by the civic leaders of Cornwall and the Isles of Scilly. In addition to the sound of the great Willis organ and the cathedral choir, music was provided by the Devon and Cornwall Police Choir, which sang Roger Quilter's 'Non Nobis Domine'. The combined forces of the Cornwall Symphony Orchestra and Penzance Orchestral Society totalled eighty instrumentalists, the majority of whom were Penzance players. This large orchestra was led by Una Bolitho, and they performed before the service began and at the end when Malcolm Arnold's 'Four Cornish Dances' were played, "in thanksgiving for the natural beauty of Cornwall". William Walton's 'Crown Imperial' March provided the processional music.

The harpist on this occasion was a lady from Teignmouth in Devon called Sheila Field. As she was also engaged to play in the forthcoming concert by the Orchestral Society she wrote to Morgan Hosking in early April expressing concern that the Society's harp, which had been used in the Cathedral, "had a dreadful buzz". This could be temporarily overcome, "by winding a piece of thread around part of the action.... 'Sea Pictures' is rather exposed and I would like to be free of buzzes"!

Prior to the Society's own concert in Truro Cathedral this problem, along with sundry others, had to be overcome. The remoteness of the organ loft necessitated the assistance of an intermediary 'conductor' to convey the beat to the organist; a page turner had to be found for the two pianists in the Saint-Saëns symphony; coach transport to Truro was needed for the Penzance subscribers. Finally, Sylvia Rowlands, the mezzo-soprano, was in the process of reviving her distinguished career after a long break to bring up her family and needed reassurance.

The buzz on the evening of Saturday 27th April 1974 came not from a faulty harp but from the excited anticipation among both the orchestra and a large audience in the lofty grandeur of Truro cathedral. Problems were set aside as the orchestra became immersed in the spiritual music of Wagner's 'Parsifal' where "Mr Hosking unravelled the prelude with the devotion of a Bayreuth conductor". Its final pianissimo soared gently into silence, the audience refraining from applause as the composer had intended. Sylvia Rowlands' rich and beautiful voice did full justice to Elgar's evocative song-cycle and for her it was, "an unforgettable experience and one I shall look back on with great joy".

The Saint-Saëns Symphony requires large forces to balance the power of a cathedral organ and involves deeper toned instruments like the cor anglais, bass clarinet and tuba. The organ and orchestra were in restrained harmony in the 'adagio' first movement, but the second movement unleashed the power of the combined forces with the pianists, Louise Sumner and Stephen Hichens, delivering glittering and virtuosic sounds from their instrument. It provided "a majestic, almost overpowering experience", according to the *West Briton* newspaper reviewer. This was the first time that Saint-Saëns' 'Organ' Symphony had been performed in Cornwall and its presentation by the Penzance Orchestral Society was, in the words of Geoffrey Self, "so fine that it was a thing to marvel at; the orchestra was, after all, a body of amateurs".

Morgan received letters of appreciation from the Dean of Truro, Rev. Henry Lloyd, and the organist, John Winter, and both expressed the hope that there would be visits from the orchestra in the future. Sadly, though members of the orchestra have been involved in other concerts there, the Orchestral Society has never returned to the Cathedral for one of their regular concerts. But who knows what the next hundred years may bring?

'Downsizing' to St Mary's Church

After providing a small orchestra for the Helston Choral Society concert on Saturday 25th May, led by Morgan Hosking, the Orchestral Society turned to the problem of where they would hold their next concert and of choosing the programmes for the 1974-75 season. There was a lot of uncertainty but finally St Mary's Church was chosen as the venue for the autumn concert. The programme presented on Friday 29th November reflected the need for music on a smaller scale due to the limited space in the church. It included an overture by William Boyce, Samuel Wesley's Fifth Symphony, and Bach's Brandenburg Concerto No. 4. The soloists, selected from the orchestra for the latter work, were Maurice Linden, violin, with Arthur Miners and Elizabeth Robertson, flutes.

In view of the fact that the cathedral concert had incurred extra expenses and made a loss of over £100 a less ambitious concert was welcome and the result was a profit which offset this loss. Press reports were very complimentary and, "the only note of sadness was in the absence of Mrs Enid Truman...who was taken ill after the final rehearsal". This was one of the very few concerts which Enid missed in over sixty years as a member of the orchestra.

St John's Hall Transformed

St John's Hall was officially re-opened on Monday 10th February 1975 at the opening night of the Operatic Society's production of 'Lilac Time', based on the life and music of Franz Schubert. Mr David Pooley, chairman of Penwith District Council, carried out the opening ceremony and welcomed the civic party. He had been the last Mayor of the old Penzance Borough which had begun the scheme and although money had not been available to carry out all the alterations planned, the change to the hall was still a radical one.

The redesigned hall looked much less picturesque, with the balcony removed and the position of the stage reversed. A new stage area had been built out behind what had been the rear wall providing much more room for performers, being sixty-five feet wide and thirty feet deep. This was very welcome to the Operatic Society, but it remained to be seen whether the notoriously difficult acoustic had been improved to make life easier for the Orchestral Society.

Penzance Orchestral Society in St John's Hall, November 2004.
Simon Cook

The new larger stage made it possible for the orchestra to be seated more spaciously, but also more conventionally. In earlier days, lack of space had meant that the double basses were positioned behind the orchestra on a raised back row. Now they were united with the rest of the strings, behind the 'cellos.

There was an atmosphere of both anticipation and celebration when the orchestra gave their first concert in the new hall on Friday 18th April 1975 and the programme was a popular one, opening with the Berlioz overture 'Le Carnaval Romain'. A young violinist, Michael Bochmann, was the soloist in the Beethoven concerto, and Brahms' monumental Fourth Symphony was played after the interval.

Michael Bochmann, aged just twenty-one, had studied with one of the Society's most popular former soloists, Frederick Grinke, and his performance of the Beethoven concerto, which had not been in the Society's programmes for nearly twenty years, met with great approval. His playing of the cadenza towards the end of the first movement had "a very personal approach, not florid or exhibitionist, but full of Beethovenesque flourishes and contrasts", and the 'Larghetto' movement had the quality of "a mezzo-soprano displaying perfect breath control". That Morgan and the orchestra both appreciated and enjoyed Michael's performance was reflected by the fact that he returned twice more as soloist, in 1979 and in 1985.

The orchestra were congratulated for their playing of the Brahms Symphony, *The Cornishman* writer feeling that the orchestra was, "in its most confident, most well-controlled form". Robert Earl was more objective, but he felt that the performance had been "particularly successful in not creating a sense of isolation that can arise between the four movements" and that there had been good work from the woodwind section throughout the evening.

Generally, the verdict seems to have been that the new hall was an improvement, but the acoustics were the subject of debate at a meeting of Penwith District Council's Finance Sub-Committee when further work on them was agreed. The debate was about when this should take place in view of other improvements still on the agenda for the future. Some minor remedial work was carried out over the years but the acoustic debate continued until, in very recent years, the orchestra made the dramatic decision to perform on the floor of the hall.

The 1975-1976 concert season once again presented Penzance audiences with programmes full of interest and variety. In November, pianist Anthony Peebles played the unusual and rarely heard 'Concerto No. 2 in A Major' by Liszt. This replaced the original choice by the committee, Rachmaninov's 'Rhapsody on a Theme of Paganini' because, having studied the score, Morgan Hosking decided it was too difficult for them to play. The Liszt, which has been described as "a symphonic poem for pianoforte and orchestra, with the sub-title, 'The Life and Adventures of a Melody'", was an inspired substitute, with its brilliant orchestration and colourful piano part. Both soloist and orchestra, and Enid Truman's 'cello playing, were warmly praised and another successful concert was completed with a performance of Beethoven's Seventh Symphony.

Rowenna Williams

Rowenna Williams, the former Miss Rowenna Maddern, was presented with a brooch and a bouquet of flowers at this concert to mark her fifty years as a member of the orchestra. Morgan Hosking would have taken especial pleasure in acknowledging Rowenna's contribution over the years for it was she, as a young girl, who had first awakened his curiosity about the violin as an instrument as she passed his home after her lessons. She remained a close neighbour of Morgan's all her life and he regularly drove her to rehearsals.

Rowenna was a prime example of the many 'rank and file' members of the orchestra who were its very life blood. She was an excellent violinist who never sought any sort of prominence, but whose devotion and commitment were unwavering. When something needed to be done on the social side of the orchestra's activities, too, Rowenna could be relied upon to do it, as in 1979 when a Grand Raffle was held to raise money to provide a new soundboard for the harp and Rowenna sold more tickets than anyone else. By the time she retired from the orchestra in 1991 her membership totalled sixty-six years, a remarkable achievement.

The major work at the spring concert was Cesar Franck's Symphony in D Minor, and the performance led Robert Earl to observe that the Penzance Orchestral Society was well equipped to achieve their ambition to play Bruckner's mighty Seventh Symphony, to celebrate their seventieth anniversary in November 1976. Timothy Brown was the guest soloist in the second of Mozart's four Horn Concertos. This was a real change of solo instrument and the capacity audience were treated to an accomplished performance.

Respighi's Suite of 'Ancient Airs and Dances No. 2', last played in 1948, was of special interest because, in addition to a full orchestra, it includes the cor anglais, harp, glockenspiel and piano duet in its scoring. The cor anglais was played by Miss Catherine Pooley and the two pianists were Enid Truman and Audrey Morcom. For many in the audience their view of the orchestra was greatly improved at this concert because tiered seating had now been installed in the rear half of the auditorium. Respighi's elaborate arrangement of music, originally written for the lute, must have been as visually fascinating for the audience as it was to listen to.

There were two big occasions for the Orchestral Society to prepare and look forward in the next two years: their own seventieth anniversary concert in November 1976, and a major concert to celebrate one hundred years since the formation of the Diocese of Truro in 1877. Morgan Hosking had been informed of this in December 1975, when the orchestra was invited to combine with the Cornwall Symphony Orchestra and a large choir to perform the 'Te Deum' by Berlioz in Truro Cathedral, at the start of a week of centenary events during May 1977, the performance to be conducted by him. He eagerly awaited this event, but was also very much looking forward to the Society's seventieth birthday concert in November when, unusually, only two works were to be played, namely Mozart's Clarinet Concerto and Bruckner's Seventh Symphony. The preparations for the latter became quite a saga in itself, briefly outlined here.

Bruckner for a Seventieth Anniversary

To conduct his orchestra in a performance of this Bruckner Symphony was one of Morgan's long dreamed of ambitions. He had to use all his powers of persuasion to get the committee to agree to it because it was likely to be a costly undertaking necessitating, for example, the engagement of four professional Wagner tuba players. Financially, the Society could afford this with their healthy deposit account, but the concerts themselves did not regularly make a profit. Nevertheless, whilst caution was not exactly 'thrown to the winds' the orchestral committee, as ever, placed their faith in Morgan's enthusiasm and vision and gave him the go-ahead. (The Wagner tuba is an instrument devised by Richard Wagner for use in his 'Ring' cycle of operas. It was intended to bridge the gap between the French horn and trombone, having a solemn and dignified sound.)

Rehearsals began, as usual, in September and in an attempt to keep costs down substitute instruments for the Wagner tubas were considered. Tenor and baritone horns were one possible solution, and then the use of euphoniums sounded promising. But these ideas fell through when the bandsmen from Camborne, who were to play them, were unable to keep the commitment due to other engagements. In the end, after many letters and phone calls, Morgan

Rehearsing Bruckner's 7th Symphony in the Bandroom, Autumn 1976.

Hosking arranged to borrow the set of four Wagner tubas belonging to the London Philharmonic Orchestra, and engaged four horn players from the Bournemouth Symphony Orchestra, who were experienced performers on the Wagner tubas. This all added nearly £75 to the expenses of the concert, but Morgan was relieved to have the problem solved in this way and delighted to have the sound of the instruments which the composer intended – if necessary he would surely have paid the expenses out of his own pocket.

In the midst of all this excitement the Society provided the orchestra for an extra week of performances by the Operatic Society from 4th – 9th October 1976. These were in celebration of their Golden Jubilee and the production was 'The Sound of Music' by Rodgers and Hammerstein. Morgan did not lead the orchestra for these performances due to his work on the Bruckner but the Operatic Society took the opportunity, in the programme, to wish the Orchestral Society every success for their seventieth anniversary concert.

Robert Earl did the Orchestral Society proud in the *Western Morning News* with a full page, illustrated article on Tuesday 21st September entitled, "Penzance Musicians' Proud Anniversary". It took the form of an historical review of the society's activities and personalities compiled from an interview he conducted with Morgan Hosking and Enid Truman, and included pictures of the orchestra during rehearsals. Nearer the event *The Cornishman* also included a preview of the anniversary concert, with a photograph of Thea King who was to be the guest soloist in the Mozart Clarinet Concerto. At long last this famous clarinettist was to perform in Penzance, twenty-three years after she had first been engaged by them but had been forced to cancel due to illness.

The Wagner tubas were collected from London by the Bournemouth musicians, and they joined the 70-strong orchestra for the final rehearsal on Thursday 25th November at 7 p.m. For the members of the orchestra this rehearsal would have been an evening of great tension and excitement. It is always thrilling but nerve-wracking to play a concerto with the guest soloist at the one and only rehearsal with them. On this occasion, too, the sound of the Wagner tubas was to be heard for the first time, a much talked-of event. Morgan would have prepared himself thoroughly and was renowned for making the best use of the time available and sticking to a practice schedule, even on an occasion such as this.

One of the oboists at this concert was David Ball, his first but far from his last appearance with the Penzance Orchestral Society, as he was destined to take over the baton from Morgan Hosking on his retirement a few years hence.

A relatively modest commemorative programme was produced for the following evening's concert, but it included a photograph of Walter Barnes and a two-page historical overview by

Penzance Orchestral Society, 70th Anniversary, November 1976. Conductor, Morgan Hosking, President, Mrs Faith Harris O.B.E. and Principal violin, Jack Glasson. Richards Bros., Penzance

Morgan. Walter Barnes' portrait would have been brought to St John's Hall, and the concert was attended by both the Mayor of Penzance and the Chairman of West Penwith District Council. Press reviews were approving, *The Cornishman* reporting Thea King's brilliance and stating that the adagio movement was, "a memorable combination of soloist and orchestra". The same writer felt that in the Bruckner Morgan Hosking had "lifted the full orchestra to some of its finest playing". The ever judicious Robert Earl felt that the orchestra's greatest success "was in scaling the heights with a sense of perception, caring and power," and that the strings provided an "insistent shimmer of sound... to create a sense of movement and development." He felt that, generally, the symphony took the players "where few amateur orchestras would be equipped to go".

This symphony was, for Morgan, the perfect vehicle with which to express his love of the romantic repertoire. Bruckner was a passionate admirer of Wagner, and the 'Adagio' movement was inspired by a premonition of that composer's death which occurred while he was writing it. This prompted him to write the 'Coda' as a memorial to Wagner, bringing the movement to a grief-stricken end. All this Morgan would have absorbed, thereby influencing his interpretation of the score through the orchestra.

It was also a fitting work to mark his thirtieth season as Conductor of the Orchestral Society. In his speech at the anniversary dinner held at the Queen's Hotel on the evening following the concert he told the assembled members and friends that he was not sure if everyone realised what had been achieved in performing the Bruckner Symphony. He appreciated the faith and trust placed in him when the decision was made to play it. In helping him achieve a life-long dream he thanked them for the memory, "which will always remain my most cherished possession".

He was presented with a set of Waterford crystal wine glasses which were also greatly cherished by him, and he would allow no one but himself to wash and dry them after use! He stressed the strength of friendship and generosity of spirit which existed within the Society and regarded this as one reason why the orchestra would endure to celebrate its centenary, a feeling echoed by the guest speaker, Mr James White, who proposed the toast to the Society.

After the dinner members and friends relaxed and enjoyed some well-earned entertainment provided by Mr Tom Waters from Mousehole. Tom, as well as being a member of the conjuror's Magic Circle, was also a steward at orchestral concerts, and later became the conductor of Mousehole Male Voice Choir for over fifteen years from 1989.

The Wagner tubas were returned safely by road transport to the LPO whose help and cooperation, along with that of the Bournemouth musicians, was acknowledged in the concert programme. And so to the end of another celebration for this remarkable group of musicians. But before their next anniversary the Society would experience the end of one era and the start of another.

With the dawning of a new year, 1977, Penzance Orchestral Society and its conductor had a very busy few months ahead. Their spring concert had been brought forward to early March to allow time to rehearse the Berlioz 'Te Deum', with its two performances in Truro Cathedral on the 6th and 7th May. But first of all Morgan Hosking was back leading the orchestra for the Operatic Society's production of Gilbert and Sullivan's 'The Gondoliers' from the 21st-26th February, their second show during the Jubilee season.

A Bit of a Punch-up!

The orchestra, normally a happy band of players, were dismayed when a fight broke out between two of the brass players during one of the final Operatic Society rehearsals. Following a pub lunch an altercation between a trumpeter and a horn player led to the former punching the latter, resulting in a badly cut lip. One of the flautists was heard to say, "most embarrassing, most embarrassing". They were ousted from the rehearsal and neither of them played for the performances, the one banned by the Musical Director, John Matthews, and the other because of his damaged lip.

A lengthy discussion at an Orchestral Society committee meeting produced a plan to call the instigator of the fight before them to explain himself. But instead of this Morgan, who felt very responsible for the conduct of his instrumentalists, invited both men to his home where they settled their differences. Later, a letter of resignation was received from the man who had thrown the punch. He had been a member of the orchestra for twenty-one years and said that he was no longer able to play because of trouble with his teeth, though he did reappear once more with the orchestra in April 1978. Trouble with teeth did seem to recur to afflict the orchestra from time to time!

A popular programme of music well-known to the orchestra was chosen for their concert on Friday 11th March 1977. The soloist was violinist, Christopher Hirons, leader of the famous Academy of St Martins in the Fields chamber orchestra, and his performance of the well-loved Max Bruch Violin Concerto was regarded as "brilliant". Haydn's 'Symphony No. 2' 'The Oxford', Glucks 'Alceste' overture, and the Suites Nos. 1 and 2 from Bizet's 'Carmen' formed the rest of the programme. According to the reviews the quality of the whole concert merited a capacity audience and the empty seats were put down to a recent visit by the Bournemouth Sinfonietta, the Operatic Society week and the earlier concert date. Morgan Hosking remarked later that he was of the opinion that 'popular' concerts did not always create a 'full house' because, "when we play Sibelius, Brahms or Bruckner we have to turn people away".

A Musical Celebration

Morgan was now able to concentrate on rehearsals for the 'Te Deum'. His thoughts on the situation, with just under two months to go, reflect some of his eager anticipation of this great event. "There is plenty to concentrate on", he reported, "two rehearsals with the combined choir... seemed to go down well, and a general air of excitement seems to prevail". He felt that Dr Edward Weymouth, conductor of the Penzance Choral Society, was doing an especially good job in training his choir, but that during his rehearsals for a recent performance of the 'St Matthew Passion', when he had been trying to restrain them from singing too loudly, he told his choristers that "you seem to be suffering from a bad attack of Berliozitis"! Practices with the Cornwall Symphony Orchestra and his own were going well and, "if we can all be fitted into the Cathedral, I have a feeling that this is going to be a great occasion".

Berlioz, in his usual flamboyant way, had dreamed of a choir of over 700 voices and an orchestra of 467 instrumentalists with 30 pianos, 30 harps, 16 kettle drums and 4 brass bands for his ideal performance of the 'Te Deum'. The Cornwall Rural Music School Friends and Concert Society, who were organising the Truro performance, neither aspired to nor had room for such fantastic forces! But they did advertise 'A Musical Celebration' involving 470 performers, including massed choirs from Falmouth, Helston, Redruth, St Austell, Penzance and four different choirs from Truro itself, a total of nearly 350 singers divided into three choirs.

The Cornwall Symphony Orchestra and Penzance Orchestral Society combined to create an orchestra of 120 players with double wind and brass, to which was added John Winter on the 'Father Willis' organ. The soloist in the 'Te Deum' was West Cornwall's own John Treleavan, listed in the programme under his real name of John Richards. Born in Porthleven he had already established his career as an opera singer having sung major roles with English National

Opera and was, in 1977, working with Welsh National Opera. His voice with its heroic, heldentenor quality was admirably suited to the one great tenor aria in the work, the prayer 'Te ergo quaesumus'. John was to become one of the greatest heldentenors of his time performing in opera houses world-wide, and noted for his interpretations of Wagnerian roles.

The musical events in Truro marked not only the diocesan centenary but also that of the city itself. Also, it was the Silver Jubilee year of Her Majesty the Queen so other music was included in the concerts to acknowledge these additional causes for celebration. The rendition of the National Anthem at the start of the concerts was, in itself, an unusually impressive one, and it received a Jubilee year tribute by being accorded programme notes.

Geoffrey Self was the conductor of the Cornwall Symphony Orchestra at this time and his growing reputation as a composer was recognised by a performance of his work, 'Noblissima Visione', a fanfare for chorus, organ and orchestra. It was specially composed for the occasion and took full advantage of the enormous musical forces at the composer's disposal. It opened with a choral statement of the words of the 'Gloria' followed by an orchestral prelude and postlude, and was intended to suggest the power and eternity of God often indiscernible through human frailty. Handel's Coronation Anthem, 'Zadock the Priest', then filled the vast space of the cathedral and prepared the audiences for the great music of thanksgiving which was to follow.

The Berlioz 'Te Deum' had been chosen for two reasons. Firstly, because it is an appropriate and major religious work of praise and rejoicing and secondly, being written on such a grand scale, it allowed the participation of a wide representation of Cornish musical organisations, which was the intention on this occasion. Its preparation necessitated a great deal of work by the conductors and singers in the various choirs and choral societies. For Morgan Hosking the challenge was huge because he had to rehearse the orchestras as well as arrange practices with the massed choirs. These groups then had to be combined into a cohesive whole at a final rehearsal before the two performances.

Many qualified commentators have remarked that courage was one of Morgan's greatest attributes as a conductor. On this occasion confidence and stamina were also required, along with a voice loud enough to be clearly heard during the rehearsal. So many people were involved, both musically and 'behind the scenes', but to him fell the ultimate, overall responsibility for successful performances and, as Geoffrey Self wrote, "his sense of the monumental easily enabled him to surmount the problems".

The performances were a resounding success, with the conductor's "concept of the work... measured to the acoustic in his timing of the great sounds of triumph from the orchestra at the climaxes", according to Robert Earl in the *Western Morning News*. John Treleavan's performance had, "a brightness and clarity of voice that rang the words to all parts of the crowded building". For those taking part it was a thrilling experience such as was rarely encountered in amateur music-making in Cornwall.

A Musical Celebration
7th and 8th May 1977

Now come all you Cornishmen, lend me your ears
All along, out along, down along lea,
In Truro, the musical feast of the years,
With John Morgan, John Richards, John Winter and 'Sin'
Geoffrey Self, Handel, Berlioz and all
Te deum laudamus and all.

Way back in December we first heard the call,
All along, out along, down along lea,
In churchroom and vestry, in schoolroom and hall,
With Cyril Lanxon, John Bawden, John Simpson, Alan Hutt,
Arthur Bending, Henry Doughty,
Ted Weymouth, Joan Perry and all,
Tibi omnes Angeli and all.

The orchestra gathered, brass woodwind and strings,
All along, out along, down along lea,
Percussionists counted, the trumpets took wing,
With John Morgan, Jack Glasson, Eileen Tombe and the rest,
Father Willis the organ and all,
Dignare Domine and all.

And so through the winter rehearsals were held,
All along, out along, down along lea,
As Spring grew the thing grew, the voices were swelled
In Helston, in Truro, in Redruth, Penzance,
In Falmouth, St. Austell and all,
Christe rex gloriae and all.

Then finally, Friday and Saturday came,
All along, out along, down along lea,
The west window glowing, the stone work aflame
In transept and Quire, in chapel and Nave,
With Bishop, Dean, chapter and all,
Te ergo quaesumus and all.

The National anthem we sang to the Queen,
All along, out along, down along lea,
Then fanfare and anthem were next on the scene,
With Te deum, Tibi omnes, Dignare, Christe rex,
Te ergo quaesumus and all,
Judex crederis esse venturus and all.

Margaret Williams 1977
(with apologies to Uncle Tom Cobleigh
and Rev. S. Baring Gould)

Back to Base

The final years of the 1970's saw the Penzance Orchestral Society resuming their normal concert routine in St John's Hall providing a series of good concerts, with excellent soloists. In November 1977 a young 'cellist, Colin Carr, played the Dvorak Concerto in B Minor. At only nineteen years old he was already making a name for himself and his performance was described as "a moving 'tour de force'". The orchestra, too, was in good form and the programme included a work for strings, Handel's 'Concerto Grosso Op.

6, No. 7', scored for 'tutti' strings throughout. Two incidental facts about this concert are that it made a profit of £129.67 which almost exactly covered the soloist's fee, and that the concert programme, from here onwards, included a short biography of the soloist.

The Choral Society held their Christmas concert on Friday 16th December 1977 in St John's Hall, and it is important to record that the leader of the orchestra was Miss J. Preston. Her name had already appeared among the viola players of the Orchestral Society's concerts in March and November and she continued as a violist with them for another two or three years, after which she transferred to the first violins. Joyce Preston was destined to become the Orchestral Society's Principal Violin and she would make a major contribution in this position.

During the exciting musical occasions of the past year and a half Morgan had felt both anxiety and impatience over the running of his business and had considered selling it. He admitted afterwards that he felt that this had been entirely due to his being, and wanting to be, preoccupied with conducting the Bruckner Symphony and the Berlioz 'Te Deum'. With this weight of musical responsibility off his shoulders the tensions eased and he abandoned the idea of selling his business and redecorated the offices instead. However, there is evidence to suggest that the passing years were taking their toll on him (he was in his sixty-fifth year) because he gave up playing in the Operatic Society Orchestra. For their 1978 production of Johann Strauss's 'The Gipsy Baron' his position as Principal Violin was taken by Maurice Linden, and a warm tribute to Morgan's years with the Operatic Society was included in the programme.

The concert which closed the 1977-78 season needed a great deal of strength and effort, with two Beethoven works, the 'Coriolan' Overture and the mighty 'Emperor' Piano Concerto, along with Arnold's 'Four Cornish Dances', and the Symphony No. 5 in E Flat Major, Op. 82 by Sibelius. With a week to go before the concert Morgan Hosking was, at last, beginning to feel that the orchestra would be able to produce a decent performance of the Sibelius symphony.

It was after considerable thought that the decision to play it had been made, because Morgan regarded it as one of the hardest tasks they had ever tackled and at times wondered if they had bitten off more than they could chew. "I think the trouble was", he wrote just prior to the concert, "that the notes and times are so complex that they had to concentrate all their minds on this, and just could not see the shape of the piece for weeks, and it was only about a couple of weeks back that they were able to relax and see what a great work it is. Now they are all thrilled. They really are a super lot of people."

After the concert on Friday 21st April, 1978, *The Cornishman* reviewer gave a good report of the Sibelius, "It required enormous concentration from conductor, and leader Jack Glasson, and the 70-strong orchestra to guide this great ship to port with its dramatic final chords". Richard Markham was the soloist in the piano concerto and his performance was enthusiastically received by the capacity audience. "His skilful chromatic runs and delicacy of interpretation made it a splendid performance", and the orchestra "gave him most capable support".

Morgan did continue to lead the second violin section for Choral Society concerts such as the one on 12th May 1978 when they gave a performance of the Beethoven 'Mass in C' as well as substantial works by Henry Purcell, Vaughan Williams and Stanford with local soloists. He felt a great sense of loyalty and obligation to their conductor, Dr Edward Weymouth, who had always supported Morgan's efforts and was particularly helpful over the Berlioz 'Te Deum' concert. In the autumn of 1977 Morgan declined an invitation to play the violin in a professional orchestra, accompanying the London Symphony Orchestra Chorus's performance of the Beethoven's 'Missa Solemnis', in Truro Cathedral. He would have enjoyed playing under the talented conductor, Richard Hickox, but the concert clashed with the Choral Society's first rehearsal.

In September 1978 rehearsals began for the next season of concerts, the first of which took place on Friday 24th November, and included some innovative features. Two soloists had been engaged with local tenor, Douglas Williams, singing two arias in the first half of the programme, 'The Flower Song' from Bizet's 'Carmen' and the lovely 'Onaway! Awake, Beloved`!' from 'Hiawatha's Wedding Feast' by Coleridge-Taylor. Douglas was probably at the peak of his form at this time and the audience would have not only enjoyed his performances but appreciated this acknowledgement of his great talent and popularity.

The visiting soloist was Keith Lovell, the well-known viola player and a founder member of the Dartington String Quartet, formed in 1958. He joined the orchestra for a performance of Berlioz' 'Harold in Italy'. The role of the viola is to depict Byron's Childe Harold wandering in the Italian countryside, encountering various scenes and experiences. It is Berlioz the dreamer at his most colourful and dramatic and the partnership between soloist and orchestra worked admirably, according to the press reports. Once more this was a new work for the orchestra and probably a first 'live' performance in West Cornwall.

Creating Conviviality

The other new feature at this concert was the introduction of a bar and provision of refreshments after the concert. Although sometimes the orchestra and friends repaired to a local hostelry after the concerts this was not regularly organised. It had been suggested in committee that concerts should have a sociable ending to them in St John's Hall when the audience, if they chose to, could mingle with the members of the orchestra. So a local licensee was asked to organise a bar in the adjoining hall, available before and after the concert as well as during the interval. Refreshments were provided, but whether Morgan's request for Cornish pasties was fulfilled has not been recorded! The idea was deemed a success and has been continued in one form or another ever since, creating an animated and friendly conclusion to the evening.

From Schumann to Gershwin

While holidaying in Wales Morgan Hosking had met a young pianist who was on the staff of the University College of Wales, Aberystwyth. Richard Simm had studied with Bernard Roberts and was a prize-winner at many prestigious competitive events including the Leeds International Piano Competition. He was an outstanding performer in both the chamber and solo music repertoire and conversations with Morgan led to his being invited to play the Gershwin Piano Concerto in F with the Orchestral Society. This formed part of a programme of contrasting music at the concert on 6th April 1979.

Opening with Schumann's Third Symphony, 'Rhenish', the first half of the concert was completed with Ann Harvey as the harp soloist in Mahler's 'Adagietto' from his Fifth Symphony, the music used in the Visconti film 'Death in Venice', starring Dirk Bogarde. The 'theme music' continued after the interval when Hamish MacCunn's concert overture, 'The Land of the Mountain and the Flood' was played, heard by television viewers in the series, 'Sutherland's Law', and the final item in the programme was the Gershwin Concerto. This was given, "a stunning duo performance", by the soloist and orchestra with Richard Simm giving, "a virtuoso display" in the jazzy rhythms and syncopations, with its more tender moods, "tellingly captured", according to *The Cornishman.*

The orchestra was congratulated for its performance of the Schumann Symphony, but while Ann Tempest's playing in the Mahler 'Adagietto' was well spoken of there was, apparently, "some untypical poor intonation" in the opening of the Mahler and the quieter passages of the Hamish MacCunn work. This was thought to be due to the dry, hot atmosphere and, overall, the concert was regarded as a great success. "It is still a remarkable record that a small town like Penzance can boast a symphony orchestra... that can cross the musical divide between Schumann and George Gershwin by its competence and sheer enthusiasm", wrote Robert Earl.

Help for the Harp

Despite its appearance at the concert the Society's harp was a cause for concern at this time. It had received another temporary repair but was in need of a major overhaul necessitating expenditure of £1,000, plus VAT. The value of the harp was £800 but an overhaul would increase this to over £2,000 so the decision was made to have the work done, and various methods of fundraising were suggested at an extra-ordinary general meeting of members called in June 1979. The major result of the meeting was that a raffle should be held during the summer months, with the prize draw to be held at the November 1979 concert. Many members donated prizes large and small and it proved very successful. The annual accounts of the Society for the year ending in June 1980 record a total of £644.47 being raised by this method. The repairs to the harp incurred a bill of over £1,200 but the instrument was then given a valuation of £3,000, thereby becoming a valuable asset to the Society

The music chosen for the opening concert of the Orchestral Society's 1979-80 season was a Handel Overture in D Minor, arranged for full orchestra by Sir Edward Elgar, the Sibelius Violin Concerto, and Beethoven's Symphony No. 3 in E Flat 'Eroica'. Rehearsals went well with good attendance and after a first 'run-through' of the Sibelius concerto Morgan was "Looking forward

to taking it to pieces this evening". Michael Bochmann had been invited back to Penzance and gave "a powerful performance" but with "moments of exquisite lyrical beauty" in the second movement of the concerto and showed his "virtuosity in the high registers of his instrument" in the final movement. The "accomplished" brass section of the orchestra received this accolade for their playing in the overture and also for some "excellent horn playing" in the 'Scherzo' movement of the Beethoven Symphony.

Robert Earl pointed out that it was unusual for an amateur orchestra to be so associated with the major works of Sibelius but that the "Penzance Symphony Orchestra's long standing identity with the composer proved a profitable experience for audience and players" at this concert on Friday 30th November. His review was wholly approving of the orchestra and soloist's performance. "Local pride in Penzance's orchestra was rightly stirred in the playing of Beethoven's 'Eroica' Symphony", which was enhanced by "notable woodwind contributions". After the interval the draw for the raffle in aid of the harp repair fund was made but no details of prize-winners have been recorded.

It was proving to be an expensive period for the Society, with soloists' fees increasing and repairs to instruments and the Bandroom needing substantial expenditure. Concert ticket prices had been raised and insurance cover did offset some of the costs of work on the building, but they still amounted to well over £1,000 during the 1979-80 financial year.

While it is sad to note the passing of some old friends of the Society during this time their legacies and gifts to the Orchestral Society were fortuitous and the £660 which was received in their memory helped keep the Society's finances stable despite major outlay. These donations resulted from the deaths of Miss Dorothy Yglesias, A. G. "Fluffie" Harrison, one of the Vice-Presidents, and their President, Mrs Faith Harris in March 1980 at the age of 92.

And so to the end of another decade with the Penzance Orchestral Society in a healthy state, musically, financially and socially. There had been great occasions, musical challenges faced, overcome and, very importantly, enjoyed. Morgan Hosking had created opportunities for his players to have the experience of performing significant and difficult works, while audiences heard major compositions in 'live' performances rarely experienced in the West Country, especially by amateur orchestras. It had been an exciting and successful ten years.

Penzance Orchestral Society at rehearsal in the Bandroom, 1976.

18

Thunder from a Clear Sky 1980-1981

Margaret Kingsley Comes Home Again

The possibility of Margaret Kingsley returning to sing Wagner with the orchestra had been discussed by her and Morgan Hosking during 1977, when Margaret had suggested she should sing Brunnhilde's 'Immolation' from the final act of 'Götterdämmerung'. Morgan's reaction to this was, "My God, what a task for amateurs", but she thought the orchestra could cope with it. However, on considering the huge instrumental forces required and the overall challenge that it represented for an amateur orchestra, Morgan felt that it would be unwise to go ahead.

By the time of her third visit as guest soloist with the Orchestral Society an alternative Wagner aria and one by Verdi had been chosen. This concert, closing the 1979-80 season, took place on Friday 25th April 1980 and music from operas formed a large part of the programme. It began with Mozart's Overture to 'Don Giovanni' which was followed by Brahms' 'Symphony No. 2 in D', the only non-operatic work of the evening. The whole of the second half of the concert was devoted to four excerpts from operas by Verdi and Wagner. First came the Prelude to Act 1 of Verdi's 'La Traviata', followed by Margaret Kingsley singing, 'O Don Fatale' from 'Don Carlos'. The Wagner items were the Prelude to Act 3 of 'Lohengrin', after which Margaret sang the Prelude and Liebestod from 'Tristan und Isolde'.

Margaret Kingsley, F.R.C.M., L.R.A.M.

In the soloist's biography the Penzance audience was brought up to date on the progress of Margaret's career. She was now singing regularly with all the major British opera companies and appearing frequently in most of the European opera houses. Among the many notable roles she performed was that of Brunnhilde in Wagner's 'Ring' cycle. In addition she maintained her concert career singing with all the main British orchestras and was teaching at the Royal College of Music.

Margaret would go on to a Professorship at the College and was awarded a fellowship in 1994. She eventually retired from public performance but still devotes her time to teaching and is renowned as a teacher and voice consultant. Many established singers world-wide owe their success to Margaret's tuition. Penzance has good cause to take great pride in Margaret's accomplishments and her life-long attachment to her town and county of birth.

The Penzance Orchestral Society began their 1980-81 season early when they took part in the St Ives Festival of the Arts, which comprised a total of eighty two events taking place during September. They presented a programme in which the main works were the Brahms Second Symphony and Beethoven's Third Piano Concerto, with Frank Wibaut as soloist. Robert Earl, in an article about the festival, spoke well of the soloist and felt that in the 'allegretto grazioso' movement of the Brahms Symphony the playing "was of the usual Penzance quality".

At the Society's September AGM significant changes among the officers took place. With the death of Mrs Faith Harris earlier in the year, they had to choose a new President. Mrs Enid Truman was elected unanimously, a fitting recognition of her life-long devotion to the orchestra founded by her father, and she continued in the office of Hon. Secretary. A new Chairman also had to be elected in place of Mr L. Graham White, and Robin Whitehead succeeded to this position. Three new Vice-Presidents were chosen, Mrs Nora Horsfall, Mrs Helen Barton and Mrs J. Harrison. Helen Barton had resigned as Hon. Librarian to the Society after twenty years in this demanding post and was replaced by Mrs Catherine Pearce, and it was agreed that Helen should receive a gift as a token of thanks for being such a wonderful Librarian for all those years.

There was nothing to indicate, at this meeting or in the months ahead, that Morgan Hosking was thinking of retiring as Hon. Conductor. If he was contemplating this he gave no inkling of it either to the orchestra or to his family and friends at this time. So rehearsals went ahead in ignorance of the fact that the coming season would, in fact, be Morgan's last. The pianist, Marlene Fleet, had been invited to make her third appearance with the Society and this concert took place on Friday 21st November 1980.

There were some empty seats in St John's Hall but, despite this, it was a successful concert. It had been ten years since Marlene Fleet's last visit, and the *Western Morning News* felt that her performance of the Grieg Piano concerto "showed the future and further development of a confident, strong player, with an individual feeling for phrasing". The concert was opened by the Berlioz overture, 'Les Francs Juges', and after the interval the orchestra played Mendelssohn's 'Symphony No. 3 in A Minor, Op 56', the 'Scottish'.

Morgan's comments following this concert are interesting and he was pleased with Marlene Fleet, who had autographed his programme with the message "Third Time Happy! Lots of love to dear Morgan". But for him the highlight of the concert was the Mendelssohn Symphony, "which exceeded my expectations, for it was a very difficult work to bring off...and the woodwind playing was quite brilliant". He held a party at his home after the concert with Marlene Fleet present and admitted to feeling very tired for two days afterwards. But he had to pull himself together by the following Friday because, as a Harbour Commissioner in Newlyn, he was involved in a Royal visit.

Morgan Meets the Queen

The Queen and the Duke of Edinburgh came to Newlyn to declare open the new Mary Williams pier which had been built, and Morgan had been given the honour of escorting the Duke for the duration of the event. It was a great day for the fishing community and village, and after the royal party had departed Morgan's harbour-side offices were 'open house' and the champagne flowed. This was followed by an official luncheon at the Queen's Hotel in Penzance after which he went back to work, though "not seriously". He revelled in it all, of course, and committed his memories of the day to paper in some detail, which is a vivid, amusing and touching record of an historic occasion. What a week!

A Concert to End an Era

There were no meetings of the Orchestral Society committee between September 1980 and May 1981 but everything was in place for the concert on Friday 10th April. The music chosen was typically imaginative, the first half consisting of two Mozart works, his overture to the 'Magic Flute' and the 'Concerto No. 4 in D', K218 for violin and orchestra, followed by the Suite 'Algeriénne' by Saint-Saëns.

The soloist was Miss Rasma Lielmane, born in Latvia but a resident of Mexico City where she was a teacher in the Mexican National Conservatory. She was of international standing as a soloist, and her playing of the concerto was described as a display of "warmth and agility with a full and rich tone". The unfamiliar work by Saint-Saëns was regarded as a very suitable vehicle for the Penzance orchestra, where its exotic nature was successfully portrayed in "an exhilarating performance...conveyed with much vigour and strength".

The climax to this concert came after the interval when just one work, the third of Vaughan Williams' nine symphonies, the 'Pastoral', was played. This beautiful and unusual work has important solos throughout, for violin, horn, and E flat trumpet, as well as the more usual woodwind solos.

The final fourth movement also requires a tenor or soprano soloist to be heard off-stage, on this occasion sung by one of the orchestra's oboists, Catherine Pearce. The E flat trumpet is not normally used in an orchestra and Christopher Harris had bought the instrument especially for the performance.

Vaughan Williams is said to have been inspired to write this great work while serving in northern France with the Medical Corps in 1916, where the landscape reminded him of rural England. A bugler practising on his instrument and sounding the seventh in error for the octave, is echoed in the trumpet cadenza in the second 'Lento moderato' movement. The tranquillity and quietude of the symphony does not reflect the horror and tumult of war but there are more forceful passages which reveal the underlying drama. The wordless soprano solos at the beginning and end of the final movement evoke the image of a girl at work in the fields and

Catherine Pearce gave a memorable performance when, in partnership with the clarinets, her solo brought the symphony to its final fading bars.

For the very few people who were, by now, aware that this was Morgan's last concert it was a moment of great poignancy. Here there was no flamboyant flourish but a gentle mood of calm and resignation, bringing the years of his conductorship, full of drama and excitement, to an end.

Morgan Hosking Lays Down the Baton

Just under a month later a committee meeting had been arranged to plan the details of the next orchestral season. This discussion was abandoned when Morgan told them of his decision to retire in favour of a younger person, and said that in David Ball he had found the man to whom he felt able to hand over. David was agreeable to this and the situation was accepted by the committee subject to the approval of the Annual General Meeting.

Following the meeting Morgan wrote a long letter to all members of the Society, telling them of his decision to retire and explaining his reasons for doing so. He said that the subject of his successor had been a source of anxiety to him, especially as there had been no Junior Orchestra for some time in which a young aspiring conductor could gain experience. David had emerged from the ranks of the orchestra as someone who had the right qualities with which to succeed him and who was a local man, committed to the musical life of the area.

Morgan admitted that it had been the hardest decision he had ever had to make but felt that it would have been selfish not to have made it, and that the orchestra and its future was much more important than any one personality within it. It was an eloquent letter but cogent and persuasive, ending with the plea for more than normal loyalty to the orchestra and support for the new conductor. Ten days later, on Friday 22nd May, the *Western Morning News* featured an article by Robert Earl on its 'Arts Review' page headed, "Baton Change 35 Years on" with a photograph of Morgan and, on Thursday 4th June, *The Cornishman* followed with a similar article but also including a picture of David Ball.

Morgan received many letters from members and friends in response to his announcement and they are a moving tribute to him, both as a conductor of the orchestra and as a man. There were tears of sadness for some but, with very few exceptions, all reassured him that they would continue to play and support David to the best of their ability. Many expressed gratitude for his encouragement and guidance when joining the orchestra as young or inexperienced players. Gladys Tranter summed this up by saying, "I do know, from many other instances, that your service has been as much to humanity itself as to music". She concluded her letter thus: "you've given so much to so many and varied people, may the bread cast on the waters come back spread with butter and jam and Cornish Cream."

A New Conductor

During the months following the retirement of Morgan Hosking the Penzance Orchestral Society showed, once again, its remarkable ability to cope with a major change. The severance of a thirty-five year old relationship had the potential to cause a major trauma within this ageing organization but this did not happen. The reasons for the problem-free continuity are not hard to find. Firstly, players remained true to their word and, as they had promised Morgan, continued their membership ready to support the new conductor. Secondly, David Ball was 'one of them', having been an oboist in the orchestra for five years, and many members had already played under his baton so he was not an alarming 'new broom'. Finally, the experienced officers and committee of the Society kept their heads and provided the administrative stability so vital at such a time.

Once Morgan had named his successor, David, already a committee member, immediately took on the mantle of musical leadership and prepared a list of works for the next season, which he presented to the committee at the end of May 1981. His formal nomination and election as the new Hon. Conductor at the September Annual General Meeting was a foregone conclusion. At the same meeting the matter of a new Principal Violin had to be resolved due to Jack Glasson wanting to retire. David had already worked with Joyce Preston as his leader, and said that he would like her in that position with the Orchestral Society and she agreed to become Principal Violin for one year. She was to continue for the next twenty-five years, and between them David and Joyce would provide a firm foundation for the orchestra as it entered the final quarter-century of its existence. But who was David Ball and what was his background and musical experience?

David Ball

David Ball.

In April 1969 an article appeared in *The Cornishman* headed "Mice gnaw Clarabella". This was the unlikely title given to an article about damage to the St Hilary Parish Church organ and the launch of an appeal for its repair. It also provided the information that Mr David Ball was the church organist. He had recently started on a career as a chemistry teacher at Redruth Grammar School where he was to become head of department.

David was born in St Erth, near Hayle, of a Lancashire born father who had moved to Cornwall at the age of sixteen. His father worked in Newlyn and met his future wife, Kathleen Eddy, whose family ran the bakery there which, until recent years, was a well-known West Cornwall 'institution'. (These Newlyn connections were, to Morgan Hosking, added confirmation of David's fitness as his successor!) Following his education at local schools and Camborne Technical College, David went on to the University of York where he graduated in chemistry. It was here that he also began his serious education in music.

By a happy accident of fate David had lodgings with a couple who were very musical. She was a semi-professional singer and he was a songman in the choir of York Minster. David, having had some piano lessons as a boy, decided he would like to take them up again and his landlord and lady, Mr and Mrs Ainsworth, arranged lessons for him. He also had lessons on the organ with an organ scholar in York Minster and became involved in the musical life of the city. He sang in the university choir and joined the York Musical Society, and on two occasions remained in York during Easter vacations to sing in Bach's 'St Matthew' and 'St John' Passions in the Minster.

After graduating he worked for a while in Exeter as a management trainee but felt that he was not making use of his science degree and trained to become a teacher. He did his post-graduate teaching course at the University of Bath and finally got a job in Redruth Grammar School, having decided that he wanted to return to Cornwall to live and work.

David had been appointed organist at St Hilary Parish Church at the age of nineteen and the next stage of his musical education came when he was back in Cornwall. He took on the conducting of the school orchestra at Redruth Grammar and at much the same time decided he wanted to learn an orchestral instrument.

While listening to a performance of Bach's 'Christmas Oratorio' in Truro he was impressed with the oboe playing in the famous 'echo' aria and went to speak to the oboist after the performance. This turned out to be none other than Anthony White, oboist in the Penzance Orchestral Society, and head of the physics department at Camborne Grammar School for Girls. When David expressed an interest in learning to play the oboe Anthony White offered to give him some lessons and lend him an instrument until he was sure he wanted to continue with it. Within twelve months David was playing in orchestras for musical productions, his first being the St Ives Operatic Society's performance of 'Rosemarie'. By 1976 he was regarded as a capable enough player to help out when the Penzance Orchestral Society had an oboe problem.

It was the Society's Seventieth Anniversary concert, when the Mozart Clarinet Concerto and Bruckner's Symphony No. 7 were played. Oboist, Liz Robertson, (the future Mrs Vosper), had broken a finger and was unable to play all the notes in the music. David was brought in as 'back up' playing in unison with Liz to cover any 'blank' notes she couldn't manage. Morgan Hosking told the duo that he had great confidence in their performance!

David was still the organist at St Hilary Church and in 1979 he became the President of the Cornwall Organists' Association. One of the obligations of the position was to organise a President's meeting with food and music. Normally this was afternoon tea followed by a recital but David decided to do something different. He planned a concert of orchestral music followed by a supper, the music being played by local musicians conducted by, perhaps, Morgan Hosking, John Simpson, conductor of Helston Choral Society, or another local conductor. He gathered the players and asked Joyce Preston to lead, and it was she who stated from the start that David was going to conduct. He had no aspirations as a conductor beyond the school orchestra, but after some thought decided he would take up the challenge and chose a programme of music and soloists.

At the first rehearsal in the Orchestral Society's Bandroom he was very nervous in front of an adult ensemble, and opened the rehearsal with Mozart's overture to The 'Marriage of Figaro'. He gave the beat to begin and they did, which, in his own words, "frightened him to death". His experience with the school orchestra had been that you had to start a piece half a dozen times before it got going! The concert at St Hilary Church on Saturday 7th July 1979 was a

David Ball rehearsing 'Music for a Summer's Evening', St Hilary Church, July 2004.

success. The audience filled the church and afterwards one of the players asked David what he was planning for the next year and when he replied that there wasn't "a next year" they said "Oh, yes there is". The concerts became an annual event under the title 'Music for a Summer Evening' and have continued to this day, raising money for many local charities in the process, and are an eagerly anticipated musical event of the summer in West Cornwall.

It was not just David's aptitude as a conductor and organiser of concerts that placed him in Morgan Hosking's mind as his successor. He saw that this young man had the right character and personality needed to direct an amateur orchestra and make it an enjoyable experience for them. David liked people and had a concern for them, as well as having a sense of humour and the ability to communicate. This spirit of friendship had been an important aspect of the Orchestral Society's music-making and members found this in their new conductor. He was caring and considerate in his dealings with them and, in return, they responded to his warmth and enthusiasm. Even when older members left the orchestra over the years David would keep in touch, visiting them and maintaining the links.

Illustrating this personal involvement with his players David recalled how Jeannette Powell, who had been a 'cellist with the orchestra since 1932, was distressed, soon after being widowed, to find that she had lost her wedding ring on returning home after a rehearsal in the Bandroom. She asked David if he would look for it the next time he was there. He immediately went to the Bandroom and carefully swept the floor but failed to find the ring. He decided to go and report the loss to the police and as he walked up the street, scuffling fallen leaves as he went, he found the ring on the pavement. Jeanette, of course, was relieved and delighted and asked David what he wanted as a 'reward' so he asked her to make him a pasty as she was a real expert. This she did and even after Jeannette had retired from playing in 1995 David would often call on her in Camborne, on his way home from school and enjoy one of her pasties.

David's 'Cornishness', too, endeared him to people and he, in turn, both valued and enjoyed being among his own people. The Orchestral Society had had a banner made to put across the front of St John's Hall to advertise the concerts and it needed repair. David took it to the sail maker in New Street in Penzance, who asked David what his connection with the orchestra was and David told him he was the conductor. "Never 'eard of 'ee", said the old man. "Well", said David, "I succeeded Morgan Hosking". "Never 'eard ob'm" said the sail maker. "He succeeded Maddern Williams", went on David, "Never 'eard ob'm" repeated the old gentleman. David tried again, "Well, he succeeded the founder of the orchestra, Walter Barnes", and this time the response was, "Everybody 'eard of 'im. He was everything to do with music". The conversation continued and David asked how long the sail maker had been in business there and the reply was typically Cornish, "shouldn' be 'ere at all, 'tis ten minutes pas' closin' time"! Time was short for the repair, but the work was carried out promptly by "the girls", all elderly ladies, and the banner restored in time to advertise the concert.

So this was the young man who bravely took over the baton intending to conduct the orchestra for a few years, but who stayed for twenty. While continuity and stability was ensured they were to be years of change, with many members succumbing to age and infirmity, costs rising as never before, and the 'turn over' of players greatly accelerated as younger members joined but quickly moved on to pastures new to pursue their education outside Cornwall. But they would be years in which celebrations would continue through the passing decades with great music and excellent soloists upholding the achievements of the past sixty-five years.

On through the Eighties and Nineties 1981-1997

David Ball's First Concert

At the first concert under their new conductor the Penzance Orchestral Society presented a generally familiar face to the large audience in St John's Hall on Friday 27th November 1981. But there were noticeable changes, chief among them being the Principal Violin, Joyce Preston, whose capable and familiar presence must have provided both confidence and reassurance to David Ball. Paddy Pinchen had retired from her position as leader of the second violins, with Helen Barton now in her place. The woodwind and brass sections, too, included some new young players but the changes were a small proportion of the whole. One minor but pleasant innovation was that the list of instrumentalists in the concert programme became less formal, with Christian names used for the first time and titles (Mr, Mrs, Miss etc) dropped.

The soloist was a young trumpeter, Philip Cesar, who performed Haydn's E flat Trumpet Concerto. He was not the Society's original choice of soloist and was still a student at the Royal Northern College of Music. The *Western Morning News* critic, Robert Earl, felt that although he produced a full sound he still lacked the virtuosity and brilliance of tone which the concerto demanded. But David Ball's debut as conductor received warm words of praise in the same report.

In Schubert's Ninth Symphony – the Great C Major – David's "firm but unflamboyant approach", had steered the orchestra through its four movements with "an unfaltering drive, warmth and energy". Glinka's overture to 'Russlan and Ludmilla', opened the concert which also included the 'Peer Gynt Suite No. 1' by Grieg. The audience was left with a feeling of relief that this new partnership between orchestra and conductor would prove to be a satisfactory one. Morgan Hosking was amongst them and felt, somewhat judiciously, that David had made "a very good start".

Following the interval Morgan found himself on stage once more, but this time as the recipient of a cheque from the orchestra and friends to mark their appreciation of his thirty-five years as conductor. David Ball paid an eloquent tribute to his predecessor and Enid Truman, as President of the Society, made the presentation. (Morgan was amused that Enid, his old friend of over fifty years, referred to him throughout her brief speech as "Mr Hosking", but this was typical of Enid's reserve and sense of propriety.) Morgan responded with both humour and sadness in his speech but stressed his confidence in David who, he said, was blessed with, "the priceless asset of Newlyn origins".

And so, having navigated through potentially troubled waters, the sturdy vessel that was the Penzance Orchestral Society unfurled its sails and went forward, once more, into calmer waters. Paul Searle-Barnes provided a "tour de force" performance of Beethoven's Piano Concerto No. 1 in C Major in April 1982 with the orchestra acquitting itself well in the other major work of the programme, Dvorak's 'Symphony No. 8 in G Major, Op 88'.

Long Service Recognitions

At this concert the first of a series of presentations, which occurred through the next few years, was made to two viola players in recognition of their fifty years membership of the Society. Gwyneth Andrewartha's first concert as a member of the orchestra had been in the spring of 1932 so she had played under all four of the Society's conductors. She had been the leader of the viola section for many years but this was to be her final concert and her ability as a player as well as her bright, friendly face would be missed. Her position was to be filled by the second recipient of a presentation that evening, Norman Truman, who had joined as a violinist in November 1931, transferring to the viola section in 1946. He was also the Society's financial backbone, having been their Hon.Treasurer since 1951. In November 1982 Jeanette Powell and Jack Glasson were similarly recognised for their fifty years service to the orchestra. Norman Truman and Jack Glasson were to continue playing for a few more years but Jeanette Powell played on in the 'cello section until 1995, and maintained her life-long connection with the Society until her death in 2005.

Recognition of a different kind was given in February 1984 to the Orchestral Society's double bass player, Mrs Nora Horsfall, and took the form of a celebration of her ninetieth birthday. A surprise party was arranged by the Society and held at Trevethoe, the lovely home of Rose Tempest, where members of the orchestra gathered and accompanied the singing of 'Happy Birthday' to greet Mrs Horsfall on her arrival. She was thought to be the oldest woman in England still playing regularly in an amateur orchestra, and this fact captured the attention of the media. As well as articles and pictures in the local press a short film of Mrs Horsfall in rehearsal was made by the BBC for the 'Spotlight South-West' programme, which she coped with graciously but felt it was "very contrived".

Nora Horsfall cutting her ninetieth birthday cake, Trevethoe, February 1984.

Nora Horsfall

Nora was born in Garstang, Lancashire, the daughter of a doctor. The family was a musical one and living far from the nearest town a music room was built so that they could make their own entertainment. During the war Nora came to Cornwall where a childhood friend was the Vicar at St Erth, a few miles from Penzance. They wanted to marry, but the Rev. Horsfall felt that Nora was not cut out to be a vicar's wife so they waited until his forthcoming retirement before doing so, but sadly he died after only three months of marriage.

Nora remained in Cornwall and joined the Penzance Orchestral Society in the autumn of 1945 as a violinist and music was to become the dominant feature of her life. She moved to Penzance, and in 1954 the orchestra needed another double bass player so Mrs Horsfall volunteered to take it up. Within a short time she was competent enough to join the double bass section, eventually becoming its leader. She was physically suited to this large instrument being a tall and upright lady, and along with Graham White and, later, Nora Page, the double bass section presented an impressive 'line-up'. Once her ability on the double bass became known Nora Horsfall was in great demand throughout the county, playing with the Cornwall Symphony Orchestra as well as many choral and operatic society orchestras in the area.

By the time of her ninetieth birthday Nora was a popular and greatly respected figure in musical circles and the wider community. She had been trained as a needlewoman at the Royal School of Needlework specialising in lace-making and tapestry and had, in her younger days, represented England in archery at national contests. Gardening was another of her interests and wherever she lived, if there was a garden, she turned it into an area of beauty, because whatever Nora Horsfall decided to do she did it well and to the best of her ability.

She had a disciplined approach to life and her days followed a strict routine with a certain amount of time allocated to various activities. There was a time for embroidery, for reading, for practising the double bass in the Bandroom, for resting, and so on. Each day was planned and the timetable adhered to. Her imposing stature and deep, cultured voice gave her an air of authority and demanded respect and she did not waste words on trivial conversation. But beneath this rather forbidding exterior was a lady of great generosity, kindness and subdued humour. Her pleasure in the party arranged for her special birthday was genuine and unfeigned, and the respect she was always accorded by members of the orchestra was combined with real affection and appreciation of a gentlewoman in the truest sense of the word. This was exemplified by the fact that most of her good friends in the orchestra would never have thought of using her Christian name, she was always "Mrs" Horsfall.

Responding to her ninetieth birthday Mrs Horsfall said, "I don't feel as old as all that and if they will still have me in the orchestra I shall be happy playing bass as long as I can". Sadly, she was a victim of an epidemic of influenza following her birthday which prevented her from taking part in the April 1984 concert and caused her to retire from further orchestral perform-

ances. At the end of her life she lived in a residential home in Penzance but continued to take a close interest in the Orchestral Society until her death in July 1990, at the age of ninety-six.

The next four concert seasons were very successful ones for the Orchestral Society, with distinguished soloists providing exciting performances. Nicholas Cox, clarinet, and Michael Evans, 'cello, presented concertos by Weber and Elgar during the 1982-83 season, and Susan Tomes played Mozart's Piano Concerto No. 23 in A Major, K488 in November 1983. These performances were complimented by varied and demanding programmes for the orchestra, including symphonies by Brahms, Schumann and Dvorak.

In April 1984 the concert featured two guest artistes, the husband and wife 'duo' of Bernard Partridge and Antonina Bialas. They were both highly regarded violinists and came to Penzance through their friendship with the family of Helen Caseley, who had recently retired from playing double bass in the orchestra. Bernard Partridge performed the Tchaikovsky Violin Concerto in the first half of the concert, and they combined to play Vivaldi's 'Concerto for two Violins, Strings and Continuo Op. 3, No. 8' after the interval. This well received concert took place despite several members of the orchestra succumbing to the 'flu epidemic, and both Enid and Norman Truman were missing from their usual seats in the 'cello and viola sections. Christopher Elston, viola player with the Duchy Quartet, and a member of the Orchestral Society for a few years before he left the area to join a Franciscan friary, replaced Norman as Principal Viola at this concert.

An Influx of Young Blood

Press reports of concerts during the early eighties often referred to an influx of younger players into the orchestra, especially among the woodwind and brass sections, which, according to Robert Earl "gave welcome sturdiness and sweetness" to these sections. This continual ingress of competent 'new blood' was due, in no small part, to the valuable work being carried out by peripatetic music teachers in the county, such as Elizabeth Robertson, Lynda Ayton and David Frost, among others. They produced able young instrumentalists and encouraged them to join groups and ensembles including the Orchestral Society. The string sections, too, benefited enormously from the ability of these trained musicians, Joyce Preston being a notable example. Many of her pupils have become proficient performers as professional violinists and their time in the Orchestral Society, even if relatively short, was always appreciated.

Two concertos were once again in the programme for the opening concert of the 1984-85 season, when the talented young horn player, Jonathan Williams, performed Richard Strauss's Horn Concerto No. 1 as well as the Concerto No. 3 in E Flat Major by Mozart. This concert also included substantial excerpts from Schubert's Incidental Music to 'Rosamunde', in which Catherine Pearce was the soloist in the 'Romance' for soprano and orchestra. The printed programme was produced with the support of local businesses, three of whom each 'donated' a page, an innovation which was to continue for a number of seasons.

The concert, held on 22nd March 1985, was a memorable one for the inclusion of a premier performance of 'The Green Cockade' by local composer and conductor, Geoffrey Self. He chose four traditional melodies identified with West Cornwall, and from these created a set of orchestral diversions full of character and colour. The composer was present to take a bow at the end of the performance, and wrote to David Ball afterwards thanking him for "midwifing my piece into life... your orchestra vindicated my transparent style of orchestration – it wouldn't come off with less confident players".

The soloist at this concert was the versatile mezzo-soprano, Susan Tyrrell, and for her visit David had gathered together a male chorus for a performance of the beautiful 'Alto Rhapsody' by Brahms. Two dozen of the area's finest tenors and basses formed the choir to sing in the final 'Adagio' movement, joining the soloist and orchestra to bring the work to its consoling conclusion. Susan Tyrrell also sang three of the songs from Elgar's 'Sea Pictures', and the concert was brought to a close by a performance of Haydn's 'Military' Symphony No. 100 in G Major.

The Orchestral Society was approaching another of its ten-yearly celebrations, but there was one more season to go. The press reports of the two concerts during the winter and spring of 1985-86 were full of praise and warmth, and heralded a promising response to the 80th Anniversary concert in November 1986. Michael Bochmann, by now pursuing a successful career as leader of the Bochmann String Quartet, returned to Penzance to play the Brahms

Violin Concerto in November 1985. The performances of both soloist and orchestra were complimented, *The Cornishman* reporting "some magical passages" in the concerto. Members of the orchestra, Joyce Preston and Pamela Rosenfeld, violinists, and Jayne Poynton, 'cello were soloists in Handel's Concerto Grosso No. 1 in G Major for strings, with the harpsichord continuo played by Russell Jory.

Oboe and cor anglais concerti were presented at the spring concert in 1986 performed by the up and coming young Greek oboist, Marios Argiros. This was a rare opportunity for the audience to hear the cor anglais as a solo instrument and Donizetti's 'Concertino in G Major', a set of variations, showed the musical colours of which the instrument is capable. The orchestra took on the challenge of playing Benjamin Britten's 'The Young Person's Guide to the Orchestra' which makes great demands on every section of the orchestra. They all shone in this set of variations on a theme by Purcell, and the performance received a great ovation.

Norman Truman.

The Death of Norman Truman

The final work in the concert was Dvorak's 'New World' Symphony and David Ball announced that its performance would be dedicated to the memory of Norman Truman, who had died just over a week before the concert. This was a great sadness for the Society and its loyal supporters because Norman, along with his wife Enid, had been at the heart of both its music-making and administration for as long as most people could remember. The Dvorak Symphony, and especially the 'Largo' movement, was a fitting tribute to Norman's fifty-five years of devotion to the Society. Later in the year a trust fund was established in his memory to help young musicians further their musical career. Following Enid Truman's death in June 2001 it was felt that her name should be adjoined to that of her late husband in the Trust's title. It remains active in helping young musicians from West Cornwall by assisting them in the purchase of instruments and their accessories.

There had been other significant losses for the orchestra to bear at this time with the deaths of Gerald Cluer and Rosemary Lane, both members of the 'cello section, and violinist Audrey Morcom, who had been in the orchestra since 1967 and was the Subscriptions Secretary at the time of her death. Also, other long-standing members retired from playing for various reasons. Marjorie Farnham and her mother who had joined the Society in 1958 moved away from Cornwall, though Marjorie did return in 1990 resuming her place in the violin section and is, happily, still playing.

Helen Barton, who had led the second violins for a number of years, retired in 1985 along with timpanist Robin Whitehead. Helen, who had been a widow for many years, and Robin had both joined the Society in 1950 and their departure after so many years drew attention to the changing face of the orchestra. But their orchestral friends were among many who welcomed the happy news of their marriage on 20th June 1987, when David Ball was the organist at the ceremony in St Erth church. The young ones came and went as the demands of their education and careers dictated, but their departure was always recorded with regret along with the hopes that they would return in the future.

On the eve of their 80th Anniversary Concert in November 1986 the Penzance Orchestral Society was in good heart. The passing years had taken its toll on a body of players which had formed a stable nucleus throughout previous decades but these changes were inevitable. Financially the Society was still benefiting from Mrs Garstin's legacy, with a substantial deposit account yielding valuable interest each year.

Concerts, generally, covered their costs though this was only possible by raising ticket prices at intervals and with the support of the subscribers, donations, and occasional grants. They retained their valuable assets in the form of the Bandroom, piano, harp, tymps and other instruments, as well as a large library of music. Overall, concerts were well attended and press reports favourable but, most importantly, the Society had the commitment and enthusiasm of its young conductor, David Ball, and its leader, Joyce Preston, supported by active and experienced committee members.

Plans for the celebratory concert had been discussed as early as May 1985 and were firmly in place by the spring of 1986 with the celebrated pianist, Yitkin Seow, engaged to play Rachmaninov's Second Piano concerto. This was not Yitkin Seow's first visit to Cornwall because he had played in a recital given at Trevethoe in 1973, held under the auspices of the Royal Overseas League. On this occasion he contributed piano works by Beethoven, Chopin, Liszt and Debussy as well as accompanying his fellow artiste, soprano Meryl Drower. Neither was it to be his one and only appearance with the Penzance Orchestral Society.

An Octogenarian Society

Eighty years that span the reigns of five monarchs... years that have seen seventeen different Prime Ministers and twenty-five governments; years when the horse, the railroad, the great ocean liners have given way in popularity to the giant in the sky, the air-liner. Events once thousands of miles away and years removed in time, flash immediately upon us by satellite. Man has set foot on the moon, performs huge calculations by computer magic. Two great wars have shaken the world and rocked accepted bases of society. Yet through all this, in a small town, a long way from seats of learning and of power, an amateur body, dedicated to music, has moved steadily from its beginnings in 1906 to its mature character today.

These words, written by Gladys Tranter, and printed in the Eightieth Anniversary concert programme, were an evocative reminder of the cause for celebration on the evening of Friday 28th November 1986 in St John's Hall, Penzance. It was the 244th concert by the Penzance Orchestral Society and all seats had been sold in advance, with queues at the door on the night. There were many old friends present among the audience, which included civic representatives from the town and district councils – both of which had contributed sums of money towards the special birthday event. Amongst them was Morgan Hosking joined, in spirit if not in the flesh, by his old friend and mentor, Walter Barnes, whose portrait was on display, acknowledging that the occasion was due to his initiative and foresight eighty years earlier.

The programme of music was well chosen to reflect both the mood of celebration and the 'style' of the orchestra over the years. Dvorak's cheerful and lively concert overture 'Carnival' opened the proceedings after the traditional playing of 'God Save the Queen', and was followed by Yitkin Seow's performance of Rachmaninov's 'Piano Concerto No. 2 in C Minor'. The second half of the concert began with Tchaikovsky's Ballet Suite 'The Sleeping Beauty', after which the string section performed 'Two Elegiac Melodies' by Grieg, based on songs which he wrote in 1880, and the concert ended with Elgar's 'Three Bavarian Dances'.

Douglas Williams, writer and musician, had written a preview of the concert and he followed it up with reports of the performance printed in both the *Western Morning News* and *The Cornishman*. He evoked the festive atmosphere and wrote of the virtuosic performance of Yitkin Seow who not only dazzled the audience with his brilliant technique but "captured the hearts and minds of a rapt audience". The soloist inspired the orchestra which "brought touches of deep loveliness to its accompaniment".

Celebrations continued a few days later with a dinner at the Porthminster Hotel, St Ives where a toast to the orchestra was proposed by Morgan Hosking. The Society's President, Enid Truman, proposed a toast to the invited guests, to which Douglas Williams made a response, and in charge of the proceedings was Michael Tunstall-Behrens as toastmaster. A splendid birthday

Penzance Orchestral Society, 80th Anniversary, November 1986, with David Ball, Conductor and Yitkin Seow, Soloist.

cake had been made and was ceremoniously cut by the orchestral leader, Joyce Preston, and there was music for dancing to round off the evening.

The Anniversary season concluded with the concert in early April 1987 when the soloist was 'cellist, Barbara Grunthal. She had participated in masterclasses with Ralph Kirschbaum and William Pleeth at the International Musicians Seminars at Prussia Cove, and was a major prize-winner. Her playing of Haydn's Concerto in C Major delighted the large audience, who also enjoyed the orchestra's performance of Sibelius's 'Finlandia' and Brahms' Third Symphony. Excellent audiences at both concerts of the season resulted in a profit at the end of the financial year of over £265, despite the Anniversary concert incurring costs of £1,380.

The Desecration of St Mary's Church

In March 1985 the people of Penzance and district were shocked by the scene following a huge fire at St Mary's Church. There was extensive damage to the beautiful interior; the marble high altar was destroyed along with the 100 year old organ, the reredos and ceiling. Twenty-four hours later, on Passion Sunday, a service was held when the vicar, Canon Robin Osborne, led prayers for the restoration of the church during its 150th anniversary year. It took two years and nearly half a million pounds to restore the building to a new, glorious resurrection from the debris of the fire, which had been started by a mentally disturbed youth

Penzance Orchestral Society was invited to give one of the concerts to celebrate its re-opening. Initially planned for the spring of 1988, it was brought forward to November 1987 due to St John's Hall undergoing electrical repairs. The programme was selected to take advantage of the newly installed organ at St Mary's, with the Saint-Saëns 'Organ' Symphony taking pride of place, and because this involved the use of a piano, Mozart's 'Piano Concerto No. 24 in C Minor. K491' was also chosen. In addition a Handel Organ Concerto, No. 4 in F Major, was to be played. Russell Jory, organist at St Mary's, involved in the planning for this concert, was the soloist in the two organ works. George Shutter, head of music at Helston Comprehensive School, was invited to perform the piano concerto and to join Louise Luing, a violinist with the orchestra, at the piano in the Saint-Saëns Symphony.

It was a memorable evening for both performers and audience alike. The re-dedicated church resounded to the music of William Walton's mighty Coronation March, 'Crown Imperial' which began the concert, providing real contrast to the more restrained mood of the Mozart piano concerto. George Shutter was well able to portray the range of emotion and colour in this work, revealing his considerable talent as a keyboard player. In his turn, Russell Jory showed off the qualities of the new organ to great effect in the Handel Concerto.

These musicians were both well known in the musical life of West Cornwall and had devoted their careers to teaching and encouraging young people to appreciate music. They also gave freely of their leisure time, George specialising in keyboard accompaniment on piano and harpsichord, and Russell as a conductor as well as organist. They had both worked with the Orchestral Society on a number of occasions and this concert was a timely acknowledgement of their great contribution to the community. Russell Jory's many years of service to music-making was recognised in September 2006, when he was awarded the Cornish Gorsedd's Music Shield

Saint-Saëns' Symphony No. 3 provided an opportunity for everyone involved to demonstrate their ability and the audience responded warmly with a standing ovation bringing an evening of thanksgiving through the joy of music to its end. Receipts were great enough on this occasion for the Society to make a substantial donation to the church and to the Malcolm Sargent Cancer Fund for Children, but still have over £150 to add to their own funds.

With this concert the next decade of the Orchestral Society was underway and the last years of the nineteen-eighties saw distinguished soloists joining the Orchestral Society. Gina McCormack played the ever-popular Max Bruch Violin Concerto, Vanessa Latarche performed Beethoven's Piano Concerto No. 4, and David Mason presented an experienced and masterly interpretation of Hummel's 'Trumpet Concerto in E Flat Major' in March 1989. This last concerto produced some amusing review headlines such as "Music taken as red!" in the *Western Morning News*, referring to the concert coinciding with Comic Relief Day and David Ball discovering a "red nose" planted on the end of his baton at the start of the concert.

The orchestra contributed performances of exciting and sometimes rarely heard works, for example Luigi Cherubini's Overture 'Anacreon' in March 1988 and Sir Charles Mackerras's arrangement of tunes from Sullivan's operettas in the Ballet Suite 'Pineapple Poll'. This had not

been played by the Penzance orchestra since 1955, which is quite surprising given the popularity of the Gilbert and Sullivan operettas in the area over many years.

A major challenge for the orchestra was taken on successfully with a second performance in 1988 of Elgar's 'Enigma' Variations. This produced moments of "inspired playing" as well as some anxious ones, according to Morgan Hosking in his occasional role as music critic for the local press. Both demanding and rarely heard 'live' in Cornwall was the Brahms 'Double' concerto which was played in November 1989 with soloists Matthew Taylor, violin and Keith Tempest, 'cello.

The 250th Concert

This concert celebrated the Orchestral Society's 250th performance and in his speech at this special concert David Ball paid tribute to the Society's founder, Walter Barnes, wondering whether he had ever visualised his orchestra giving its 250th concert. Two familiar faces were missing from the ranks of the orchestra that night, as both Enid Truman and Michael Tunstall-Behrens had decided to retire as playing members. They were present to receive gifts as a token of their long service and the affection in which they were held. David also acknowledged his debt to officers of the Society such as Rose Tempest their Hon. Secretary, Elizabeth Rowe, the Librarian and especially his Principal Violin, Joyce Preston. Joyce had already received public acknowledgement of her contribution to the musical life of Cornwall a year earlier when she had been awarded the Gorsedd Shield for music.

The years rolled inexorably onwards taking the Penzance Orchestral Society through the final concert seasons of the twentieth century in which talented young soloists, at the beginning of promising careers, delighted Penzance audiences. Some were known to the area, either because of local connections, such as Neil McLaren who had been principal flautist with the Cornwall Youth Orchestra, or from their performances during the International Musicians Seminar at Prussia Cove. Others were more experienced and well-known, such as the viola player, Keith Lovell, who played Berlioz' 'Harold in Italy' with the orchestra in April 1992 just as he had done fourteen years earlier.

This spring season concert had to be held in St Mary's Church due to it being General Election Day when St John's Hall was in use for the election count. Geoffrey Self was once more in the audience to listen to the performance of his suite, 'Mr Playford's Fancy', based on familiar tunes and dances published by John Playford in the late seventeenth century. In a letter to David Ball following this concert Geoffrey, in typically modest fashion, said that his composition did not offer any great thoughts, "only confections to tickle the palate, but the care you... lavished on them is deeply appreciated".

It was party time once again, on 21st October 1992, for another nonagenarian member of the orchestra. Gladys Tranter had been a member of the 'cello section since 1963 and had now reached her ninetieth birthday. The orchestra responded with a surprise party at Trevethoe where many old friends gathered. There was music, of course, and birthday tributes to Gladys made by David Ball, Enid Truman and Morgan Hosking, as well as gifts, supper and a birthday cake.

Gladys M. Tranter ('Trant')

Close friends and former pupils of Gladys knew her by the name of 'Trant', which she encouraged people to call her. But to others she was always 'Miss Tranter', though this in no way indicated any lack of affection. When she died, early in 2000 at the age of ninety-seven, her life and career in Penzance received the public acknowledgement it so richly deserved. Her thirty-six years as an English teacher and senior mistress at Penzance Girls' Grammar School, her Presidency of the Penzance Choral Society and membership of the Orchestral Society, her many other interests and skills in painting, pottery, needlework and nature, all contributed to a portrayal of a remarkable lady.

Her funeral service at Penmount Crematorium, Truro, led by her close friend and colleague, Vivienne Mostyn, revealed the many facets of her personality which made Gladys Tranter so universally loved and respected. Later, her memory was preserved in the form of a sundial erected in Penlee Gardens, Penzance, commissioned by the Old Girls' Association of the Girls Grammar School. Its inscription, "She Enlightened Our Lives" is true for her many former pupils, and her active and productive life in nearly forty years of retirement enriched all those who knew her.

Gladys Tranter at her ninetieth birthday party, Trevethoe, October 1992.

It was not until she retired from teaching, in 1963, that Gladys Tranter joined the orchestra after she had been having 'cello lessons with Enid Truman for some time. But her links with the Orchestral Society spanned many previous decades. She had known Walter Barnes in her early days as a teacher, when her school productions of drama and opera involved him as musical director, as has been described. A regular member of the audience for orchestral and choral concerts in the town she knew the musical scene of Penzance and its personalities very well. She was, therefore, well qualified to write brief accounts of the Orchestral Society's history, as she did in 1966 and 1986 in its anniversary programmes. These comprehensive but concise and entertaining summaries show Gladys's imaginative use of language and were a valuable contribution to these special concerts.

Miss Tranter took an active interest in the running of the Orchestral Society, frequently sitting on its committee, and was a prime mover in organising members to produce goods for sales of work and bazaars when fund raising was needed. Even after retiring from playing in the orchestra in 1993 she would come by taxi to sit in on rehearsals and followed progress with keen interest.

Her skills as an artist and needlewoman were also at the disposal of the Orchestral Society, when she worked with Enid Truman, or on her own, to create beautifully embroidered panels for presentation to prominent members of the Society on significant occasions. These skills were in evidence in her own home in St Michael's Terrace, too, where the door was always open, literally, to her many friends. A visit to Trant was a delight and in her declining years, though physically frail and incapacitated, her lively interest in everything and everybody never dimmed. Her long memory and ever-present sense of humour, combined with courtesy and concern, also remained for guests to enjoy. Her generosity of spirit is epitomised in her letter to David Ball following the birthday party – "it was a lovely, lovely evening....thank you – not just for one evening"!

Yitkin Seow to the Rescue

The 1992-93 season was a very successful one for the Society both musically and financially with both concerts making a profit after expenses were paid. Violinist Laurence Jackson was the soloist in Beethoven's Violin Concerto in the autumn, and Yitkin Seow returned to Penzance for the April 1993 concert. This was a welcome surprise for the orchestra because the young Bulgarian born pianist, Lora Dimitrova, had been invited to play the Second Piano concerto by Brahms. However, she was expecting a baby, and had become too exhausted to carry out her engagements, and the Penzance Orchestral Society were left with only about a week to replace her with another soloist who could perform the concerto.

Agencies were approached and one said that Yitkin Seow was available but that he was not terribly familiar with the Brahms and would need to use the score. Russell Jory was asked to turn pages for this internationally renowned pianist, but by the time Yitkin Seow arrived for the final rehearsal he had done his homework and didn't need the music. His performance inspired the orchestra to rise to the occasion which Douglas Williams regarded as, "among the great accomplishments of the Society in its 81 year history".

A Final Tribute to Morgan Hosking

Morgan's death on 14th September 1993 was noted by the Society at their Annual General Meeting a month later when it was announced that the next concert would be a memorial to him, and that a performance of Wagner's 'Siegfried Idyll' would be specifically dedicated to his memory. This took place on Friday 26th November, when Michael Chapman, principal bassoon with the Royal Philharmonic Orchestra, was the soloist. A photograph of Morgan in his well-remembered white dinner-jacket accompanied a three page tribute in the concert programme written by Miss Tranter. The music chosen for this concert, in addition to the 'Siegfied Idyll', would have pleased Morgan, comprising works from the post-classical and romantic repertoire and included two dances from George Lloyd's opera 'John Socman'.

Once asked what he would like to do on his eightieth birthday Morgan had jokingly replied that he would like to conduct Wagner's 'Siegfried Idyll'. He died just two weeks before

reaching this birthday so it was entirely appropriate that the music was played at his memorial concert and there was a period of silence at its conclusion in place of the usual applause. The choice of music by George Lloyd was a timely coincidence, bearing in mind that he and Morgan Hosking had been young violinists together in the orchestra and Morgan had followed the composer's career with interest and pride.

Douglas Williams, writing in the local papers, referred to these associations with Morgan Hosking in his review of the concert, and spoke admiringly of Michael Chapman's performance of the Weber concerto. He brought an "apparent effortless ease and quality" and "a stream of delightful melody" to the rarely heard work. The orchestra's performance of the 'Siegfied Idyll' captured its mood of romance and mystery, which contributed to a poignant occasion for both players and audience as they paid their musical respects to their late 'maestro' and friend.

Morgan Hosking.

Home-Grown Soloists

Soloists with local connections or of Cornish birth were to the fore at concerts during 1994 and 1995. In March 1994 a rarely performed work by Mozart, his 'Concerto for Two Pianos and Orchestra', was performed by two gifted pianists both of whom lived and worked in Cornwall. Peter Jolley, an exponent of the organ and harpsichord as well as the piano, was Head of Music at Penwith College, Penzance and his partner in the Mozart, Paul Comeau, was well known in Cornwall as a soloist and piano teacher. The presence of two pianos on the stage of St John's Hall was an unusual spectacle for the audience, with further drama in the orchestral works by Rossini, Beethoven, Rimsky-Korsakov and Borodin – his Symphony No. 2 in B Minor.

One of Europe's finest harpists, Susan Drake, gave a "double bill" at the November 1994 concert when she played Handel's 'Harp Concerto No. 6', better known as an organ concerto but admirably suited to the harp. A late work for harp and orchestra by Saint-Saëns, the 'Morceau De Concert' was the second 'concerto' by Susan Drake which provided "further evidence of (her) exceptional talent", according to the *Western Morning News*. The Society again recognised the occurrence of Children in Need coinciding with its concert, and the income from programmes sales was donated to the cause on this occasion.

The two soloists at the next concert in April 1995 were both natives of Penzance. It was a proud evening for the Orchestral Society, and especially its Principal Violin, Joyce Preston, because the violin soloist, Kay Chappell, was one of her former pupils, and had been a member of the orchestra before leaving the town to pursue her studies at Chetham's School in Manchester. Kay maintained her links with music in West Cornwall and reappeared in the orchestra from time to time, and had already appeared as a soloist in the town with the St Mary's Sinfonia in 1990 and 1992. On this occasion she played Beethoven's 'Romance in F' for violin and orchestra which was "quite lovely in its lyric quality, and impeccable intonation" and her performance of Sarasate's spectacular 'Zigeunerweisen' showed "virtuoso playing of the highest quality".

Local boy, Richard Jackson, made his first appearance in St John's Hall as a teenager and now returned as a highly acclaimed baritone soloist. He was particularly well known as a founder member ofThe Songmaker's Almanac, with pianist Graham Johnston, but had also sung with major opera companies as well as teaching at prestigious music colleges in England. He sang Mahler's song-cycle 'Lieder eines fahrenden Gesellen' (Songs of a Wayfarer) and Strauss's beautiful song, 'Morgen', as well as the 'Salt Water Ballads', a setting by Frederick Keel of four poems by John Masefield. Less expected from this accomplished lieder singer was his choice of Bach's 'Gebt mir meinem Jesum wieder' from the St Matthew Passion, but it surely pleased the choral singing members of the audience. As well as accompanying the soloists the orchestra began the concert with William Alwyn's 'Suite of Scottish Dances', and ended it with a performance of Brahms' 'Symphony No. 4'.

Once more the Orchestral Society was approaching an anniversary, with the 1996-1997 season on the horizon. But there were two more concerts to go and piano and clarinet were the solo instruments chosen for the 1995-96 season. Andrew West returned, in the midst of a burgeoning career, to perform the Beethoven 'Piano Concerto No. 3 in C Minor' at the November 1995 concert. In March 1996 the young Guy Cowley, heard at Prussia Cove two years earlier, played two clarinet works with the orchestra, the 'Concertino Op. 26' by Weber and Rossini's 'Introduction and Variations'.

As the Orchestral Society prepared for its ninetieth anniversary concert on Friday 22nd November 1996 there was little doubt about its continuity and survival. But the preceding years had not been without their problems and anxieties and some of these, along with administrative achievements and changes, merit some attention.

Behind the Scenes 1986-96

In any orchestra the essential component is, of course, its instrumentalists; they are what audiences hear and provide the image of the organisation which remains in the memory. Even a conductor has no function without them and, in most amateur orchestras, one of his areas of responsibility is to select and gather together musicians to make up a balanced ensemble.

During David Ball's conductorship of the Orchestral Society this task became more time-consuming and difficult than ever before. An analysis of orchestral members shows a much greater 'turnover' of players from the mid-nineteen eighties onwards in all sections of the orchestra. The passing years were taking effect with many long-serving players retiring. Around a nucleus of established members each section shows new names appearing, some to remain for lengthy periods, others coming and going more fleetingly.

This, in itself, was not a problem because many of the incoming instrumentalists were very able and an injection of new blood was both healthy and desirable. Press reports frequently commented on the appearance of new, younger players and the resulting improvement of sound in this or that section of the orchestra. However, recruitment was not always easy and the committee minutes often refer to this problem. Advertising in the local press yielded little response and often the best source of instrumentalists was through the peripatetic teachers in the orchestra who brought in their ablest pupils. It was an on-going problem and David, who found the onerous task of ringing or writing to potential players increasingly burdensome, was grateful when others, such as Piers Owen during the late nineties, were willing to help with this work.

Irregular attendance at rehearsals was another recurring problem, and in November 1996 David expressed real concern for the orchestra's future. The tendency was that those asked to play would not commit themselves to coming regularly to rehearsals until late in the rehearsal period. This not only caused them to be ill-prepared for a performance but was unfair on regular attenders and on David as conductor. If sections were weak or lacked players completely, as could happen among the woodwind and brass, satisfactory steady progress was impossible with work on the music needing to be repeated for those who had missed previous practice sessions.

There were plenty of young instrumentalists available, but also the opportunities for them to play in other groups had increased over the years. Their commitment was no longer to one organisation and so their musical energies were dispersed and fragmented. The more experienced, professionally trained instrumentalists and teachers had many demands on their time, too, and with greater expertise sometimes felt that they did not need so much rehearsal time as the true amateurs. This may well have been the case, but creating the unity and cohesion needed to maintain standards of performance was very difficult under these patchy rehearsal conditions.

Development and change in the musical life of West Cornwall, which affected performing musicians, were also reflected in the audiences at Orchestral Society concerts. These fluctuated from season to season and could not be confidently predicted. Press reports occasionally commented on empty seats in St John's Hall, and in December 1992 a supportive member of the audience wrote to *The Cornishman* pointing out the outstanding performance of the violin soloist, Laurence Jackson, but chastising the musical public for not filling the hall to ensure future concerts.

Concert seasons more often than not covered their costs despite a relentless increase in soloist's fees and overall expenses. Some years saw a substantial profit, as at the end of 1991, when £791 was contributed to the Society's income from concert profits. When losses

occurred they could sometimes be explained, as in the spring of 1992 when the concert had to be held in St Mary's Church and a smaller seating capacity combined with a bad night of weather resulted in a loss of over £280. In other years concert losses reflected a financial year when overall revenue did not match the necessary expenditure, for no obvious reason.

Another noticeable decline during these years was in the number of subscribers to the Society. These regular supporters had not been listed in the concert programmes for over twenty years, but they continued to exist, and the income from tickets bought by them has been recorded in the annual accounts. In 1964 the subscribers totalled 194 but by 1996 this figure had dropped to 39. Even by 1986 ticket sales to subscribers had reduced considerably as a proportion of total tickets sold, and this trend continued.

As names disappeared from the subscriber's list they became more difficult to replace. It was no longer an era when subscribing to the Orchestral Society was seen almost as a social obligation among the music-lovers of Penzance and district. Potential concert goers were presented with many other musical events of high quality and felt able to distribute their patronage freely and spontaneously without making a commitment to any particular one.

Members' subscriptions caused problems, too, with frequent pleas at annual general meetings for them to be paid promptly and discussions in committee meetings as to whether they should be raised. As David Ball reminded members in 1989, when the membership subscription was £5, this was excellent value for money when compared with fees to join a London orchestra which were often as high as £40.

Ticket prices were raised on an irregular basis between 1986 and 1996. At the start of this period they stood at £2 and £1.50 and by the end of it had risen to £4.50 and £3.50. By this time the raised seating area in St John's Hall had been improved, with roomier more comfortable seats, which had slightly reduced the audience capacity so this had to be borne in mind. But it was the steady increase in soloists' fees and printing and advertising costs that necessitated rising ticket prices. Concert expenses went from just over £1,000 to well over £2,000 during these years.

The Penzance Orchestral Society was fortunate that it had a financial 'buffer' in the form of a capital sum which had been greatly boosted following the sale of Mrs Garstin's violin in 1972. It was kept very much as a reserve fund but was occasionally used when major expenditure became necessary.

In 1989 the Society became aware that two new pedal type tympani drums were needed and fund-raising ideas were put forward. This matter was discussed during the next two years but it was not until 1992 that the new tymps were acquired. One of the main fund-raising events was when Lord and Lady St Levan offered the Society an 'open day' on St Michael's Mount during the summer of that year, when £569 was raised. Expenditure on the tymps was nearly £2,500 but the reserve fund was there to bear this great cost.

Following the retirement of Norman Truman from the position of Hon. Treasurer in 1984 the post was held by Wilson Sadler, who alternated between the second violin and double bass sections. He left the Society in 1986 and Mr Peter Sanders, who was not a member of the Society, held the post until pressure of work forced him to resign during the 1989-90 financial year. Mark Belfied, another non-instrumentalist but with three family members in the orchestra, took over and remained as Hon. Treasurer for nine years.

There were other changes among the officers of the Society during the eighties and early nineties. After twenty years as the orchestra's Hon. Librarian Helen Barton gave up this demanding job in 1980 and was succeeded by Catherine Pearce who, in turn, was followed by Elizabeth Rowe in 1983. She carried out this work with diligence and efficiency until 1991. Sally Bardsley, 'cello and Geoffrey Pearson, clarinet, took over from her as joint Hon. Librarians and have continued until the present time, becoming Mr and Mrs Pearson along the way.

At the same time as her husband, Enid Truman retired from her position as Hon. Secretary in 1984, after an amazing twenty-four years, when Helen Caseley, a former member of the double bass section, replaced her in this demanding role. (Helen was often referred to as 'young Helen' to avoid confusion with her mother, Helen Barton). She handed the work on to Rose Tempest in 1985 who devoted twelve years to this important post.

During this period, Enid Truman continued as the Society's President, while the position of Committee Chairman was a more 'moveable feast' with various senior members of the Society being elected to the post. The position of Subscribers' Secretary was held by Catherine Pearce throughout these years until Eileen Woolmington took over from her in 1996. In the early nineties it was felt that someone should take on the publicity work for the concerts and Elizabeth Gregg, viola, was responsible for this until 1996.

These, then, were the willing souls who laid the plans for the forthcoming concert in celebration of the ninetieth season of the Penzance Orchestral Society and rehearsals got under way, as usual, in September 1996. It was not until the August of that year that the music was chosen, and although two works for piano soloist and orchestra were programmed the pianist still had to be announced. By the time the annual prospectus was distributed to Subscribers in the autumn the chosen soloist was Marie-Noëlle Kendall, a pianist with impressive credentials and an international reputation.

Ninetieth Anniversary

"Quality and elan from ninety-year-old!" was the headline given to Douglas Williams' report of this remarkable occasion, accompanied by a photograph of the soloist and orchestra on stage. The evening of Friday 22nd November 1996 saw many distinguished guests in the audience, including the Mayor of Penzance, Mrs Primrose May, Councillor Mrs Sonia Menadue representing the Penwith District Council, Lord and Lady St Levan, and eighty-six-year-old Enid Truman, whose life spanned all but three years of the Orchestral Society's existence.

The printed programme was a fairly modest one for such an important birthday; for some years 'mass produced' covers with the Walter Barnes logo had been in use to keep printing costs to a minimum. But photographs of the Society's four conductors, its leader, Joyce Preston and the solo pianist, as well as a list of Subscribers was added to the usual programme notes, with names of the orchestral members and a list of acknowledgements.

Musically it was an evening of celebratory sparkle and dignified splendour. The evening began, as always, with the National Anthem, then the concert opened with the overture, Franz von Suppe's 'Light Cavalry', which made a rousing and triumphant beginning. Marie-Noëlle Kendall then enthused the audience by a brilliant performance of the Grieg 'Piano Concerto in A Minor', with the orchestra giving sympathetic accompaniment. To provide the musical champagne bubbles both soloist and orchestra "rippled to their hearts content" in the delightful 'Scherzo' movement from Henry Litolff's 'Concerto Symphonique No. 4' which brought the first half of the concert to its end.

After the interval the orchestra "brought sustained playing of a high standard", to its performance of Beethoven's mighty 'Symphony No. 3 in E Flat', the 'Eroica'. David Ball and his orchestra conveyed the varied emotions of the symphony with "integrity and deep understanding". There was a string section of thirty-six and a total of over fifty members forming the orchestra on this occasion with players old and young combining their talent and skill to rise to the occasion. There was little doubt that the Penzance Orchestral Society would adapt to change and surmount on-going problems as it headed for the millennium.

The ninetieth concert season ended in March 1997 with a performance of some length but full of delight and variety, comprising music by Rossini, Mendelssohn, Elgar, Respighi, Saint-Saëns and Haydn. The soloist was the distinguished violinist, Leo Payne, whose career embraced solo, chamber and orchestral playing. He had been the leader of many prestigious orchestras and Professor of Violin at the Guildhall School of Music. On this occasion he was the soloist in Mendelssohn's ever-popular Violin Concerto and also the Saint-Saëns 'Introduction and Rondo Capriccioso'.

20 To the Millennium and Beyond 1998-2003

With the exception of Imogen Trimer, oboe, and Michael Evans, 'cello, all the soloists who played with the Penzance orchestra during the years taking it through to the twenty-first century were drawn from the talented pool of musicians living and working in West Cornwall. David Ball pointed out the high cost of engaging soloists to the Committee in June 1997, which had reached an average of £900 a season. They responded quickly to an offer from the National Federation of Music Societies for an oboe soloist who would play the Strauss Oboe Concerto free of charge, and Imogen Trimer was invited to Penzance in November 1997. She was in great demand internationally as a soloist and chamber performer, so the orchestra were fortunate to get her.

David Ball's suggestion that local soloists should be used in an effort to control rising expenses was acted upon over the next three seasons with notable success. In April 1998 Margaret Green, well known as a contralto soloist in the South West and a member of Duchy Opera, sang Elgar's 'Sea Pictures' in a concert which devoted its first half to English composers. Professional free-lance oboist, Peter O'Connor, who had friends in West Cornwall and often came down to play in local musical productions and concerts, offered his services to the Orchestral Society, once again free of charge. He performed two works in December 1998, the Mozart 'Flute Concerto in G' and the showy 'Concertino in D' by the French composer Cécile Chaminade. The whole programme in this concert contributed to a 'Christmas Proms' atmosphere opening with the Grand March from Verdi's 'Aida', followed by light and tuneful items, and closing with the 'Fantasia on Sea Songs' arranged by Sir Henry Wood.

Michael Evans, the distinguished 'cello soloist and teacher, returned to Penzance after sixteen years in March 1999 and presented another 'double bill', consisting of Saint-Saëns' 'Cello Concerto in A Minor' and the beautiful 'Kol Nidrei' by Max Bruch. These four concerts provided a great variety of music in their programmes, representing composers from many countries.

The concert which took place on Friday 19th November 1999 was chosen as the one to mark the millennium, and it was decided by the Committee that the programme should consist of music by British composers. They were also delighted to accept an offer from local musician, Miles Baster, to come and play the Elgar Violin Concerto with the orchestra. He was keen to do this and was willing to work with the orchestra in rehearsals. This set the scene for a very special occasion which would celebrate the Society's 270th, concert as well as the turn of the second millennium.

Miles Baster

From the time of his retirement in 1995, when Miles Baster returned to Cornwall, he contributed greatly to the musical life of the area, playing in chamber music groups and performing concerti and other major works with ensembles such as the St Mary's Sinfonia and David Ball's 'Music for a Summer Evening' concerts.

His 'pedigree' as a violinist was impeccable, and though not a native of Cornwall his association with the county went back to childhood when the family came to live in the Penzance area after spending holidays there. Miles' mother joined the Orchestral Society in the autumn of 1941 and remained a member until 1949 when she had to move away. Miles, born in Croydon in 1935, attended St Erbyn's School in Penzance and had his first violin lessons in Marazion with Olga Bennett. By the time he was twelve years old Miles was a member of the

Orchestral Society, playing in three concerts during 1948 and 1949. He was at this time travelling to London to study with the great violinist, Albert Sammons, and soon became leader of the National Youth Orchestra of Great Britain which had been formed in 1947. At the Royal Academy of Music his tutor was Frederick Grinke, soloist with the Orchestral Society in June 1949. Miles went on to further study at the prestigious Julliard School of Music in New York where he had the good fortune to study under Louis Persinger, the renowned violin teacher and chamber music specialist, who had tutored the young Yehudi Menuhin.

Miles Baster.

Miles Baster was proud of his Scottish ancestry and family connections with Edinburgh and it was here, from 1959, that he established his career. He was the founding leader of the Edinburgh String Quartet and their performances took him all over the world. They produced many recordings as well as radio and television broadcasts. Music, and chamber music especially, was his life. He regarded himself as of secondary importance to that of the music, yet his musicianship, beautiful tone and generosity of spirit made his performances memorable. David Ball, who worked with Miles on many occasions, said that he made his fellow performers feel that they were "ten times as good as they really were". This charming and generous man would never accept any payment for his performances.

Since his earliest days with the Penzance Orchestral Society he had cherished an ambition to return and perform the Elgar concerto with them. So it was fitting that it should be on an auspicious occasion that this ambition was realised. For the orchestra and David Ball it was the thrilling culmination of rehearsals in which the soloist guided them through the work – a rare experience. The performance of the Elgar was preceded in the first half of the millennium concert by Hamish MacCunn's 'Land of the Mountain and the Flood', 'Four Cornish Dances' by Malcolm Arnold, and Vaughan Williams' 'English Folk Song Suite'. Miles Baster died in October 2004 at the age of sixty-nine after which an obituary was printed in *The Cornishman* paying tribute to this fine musician, accompanied by a photograph of him holding, most probably, his beloved Landolfi violin.

For the opening concert of the new century, on Friday 7th April 2000, pianist Paul Comeau returned to play Rachmaninov's Second Piano Concerto. The orchestra gave performances of the 'Hebrides' overture by Mendelssohn and Brahms' 'Symphony No. 2'. This popular but demanding programme resulted in queues forming at the box office in St John's Hall. *The Cornishman* reviewer gave the concert a commendable report pointing out that such performances were likely to be the only ones heard in the area with no large professional orchestras visiting the far west of Cornwall. For this reason "support of our own home-grown music-makers is vital to the cultural wealth of the country. Well done, Penzance Orchestra!" it concluded.

Another local soloist appeared with the orchestra in November 2000 when Geoffrey Pearson, their principal clarinettist, performed Weber's 'Clarinet Concerto No. 1 in F Minor'. Geoffrey, a former Royal Marine Bandsman, was for many years a member of the band of Her Majesty the Queen's Royal Yacht, *Brittania*. He is also an able viola player and plays regularly in one or other capacity with most of the major instrumental ensembles in the county. He had appeared as a clarinet soloist on many occasions but this was his first solo appearance with the Penzance orchestra.

Since 2001 it has become the practice of the Society to engage young musicians at the outset of their careers as soloists. Often post-graduate students from the Royal Academy of Music some of them have also attended the IMS seminars at Prussia Cove. Lan Yao, piano, Beate Altenburg, 'cello, and Maria Martinova, piano, came to Penzance in 2001 and 2002, each performing a major concerto for their chosen instrument.

The concert on 15th March 2002 in which Maria Martinova performed Beethoven's 'Piano Concerto No. 4' was a significant one. The concert had to be held in St Mary's Church which meant that the church organ was available, so a programme was selected to include Edward Elgar's work 'Sursum Corda' for organ, strings, brass and tympani, with Russell Jory as organ soloist. Schubert's 'Rosamunde' Overture and Schumann's Fourth Symphony completed the programme. It was not generally known at the time but this was to be David Ball's last concert with the Orchestral Society.

A Bolt from the Blue

David announced his intention to resign as conductor at the Annual General Meeting in May 2002. It was an unexpected blow for the Society because David, like his predecessors, had become synonymous with the orchestra and there was no obvious successor. His reasons for

deciding to retire were understandable: he had recently retired from full-time teaching and felt the need to be free of such a time-consuming commitment. He had been the conductor for over twenty years, which was an admirable contribution by any standards, and he thought that someone with new ideas would bring a renewal of energy to the orchestra. His total dedication, over the years, was often remarked on by members such as Elizabeth Rowe who said that "no one has the remotest idea of how much he does". There is no doubt that David's devotion, enthusiasm, and concern for the Society as a whole, is a vital factor in its continuing existence.

Retirement had been well earned by David Ball but he did not intend to remove himself from the orchestral scene completely. He resumed his place as an oboist in the orchestra and continued to conduct many of his former musicians at the ever-popular summer concerts at St Hilary, which are still taking place. David's contribution to the musical and cultural life of Cornwall was recognised in 2001 when, on the recommendation of the Orchestral Society, he was made a Bard of the Cornish Gorsedd. That this honour had been bestowed on him through the support of his players meant a great deal to David.

The Orchestral Society was now in the difficult position of having to find someone to conduct their forthcoming concert season with rehearsals due to start in September. The committee acted quickly and engaged David Frost to take them through the autumn practice session and concert.

Enid Truman.

David Frost is well known throughout Cornwall as a conductor, teacher and composer. He is employed by the county music service as the team leader for brass teaching, but has also taught the trumpet at Dartington College, organised in-service training for the Guildhall School of Music and Drama and been an examiner and adjudicator. In this busy life he has also found time to conduct the Cornwall Youth Orchestra, the St Mewan Sinfonia, the Duchy Opera and Duchy Ballet. He attended a committee meeting in June 2002 to discuss the programme for the autumn concert.

This concert, on Friday 29th November 2002, was also held in St Mary's Church, Penzance as a result of a discussion at the AGM in May. It was felt that the acoustics in St John's Hall were unsatisfactory and the possibility of using St Mary's Church instead led to the decision to alternate between the two venues, beginning with the November concert. With David Frost as the guest conductor the concert featured the twenty-year old 'cellist, Oliver Coates, as soloist. This already busy and enterprising young musician performed the Elgar 'Cello Concerto, and the rest of the programme consisted of Rossini's overture to 'The Barber of Seville' and Beethoven's Sixth Symphony, the 'Pastoral'.

During the summer and autumn prior to this concert an unusual number of committee meetings had taken place. Of prime importance was the problem of a future conductor. Eventually it was decided that Judith Bailey should be asked to conduct the spring 2003 concert as a 'one-off' while deciding who should be offered the post on a more permanent basis. Judith agreed to this and attended a committee meeting on 13th November 2002 when a programme for the concert on 11th April 2003 was confirmed.

The Death of Enid Truman

During the first three years of the new century there had been a number of significant matters for the officers and committee of the Orchestral Society to deal with in addition to David Ball's retirement. In June 2001 the Society's President, Enid Truman, died aged ninety-one. She had retired from the 'cello section of the orchestra in 1989 and this was acknowledged with a presentation at the 250th concert in November of that year. Enid continued to take a keen interest in the Society, attending concerts and being concerned for its future. Increasing physical frailty meant that she spent the last period of her life in a residential home,, but she was still able to enjoy a party in honour of her ninetieth birthday held at Trevethoe in May 2000.

Her death was a great sadness to her many friends and colleagues in the orchestra and the wider musical scene in West Cornwall. A final link had been severed in the chain of history stretching back over ninety-five years to the birth of the Society. Enid had devoted her adult life to its activities and through this to the memory of her father, Walter Barnes. It is fair to say that this story of the Penzance Orchestral Society is also Enid's story because she was always at its heart.

Enid's successor as President was discussed by the committee in September 2001, and the two names suggested were Nora Page and Rose Tempest.

Nora Page

Nora had joined the orchestra as a double bass player in 1969, having been a pupil of both Enid Truman and Mrs Horsfall. She was one of its most faithful servants and admitted that, having become involved with the Society, its music-making and friendship had changed her life. She contributed in many ways, not least by taking on the mundane but essential responsibility for setting out chairs, music stands etc for rehearsals in the Bandroom over many years. Her husband, Geoffrey, was also a supporter of the orchestra and was one of the regular stewards at the concerts for many years. Failing health forced Nora to retire from the orchestra in 2001 and it was felt unfair to impose the obligations of Presidency upon her so she was granted Life Membership of the Society as a gesture of gratitude and respect. She was a welcome member of concert audiences, even when she was confined to a wheelchair, and her funeral on 20th December 2002 was attended by her many friends in West Cornwall.

Rose Tempest was invited to become the Society's next President, and for many reasons no more suitable person could have been chosen.

Rose and Horace Tempest.

Rose and Horace Tempest

Rose and her husband, Horace, came to West Cornwall in 1958 when Horace decided to transfer his schools photography business from Nottingham to Trevethoe Manor, near Lelant. Here he was able to accommodate his headquarters and family home in one place, and also build an airstrip. Horace was an experienced pilot and used his aeroplanes for both business and pleasure.

Already a capable string player, Horace joined the Orchestral Society in 1961 and, over the years, played the violin, 'cello, double bass and viola in the orchestra. When he transferred to the viola section in 1974 he became known for using a large viola which he played in 'cello-like style between his knees. This style of instrument had first been introduced in 1876 by Hermann Ritter and was used in Wagner's orchestra at Bayreuth. It was known as the 'viola alta' and a revival of interest in it had prompted Horace to acquire one, though he did have a more conventional viola as well.

Rose Tempest was taught to play the 'cello by Enid Truman and joined the Junior Orchestra during the time when Enid was its conductor. She became a member of the senior orchestra in 1968 and has been a regular member of the 'cello section ever since. Rose and Horace both served as committee members over the years and Rose was the Society's Hon. Secretary from

Chamber music at Trevethoe. Left to right: *Maurice Linden, Norman Truman, Horace Tempest playing his 'viola alta' and Rose Tempest.*

1985-1998. Horace Tempest died in August 1979 and the couple's constant support and help to the Society was acknowledged by Rose being made a Vice-President later that year.

The 'State of the Bandroom' and Piers Owen

A major preoccupation with the committee was the state of the Bandroom. The soundness of its structure, security, dampness in the cupboards where the music was stored, and the toilet facilities, were all causes for concern. As early as October 1998 a sub-committee was formed to look into the problem, namely David Ball, Piers Owen and Mike Higgs. However, it was not until the autumn of 2001 that work began after Piers Owen volunteered to carry out the extensive repairs. He was not a qualified builder but felt that he had the skills required and the spare time and energy to offer the Society in an attempt to keep the financial outlay to a minimum. His schedule of work and estimate of costs was accepted and over the next year and a half the interior of the building was completely refurbished. The cost of the work done by Piers, with the help of John Care in electrical installations, came to between £2,000-£3000. When completed the Bandroom was transformed and made a much more attractive venue for rehearsals as well as for potential tenants.

Piers also helped Sally and Geoff Pearson, the librarians, to tidy up the Society's library of music which involved drying it out, sorting, and then providing proper packaging within the cupboards. This input of time and effort by Piers, over a long period of time, indicates a real commitment to the Society and its future. He remains an active member of the orchestra as a double bass player.

The finances of the Society remained fairly healthy during these years, boosted in 2001 by the sale of Elizabeth Rowe's viola, which had been bequeathed to them following her death in 1999. However, the expenditure incurred over the repairs to the Bandroom did result in a low point being reached in the autumn of 2002 and there was even a suggestion put forward by a member of the committee that the Bandroom should be 'released', presumably meaning that it should be sold.

Generally, the sale of assets was not approved of but later in the year Ann Tempest, the Society's harpist, suggested that perhaps the orchestra's harp could be sold. She had the instrument valued and it was given an auction valuation of between £2,500-£3000. When the question of whether the Society wanted to sell it was discussed, the committee voted in favour of doing so. Ann offered to buy it from the Society and in November 2002 the Treasurer, Stephen Bray, reported to the committee that he had received a cheque from the Tempest family in payment for the harp, but including £2,000 as a donation in memory of the late Horace Tempest.

This was a gesture which reflected the generosity to the Society of Horace himself over the years, and was a much appreciated reinforcement to the Society's depleted funds. These were also boosted by a £2,000 rebate from the electricity board which had given an incorrect reading on the Bandroom electricity meter! Both members' subscriptions and concert ticket prices were raised, as well as the hire charge for the Bandroom. Also at the AGM in September 2001, it was decided to adopt the term 'Friend' instead of 'Subscriber' to the Society and that the Friends' annual subscription should be raised to a minimum of £5. All these forms of income contributed to a greatly increased sum in the Society's bank account by the end of the 2003 financial year.

While on matters of administration it should be noted that the elderly Penzance Orchestral Society was doing its best to keep abreast of technological advances. In May 2002 it was suggested that the possibility of creating a website for the Society should be investigated. This was agreed, with a maximum sum placed on expenditure to be incurred. It took some time to achieve but the website has now been 'up and running' for some time. It is an interesting source of information about the Society, its history and current activities, with illustrations of the orchestra.

Change and Continuity

For the Penzance Orchestral Society the 2002-2003 season was an interregnum, with two guest conductors, David Frost in November 2002 and Judith Bailey in April 2003. The rehearsal period leading up to the April concert was by way of a probationary period for both the orchestra and conductor. The Society was seriously considering asking Judith to be their next conductor and each of them was able to use the time to assess their response to one another, The programme was a popular one, opening with Humperdinck's 'Hänsel und Gretel' overture, followed by Max Bruch's 'Violin Concerto No. 1 in G Minor'. The soloist was the young Israeli violinist, Sivann Zelikoff, a post-graduate student at the Royal Academy of Music with an already impressive list of awards and performances to her credit. Dvorak's Eighth Symphony formed the second half of the concert.

The orchestra was obviously satisfied with their guest conductor because they invited her to accept the position on a permanent basis. At the annual general meeting a month later Judith reported that she had enjoyed working with the orchestra, had been delighted with the concert and the soloist, and confirmed her acceptance of the Society's invitation.

It was with pleasure and relief that the committee and members welcomed Judith as the fifth conductor of the Orchestral Society. They knew that they had found an admirable, professionally trained and experienced musician to take them forward, and Judith also had the added attribute of having been born and bred in Cornwall! She was already well known in Cornish musical circles and had been conducting the Cornwall Chamber Orchestra since September 2002.

Judith Bailey, ARAM, B Mus (Lond), GRSM, LRAM, ARCM.

Judith's academic success and musical career is outlined on the Penzance Orchestral Society's website which provides an excellent introduction to her many and diverse achievements. Born in Camborne in 1941 Judith is the daughter of the late Mr and Mrs J. R. Bailey whose bakery business was well known in the town. Her parents were both musical and were closely associated with Camborne Wesley Chapel where Judith sang in the choir for many years, as did her mother. Reg Bailey, her father, had been an organist and was also an able pianist. He is remembered as a prominent and community minded citizen who, in 1961, became the Chairman of the Camborne and Redruth Urban District Council. This year of special distinction ended sadly when Reg Bailey died almost at the exact hour of the end of his period of office in 1962.

Judith Bailey. Cornwall & IOS Press

Showing early promise as a musician, Judith's talent flourished during the years she attended Truro High School for Girls. Here there were gifted music teachers such as Miss Eleanor Buddle, a viola player and Judith's piano teacher from the age of seven to eighteen years old. Miss Ethel Broad, 'cello, also taught at the High School, and both she and Eleanor Buddle had been members of the Penzance Orchestral Society.

Also on the staff was another Penzance player, Charles Simmons, a woodwind teacher and an oboist in the orchestra for a brief period in the mid-nineteen fifties. He taught Judith to play the clarinet and must have been very proud of his pupil as her name began to appear among lists of prize-winners and performers in the Cornwall Music Festival. In 1959 Judith won the overall Junior Music Award and, at a special evening concert given during the Festival's Golden Jubilee celebrations in Truro that same year, she performed in a clarinet trio alongside such well known Cornish musicians as Kenwin Barton, baritone, Muriel Peters, soprano and the renowned Treviscoe Male Voice Choir.

Judith had always been aware of the Penzance Orchestral Society and had attended its concerts with her family. She remembers hearing performances by John Vallier, Alan Loveday and Harriet Cohen in the early days of Morgan Hosking's conductorship. Then, in 1957, a course for string players was held in Truro under the auspices of the newly formed Cornwall Rural Music School and a piano concerto was among the works being studied. As an accomplished young pianist Judith was asked to play the solo piano part during the course and it was then that she had her first encounter with instrumentalists from the Orchestral Society.

Music was becoming a very important part of Judith's life but she was equally talented in art and quite early on in her High School years she was wondering which of these two areas of creativity she should pursue as a career. By the age of thirteen she had decided that it had to be the music profession because she could endure a few days without painting but none without music. However, Judith has retained her love of painting enjoying it as a leisure activity.

As a student at the Royal Academy of Music from 1959 to 1964 Judith continued with the clarinet and piano and also studied composition and conducting. On completion of her studies she worked for a few years as a peripatetic woodwind teacher for the Hampshire Music Education Service, based in Winchester. But she found that she did not have a true vocation for teaching children and in 1971 made the brave decision to become a freelance musician.

She remained in Hampshire and built up a busy and varied career which incorporated conducting, teaching in the field of adult education, adjudication, and clarinet playing. Staying in Hampshire was a practical decision for Judith because it provided her with a wider sphere of activity in which to earn a living; surrounding counties provided opportunities for work whereas Cornwall's isolation prevented this.

Judith kept in very close touch with musical activities in Cornwall, nevertheless, returning

frequently to take part in them. For example, in 1963 during her summer vacation, she was invited by Maisie and Evelyn Radford to be their clarinettist for the Falmouth Opera Singers production of Mozart's 'La Clemenza de Tito'. This was not Judith's only appearance under the baton of the remarkable Maisie Radford, but she recalls it as especially memorable due to her providing the elaborate clarinet obbligato in the aria 'Parto, parto' sung by tenor, David Galliver, in the role of Sextus.

Composing music has always been a compulsive force in Judith's life, and while at the R.A.M. two of her works were performed, a trio for clarinet, viola and piano and a violin and piano sonata. She had also written an anthem for Camborne Wesley Chapel choir which they performed under her direction. Later she was asked to write music for a Cornwall Youth Drama Service production of Brecht's play, 'The Caucasian Chalk Circle', and Judith herself conducted its performance. In 1967 she was awarded the Lorgh Vras Cup at the Cornwall Music Festival for a composition of a choral setting of words relating to Cornwall.

These are just a few examples of a considerable 'oeuvre' of music which Judith has composed. Much of it has been inspired by her native Cornwall and music for wind instruments has featured prominently. Her symphonies and other orchestral works were performed by the orchestras she conducted in Southampton and Petersfield. The Orchestral Society has also performed Judith's music; her 'Penwith' overture was an appropriate work with which to open their programme in November 2006 at the first of the Society's two concerts during its centenary season.

The year 2001 was a significant one for both Judith Bailey and the Penzance Orchestral Society. Firstly, Judith received the honour of being awarded the Associateship of the Royal Academy of Music, which is granted only to those of the Academy's past students who have achieved distinction in their musical career. It was a timely acknowledgement of her great contribution to her profession and a vindication, if any was needed, of her courage, thirty years earlier, in foregoing the security of a salaried teaching post in favour of a more personal and fulfilling career path. Secondly, having reached the age of sixty Judith again felt the need for a change of direction in her life and she decided to return to live permanently in Cornwall.

Here she settled into her house by the sea in Gwithian, long established as a family holiday home, and resumed old friendships and created new ones. Soon after this David Ball discovered her as a clarinettist and asked her to join the Orchestral Society. She had already played with the Society's first clarinet, Geoffrey Pearson, and joined him for the rehearsal session leading to the concert in November 2001. Little did Judith or anyone else realise that within two years she would be standing in David's place on the conductor's rostrum.

She did not remain a member of the Orchestral Society because she decided to take a belated 'gap year' and during the next twelve months spent time rediscovering Cornwall, attending musical performances and generally reacquainting herself with the county and its culture. This she enjoyed with her long-time friend and companion, Isobel Young, whose death in November 2003 endowed the year with special meaning and poignancy. By the autumn of 2002 Judith was prepared to resume her musical activities, greatly to the benefit of music in West Cornwall generally and the Penzance Orchestral Society in particular.

Judith Bailey's succession to the position of conductor of the Penzance Orchestral Society embodies the words chosen for this chapter heading. 'Change' is represented in two major ways: by Judith being the first woman conductor in the Society's history and, apart from the relatively short tenure of Maddern Williams, its first to have been professionally trained. These would both seem to be very positive and worthwhile developments as the Society progresses into the twenty-first century. 'Continuity' is evident from Judith's Cornish birthright, her contribution to Cornish music-making over many years, and her links with the Orchestral Society and its instrumentalists. Above all, she upholds the Society's long held 'raison d'être', that the orchestra should exist to foster an enjoyment and love of music for both its performers and the community which provides its audiences.

21

Finale

Modern Times, 2004-2006

In the years approaching its centenary season the Penzance Orchestral Society and its new conductor, Judith Bailey, continued to provide the music lovers of West Cornwall with concerts of substance and quality. Between November 2003 and March 2005 young soloists came to Penzance performing concerti for piano, French horn and violin. On the 2nd April 2004 the lovely young soprano, Julia Riley, performed the Berlioz song cycle, 'Nuits d'Été' which suited the mezzo-soprano quality of her voice, and which she sang with "sincerity and skill" according to Douglas Williams, writing in *The Cornishman* newspaper.

This article was headed, "Orchestral Society abandons the stage", referring to a dramatic innovation at the concert. Following dissatisfaction with the acoustics of St John's Hall and the occasional use of St Mary's Church as an alternative venue, it was finally decided by the committee that St John's Hall was the better auditorium. At the 2003 annual general meeting the idea of placing the orchestra on the floor of the hall was suggested.

This was not an entirely novel idea because Rosemary and Michael Tunstall-Behrens had put forward a similar idea to David Ball in 1989, accompanied by a diagram. Michael had felt that playing on the stage of St John's Hall caused the loss of many finer points in the music because the sound was not well projected into the hall. So in April 2004 the orchestra moved to the floor of St John's Hall as an experiment.

It was deemed a success by Douglas Williams in his article and also by the orchestra members and the practice has continued. To compensate for the reduced seating capacity ticket prices were raised, but the audience, sitting on the raked seating, were rewarded by a much better view of the orchestra and soloist and, most importantly, improved sound quality.

Playdays

Another innovative idea agreed upon in committee in early 2004 was to hold a Playday. The aim was to get young instrumentalists together with members of the Orchestral Society to play music alongside each other. It was hoped that this would encourage budding musicians as well as boost the Society's audiences at concerts and foster future membership. The original suggestion had come from Making Music for Youth, part of the National Federation of Making Music (as the N.F.M.S. had been renamed), who provided funding for the event.

The Penzance Orchestral Society's first Playday was held in the Hayle Community School on Saturday 16th October 2004. The school had offered the use of their new music and drama studio and Making Music's officer for the South West, Jason Thornton, directed the music. Over a hundred musicians took part, with pupils from schools all over West Cornwall performing with their more experienced peers. The Orchestral Society was one of about twenty similar societies nationwide which took part in the Making Music for Youth project.

Penzance Orchestral Society's Playday, October 2005.

The music chosen for the occasion had two elements, firstly, popular themes from film classics like 'Jurassic Park' and 'Lord of the Rings' which the children would recognise and enjoy and, secondly, excerpts from items which would be performed by the Orchestral Society at their forthcoming concert. These were Judith Bailey's 'Havas – a Period of Summer', which is a three-movement suite inspired by Cornish legends, and the 'Symphony No. 2 in D' by Sibelius.

The Playday was a great success and a whole page of colour photographs accompanied an article by Maurice Stevens in the following week's *Cornishman* newspaper. It has become an annual event for the orchestra held with or without financial assistance from Making Music. If no funding is available a small charge per head is levied to cover the costs. In 2006 the venue changed to the Humphry Davy School in Penzance following its designation as a Specialist Music College. Playday 2006 on Saturday 14th October was the Penzance Orchestral Society's

contribution to the 'Listen Up! Festival', sponsored by BBC Radio 3, Making Music, and the Association of British Orchestras.

It was noted at an Orchestral Society committee meeting in January 2006 that there had been audience members attending concerts as a direct result of Playdays. Having attained an acceptable standard of playing, young musicians are welcomed into the orchestra through this enterprising scheme. It perpetuates the Society's long tradition of collaboration with local schools, whose pupils are now entitled to attend concerts free of charge, and their parents at a reduced rate.

There have been important changes among the principal officers and musicians in the Society during recent years. Jayne Poynton succeeded Rose Tempest as Hon. Secretary in 1998 and held the post for four years until ill health forced her to retire. At the annual general meeting of 2003 Elizabeth Gregg, a member of the viola section since 1988, succeeded Jayne and remains the Society's efficient and enthusiastic Hon. Secretary. Jayne Poynton had been an active member of the Society since 1975 as a 'cellist and, apart from a short break, leader of that section from 1983. Sally Pearson became Principal 'cello in April 2003. The post of Hon. Treasurer also changed, with Iain Vosper taking over this major responsibility in 2004 from his fellow horn player Stephen Bray.

Iain Vosper

Iain has been closely associated with the Penzance Orchestral Society all his life. His aunt, Miss Lilian Keast, had joined the orchestra in 1954 as a violinist. She transferred to the oboe in 1955 then flute in 1963 but not without a flirtation with the percussion section in May 1960! She read maths at Girton College, Cambridge and returned to Penzance in 1950 to teach at West Cornwall School.

French Horns and Oboe in rehearsal, with Iain Vosper nearest to the window.

Iain was, in his own words, "required to learn a musical instrument" as a child and ran the whole gamut of those available, rejecting them all. Miss Keast took him to an orchestral rehearsal in 1956 when he was eight years old. He remembers the kind and welcoming people but nothing at all about the music. Revelation came at the end of the rehearsal when, on leaving the Bandroom, Iain saw Michael Tunstall-Behrens climbing into his Lagonda car, "holding the most wonderfully shaped instrument – his French horn". Recognising Iain's enthusiasm his aunt borrowed the orchestra's spare horn and taught him the rudiments of playing it. He gained some proficiency and soon joined the Junior Orchestra where he was greeted and encouraged with, "enormous patience" by the older players.

By the time he was twelve, in 1960, Iain was to be found playing the French horn in the main orchestra, listed in the programme as "Master Iain Vosper". He was a regular member of the Society until he joined the Royal Navy in 1966 when he stopped playing for about fifteen years. He took up the horn again when he had become senior enough in the service, "not to care about making a loud noise in a confined space"! This confidence combined with greater proximity to Penzance enabled Iain to resume his membership of the orchestra in the nineteen eighties.

On his retirement in 2004 Iain came to live permanently with his family in Perranuthnoe and at that year's annual general meeting he was elected to the post of Hon. Treasurer and remains so at the present time.

Making a greater impact on the orchestra, musically, was the decision made by Joyce Preston, following the Orchestral Society's concert in November 2005, to retire as their Principal Violin. She had been sitting on the 'first desk' for nearly twenty-five years throughout David Ball's conductorship and continued to provide stability and continuity during Judith Bailey's early concerts. She had become the sheet-anchor of the orchestra and her familiar presence would be sorely missed.

Joyce Preston

Joyce was born in Bradford, Yorkshire, but when she was about eight years old her family moved south to Essex. Following her school career, during which she had become a talented music pupil, she went on to the Royal Academy of Music in 1944. She had a number of well-known violin teachers, namely Marjorie Hayward, Sydney Robjohns and Harold Fairhurst. The latter was, of course, a favourite soloist with the Penzance Orchestral Society and its audiences, appearing in four concerts between 1927 and 1941; he was described by Kathleen Frazier as, "that most beautiful violinist". Little did he know, when teaching Joyce Preston, that she would one day become the leader of the orchestra so familiar to him in Cornwall.

Joyce Preston.

Joyce was unable to continue postgraduate studies at the Academy because places there were at a premium due to the number of musicians returning from the Second World War wanting to resume their musical education. But her study of the violin continued with Sasha Lasserson, David Martin and Frederick Grinke. She regarded Sasha Lasserson as the best and most influential of her teachers but it was an impressive well of talent and experience from which to draw out her own expertise. David Martin was a soloist with the Orchestral Society in November 1959 and Frederick Grinke was their soloist on two occasions in June 1949 and May 1961.

Joyce Preston began to earn her living as a freelance orchestral leader but then took on a permanent post at the Ursuline Convent High School in Brentwood. Coincidentally, this was a school attended by Eileen Woolmington who was to join the 'cello section of the Penzance Orchestral Society in 1993. Joyce and Eileen became very good friends and remain close neighbours in their peaceful valley near St Just. Joyce remained at the school in Brentwood for thirteen years and the final phase of her career began when she moved to Cornwall. She became a peripatetic string teacher for the Cornwall Music Education service in 1976, then under the leadership of the unforgettable Henry Mills, with responsibility for the west of the county.

During her years of teaching in West Cornwall Joyce has made an enormous impact on the development of string playing in the area. Countless numbers of young musicians have benefited from her skill and experience and many have gone on to have successful careers as performers, some returning to Penzance as soloists with the orchestra. She also created opportunities for her pupils to experience playing in groups and public performances. For example, she and a friend, Pamela Rosenfeld, founded the St Cecilia Ensemble, a string orchestra made up of their most talented pupils. (Pamela Rosenfeld made a valuable contribution to the Society as Principal of the second violin section from 1985-1988).

In 1980 Joyce founded the Cornwall Chamber Orchestra which comprised gifted students and talented mature players from all over the county. Under the baton of Dr. Edward Weymouth, followed by Russell Jory and currently conducted by Judith Bailey, the Chamber Orchestra has performed throughout Cornwall raising money for many charitable causes. Joyce also led the St Mary's Sinfonia, established by Russell Jory in 1987, for nearly twenty years.

She joined the Orchestral Society in the autumn of 1976, appearing as a violist in their 70th Anniversary concert on Friday 26th November. In November 1979 she transferred to the first violins and when David Ball became the conductor in 1981 he asked Joyce to become his leader. She was the Society's Principal Violin until November 2005, and during that time brought quality and cohesion to the orchestra's playing.

In this impressive contribution to music-making in Cornwall Joyce's Yorkshire roots often surfaced along with her dry sense of humour. David Ball recalled having problems with a member of his orchestra, who shall remain nameless, and asked Joyce to help. Joyce responded that the person in question, who was known to be from Yorkshire, "probably came from Doncaster"! Her reserved and quiet personality revealed true north-country veracity and loyalty on occasions. She would defend her conductor if he was ever shown at a disadvantage by a soloist, not being afraid to point out to them that it was they who were at fault.

In 1988 Joyce Preston's selfless devotion to musical education and public performance was recognised when she was awarded the Music Shield by the Cornish Gorsedd of Bards for her services to music in the county. Later, in 1997, she was welcomed as a Bard of the Gorsedd at their meeting in Bodmin. She chose as her bardic name, 'Fyllores Pow Evrok', meaning 'Violinist from Yorkshire'. As Joyce hands over some of her many responsibilities she can be sure of the continuing respect, affection and gratitude which she has generated over the years amongst her fellow musicians and audiences in West Cornwall.

On Joyce's retirement as Principal Violin two young violinists were approached about succeeding her as leader of the Orchestral Society. Christine Judge had joined the second violin section in 1999 but quickly moved into the first violins where she played on the front desk with Joyce. Christine is a peripatetic string teacher with the county music service. The other candidate was Ruth Boulton, an ex-professional violinist who had joined the orchestra on coming to Cornwall to live in 2004.

They were both willing to take on the role of leader but with some reservations. Christine was unsure about being permanently in such a prominent position and Ruth had a young family to consider. It was decided that they should share the Principal Violin's duties and responsibilities as co-leaders. So, with this example of 'job-sharing', the Penzance Orchestral Society is once more showing its ability to adapt to change and the demands of the twenty-first century.

The 2005-2006 season was something of a harbinger to the Penzance Orchestral Society's centenary, for in its chosen works and soloists it exemplified a number of the Society's characteristics. Both concerts took place in St John's Hall and the first, on Friday 18th November 2005, opened with Schubert's 'Unfinished' symphony. This was an old favourite in the orchestra's repertoire having been performed on at least ten previous occasions. The concert concluded with Elgar's concert overture, 'In the South', and of his overtures the most often played by the orchestra, first performed by them in 1933. It is a substantial composition, lasting nearly twenty minutes, with vivid musical colouring and moods, making it a challenge for any amateur orchestra.

The soloist at this concert was Laurence Perkins, bassoonist, representing the Society's tradition of bringing eminent and internationally acclaimed performers to Penzance. He played Weber's 'Bassoon Concerto in F, Op. 75' in a version revised by himself to bring the work closer to Weber's original intentions than the more usually heard edition arranged by Weber's publishers. *The Cornishman* reported his performance in this, as well as in the Elgar 'Romance for Bassoon and Orchestra, Op. 62', as "superb" and "his personality made watching and listening to him a real joy".

In early April 2006 the programme included a first performance by the Society of Dvorak's 'Symphony No. 6 in D Major, Op. 60'. Many of Dvorak's symphonies had been played over the years but not the Sixth until this concert. The first half of the concert opened with Brahms' 'Academic Festival Overture, Op. 80', which was followed by the Tchaikovsky 'Violin concerto in D, Op. 35' played by soloist, Jane Gordon.

In engaging Jane, the Society was fulfilling two of its regular commitments, firstly by inviting soloists with local connections to perform in Penzance and, secondly, by engaging young musicians who were on the threshold of their careers. Jane had lived in Penzance as a child and attended the School of St Clare in the town. She had been a violin pupil of Joyce Preston and then gone on to graduate from the Royal Academy of Music in July 2003. During her post-graduate studies at the Academy she won many prestigious awards, and further competition prizes confirmed her outstanding talent. Her early career, including a Wigmore Hall debut as a member of the Rautio Piano Trio and a live performance on BBC Radio 3, indicates a successful and promising future.

Joyce Preston, playing in the viola section at this concert, must have been very proud of her former 'protégée' who performed the demanding Tchaikovsky concerto with, "complete assurance". She vividly portrayed the lyricism and passion in the concerto and Kenneth Northey, a well known local musician, wrote in his review that the emotion in her performance "came from a girl in a red dress playing with an absorbed composure". The large audience responded warmly to Jane's playing, resisting the urge to applaud at the end of the first movement, simply expelling an audible gasp of excitement but releasing their appreciation in vociferous cheers and clapping at the end.

Judith Bailey, conducting her seventh concert with the Orchestral Society, also received complimentary words from the reviewer. The performance once again showed, "what a fine conductor she is", and in the concerto her skill was especially evident where she had, "brought the orchestra into such fine rapport with the soloist".

Judith Bailey being admitted to the Gorsedd of Bards, September 2005.

Judith's contribution to the musical life of West Cornwall was recognised in September 2005, when she was received into the Cornish Gorsedd of Bards at its Wadebridge ceremony. Judith was one of fourteen new Bards to be welcomed that year and she took the Bardic name 'Gedyores Menestrouthy', meaning 'Orchestral conductor'. With this distinction Judith was upholding the Society's honour of having all five of its conductors created Bards of the Cornish Gorsedd.

"Plus Uno Maneat Perenne Saeclo"

To use a quotation from the Latin poet Catullus may seem both extraordinary and pretentious in a book about an amateur orchestra. But there is little that is ordinary about the Penzance Orchestral Society; its history provides plenty of evidence to support this view. Some have claimed that it is a 'unique' organisation but other amateur orchestras have existed for over one hundred years, though they are rare. They, too, will have their own individuality and one should not be regarded as more, or less, important than another. Nevertheless, the Penzance orchestra is very special and any claim to uniqueness is not without justification.

The fact that the Society has endured for so long in its geographical isolation and remoteness is remarkable. It has had to rely on a relatively small population to provide an audience because, after all, two thirds of its catchment area is covered by the English Channel or the Celtic Sea. This insularity has also limited its recruitment of members to the county of Cornwall alone. However, that county's appeal has resulted in many musicians choosing to live there in retirement, thus providing a source of professionally trained and talented instrumentalists to sustain and maintain standards. More recently peripatetic teachers have also chosen Cornwall as an attractive place to live and work, discovering in the Society a welcome opportunity for orchestral playing.

The people of Cornwall have always been of a resourceful and self-reliant nature from necessity. They have had either to create their own entertainment or support others doing so, often both. This energy and loyalty has contributed greatly to the orchestra's survival. It provided a rare chance to hear live performances in its pre-war years, thereby establishing it as an essential cultural amenity in the area. This firm foundation of audience support has, on the whole, remained secure which is a testimony to the Society's continued striving for excellence and value for money.

The Orchestral Society itself quickly assumed a sense of identity. The name of Penzance in its title soon became a source of pride both to members and its supporters. Always conscious of its civic pride and position the town welcomed the emergence and development of the orchestra. In its turn, the Society was willing, when asked, to be involved in formal municipal events, support charitable causes in both war and peacetime, and contribute to other musical community activities. In providing an orchestra for the Choral and Operatic Societies it has been indissolubly linked with the major musical occasions in the town for over a century. For the duration of its existence, with a few exceptions for legitimate reasons, its concert venue has been St John's Hall in the town's imposing municipal building.

Penzance, showing three of the orchestra's homes: St John's Hall (top left), The Market House (top right of centre) and The Bandroom in Queen Street (bottom, right of centre). Morrab Library, Penzance

This sense of community responsibility has manifested itself in the Orchestral Society's encouragement and fostering of young people in its music-making; not only through the formation of the Junior Orchestra but by its constant awareness that children should have access to its concerts. The large attendance of schoolchildren at its afternoon concerts for a token charge sowed the seeds of many future instrumentalists and music-lovers; music for concert programmes was frequently chosen with the school music curriculum in mind. Through the involvement of music teachers in the orchestra their pupils were encouraged to join its ranks and, more recently, the introduction of the Playday is perpetuating this long-held concern within the Society for the musical future of its community.

The acquisition of its Bandroom was a courageous and sagacious decision by the Society, giving it an unusual position among amateur orchestras. Not only is it a valuable asset but it has provided a permanent home for its rehearsals and activities and a storage place for instruments, music and photographic memorabilia. It has, in addition to these practical considerations, given the Society a sense of responsibility and continuity. This has been an added dimension to the running of its affairs, not without problems and anxieties but creating, indirectly, further bonding within the structure of the Orchestral Society. It has also provided a venue for many disparate bodies, ranging from various other musical groups to dog training classes, art exhibitions, and the Society of Friends. Within the historic fabric of Penzance one of its ancient buildings has been preserved and put to good use by the Society.

There can be few other orchestras, amateur or professional, who have existed for one hundred years with only five conductors during that entire time. The remarkable fact is that three of them incorporated over ninety of those years within their periods of conductorship. This, alone, must give substance to the Orchestral Society's unique character.

It must also be an important reason for its longevity and stability, and the Society's centenary season provides the appropriate occasion to acknowledge, nowadays, a rarely expressed indebtedness to the late Walter Barnes, Maddern Williams and Morgan Hosking. These outstanding men formed, nurtured and developed the Society in their different ways and this inheritance was preserved and carried on by David Ball, happily still a member of the orchestra. The incredible commitment and devotion by these four musical heroes has provided the legacy now in the hands of Judith Bailey and the officers of the present Society.

David Ball and Morgan Hosking, circa 1991.

Society – a word used by many other musical bodies in their title, but never better exemplified than by the Penzance Orchestral Society. Throughout its history the orchestra has been led by musicians and administrators of talent and integrity, who have brought it through years of success as well as periods of turbulence. Within its membership the threads of friendship, care and support for each other have created a huge 'family' of people. Those no longer with us are not gone and forgotten, but remain links in the long chain of men and women who, through their mutual love of music, have brought the Society safely through its ten decades.

It should be a matter of enormous pride to the present members of the Penzance Orchestral Society that they are a part of its centenary season. The concerts and events being held mark not only the completion of one century of music-making by the Society, but also the dawning of a second. The words of Catullus should be the wish of everyone concerned and interested in the future of orchestral music in Cornwall:

"May it live and last for more than a century".

Penzance Orchestral Society in their Centenary season, November 2006. Simon Cook

Appendices

Penzance Orchestral Society Instruments 1907–2007

Penzance Orchestral Society Officials 1907–2007

Penzance Orchestral Society Soloists and Guest Artistes 1907–2007

Penzance Orchestral Society Works Performed 1907–2007

Notable Families within the Penzance Orchestral Society

Calling in the Troups!

A Bardic Connection

Bold Amateurs

Appendix 1

Penzance Orchestral Society Instumentalists 1907-2007

Notes:

1. If a person played more than one instrument their name is included in each section.
2. The year shown indicates the first appearance of the name in a section of the orchestra.
3. Where Christian names of women are known no titles are used. Where women are known to have played under maiden and married names the married name is used with maiden name indicated.
4. The title 'Musician' indicates a member of the Royal Marine Band, but the designation was not always given.
5. This list has been compiled from available records: it may contain omissions and inaccuracies which, inevitably, occur over such a long period.

VIOLIN

Adams, Grace 1941
Alexander, Gail 1998
Anderson, Mrs K. 1946
Andrewartha, Enid 1944
Andrews, D. 1962
Atkinson, Helen 1937
Baic, Kenneth 1932
Balmford, Hurst 1924
Barnes, Jonathan C. 1924,1963
Barnes, Susan-Ann 1986
Barton, Helen 1950
Baster, Mrs M. 1941
Baster, Miles 1948
Bazeley, Peggy 1926
Beadsworth, George 1909
Beadsworth Winifrede 1913
Beaghan, Miss G. P. 1958
Bcats, Felicity 1989
Bee, Connie 1971
Beecroft, Frank 1925
Belfield, Jane 1988
Belfield, Sinead 1990
Bennetts, Barry 1909
Benney, J. 1955
Biles, Miss 1911
Binnet, Mrs 1920
Birch, Lionel 1909
Bird, G. H. 1952
Blackwell, H. M. 1911
Blight, Miss K 1935
Blundy, Peter 2005
Boase, J. 1922
Bolitho, Una née George 1958
Bosanko, Miss G. 1933
Bosence, Mabel 1912
Boulton, Ruth 2004
Boyns, J.S. 1914
Brain, Penny 2001
Brewer, Leonard 1909
Bridle, Maud 1924
Brodie, A.C. 1942
Broom, Mrs J. 1970
Brown, G. A. 1966
Bruce, Mrs L. H. 1960
Burdett, Mrs Derek 1939
Cadwallader, Winifred 1974
Care, John 1954
Carling, Gwen 1922
Carr, Pat 1930
Carr, Mrs Rex 1926
Cave-Day, G. 1931
Champion, T. Tumer 1907
Chappell, Clare 1982
Chappell, Godfrey 1982
Chappell, Kay 1982
Chappell, Stan 1990
Clark, Christine 1979
Clotworthy, Percy 1945
Cocking, M. 1925
Cole, Lieut. Spear 1909
Colegate, Mr 1922
Coleman, Mr 1914
Coleman, Iola
née Keskeys 1932
Collins, Marjorie 1985
Cooper, Alison 1987
Costello, S. 1942
Couch, W. J. 1925
Cox, Jemma 2004
Crawley, V. 1974
Crothers, Miss P. 1963
Crowle, Miss L. E. 1944
Cullimore, Robert 2000
Curnow, Mrs W. 1955
Dakin, Ann 1937
Daves, Miss 1912
Davies, Mrs D. J. 1938
Davies, Sgt. Major Hubert 1942
Davies, Justine 1996
Deason, George 1961
De Chabot, Siegfried 1967
Denyer, Geoffrey 1986
De Pury, Sally 1963
Derham, M. 1964
Derici, Helen 1994
Dixon, Dolly 1964
Dobson, Emily 2003
Dodge, Kathryn 1995
Dore, Frank 1942
Down, Sarah 2000
Drake, F. W. 1941
Dunster, Mrs M. E. 1973
Dussek, Molly 1995
Eddy, Paul 2004
Edwards, Janet 1991
Elliston, Miss H. 1935
Emmott, Miss 1925
England, Edward 1972
England, I. 1925
Ennor, Kathleen 1967
Eva, Annie 1939
Eva, W. H. 1912
Evans, Catherine 1982
Fairhurst, Enoch 1945
Farnham, Marjorie 1958
Fell, J. C. 1971
Finch, P. J. A. 1941
Firth, A. W. 1909
Fishwick, Irene
née Trewhella 1922
Foss, Mary 1940
Frazier, Kathleen 1924
Freeman, Zoe 1985
Frost, Karen 1986
Fry, Miss M. 1938
Gadd, Elvira M. 1971
Gadd, K. 1971
Garrod, C. 1970
Garstin, Lilian 1924
Geeson, Mrs 1922
George, Beryl 1925
Glasson, Jack 1932
Glendinning, Albert 1986
Glendinning, Sue 1986
Green, Mrs 1920
Grose, F. B. 1931
Grosse, B. 1946
Hadfield, Adrienne 1940
Hall, C. E. 1935
Hall, Ernest 1946
Hampton, Victoria 2003
Hardy, Marian 1964
Harper, Miss B. 1972
Hartley, Frank 1948
Harvey, Caroline 1964
Harvey, Miss J. 1960
Heath, Frank 1909
Herbst, Ludwig 1941
Herschel, Mary 1988
Hewins, E. J. 1943
Higgins, Norman 1986
Hillman, Miss 1922
Hinchcliffe, Gill 1992
Hiscox, Phyllis 1913
Hoadley Daniel 1985
Hoblyn, William 1907
Hocking, May
née Stewart 1911
Hodge, Mr 1929
Holden, Margery 1922
Hollands, Joyce 2003
Holme, Willie 1928
Holmes, Lucy 1991
Horsfall, Nora C. 1945
Hosking, J. Morgan 1929
Hosking, W. H. 1927
Howarth, Osbert 1907
Howells, Jonathan 1992
Hugh-Jones, Carenza 1991
Hughes, Doris 1930
Humphrey, Miss 1925
Huntingford, Rodney 1928
Hurley, A. 1907
Hurrell, Mr 1936
Ingham, Dorothy 2002
Jacob, Mrs 1935
Jacoby, Jonathan 1994
James, Christopher 1996
James, Desmond 1939
James, Ivan 1928
Jasper, Bridget 1984
Jeltes, Raymonde de 1939
Jenkins, Lucy 1991
Joel, Mrs 1948
John, Miss 1912
Johnson, H. W. 1951
Johnston, P. 1951
Jones, Gillian 1989
Joscelyn, Dr. M.V. 1947
Jowett, J. D. 1952
Judge, Christine 1999
Keast, Mrs 1939
Keast, E.V. 1911
Keast, Lilian R. 1954
Keating, Mrs P. 1980
Kent, Winifred 1940
King, Miss M. 1965
Laity, Celia 1926
Larry, Helene 2005
Latham, Frank 1940
Lawrence, L. 1943
Leighfield, Miss 1922
Lewis, Miss E. 1967
Ley, R. M. 1949
Lichy, Roger 1982

Lidgey, Miss M.	1922
Linden, Maurice	1974
Lloyd, George	1930
Luing, Louise	1987
Lukashevitch, Olga née Bennett	1927
Lynch, Alyssa	2005
McCraith, Mrs L.	1974
McDonnell, Clare	1937
MacGuire, Mrs J.	1972
Mackenzie, F. H. M.	1957
Main, Georgina	1911
Major, Kathryn	1983
Major, Susannah	1986
Martin, Mrs E. E.	1963
Martin, Fred	1919
Martin, T. Jun	1920
Martin, Tracey	1995
Matthews, Alison	2000
Matthews, Mark	1987
Matthews, Paul	1986
May, Isabel	1996
May, Miss M.	1934
Mollard, Clifford	1927
Montague-Smith, Philip	2000
Moore, Jeremy	1982
Moore, Margaret	1924
Moore, Capt. W. J.	1967
Morcom, Audrey	1967
Morgan, C.	1911
Morris, Ariel	1940
Morris, Miss G. M.	1913
Murgatroyd, Miss	1940
Murphy, Miss E.	1956
Murton, Claudia	1994
Murton, Stephanie	1996
Nicholas, C. F.	1924
Nicholls, Amanda	2003
Nicholls, Clarice	1945
Nicholls, Hetty	1939
Nowell, Ada	1946
Nunn, Louie	1923
Nunn, Violet	1911
Nutt, Mr	1907
Nye, Jason	1986
Ogilvie-Gaskell, A.	1931
Oliver, Miss	1914
Owen, Jean	1937
Page, Esme	1985
Pangborne, R.	1959
Parker, David	1996
Parsons, Mrs A.	1955
Partington, F. H.	1922
Passmore, Mrs	1922
Paul, Kathleen	1925
Pearce, Mrs M.	1971
Pearce, R.	1976
Pendlebury, Peter	1993
Penrose, Miss V. L.	1978
Phillips, H.	1913
Pinchen, Loveday née Harris	1933
Polglase, Percy	1909
Pollard, Sam	1926
Poole, W. V.	1938
Porter, Jacob	2004
Poulter, Emma	1987
Powell, Mrs G.	1936
Preston, Joyce	1979
Prisk, Janet	1993
Proctor, Phoebe	1976
Quick, Hilda	1922
Quillisch, Gesine	1992
Quirke, Miles	1962
Rablen, Harold	1951
Radford, Miss M.	1944
Radford, P.	1971
Rapson, Jenny	1995
Rayner, Miss	1914
Reynolds, Dora	1960
Rich, Avril	1981
Rich, Mrs B. E.	1955
Rich Mrs Gregory	1936
Rich, Mrs William	1937
Richards, Mr	1907
Richards, Carrie	1997
Richards, Sheila	1961
Rickards, John	1981
Riddle, D. K. P.	1942
Robbins, P.	1949
Robinson, Mrs Arthur W.	1911
Robinson, Miss E.	1929
Rogers, E. A. Gordon	1907
Rosenfeld, Pamela	1985
Rowbotham, Bronwen	1922
Rowe, Master B.	1909
Rowe, Miss C.	1945
Rowe, J.	1921
Rowe, Percy	1914
Rundle, Mary	1934
Ryder, L.	1969
Sadka, Matthew	1985
Sadler, Wilson	1980
Salmon, Mrs M.	1971
Schultz L.	1971
Scott, Miss	1921
Searle, R. H.	1909
Sell, Deborah	2003
Shakerley, G. H.	1928
Shepherd, Elizabeth	1995
Skinner, Ruth	1983
Smith, Miss V.	1949
Sowden, Mrs M. E.	1958
Start, Nellie	1948
Stephens, Miss C.	1974
Steuart, Mrs D.	1919
Stone, Dolly	1924
Swift, Eileen	1982
Swift, Ian	1982
Swift, Richard	1982
Tamblyn, Derek	1946
Tamblyn, Frank	1930
Tempest, Ann née Harvey	1957
Tempest, Horace	1961
Thomas, Joan	1998
Thompson, Miss E.	1934
Thompson, Stuart	1925
Thorne, Alan	1911
Thornley, Mrs M.	1929
Todrick, Mrs E. K.	1932
Tombe, Eileen	1974
Tonkin, Lilian	1931
Tonking, Isobel	1938
Toy, Dorothy	1931
Tregaskes, Alan	1989
Tregenza, Mrs W. C.	1927
Treglown, J.	1946
Trevena, Mrs K.	1945
Trounson, W.	1907
Truman, Norman	1931
Trythall, E.	1920
Tudor, Miss A.	1967
Tunstall-Behrens, Rosemary	1966
Tyreman, Hilary	1995
Uren, Diana	1940
Ursell, Evelyn	1937
Verran, Mrs C.	1950
Vosper, Jack	2002
Wardle, Alex	2000
Warren, Mr	1907
Watson, Amelia	2004
Watson, M.	1969
Webb, L. A.	1942
Webber, Miss	1922
Webber, Mrs D.	1914
Wellington, Musician	1910
West, R. H.	1925
West, R. S.	1923
Weymouth, Edward	1934
Wheeler, Betty	2005
White, Martin	1993
Whitt, Mrs	1951
Willacy, James A.	1946
Williams, B.	1937
Williams, G. E.	1941
Williams, Miss H. V.	1930
Williams, Mrs M.	1954
Williams, Dr. M. Fischer	1966
Williams, Rowenna née Maddern	1925
Willis, Musician	1910
Winters, Amanda	1996
Winters, Simon	1998
Wood A.	1970
Woodcock, Stephen	1989
Woolcock, Kenneth	1929
Woolfrey, J. H.	1952
Yardley, C. H.	1912
Yeadon, Evelyn M.	1944
Young, Mrs Mackworth	1923
Ziolo, P.	1972
Zybach, Pollyanna	1983

Viola

Andrewartha, Gwyneth	1932
Atkinson, Helen	1937
Balkwill, Susan	1995
Barnes, Anton	1985
Barwell, Miss	1975
Belfield, Toby	1988
Bennetts, Barry	1907
Bolitho, Una née George	1974
Buddle, Eleanor	1936
Carling, Gwen	1924
Champion, T. Turner	1909
Chase, Matthew	2001
Collins, Caroline	1987
Collins, Mrs R. J.	1935
Congreve, Miss	1914
Crompton, Jo	2005
Dalling, Musician	1910
Dussek, Molly	1998
Edwards, Louise	1985
Elston, Christopher	1979
Farmer, Zoe	1999
Findlay, Andrew	2001
Flyckeberg, Charlotte	1985
Gadd, Elvira	1973
Gilardoni, C.	1909
Gregg, Elizabeth	1988
Gundry, Kitty née Laity	1925
Guthrie-Smith, Peter	1950
Hall, James	1933
Hardy, Marian	1968
Harper, Romola	1981
Harris, Faith	1923
Harrison, C.	1913
Harvey, Mr	1927
Harvey, Guernsey	1932
Harvie, Caroline	2002
Haswell, J. D.	1950
Hodson, Miss	1930
James, Ivan	1934
King, Miss M.	1966
Lloyd, Rosemary	1920
McCraith, Mrs L.	1974
Macdonnell, Ellie	1999
Main, Georgina	1920
Nye, Annette	1992
Page, Esme	1985
Parker, David	1998
Pearson, Geoffrey	1988
Poole, W.	1971
Poulter, Helen	1988
Preston, Joyce	1976
Prichard, Miss	1926
Rablen, Harold	1958
Radford, P.	1976
Rice, Hilda	1940
Richards, Claire	1986
Rogers, E. George	1910
Rowe, Elizabeth	1959
Rundle, Mary	1963
Scott, May	1936
Shakerley, G. H.	1925
Shepherd, Elizabeth	1982
Shewell, Richard	1986
Smeaton, Mr	1913
Stapley, Miss	1911
Steuart, Mrs D.	1914
Tamblyn, Derek	1955
Tempest, Ann née Harvey	1978
Tempest, Horace	1974
Thorne, Mary	1957
Tracy, Mary F.	1957
Truman, Norman	1946
Vercoe, Marjorie	1930
White, Winifred M.	1937
Willacy, James A.	1946

Wood, A	1935
Wright, Phillipa	1982

'Cello

Arthur-West, Monica	1931
Baldry, Miss	1931
Barkworth, R. C.	1936
Bartlett, May	1924
Bauman, Blanche	1945
Berkowitz, Saul	1993
Blight, Miss W.	1913
Brett, Katy	1997
Broad, Ethel	1941
Brown, Andrew	1987
Brown, Mrs G.	1947
Brown, J. Weyman	1922
Carr, Thompson	1923
Cavanagh, Miss B.	1973
Chapple, E. J.	1931
Clarke, Rachel	1929
Cleave, Miss H.	1953
Cleur, G. D.	1971
Cock, Mrs R.	1969
Codyre, Kathleen	1942
Collins, R. J.	1938
Cooke, Iris	1927
Cox, Doris	1923
Curnow, Demelza	2003
De Bever, Monsieur	1914
Derici, Joyce	1994
Derrington, David	1963
Dunkley, Miss	1925
Farnes, Rod	1990
Farnham, Christine	1958
Fido, Enid	1958
Forbes, Stanhope A.	1909
Gale, Patrick	2003
Gleeson, Phyllis	1925
Graham-Jones, Ian	1966
Green, Miss C. D.	1970
Grimer, Miss F.	1962
Hallward, A. W.	1926
Hanson, Anthea	1981
Harris, C.	1974
Herschel, Sarah	1988
Hoadley, Ben	1987
Holdsworth, J.	1924
Hooper, Gerald	1987
Hoskins, R. A.	1909
Kilty, James	1998
Lane, Rosemary	1981
Leaman, P. J.	1960
Luke, Herbert	1929
McCreery, Ethel	1940
McDonnell, Doreen	1938
Moir, H.	1913
Morris, B.	1967
Nalder, Hugh	1939
Nicholls, W. S.	1907
Norris, J. L. B.	1935
O'Brien, K. J.	1944
Padel, Oliver	1973
Page, Dr. J. Basil	1913
Park, Jim	1986
Pearson, Sally née Bardsley	1985
Pike, Charlie G.	1919
Porter, Amy	1932
Powell, Jeanette née Davey	1932
Poynton, Jane	1975
Price, Honor née Harris	1933
Robinson, Hannah	2003
Rundle, Kathleen	1933
Shilan, W. F.	1947
Short, E. A.	1907
Slater, Margaret	1940
Swift, Eileen	1984
Taylor, Mrs D. Mascie	1934
Tempest, Horace	1962
Tempest, Rose	1968
Thomas, Vivien	1931
Thompson, Roy	1928
Tranter, Gladys M.	1963
Trudgeon, J. H.	1921
Trudgian, Stacey	1991
Truman, Enid née Barnes	1928
Tunstall-Behrens, Peter	2002
Ware, Mrs Herbert	1948
Webb, Ernie	1994
White, Cecil	1931
White, Miss A.	1957
Woolmington, Eileen	1993
Young, Lawrence	1923

Double Bass

Allen, Jack	1921
Arthur-West, E.	1931
Barber, F. J.	1959
Bassett, F.	1968
Bennetts, Lynda	1993
Bretherton, F.	1963
Bridgland, A.	1966
Butterfly, Patrick	1994
Caseley, Helen	1970
Caswell, Hamilton	1972
Chamberlain, H. T.	1941
Collins, Peter	1979
Comber, Phaedra	1993
Couch, Mrs L.	1950
Craven, J.	1919
Curnow, Zoe	1993
Eastland, A. E.	1968
Eilertsen, Lydia	1995
Engleheart, John	1938
Hamilton, Carolyn	1998
Higgs, Michael	1984
Hill, C.	1927
Hofler, Herr Fritz	1907
Horsfall, Nora C.	1954
Hosken, Timothy	1979
Kellow, L. T.	1964
Kelly, Sian	2004
Ledger, T.	1952
Littlepage, Musician	1910
Locker, Claudia	1993
Manning, J. C.	1932
Manning, Stephen	1987
Manning, W.	1925
Neal, Rebecca	1991
Nye, Maurice	1992
Owen, Piers	1994
Page, Nora	1969
Raymond, Julie	1992
Sadler, Wilson	1978
Sainsbury, H.	1922
Slatford, Rodney	1969
Steer, Hannah	1995
Tempest, Horace	1969
Thewlis, R	1962
Tregarthen, N.	1931
Truscott, J. C.	1911
Uren, Peter	1940
White, G. Howard	1909
White, Graham L.	1935
Williams, William B.	1925
Yardley, C. H.	1913

Flute/Piccolo

Ableman, Sarah	2004
Beare, Natalie	1993
Benney, Jane	1989
Besley, Susan	2003
Blundy, Nathan	1996
Bota, Maria	1982
Bradbury, H.	1909
Briton, Musician W. H.	1948
Campbell, Jennet	1983
Capon, Miss L.	1975
Corrison, Alex	1907
Crawshaw, Joanna	1999
Curnow, Tamara	1992
Davey, Maureen	1986
Du'Sautoy, Jennifer	1993
Eden, Musician H. L.	1948
Edwards, H.	1949
Engel, H. B.	1969
Fry, Claire	1986
Gower, E. Fagg	1922
Grant-Johns, Alan	1991
Greebe, M. E.	1940
Gwynne, Helen	1964
Hodson, F. H.	1911
Hopkinson, L.	1958
Ingram, G. M.	1963
Jones, Charlie	1956
Jones, Sharyn	1999
Keast, Lilian R.	1963
King, R.	1962
Lewin, A. E.	1930
Lewis, Tom	1987
Lloyd, William A. C.	1924
Matthews, Abby	1998
Miners, Arthur	1932
Morgan, Rev. T.	1909
Murray, Mr	1938
Murray-Hanley, Sarah née Murray	1974
Mutlow, Adrian	1995
Nicholls, Maureen	1994
Oates, B.	1960
Oswald, Geoff	2004
Pascoe, Deborah	1985
Pengelly, J.	1923
Phillips, Leo	1943
Poznansky, Gillian	1998
Poznansky, Jonathan	2002
Prowse, M.	1981
Purchase, Holly	2006
Richards, Tracey	1984
Roberts, Ann	1986
Solomon, M.	1949
Stewart, Barbara	1945
Thomas, Rebecca	2005
Tredinnick, Jennie	2000
Turner, F.	1950
Vosper, Elizabeth née Robertson	1982
Ward, Musician C.	1909
White, Miss P.	1976
Whitehead, Robin	1950
Whitlock, Dr. F. A.	1952
Wood, Mr	1930
Wood, Michael	2004

Clarinet/Bass Clarinet

Ableman, Sarah	1995
Allen, S.	1971
Allum, Ktiskin	1992
Aspinall, C. H.	1942
Bacher, Mr	1907
Bailey, Judith	2001
Bartlett, Dr. D.	1975
Bateman, A.	1941
Bryant, Julia née Favell	1971
Carder, R.	1972
Cardew, Michael A.	1924
Chubb, W. B.	1949
Clarke, O.	1966
Clay, William	1922
Clemence, Mr	1911
Conboye, Jo	2001
Crompton, Jo	2005
Dolbear, A.	1926
Elkan, G.	1960
Elston, Janet	1982
Farnham, Michael T. E.	1958
Fitkin, G.	1980
Fryer, Miss A.	1969
Fussel, Miss A.	1959
Geidt, W. R.	1961
Grover, J. A.	1962
Hailey, Teresa	1993
Hewson, Miss V.	1960
Hollywood, Jo	1985
Josling, Melanie	1989
Latham, Frank	1907
Laurence, G.	1932
Lawrence, G.	1912
Lever, J.	1979
Lewis, N.	1947
Lupton, P.	1943
Lynch, Clare	2002
McSweeney, J.	1971
Martin, Karen	1994
Matthews, Musician	1910
Matthews, Alison	1983
Mayne, John	1946
Moore, Mrs P.	1974
Negus, L. A. W.	1953
Olfzewsky, Katie	1994
Ovenden, L. E.	1961

Page, J. 1966
Pawlyn, Miss M. 1964
Pearson, Geoffrey 1994
Richards, Miss C. 1981
Roberts, A. 1922
Rogers, Matt 2005
Rowe, Arthur 1933
Rowe, Deborah 1985
Sainsbury, H. 1909
Sargent, Paul 1970
Singh, Mrs P. 1979
Skinner, S. 1976
Smith, A. 1946
Thompson, Jackie 2003
Tonkin, A. 1952
Ursell, Victor 1931
Vosper, Elizabeth née Robertson 1974
Weeks, Musician 1910
White, F. 1947
Willey, E. G. 1962
Woodhouse, H. 1973

Oboe/Cor Anglais

Andrews, Malcolm 1994
Ball, David 1976
Blewett, Lorna 1986
Boyd, Ann C. 1962
Bradley, Gilbert Leslie 1926
Brien, Albert 1922
Clark, Miss R. 1981
Clementson J 1962
Dennis, H. 1909
Doughty, Francesca 1972
Giles, Miss P. 1960
Halllwell, J. 1923
Harris, Cameron 1992
Henderson, Gavin 1992
Howells, Elizabeth 1984
Jones, Ruth 1995
Keast, Lilian R 1955
Knuckey, Lauren 2005
Kowalewsky, Lutz 1992
Laurence, G. 1931
MacDonald, K. J. 1964
McMullen, Miss J. 1965
Mole, Margaret 1957
Ollson, Miss A. A. 1962
Overton, B. 1966
Pascoe, Mark 1989
Pearce, Catherine née Pooley 1974
Pengelly, Cyril 1922
Polkinghorn, M. 1981
Poznansky, Jonathan 1998
Ricketts, W. 1956
Roberts, Rebecca 1991
Simmons, Charles 1954
Smith, Miss A. 1980
Taylor, Charles L. 1907
Ursell, Victor 1931
Vosper, Elizabeth née Robertson 1972
White, Anthony 1968
Wicks, Musician Stanton 1922
Williams, Miss H. 1968
Woolner, Miss A. 1976

Bassoon

Adrian, R. 1969
Alker, J. 1957
Ayton, Lyn 1980
Baker, C. J. 1907
Baldry, Kathryn 1981
Bearman, J. C. 1967
Blower, S. 1965
Boyle, M. 1956
Camden, D. 1959
Chalmers, S. 1966
Cleave, Miss H. 1960
Cooper, L. 1962
Corin, Tom 2005
Densham, Miss C. 1963
Evins, W. 1947
Fletcher, Mrs J. 1979
Francis, P. 1959
Gadsdon, Kim 1990
Gibson, Rebecca 2003
Goldsworthy, Julia 1999
Gurney, Samantha 1984
Hall, Susan. 1953
Haskins, A. D. 1952
Hatherill, S. E. 1951
Head, L. 1950
Hedley, J. A. 1965
Hereward, D. 1971
Holmes, R. G. 1926
Howarth, M. A. 1964
Johnson, D. W. B. 1962
Johnston, A. 1932
Johnston, L. 1928
Jones, Paul 2003
Kingshott, Brigit 1998
Knight, Lester 2004
Latham, Frank 1909
Lee, J. 1973
Miles, Mrs J. 1973
Milne, P. 1963
Murrey, Miss P. 1972
Piper, W. 1931
Poznansky, Jonathan 2003
Rance, Jessica 2004
Sargent, Paul 1968
Scott, D. G. 1961
Shirley, D. 1980
Stallard, Mr 1935
Stewart, Elizabeth 1997
Tonkin, A. 1958
Tregloyn, Musician T.G. 1948
Vosper, Elizabeth née Robertson 1976
Walker, G. 1956
Willey, E. 1968
Williams, Pat 1992
Woolner, Miss A. 1968

Saxophone

Peters, Steven 1983
Tonkin, A. 1960
Williams, W. F. 1947
Woolcock, Kenneth 1932

French Horn

Abbott, P. J. 1951
Adams, Andrea 1982
Adams, Teresa 1981
Alford, J. P. 1968
Arden, F. H. 1951
Ardis, J. 1949
Austen, E. 1979
Bainbridge, Becky 1991
Baker, Paul 1986
Beare, W. J. 1911
Bell, D. 1973
Borrows-Watson, J. 1975
Bowditch, F. H. 1912
Bray, Stephen 1998
Brown, Shirley 2001
Brown, Stanley 1939
Bunt, C. 1975
Carter, Tamsin 1993
Chamberlain, Lisa 1994
Collins, D. F. 1957
Crutwell, Percy 1919
Davies, Sgt. Major Hubert 1944
Dawes, A. 1946
Doo, R. 1978
Elford, Musician 1910
Fergusson, J. 1980
Fletcher, Stuart 1985
Floyd, Denzil 1990
Gurr, Peter 1985
Hamilton, Mr 1912
Hammond, David 1985
Healey, Thomas 1916
Hodge, Miss M. 1965
Hortin, Christopher 1989
Hosking, W. J. 1914
Hugh-Jones, Rupert 1991
James, Steven 1989
Jewell, A. 1942
Kimberly, E. W. 1962
Kitley, David 2002
Laslett, Catherine 1995
Leisk, Rachael 2002
Lowry, D. L. 1948
Marsh, D. 1958
Marshall, Emily 1984
Martin, F. 1912
Mathewman, Mr 1933
Matthews, Morwenna 2002
Mattingly, C. F. 1960
Miller, J. 1953
Moon, Willie 1928
Moulton, J. W. 1912
Moyle, Sarah 1998
Nicholls, Alfred 1922
Oates, E. H. 1938
Oates, W. E. 1929
O'Dell, Jacqueline 1982
Offord, J. 1969
Parkinson, Jane 1983
Parsons, William 1924
Pike, Lynette 1995
Rawlings, A. 1927
Richardson, A. W. 1973
Rogers, J. 1967
Saunders, A. 1977
Smith, J. 1937
Smith, Musician J. 1948
Smith, Jeremy 1996
Smith, R. 1964
Stephens, Natalie 1987
Stepney, Musician 1910
Stobart, J. 1972
Sumpster, Mr 1913
Thomas, Rebecca 1999
Tonkin, Miss J. 1968
Tunstall-Behrens, Michael 1954
Turnbull, John 1940
Vosper, Iain 1960
Vosper, Jenny 2000
Ward, G. L. 1973
Waters, D. J. 1967
Wear, D. 1977
West, D. 1980
Willey, E. 1966
Williams, J. T. 1966
Willmett, Mr 1926
Wills, Roger 1981
Wilson, J. 1972
Wilson, R. C. 1963

Trumpet/Cornet

Ampleford, David 1996
Austen, John 2005
Ball, Eric 1931
Barton, Caroline née O'Dell 1977
Bassett, Neil 1982
Batten, J. 1909
Bedding, J. 1952
Bennett, Reg 1990
Blewett, M. 1907
Brown, Stanley 1940
Caless, T. 1957
Carter, Jonathan 2002
Couch, Michael 1986
Crenell, William 2001
Curnow, Zoe 1994
Dark, Sam 2000
David, Paul 1984
Davis, Katherine 1999
Driver, B. 1981
Evans, Owen 2006
Flynn, Mr 1907
Gregory, I.G. 1955
Hagen, Kirsten 2003
Hamley, John C. 1945
Harris, C. 1964
Harris, J. 1973
Henry, G. D. 1929
Jewell, A. 1927
Johns, Norman 1987
Kellow, Vicky 1999
Kennedy, W. 1951
Le Lacheur, D. 1950
McGuinness, T. 1931
Martin, Victor 1932
Matthews, Arthur J. 1909
Mitchell, J. 1954
Mitchell, S. 1953
Nicholls, A Jnr. 1919

Nicholls, C. 1970
Penrose, W. 1965
Pritchard, Michael 1986
Ray, M. 1969
Richards, A. G. 1926
Rutter, Natasha
née Mead 1981
Rutter, Neil 1988
Seabourne, R. 1914
Smith, R. 1966
Steward, D. 1969
Strutt, Cyril 1960
Thomas, E. 1929
Thomas, Paul 2001
Tomkinson, Mandy 2004
Tonkin, D. 1976
Vague, D. 1971
Warren, John 1937
Warren, Vivian 1936
Williams, T. 1958
Williams, W. E. B. 1926
Willis, Bibba 1999
Woods, Roland 1990
Worth, W. H. 1942
Wright, R. 1914
Yarwood, R 1980

Trombone
Allen, Harry 1962
Andrew, Steve 1995
Annear, Andrew 1992
Ashton, E. 1980
Barnes, Anton 1993
Bennetts, D. 1954
Bennetts, W. 1943
Bowditch, C. G. 1911
Brind, Colin 1993
Buist, Barry 1994
Clift, W. 1953
Davies, D. D. 1956
Davies, Ian 1998
Douglas, Paul 1982
Dyer, Kevin 2004
Evans, Chris 1994
Farley, P. A. 1967
Fletcher, Diana
née Toy 1982
Firth, Donald 1922
Galbraith, Deborah 1999
Gillis, John 1925
Hannam, P. 1951
Harvey, G. 1972
Higgs, Michael 1983
Hughes, D. 1977
Jones, D. Melville 1927
Kessell, Herbert 1929
Little, Mark 2002
Loukes, David 1991
Magarr, J. 1980
Marks, E. R. 1968
Nathan, Nigel 1999
Nicholas, David 1986
Nicholls, M. 1975
Nicholls, Richard 1907
Nimmon, Ben 1996
Perkins, Michael 1991
Prowse, W. B. 1930
Randall, Rachel 1998
Randall, Roger 1998
Richards, Glyn 1999
Roach, C. H. 1913
Rosevear, George 1924
Smith, Simon 1990
Stone, W. S. 1929
Stunnel, S. 1981
Teague, Andrew 1998
Thomas, Jeff 1984
Tonkin, Thomas M. 1956
Toy, Miss E. 1982
Tremayne, I. 1972
Trudgeon, N.V. 1922
Wadsworth, G. 1954
Williams, Mr 1926
Wills, Roger 1988

Tuba
Ashton, Mr 1926
Bennetts, T. 1958
Bunney, D. 1973
Davies, Ian 2004
Donohew, Barnaby 2005
Evans, T. 1981
Hosking, Charles 1924
Lawry, J. 1966
Nicholls, Alfred 1923
Paul, George 1928
Probert, J. 1931
Pryor, J. 1932
Stobart, H. 1976
Thomas Eric 1984
Thomas, Stephen 1986
While, Ian 2001
Williams, John 1925

Wagner Tuba
Hennessy, I. 1976
Pfaff, M. 1976
Sampson, B. 1976
Thomas, R. 1976

Euphonium
Nicholls, Alfred 1907

Drums
Edwards, J. 1912
Gendall, H. 1926
Hosking, C. 1907
Nicholls, Richard 1924
Nicholls, W. H. 1909
Nicholls, W. T. 1925

Tympani
Bassett, Tom 2005
Edwards, Michael 1993
Frith, Martin 1995
Hamilton, Ross 1993
Hughes, Elizabeth 2004
Masser, Guthrie 2002
Robinson, Elizabeth 2003
Rowe, Natalie 1999
Smith, Adam 1998
Stewart, Leonard 1919
Weekes, John 1969
Whitehead, Robin 1959
Wilshaw, Alf 1970

Percussion
Aldous, Mark 1994
Andrews, Miss R. 1978
Ayerst, Richard 1994
Baker, C. J. 1908;1948
Bamforth, Louise 1983
Barton, Miss B. 1976
Beardmore, Bernard 1930
Blundy, Adam 1996
Brown, Marie 1941
Caseley, Bridget 1974
Collins, J. 1947
Dyer, Anna 1985
Eva, B. 1955
Fitkin, G. 1979
Gendall, F. 1938
Gendall, H. 1933
Grebe, Eric 1946
Gwynn, Miss H. 1964
Haines, Tom 1994
Hamilton, Ross 1993
Hichens, S. 1953
Hiley, Michelle 1986
Hockings, D. 1978
Hough, Calie 2005
Jacoby, Jonathan 1992
Jacoby, Mrs S. 1979
Keast, Lilian R. 1960
Keech, Miss V. 1971
Loring, Miss S. 1967
Luke, R. 1959
Mitchell, John 1989
Nicholls, Alfred 1928
Nicholls, Richard 1924
Nicholls, W. H. 1924
Nicholls, W. T. 1925
Nye, Jason 1987
Paul, George 1929
Pawlyn, Miss M. 1964
Paynter, Tom 1946
Probert, J. 1931
Pryor, J. 1932
Rapson, Jo 2006
Rhodes, Helen 1994
Robinson, James 1986
Rosewarne, Mark 1991
Rowe, Mr B. 1935
Rowe, David 1984
Shannon, Duncan 1989
Smith, Adam 1998
Stewart, Barbara 1941
Stewart, Ben 1994
Stewart, Leonard 1919
Sutherland, Zelda 1982
Tellam, Andrew 1990
Terry, Brenda 1959
Thomas, D. 1947
Vennings, Tony 1990
Walker, Marie 1990
Weeks, Stephen 1990
White, Miss E. 1964
Whitehead, Robin 1955
Williams, G. 1948
Williams, J. 1911
Williams, William E. 1924
Wilshaw, Alf 1960
Wycherly, James 1986

Piano/Accompanists
Frazier, Kathleen 1926
Jory, Russell 1983
Luing, Louise 1987
Robinson, Alfred W. 1907
Truman, Enid
née Barnes 1928

Organ
Main, Georgina 1919
Robinson, Alfred W. 1907

Harpsichord
Simons, John 1938
Wilkinson, Eleanor 1934

Harp
Bennetts, W. 1909
Field, Sheila 1974
Robinson, Alfred W. 1923
Ross, Ann 1955
Seton, Miss A. 1947
Tempest, Ann
née Harvey 1956

Banjo
Richards, Rex 1985

Harmonica
Collins, J. 1947

Appendix 2
Penzance Orchestral Society Officials 1907-2007

Notes:

1. Minutes of the Society's committee meetings and annual members' meetings are not available prior to 1933. Earlier records are either lacking or uninformative resulting in incomplete lists in some cases.

2. Vice-Presidents were either senior or long-serving members of the Society or supportive members of the public. They are not listed here due to inconsistency of records.

3. Occasionally the title of 'Life President', 'Life Member' or 'Honorary Member' was bestowed upon a member who had merited it. Inconsistency of recording the names makes a listing difficult but they were normally members who were prominent in the Society's history.

4. Between the years 1934 and 1945 'Patrons' were named on concert programmes. They included Brig-Gen. the Lord St Levan, 1934-1941; Frank Latham, 1942-1945; Lt. Col. the Lord St Levan, 1943-1945 and Sir Henry Wood, 1943-1944.

5. * indicates an officer who was not a member of the orchestra.

President

1907-1941	Frank Latham
1941-1953	Alfred W. Robinson
1953-1954	Mrs Charles Williams
1954-1968	Miss Winifrede Beadsworth
1968-1980	Mrs Faith Harris, M.B.E.
1980-2001	Mrs Enid Truman
2001-	Mrs Rose Tempest

Conductor

1907-1942	Walter Barnes
1942-1946	R. J. Maddern Williams
1946-1981	J. Morgan Hosking
1981-2002	David Ball
2002-2003	David Frost and Judith Bailey (Guest conductors)
2003-	Judith Bailey

Principal Violin (Leader)

1907- ?	Osbert Howarth
1914	Miss May Stewart
1919-1927	Miss May Stewart
1927-1946	Lilian Garstin
1939-1946	Miss Winifrede Beadsworth (Acting Principal during World War II)
1946-1948	Kendal Baic
1948-1950	Iola Coleman
1950-1972	Lilian Garstin
1972-1973	Connie Bee
1973-1981	Jack Glasson
1981-2006	Joyce Preston
2006-	Ruth Boulton and Christine Judge (joint Principals)

Treasurer

1907- ?	Osbert Howarth
1908-1912	not named
1912-1944	A. W. Firth
1944-1951	G. L. Bradley
1951-1984	Norman Truman
1984-1987	Wilson Sadler
1987-1989	Peter Sanders *
1889-1998	Mark Belfield *
1998-2004	Stephen Bray
2004-	Iain Vosper

Secretary

1907-1908	E. A. Gordon Rogers
1908- ?	J. F. Brock
1912- ?	R. A. Hoskins
1919-1922	Georgina H. Main
1922-1925	Leonard Stewart
1925	Georgina H. Main/R.A. Hoskins
1926-1933	Georgina H. Main
1933-1934	Miss Lilian Tonkin
1934-1938	H. D. Morris *
1938-1939	J. O. Volk *
1939-1940	H. D. Morris *
1940-1941	Mrs H. D. Morris *
1941-1942	R. H. Pezzack *
1942-1943	Miss Lilian Tonkin/A. W. Firth
1943-1945	Rev. H. E. Gardner *
1945-1946	R. L. Yeadon *
1946 Jan-June	Miss Green *
1946 July-1947	J. Morgan Hosking
1947-1949	Miss Adrienne Hadfield
1949-1955	Frank Hartley
1955-1960	Miss Adrienne Hadfield
1960-1984	Enid Truman
1984-1985	Helen Caseley
1985-1998	Rose Tempest
1998-2003	Jane Poynton
2003-	Elizabeth Gregg

Librarian

1913- ?	C. H. Yardley
1924-1931	J. G. Beadsworth ('Concert Director' 1931-1932, a fleeting post!)
1931-1932	Thomas Weaver
1932-1934	J. G. Beadsworth/Stuart Thompson

1934-1935	Stuart Thompson
1935-1938	Bernard Williams
1939 (part year)	A. W. Murray – Acting Hon. Librarian
1939-1941	C. J. 'Jerry' Baker
1941-1951	Helen Atkinson
1951 (part year)	J. Treglown
1951-1960	Enid Truman
1960-1980	Helen Barton
1980-1983	Catherine Pearce
1983-1991	Elizabeth Rowe
1991-	Sally and Geoffrey Pearson

Committee Chairman

This was not a clearly defined post until 1946 prior to which a member of the committee was 'elected' to take the chair at meetings.

1946-1963	L. Graham White
1963-1969	not named
1969-1979	L Graham White
1979-1984	not named
1984-1985	Robin Whitehead
1985-1988	Ann Tempest
1988-1991	Peter Collins
1991-1993	Mike Higgs
1993-1997	John Care
1997-1998	Sheila Richards
1998-	Mike Higgs

Subscribers/Friends Secretary

This work was carried out by committee members and the Hon. Treasure until 1948 when the post was created. Miss Winifrede Beadsworth took this office from 1948-1953 when the work reverted to the Hon. Treasurer. It did not appear as a named post again until 1984.

1984-1986	Audrey Morcom
1986-1987	Rose Tempest (Acting Secretary)
1987-1996	Catherine Pearce
1996-	Eileen Woolmington

Appendix 3

Penzance Orchestral Society Soloists and Guest Artistes 1907-2007

Notes:

Except for concerti, solo performances by members of the Penzance Orchestral Society, for example in concerti grossi, are not included.

Members of the Penzance Orchestral Society who conducted their own compositions are not included under 'Guest Conductors'.

Violin

Barnes, Walter	1908;1937
Baster, Miles	1999
Beadsworth, Winifrede	1940
Beyers, Zoe	2005
Bialas, Antonina	1984
Bochmann, Michael	1975; 1979; 1985
Chappell, Kay	1995
Cummings, Diana	1971
Fairhurst, Harold	1927; 1930; 1932; 1941
Fairless, Margaret	1925
Fry, Marjorie	1940
Garstin, Lilian	1939
Gordon, Jane	2006
Grinke, Frederick	1949; 1961
Gruenberg, Erich	1952
Hirons, Christopher	1977
Howard, Penelope	1968
Jackson, Laurence	1992
Jeltes, Raymonde	1940
Jenkins, Tom	1955
Kent, Winifred	1940
Lielmane, Rasma	1981
Lockhart, Elizabeth	1945
Loveday, Alan	1947; 1951; 1956
Lucas, Hilda	1909
McCormack, Gina	1988
Martin, David	1959
Mason, Frances	1965
Moldawsky, Sonia	1933
Partridge, Bernard	1984
Payne, Leo	1991; 1997
Pini, Carl	1957; 1962
Sammons, Albert	1934
Stewart, May	1914
Taylor, Matthew	1989
Thomas, Ronald	1967
Wilde, Barry	1970; 1973
Zelikoff, Sivann	2003
Zorian, Olive	1942

Viola

Bucknall, Joan	1968
Lovell, Keith	1978; 1992

'Cello

Altenburg, Beate	2001
Alvin, Juliette	1940; 1948
Bartlett, May	1926
Carr, Colin	1977
Coates, Oliver	2002
Cummings, Douglas	1968
De Bever, Monsieur	1914
Evans, Michael	1983; 1999
Grunthal, Barbara	1987
Harvey, Keith	1972
Hooton, Florence	1960
Hopkins, Louise	1991
Piggott, Audrey	1936
Pini, Anthony	1955; 1957
Sharpe, Cedric	1931
Tempest, Keith	1989

Guitar

Gregory, Charles	1971

Flute

McLaren, Neil	1990
Miners, Arthur	1950
O'Connor, Peter	1998

Clarinet

Cowley, Guy	1996
Cox, Nicholas	1982
Ferrar, Jenny	2006
King, Thea	1976
Pearson, Geoffrey	2000
Waters, Stephen	1953

Oboe/Cor Anglais

Argiros, Marios	1986
Brien, Albert	1950
Rothwell, Evelyn	1958
Triner, Imogen	1997

Bassoon

Chapman, Michael	1993
Perkins, Laurence	2005

French Horn

Brown, Timothy	1976
Palmer, James	2004
Williams, Jonathan	1984

Trumpet/Cornet

Cesar, Philip 1981
Eskdale, George 1946
Mason, David 1989

Harp

Drake, Susan 1994
Quinney, Enid 1950

Piano

Bamford, Stephanie 1973
Caplan, Freda 1943
Cohen, Harriet 1956
Cole, Maurice 1954
Comeau, Paul 1994; 2000
Fatichenti, Marco 2003; 2007
Fleet, Marlene 1967; 1970; 1980
Ford, Diana 1948;1952
Frazier, Kathleen 1926; 1949
Hambourg, Michal 1945
Hichens, Stephen 1974
Horsley, Colin 1961
Jolley, Peter 1994
Jory, Russell 1983
Katin, Peter 1966
Kendall, Marie-Noelle 1996
Latarche, Vanessa 1988
Loveridge, Iris 1963
Marckham, Richard 1978
Martinova, Maria 2002
Mason, Berkeley 1947
Moores, John 1948
Nunn, Violet 1923
Peebles, Antony 1975
H.H. Ranee Margaret of Sarawak 1927
Searle-Barnes, Paul 1982
Sellick, Phyllis 1942
Seow, Yitkin 1986; 1993
Shutter, George 1987
Simm, Richard 1979
Simons, John 1937; 1938
Sumner, Louise 1948; 1974
Tomes, Susan 1983
Tonking, Ethel 1913
Truman, Enid née Barnes 1934; 1948; 1953
Vallier, John 1950; 1959; 1969
Weingarten, Joseph 1949; 1964
West, Andrew 1990; 1995
Wibaut, Frank 1972; 1980
Wilde, David 1966
Yao, Lan 2001

Harpsichord

Simons, John 1938
Wilkinson, Eleanor 1934

Organ

Jory, Russell 1983; 1987; 2002
Thomas, E. Fugler 1934
Winter, John 1974

Singers

Ball, Eric Bass 1932
Bannerman, Betty Soprano (?) 1932
Barlow, Tom Tenor 1914
Barton, Kenwin Baritone 1949
Bazeley, Peggy Soprano 1931
Bollard, Archibald Bass 1920
Branwell, Alfred Bass/Baritone 1911;1912
Brookesbank, Margaret, née Rich Soprano 1922;1928
Cameron, John Baritone 1963
Cardell, Harry Tenor 1914
Carfax, Marion Mezzo-soprano 1924
Carnegie, Austen Baritone 1939
Chitty, George Tenor 1951
Cooke, George Bass/Baritone 1939
Craig, Charles Tenor 1960
Cresser, A. Victor Bass 1923
Dapp, Dorothee Soprano 1919
Davey, John ? 1907
De La Cote, Fifine Soprano 1913
Dunn, Jack Baritone 1946
Dyer, Lorely Soprano 1950
Edwards, Clarice Soprano 1927;1934
Elliott, Victoria Soprano 1953;1956
Ellis, Kenneth Bass 1941;1950
Ellis, Nellie Soprano 1908
Fishwick, Bernard Baritone 1930;1933;1937
Garner, George Tenor 1929
Gowings, Leonard Tenor 1936
Green, Margaret Contralto 1998
Grohn, Nora Soprano 1936
Hale, Una Soprano 1964
Hall, Kitty Soprano 1939
Hallward, Marjorie Mezzo-Soprano 1926
Hancock, Joan Contralto 1953
Hargreaves, Mrs Spencer ? 1921
Harvey, Elise Mezzo-Soprano 1951
Heyner, Herbert Baritone 1926
Inglewood Jenkin, Miss E Contralto 1910
Inia Te Wiata Bass 1957
Jackson, Richard Baritone 1995
Jasper, Charles Baritone 1915
Jones, Trefor Tenor 1934
Kingsley, Margaret Soprano 1962; 1966; 1980
Lewis, Gladys Soprano 1951
Lowe, Marion Soprano 1958
Luxon, Benjamin Baritone 1965
McEachern, Malcolm Bass 1935
McFadyean, Mrs Gavin Soprano 1920
McKenna, John Tenor 1931
Maynard, Aldrovand Tenor 1921
Morton, Frida Soprano 1940
Nunn, Violet Soprano 1912
Nuttall, Lucy Contralto 1924
Osborne, Mrs Tom Contralto 1911;1915
Parker, Linda Soprano 1943
Pearce, Catherine Soprano 1984
Perry, E. S. Bass 1908
Peters, Muriel Soprano 1947
Pollak, Anna Soprano 1954
Reach, Edward Tenor 1946
Rich, Margaret Soprano 1922
Riley, Julia Soprano 2004
Roberts, Alma Contralto 1914
Roberts, Beatrice Contralto 1909
Rowbotham, Bronwen Soprano 1923
Rowlands, Sylvia Mezzo-soprano 1974
Sandow, Helen Contralto 1937
Searle, Minnie Soprano 1912
Sellers, Gertrude Contralto 1909
Severn, Margaret Contralto 1929
Sutherland, Oriel Mezzo-Soprano 1969
Taylor, Mrs C. L. Soprano 1908
Thomas, Eric L.V. Baritone 1922; 1925; 1930
Tregoning, R.V. Baritone 1920; 1925
Tregoning, Sara Contralto 1907
Tregunna, Louis Baritone 1940
Truscott, J. C. ? 1907; 1927
Tyndale, Amy Mezzo-soprano 1911
Tyrrell, Susan Mezzo-soprano 1985
Vallé, Gaby Soprano 1935
Watcyns, Watcyn Baritone 1928
Wendon, Henry Tenor 1938
White, Ernest Bass, 1909;1912;1913
White, J. K. Tenor 1912
Williams, Douglas Tenor 1978
Williams, Mabel Soprano 1931
Worth, Vivian Soprano 1933

Groups

Male Voice Choirs: *Heamoor; Ludgvan; Marazion; Pendeen* 1942-1944
Male Chorus 1985
Penzance Girls' Grammar School *Madrigal Group* 1951
Penzance Operatic Society *Male Chorus* 1933;1935;1937
Royal Marine Band Plymouth *Principals* 1910

Guest Conductors

Bailey, Judith 2003
Frost, David 2002
Ormond, Guillame 1933
Redmond, Reginald 1934;1937
Rivers, Dr. Charles 1927
Robinson, Stanford 1950
Ware, Herbert 1948

Appendix 4

Penzance Orchestral Society Works performed 1907-2007

Notes:

1. All instrumental and vocal solos have been excluded unless of significance.

2. This list has been compiled from available records; omissions and inaccuracies are inevitable over such a long period of time.

Composer	Work	Year(s)
Alwyn, William	Suite of Scottish Dances	1995
Arcadelt, Jacques	Ave Maria, arr. for string orchestra by Walter Barnes	1931; 1932; 1935; 1939; 1950
Arensky, Anton S.	Variations on a theme of Tchaikovsky	1951
Arne, Thomas	Air and Gigue	1956
Arnold, Malcolm	Beckus the Dandipratt	1969
	Little Suite No. 1	1967
	Four Cornish Dances	1978; 1999; 2006
Atkinson, Rev. C. Daly		
	Symphonic Poem 'Flora Day at Helston'	1937
Bach, Johann Sebastian		
Overture:	To a Secular Cantata	1930; 1931
Concertos:	No. 1 in D Minor for Piano	1948
	No. 14 in F Minor for Piano	1953
	in D Minor for 2 violins	1922
	Brandenburg No. 2 in F	1946
	No. 3 in G	1960
	No. 4 in G	1974
	No. 5 in D	1950
Suites:	No. 3 in D	1933; 1936; 1941; 1948; 1950; 1951; 1954
	The Wise Virgins arr. Walton	1973
Quartet:	Meditations on the 1st Prelude, for Violin, 'Cello, Harp and Organ, arr. Gounod	1919
	Prelude, orch. Maddern Williams	1943
Bailey, Judith	Havas – a Period of Summer	2004
	Penwith Overture	2006
Baker, C. J. (arr.)	Arabesque	1911
Barber, Samuel	Adagio	1948; 1952; 1969
Barbirolli, Sir John (arr.)		
	Concerto for Oboe and strings on themes of Pergolesi	1950
Bazzini, Antonio	Overture to 'Saul'	1921; 1923
Beethoven, Ludwig van		
Overtures:	Egmont	1914; 1919;1922; 1938; 1956; 2000; 2005
	Cariolan	1964; 1978
	Prometheus	1930; 1940; 1967; 1994
	Leonore No. 3	2007
Concertos	Piano: No. 1 in C Major	1982
	No. 3 in C Minor	1927; 1966; 1980; 1995
	No. 4 in G Major	1943; 1952; 1988; 2002
	No. 5 in E^{b} Major 'Emperor'	1948; 1963; 1978
	Violin: in D Major	1930; 1947; 1956; 1975; 1992
	Romance in F Major for Violin and Orchestra	1937;1995
	Three Equali for Trombones	1931
Symphonies:	No. 2 in D Major	1931; 1945; 1949
	No. 3 in E^{b} Major 'Eroica'	1929;1936; 1963; 1979; 1996; 2005
	No. 5 in C Minor	1911; 1913; 1921; 1927; 1931; 1939 (Finale) 1942; 1950; 1969; 1984
	No. 6 in F Major 'Pastoral'	1938; 1953; 2002
	No. 7 in A Major	1913; 1975; 1991
	No. 8 in F Major	1971
Benjamin, Arthur	Jamaican Rumba	1965
Berlioz, Hector		
Overtures:	A Roman Carnival	1929; 1948; 1962; 1975
	Les Francs-Juges	1980
	Rob Roy	1995
Symphony:	Harold in Italy	1978; 1992
	Marche au Supplice from Symphonie Fantastique	1932
	The Royal Hunt and Storm from 'Les Troyens'	1969
	Three Excerpts from 'La Damnation de Faust'	1929
	Hungarian March from 'La Damnation de Faust'	1931; 1964
Song Cycle:	Les Nuits D'Été	1969; 2004
Berwald, Franz	Sinfonie Singulière (Symphony No. 3 in C Major)	1970
Binding, E.	Nautical Selection 'A Life on the Ocean Wave'	1940
Bizet, Georges	L'Arlèsienne suites Nos. 1 and 2	1927; 1932; 1936; 1947; 1953; 1983
	Carmen suites Nos. 1 and 2	1946; 1960; 1977; 1996
	Selection from 'Carmen'	1909; 1913
Blackenburg	March: Abschied des Gladiatoren	1908
Bliss, Sir Arthur	Suite from the music for the film 'Things to Come'	1937; 1953
Blon	Morceau: Sizilietta	1907
	March: With British Colours	1908
Boccherini, Luigi		
Concerto:	'Cello: in B^{b} Major	1940
	'The Celebrated Minuet'	1925; 1928
Boëllmann, Léon	Symphonic Variations for	

Composer	Work	Year(s)
	'cello and orchestra	1931
Boieldieu, Adrien	Overture to 'Le Calife de Bagdad'	1907
Borodin, Alexander P.		
Overtures:	In the Steppes of Central Asia	1930; 1931; 1950
	Prince Igor	1958; 1972; 1982; 2001
Symphony:	No. 2 in B Minor	1994
	Nocturne for String Orchestra, arr. Sargent	1955
	Polovtsian Dances from 'Prince Igor'	1935
Boyce, William		
Overture:	No. 6 in D Minor	1974
Symphony:	No. 7 in B^{b}Major	1947; 1953
Brahms, Johannes		
Overtures:	Academic Festival	1927; 1961; 2006
	Tragic	1963
Concertos:	Piano: No. 2 in B^{b} Major	1970; 1993
	Violin: in D Major	1927; 1945; 1965; 1985; 2005
	Violin and 'Cello: in A Minor	1957; 1989
Symphonies:	No. 1 in C Minor	1972; 1982; 1998; 2003
	No. 2 in D Major	1980;1990; 2000
	No. 3 in F Major	1987; 2007
	No. 4 in E Minor	1975; 1995
	Variations on a theme by Haydn 'St Anthony'	1951
	Hungarian Dances: Nos. 1, 3 and 10	2000
	No. 2	1912
	Nos. 5 and 6	1948; 1992
	Two Hungarian Dances in G Minor and D	1910; 1912; 1921; 1925
	Alto Rhapsody for Contralto and Male Chorus	1985
Britten, Benjamin	Simple Symphony	1959
	Soirees Musicales	1964
	The Young Person's Guide to the Orchestra, (Variations and Fugue on a theme of Purcell)	1986
Bruch, Max		
Concerto:	Violin: No. 1 in G Minor	1933; 1934; 1942; 1951 1959; 1977; 1988; 2003
	Scottish Fantasy in E Flat	1991
	'Cello: Kol Nidrei	1914; 1999
Bruckner, Anton	Symphony No. 7 in E Major	1976
Butterworth, George		
	The Banks of Green Willow	1960; 1998
	A Shropshire Lad	1957; 1990
Chaminade, Cécile		
	Flute Concertino in D	1998
Cherubini, Luigi		
Overtures:	Anacrèon	1988
	Medea	1933
Chopin, Frédéric		
Concertos	Piano:No. 1 in E Minor	2001
	No. 2 in F Minor	1966; 1990
Clemens, Matthew		
	Orchestral Variations on an original air	1921
Coates, Eric	Miniature Suite	1912; 1915
	London Every Day Suite	1961; 1991
Coleridge-Taylor, Samuel		
	Othello Orchestral Suite	1919; 1920; 1925; 1941
	Hiawatha Ballet Music	1924; 1940
Copland, Aaron	Variations on a Shaker Melody	1999
Corelli, Arcangelo	Concerto for oboe, arr. Barbirolli	1958
	Concerti grossi for chamber orchestra Nos.1 and 2	1938
	Concerto grosso No. 8 in G Minor 'Christmas Concerto'	1961
Davies, Walford	Solemn Melody	1914; 1919; 1942
Debussy, Claude	Petite Suite, arr. Henri Busser	1936; 1956
	Petite Suite, arr. H. Mouton	1973
Delibes, Léo	Coppelia Ballet suite	1911; 1921; 1924; 1931; 1954; 1983; 1998
	Sylvia Ballet Suite	1914; 1938; 1958
	La Source Suite	1920
	Le Roi s'amuse Suite	1940; 1963
Delius, Frederick	On Hearing the First Cuckoo in Spring	1949; 1951 1964; 1982
	Summer Night on the River	1951; 1982
	Intermezzo from 'Fennimore and Gerda'	1961; 1998
	Intermezzo from 'Hassan'	1957
	The Maids of Cadiz	1950
	La Calinda, dance from 'Koanga'	1947; 1974; 1985
	The Walk to the Paradise Garden, intermezzo from 'A Village Romeo and Juliet'	1962; 1972; 1988
Donizetti, Gaetano		
	Concertino in G Major for Cor anglais	1986
Dvorak, Antonin		
Overture:	Carnival Festival overture	1986
Concertos:	'Cello concerto in B Minor	1955; 1977; 1991; 2001
	Romance in F Major for violin and orchestra	1971
Symphonies:	No. 5 in F Major, Op. 76	1958
	No. 6 in D Major, Op. 60	2006
	No. 7 in D. Minor, Op. 70	1971; 1983
	No. 8 in G Major, Op. 88	1928; 1949; 1964 1982; 1994; 2003
	No. 9 in E Minor, Op. 95 'From the New World'	1924; 1925; 1929; 1937 1946; 1954; 1962; 1986
	Humoreske	1922
	Serenade in E Major, Op. 22	1953
	Slavonic Dances Nos. 2 and 4 Op. 46	1957
	Slavonic Dances Nos. 6 and 8 Op. 46	1938
Elgar, Sir Edward		
Overtures:	Cockaigne (In London Town)	1967
	Froissart	1987
	In the South (Alassio)	1933; 1965; 1989; 2005
Concertos	Violin: in B Minor	1973; 1999

'Cello: in E Minor 1948; 1960; 1983; 2002
Romance for Bassoon and Orchestra 2005

Chanson de Nuit and Chanson de Matin Op. 15 Nos. 1 and 2 1997
Elegy 1923; 1934
Imperial March 1924; 1951
Introduction and Allegro 1950
Pomp and Circumstance March No. 4 1928; 1937; 1942; 1991
Pomp and Circumstance March No. 5 1993
Serenade 1945; 1946; 1949; 1953; 1967
Sursum Corda (Elevation) 2002
Three Bavarian Dances 1929; 1930; 1935; 1949; 1954; 1986
Variations on an Original Theme 'Enigma' 1929(Dorabella); 1969; 1988
The Wand of Youth Suite No. 2 1946; 1956; 1978

Song Cycle: Sea Pictures 1974; 1985; 1998

Falla, Manuel de El amor brujo 1953
Nights in the Gardens of Spain 1967

Fauré, Gabriel Pelléas et Mélisande Suite 1955

Finzi, Gerald Dies Natalis 1951

Flotow, Friedrich
Overture: Stradella 1907

Foulds, John Herbert
Lament from Keltic Suite Op.29 1920; 1926; 1941

Franck César Variations symphoniques 1964
Symphony in D Minor 1976

Friedemann Slavonic Rhapsody 1921; 1943

Ganne, Louis Invocation for string orchestra and harp 1923
Marche Lorraine 1939

German, Edward Welsh Rhapsody 1923
Three dances from Henry VIII 1913; 1998
Three dances from Nell Gwyn 1950

Gershwin, George Piano concerto in F Major 1979

Glinka, Mikhail Ivanovich
Overture: Ruslan and Ludmilla 1944; 1981; 1996

Gluck, Christopher Willibald
Overtures: Alceste 1977
Iphigénie en Aulide, arr. Wagner 1926; 1934; 1939 1951; 1962

Gavotte and Musette from 'Armide' 1931

Gossec, Françoise-Joseph
Gavotte in D Major 1931

Gounod, Charles
Overtures: Mireille 1909
La Reine de Saba 1915

Ballet music from 'Faust' 1955

Funeral March of a Marionette 1907; 1908
Meditation on the 1st Prelude of J. S. Bach 1919; 1920
Selection from 'Faust' 1908; 1915

Grainger, Percy Handel in the Strand 1983
Irish Tune from County Derry 1919; 1920; 1921; 1926; 1939
Mock Morris 1939; 1949; 1983
Molly on the Shore 1983
Shepherd's Hey 1943; 1983

Grieg, Edvard
Concerto Piano: in A Minor 1913; 1923; 1942; 1949 1959; 1980; 1996; 2003

Holberg Suite 1943; 1948; 1961
Peer Gynt Suite No. 1 1922; 1923; 1928; 1939; 1981
Peer Gynt Suite No. 2 1957
Sigurd Jorsalfar Suite 1913; 1940; 2001
Two elegiac melodies 1924; 1937; 1947; 1986
Two pieces for string orchestra 1923
Selection from the works of Edvard Grieg 1908; 1911

Haines, Herbert E.
March Triumphant 'The London Scottish' 1940

Handel, George Frederick
Overtures: Berenice, arr. Bantock 1951
The Occasional 1941
In D Minor, arr. Elgar 1953; 1979
Concertos Organ: No. 4 in F Major, Op. 4 1987
Harp: No. 6 in B^b Major, Op. 4 1994
Concerti Grossi: No. 1 in G Major, Op. 6 1985
No. 3 in C Minor, Op. 6 1947
No. 7 in B^b Major, Op. 6 1977

The Faithful Shepherd Suite, arr. Beecham 1964; 2000
The Gods Go A-Begging, Ballet Suite, arr. Beecham 1962; 1982
Water Music Suite, arr. Harty 1927: 1937; 1943; 1967

Haydn, Franz Joseph
Concertos 'Cello: in C Major 1987
in D Major 1936
Oboe: in C Major [attributed but doubtful] 1958
Trumpet: in E^b Major 1946; 1981
Symphonies: No. 6 in D Major 'Le Matin' ('Andante' movement only) 1939
No 85 in B^b Major 'La Reine' 1965
No 88 in G Major 1945
No. 92 in G Major 'Oxford' 1924; 1931; 1941 1943; 1945; 1977
No. 94 in G Major 'The Surprise' 1992
No. 99 in E^b Major 1959
No. 100 in G Major 'Military' 1933; 1985
No. 103 in E^b Major 'Drumroll' 1926; 1997
Toy Symphony [attributed but doubtful] 1941

Holliday, John C. The Geeze Dance 1926; 1942
Skipton Rig 1926
Songs: Sea Lights; The Privateersman (Words by Crosbie Garstin) 1926

Composer	Work	Year(s)
Holst, Gustav	A Somerset Rhapsody	1965
	St Paul's Suite	1924; 1947
Howarth, Osbert		
Song:	My Lady's Garden	1907
Hummel, Johann Nepomuk		
	Trumpet concerto in E^b Major	1989
Humperdinck, Engelbert		
Overture:	Hänsel und Gretel	1938; 1949; 1970; 1985; 2003
	Dream Pantomine from 'Hänsel und Gretel'	1913; 1923; 1925; 1932
	Suite from 'The Miracle'	1928
Jacob, Gordon	Denbigh Suite	1959
Järnefelt, Armas	Berceuse	1914; 1915
	Praeludium	1911; 1920; 1921; 1925; 1928; 1935; 1943; 1997
Lacombe Paul	Suite Espagnole 'La Feria'	1923; 1935; 1949
Lalo, Edouard	Symphonie Espagnole	1949
Larsson, Lars-Erik	Pastoral Suite	1958
Lehár, Franz	Gold and Silver Waltz	1908
Leutner	Fest Overture	1908
Liszt, Franz		
Concertos	Piano: No. 1 in E^b Major	1937
	No. 2 in A Major	1975
	Les Préludes	1964
	Hungarian Rhapsody No. 1	1961; 1968
	Hungarian Rhapsody No. 2	1923
Litolff, Henry	Scherzo from the 4th Symphonic concerto	1996
Lloyd, George		
Symphony:	No. 1 in A Major	1932
Aria:	Light darkens not the world, from 'The Serf'	1938
	Two dances from 'John Socman'	1993
Luigini, Alexandre		
	Ballet Egyptien suite	1909; 1911; 1912; 1924
	Ballet Russe suite	1939
MacCunn, Hamish		
	Land of the Mountain and the Flood	1955; 1979 1992; 1999
Mackenzie, Sir Alexander Campbell		
	Benediction	1921
	Britannia Overture	1914
Mahler, Gustav	Adagietto from Symphony No. 5	1979; 1993
Mancinelli, Luigi	Triumphal march from 'Cleopatra'	1922; 1923; 1931; 1935
Mascagni. Pietro	Selection from 'Cavalleria Rusticana'	1909; 1910; 1914; 1920

Composer	Work	Year(s)
Massenet, Jules	Ballet music 'Le Cid'	1930; 1947; 1954
	Suite No. 4 'Scènes pittoresques'	1950
	The Last Sleep of the Virgin from 'La Vierge'	1971
	The Prelude and Clair de Lune from 'Werther'	1921; 1922; 1935
Mendelssohn, Felix		
Overtures:	A Midsummer Night's Dream	1949
	Hebrides 'Fingal's Cave'	1931; 1935; 1947; 1954 1977; 2000
	Ruy Blas	1912; 1924; 1942; 1950; 1959; 1970
	In C Major for Wind Instruments	1994
Concertos	Piano: No. 1 in G Minor	1972
	Violin: in E Minor	1925; 1941; 1955; 1997
Symphonies:	No. 2 in B^b Major 'Lobgesang' (3 movements)	1908
	No. 3 in A Minor 'Scottish'	1912; 1960; 1980
	No. 4 in A Major 'Italian'	1937; 1958; 1997
	No. 5 in D Major 'Reformation'	1993
	A Midsummer Night's Dream, complete Incidental Music	1951
	A Midsummer Night's Dream Suite	1930
	March from 'Athalie'	1907
	War March of the Priests	1907
Meyerbeer, Giacomo		
	Grand March 'Schiller'	1911
	Selection 'Les Huguenots'	1907
Monckton, Lionel	Selection 'A Country Girl'	1908
Mozart, Wolfgang Amadeus		
Overtures:	Don Giovanni	1980; 1997
	The Impresario	1966
	Il Seraglio	1958
	The Magic Flute	1932; 1941; 1948; 1969; 1981; 1988; 1999
	The Marriage of Figaro	1928; 1929; 1931; 1943;1946; 1955; 1990
Concertos	Piano: No. 12 in A Major K414	1956
	No. 20 in D Minor K466	1964
	No. 21 in C Major K467	1973
	No. 23 in A Major K488	1945; 1983
	No. 24 in C Minor K491	1987
	2 Pianos: No. 10 in E^b Major K365	1994
	Violin: No. 3 in G Major K216	1971
	No. 4 in D Major K218	1932; 1967; 1981
	Flute: No. 1 in G Major K313	1990; 1998
	Flute and Harp: in C Major K299	1924 and 1926 ('Andantino' movement); 1950
	Clarinet: in a Major K622	1953; 1976; 2006
	Oboe: in C Major K314	1986
	Horn: No. 2 in E^b Major K417	1976
	No. 3 in E^b Major K447	1984
	Sinfonia concertante for 4 wind instruments K297B	1929
	Sinfonia concetrante for violin and viola K364	1968
Symphonies:	No. 34 in C Major K338	1948
	No. 35 in D Major K385 'Haffner'	1925
	No. 36 in C Major K425 'Linz'	1923; 1940; 1957; 1996
	No. 39 in E^b Major K 543	1927; 1944
	No. 40 in G Minor K550	1930; 1936; 1946; 1973

No. 41 in C Major K551 'Jupiter' 1938; 1943; 1991

Eine Kleine Nachtmusik K 525 1942
Suite for strings, ed. Barbirolli 1949; 1950
Gloria from Twelvth Mass 1907
Minuet in D Major 1911

Mussorgsky, Modest Petrovich
Gopak 1944

Nicolai, Otto The Merry Wives of Windsor overture 1960; 1975; 1992; 2004

Nonuwieski March 'Under Freedom's Flag' 1915

Oates, Ernest Henry
Introduction to Act II of 'Andromeda' 1951
Introduction to Act III of 'Andromeda', 'Perseus at the Rock' 1932; 1951
Prelude and Final Scene from 'Andromeda' 1936

Offenbach, Jacques
La Belle Hélène overture 1954
Barcarolle from the Tales of Hoffmann 1908

Pachelbel, Johann Canon and gigue in D Major 1997

Paderewski, Ignacy Jan
Chants du voyageur 1909

Paganini, Nicolò Violin concerto No. 1 in D Major 1970

Paynter, Tom Newlyn Suite 1947

Ponchielli, Amilcare
Dance of the Hours from 'La Gioconda' 1935; 1957; 1963

Prokofiev, Sergey Symphony No. 1 in D Major 'Classical' 1950

Purcell, Henry Suite for strings arr. Barbirolli 1946; 1947
Suite from 'King Arthur' arr. Herbage 1951; 1953
Trumpet Voluntary arr. H. Wood [then attributed to Purcell] 1934

Quilter, Roger A Children's Overture 1971

Rakhmaninov, Sergey
Piano Concerto No. 2 in C Minor 1934; 1961; 1986; 2000

Ravel, Maurice Pavane pour une Infante Défunte 1972
Toccata from 'Le Tombeau de Couperin' 1938

Redman, Reginald
From a Moorish Village Suite 1934
Pan's Garden – an Idyll 1937

Resphigi, Ottorino
Ancient Airs and Dances:
Suite No. 1 1934; 1997
Suite No. 2 1948; 1976
Suite No. 3 1960

Rimsky-Korsakov, Nikolay
Russian Easter Festival overture 1994
Introduction and March from 'Le Coq D'or' 1955
Dance of the Tumblers 1942
Scheherazade 1959

Rossini, Gioachino
Overtures: Barber of Seville 1943; 1957; 2002
Italian Girl in Algiers 1911; 1959; 1976
La Cenerentola 1997
La Scala di Seta 1934; 1964
Semiramide 1946; 1955; 1978
Tancredi 1971; 1994
Thieving Magpie 1960
William Tell 1910; 1913; 1933; 1948
Introduction and Variations for Clarinet in C Major 1996
La Boutique Fantasque Suite, arr. Respighi 1946; 1958; 1985
William Tell ballet music, arr. Godfrey 1950
William Tell ballet music 2001

Sabathil Mauerblumchen 1907

Saint-Saëns, Camille
Concertos Piano: No. 4 in C Minor 1954
Cello: No. 1 in A Minor 1999
Harp: Morceau de concert in G Major 1994
Violin: Introduction and Rondo capriccioso in A Minor 1952; 1967; 1997
Symphonies: No. 3 in C Minor 'Organ' 1974; 1987

Carnival of the Animals 1948
Danse Macabre 1936
Suite Algérienne 1981

Sarasate, Pablo Zigeunerweisen for violin and orchestra 1995

Scarlatti, Alessandra
Suite arr. M. Esposito 1949

Scarlatti, Domenico
Four Pieces arr. M. Esposito 1953

Schubert, Franz
Overtures: in D Major 'In the Italian Style' 1973
Rosamunde 1909; 1912; 1921; 1931; 1953; 1965; 2002
Symphonies: No. 5 in B^b Major 1947; 1967
No. 8 in B Minor 'Unfinished 1909; 1910; 1911; 1920; 1922; 1923; 1928; 1934; 1939; 1942; 1954; 1993; 2005
No. 9 in C Major 'Great' 1935; 1951; 1981

Selections from the Incidental Music to 'Rosamunde' 1930; 1941; 1984
March Militaire 1909; 1910
Moment Musical 1932

Schumann, Robert
Overture: Manfred 1993
Concertos Piano: in A Minor 1926; 1938; 1969
'Cello: in A Minor 1968
Symphonies: No. 1 in B^b Major 'Spring' 1967; 1983; 1995
No. 2 in C Major 1999
No. 3 in E^b Major 'Rhenish' 1979; 1989
No. 4 in D Minor 1972; 1988; 2002

	String Quintet 'Traumeri'	1909
	'Liebesgarten', arr. for string orchestra W. Barnes	1935; 1940; 1948
Self, Geoffrey	The Green Cockade	1985
	Mr Playford's Fancy	1992
Shostakovich, Dmitry		
	A Festival Overture	1966
Sibelius, Jean		
Concerto	Violin: in D Minor	1962; 1979
Symphonies:	No. 1 in E Minor	1968
	No. 2 in D Major	1973; 1989; 2001; 2004
	No. 5 in E^b Major	1978
	Elegie from 'King Christian' suite	1950
	Finlandia	1911; 1912; 1915; 1919; 1922; 1923; 1928; 1931; 1937; 1940; 1952; 1987; 2001
	Karelia suite	1959; 1990
	The Swan of Tuonela	1967; 1991
	Valse Triste from 'Kuolema'	1911; 1912; 1915; 1920; 1931
Smetana, Bedrich		
Overture:	The Bartered Bride	1945; 1952
	Vltava (Moldau)	1928; 1934; 1938; 1952; 1965; 1988
	Dance of the Comedians	1945
	From the Woods and Fields of Bohemia	1962
Smyth, Dame Ethel		
	Two Interlinked French Melodies	1952
Strauss, Johann	The Blue Danube	1927; 1933; 1937; 1944
	Radetzsky March	1990
	Roses from the South	1939
	Tales from the Vienna Woods	1989
Strauss, Richard		
Concertos	Oboe Concerto	1997
	Horn: No. 1 in E^b Major	1984
	No. 2 in E^b Major	2004
Stravinsky, Igor	Pulcinella suite	1961
Sullivan, Sir Arthur		
Overtures:	Di Ballo	1966; 1991
	The Yeoman of the Guard	1969
	Selection from 'The Yeoman of the Guard'	1912; 1939
	Pineapple Poll ballet suite, arr. Mackerras	1956; 1989
Suppé, Franz Von		
Overtures:	Light Cavalry	1996
	Poet and Peasant	1907; 1915
Svendsen, Johan	Norwegian Rhapsody No. 1 Op. 17	1922; 1952
Tchaikovsky, Piotr Ilyich		
Overtures:	1812	1924
	Romeo and Juliet	1956; 1966
Concertos	Piano: No. 1 in B^b Minor Op. 23	1950; 2007
	Violin: in D Major Op. 35	1961; 1984; 2006
	'Cello: Variations on a Rococo theme Op. 33	1926; 1931; 1972
Symphonies:	No. 2 in C Minor 'Little Russian' Op. 17	1970; 1984
	No. 4 in F Minor Op. 36	2004
	No. 5 in E. Minor Op. 64	1952; 2006
	No. 6 in B Minor 'Pathetique' Op. 74	1926; 1932; 1966
	Suite No. 4 in G Major 'Mozartiana' Op. 61	2000
	Nutcracker Suite Op. 71a	1911; 1913; 1921; 1933; 1963; 1992
	Sleeping Beauty Suite	1945(Waltz); 1957; 1986
	Swan Lake Suite	1930; 1947; 1955; 1990
	Andante Cantabile (from string Quartet No.1 in D Major Op.11)	1910; 1920; 1922; 1942
	Capriccio Italien in A Major Op. 45	1994
	March Slave in B^b Major Op. 31	1926
	Serenade in C Major Op. 48	1941; 1949; 1974
	Waltz and Polonaise from 'Eugene Onegin'	1912; 1914; 1921, 1924; 1936; 1941; 1951;1961; 1995
Thomas, Ambroise		
Overtures:	Mignon	1923; 1925; 1929
	Raymond	1911; 1919
Toselli, Enrico	Serenata Celebre	1923
Valverde, Joaquin	Selection from 'La Gran Via'	1908
Vaughan Williams, Ralph		
Symphonies:	No. 3 'Pastoral'	1981
	No. 5 in D Major	1968
	English Folk Song Suite, orch. G. Jacob	1999
	Fantasia on a Theme by Thomas Tallis	1965
	Five Variants of 'Dives and Lazarus'	1958
	The Lark Ascending	1951
Verdi, Giuseppe		
Overtures:	The Force of Destiny	1963; 1972; 1982
	Nabucco	1932; 1990
	The Sicilian Vespers	1930; 1931
	Grand March from 'Aida'	1998
	Prelude to Act 1 of 'La Traviata'	1980
	Selection from 'Il Trovatore'	1907
Vivaldi, Antonio		
Concertos	Violin: in A Major	1939; 1952
	Two Violins: No. 8 in A Minor Op. 3	1984
	Four Violins: No. 10 in B Minor Op. 3	1940
	Guitar: in D Major	1971
Wagner, Richard		
Overtures:	A Faust Overture	1927; 1933
	Die Meistersinger von Nürnberg	2004
	Rienzi	1929; 1935; 1947; 1968; 1984
	Tannhäuser	1922; 1923; 1953
	Siegfried Idyll	1933; 1939; 1952; 1962; 1974; 1993
	Vorspiel from 'Lohengrin'	1909; 1925

Appendix 6
Calling in the Troups!

In most amateur orchestras there are occasions when instrumentalists have to be brought in from outside their membership to stiffen the ranks of a section or provide an unusual instrument for a particular work. The Penzance Orchestral Society is no exception and from its earliest concerts the support of players from the Penzance Military Band, the Devon and Cornwall Light Infantry Band, based in Bodmin, or the Royal Marine Band in Plymouth was needed from time to time.

In October 1909 the help of the local band was recognised when the Society's concert was for the benefit of the conductor of the Penzance Military Band, Mr Alex Corrison. There was also the special concert on Easter Monday in March 1910 when the Royal Marine Band contributed ten members to the orchestra and were invited to provide all the section leaders.

It was usually the woodwind and brass sections which needed to be strengthened but even the strings were occasionally boosted. For example, C. G. (Charlie) Pike from the Royal Marines was a regular member of the 'cello section from 1919 to 1923. An able and popular 'cellist he often performed solos with the orchestra and became a frequent artiste at concerts arranged by other organisations in the area.

These links, forged so early in the Society's history, continued but mainly with the Royal Marine Band. One of their players, Jerry Baker, was the Penzance orchestra's regular bassoonist and would have been a convenient 'go between'. There were always 'pros' and 'cons' to be considered. For instance, the Devon and Cornwall Light Infantry charged less for their services but were not so reliable. In 1948 horn and clarinet players from the D.C.L.I. had failed the Orchestral Society at the last moment and the Royal Marines had come to the rescue but were, "much more expensive than the D.C.L.I."! The year before, the D.C.L.I. had been unable to guarantee providing instrumentalists due to a possible tour of duty at the time of the concert. So it was to the Royal Marines that the Society more regularly applied for assistance.

According to Marjorie Farnham, who joined the orchestra in 1958 and served on its committee, Morgan Hosking got to know the commanding officer of the Royal Marine Band very well. He only had to telephone him for help and the response would be, "Of course, Morgan, we'll send down whatever you want". If any of the music they were to play was especially difficult Morgan would travel to the barracks in Plymouth to rehearse their parts thereby only requiring them to attend the final orchestral rehearsal and concerts. He never recalled having any problems with these professional musicians despite their being many different players over the years.

In December 1948 the concert programme included, among those to whom the Society owed their thanks, the note that "Royal Marines appear by kind permission of Colonel E. St J. Brockman and Officers Royal Marines, Plymouth". This was a rare acknowledgement but there had been a considerable number of 'stiffeners' in that concert with two flautists, Musicians H. L. Eden and W. H. Briton, one bassoonist, Musician T. G. Tregloyne and one French horn player, Musician J. Smith. It was also unusual to list them in the programme as 'Musician....' so perhaps it was felt that a special mention was due in recognition of regular support over many years.

In later decades, with the emergence of peripatetic wind and brass teachers in Cornwall the need for recourse to the Royal Marine Band lessened. By the time of David Ball's conductorship their help was no longer called upon.

Appendix 7
A Bardic Connection

Gorseth Byrth Kernow, the Cornish Gorsedd of Bards, was inaugurated by Pedrog, Archdruid of Wales, on 21st September 1928. The ceremony was held at Boscawen-un, the Bronze Age stone circle near St Buryan, a few miles from Penzance. Prior to this Cornish bards had been created but initiated either in Wales or, less often, in Brittany. The Cornish Gorsedd, though allied to those of Wales and Brittany exists to give expression to the spirit of Cornwall, to encourage the study of its history and language and to foster its literature, art and music.

From its earliest years the Gorsedd initiated bards who were members of the Penzance Orchestral Society with A. W. Robinson, the Society's harpist, installed in 1929 as Telenner Kernow, meaning Harpist of Cornwall. In 1931, at the annual Gorsedd ceremony in Penzance, Walter Barnes' contribution to the musical life of the county was recognised. He was endowed with the bardic name Pen Ylow, meaning Chief of Music. Over ten decades many other members of the Society and some of its soloists have received this distinction. Occasionally it has been recognition for achievements in areas other than music. For example, Michael Cardew, the potter who was a clarinettist in the orchestra, took the bardic name Myghal an Pry, which means Michael of the Clay.

All five conductors of the Orchestral society have been installed as Bards of the Cornish Gorsedd:

Walter Barnes, Pen Ylow (Chief of Music), Penzance 1931

R. J. Maddern Williams, Madern Pendyn (Maddern of Pendeen) Truro 1942

J. Morgan Hosking, Ylowvester (Master of Music) Callington 1959

(Morgan had wanted his bardic name to be Man of Music but was told, erroneously, that this was the name chosen by Walter Barnes)

David Ball, Mab Kymygieth Hag Ilow (Man of Chemistry and Music) St Columb 2001

Judith Bailey, Gedyores Menostrouthy (Orchestral conductor) Wadebridge 2005

Scos an Orsedd, the Gorsedd Music Shield.

The Council of the Gorsedd makes a number of annual music awards and members of the Orchestral Society have been among the award-winners over the years. The most prestigious of these is Scos an Orsedd, the Gorsedd Music Shield, which was inaugurated in 1935 and is awarded to those who have given outstanding service to music in Cornwall. The recipient is usually chosen upon the recommendation of the Cornwall Music Festival Committee, an institution which has always maintained close links with the Gorsedd of Bards. Members of the Penzance Orchestral Society and musicians associated with it who have received the Gorsedd Music Shield are:

Eleanor Buddle 1969

Hon. Jennet Campbell 1989

Dr. Edward Weymouth 1964; 1974

David Frost 1996

J. Morgan Hosking 1967

Russell Jory 2006

Joyce Preston 1988

Maisie Radford 1971

Geoffrey Self 1981

Douglas Williams 1985

Eileen Woolmington 1986

Appendix 8
'Bold Amateurs'

Reproduced below and on the following page are letters exchanged between Oliver Price, Chairman of the Falmouth 3 Arts Committee and husband of Honor Price, member of Penzance Orchestral Society, and Noel Vinson, Editor of The *Western Morning News* newspaper, during November and December 1950. This was the forerunner to the long debate in the press about amateur musicians described in Chapter 11.

1

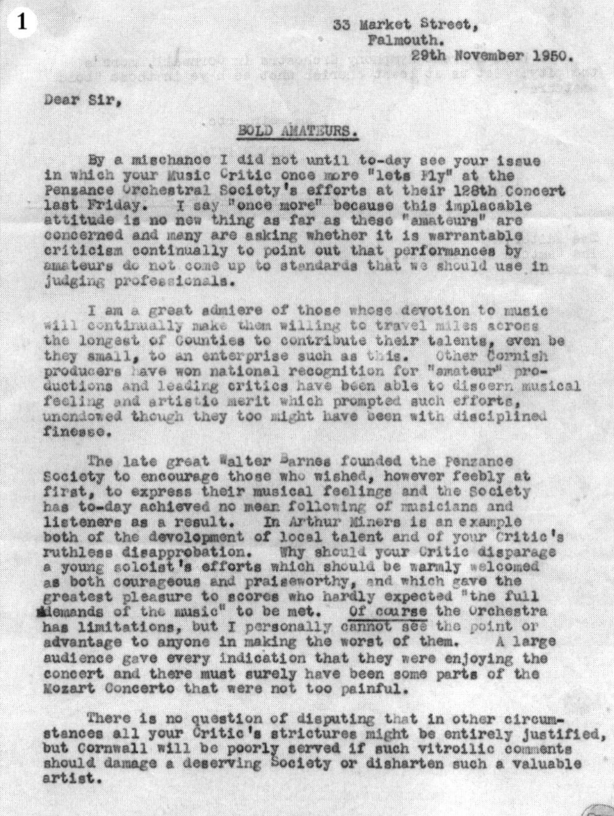

33 Market Street,
Falmouth.
29th November 1950.

Dear Sir,

BOLD AMATEURS.

By a mischance I did not until to-day see your issue in which your Music Critic once more "lets Fly" at the Penzance Orchestral Society's efforts at their 128th Concert last Friday. I say "once more" because this implacable attitude is no new thing as far as these "amateurs" are concerned and many are asking whether it is warrantable criticism continually to point out that performances by amateurs do not come up to standards that we should use in judging professionals.

I am a great admiere of those whose devotion to music will continually make them willing to travel miles across the longest of Counties to contribute their talents, even be they small, to an enterprise such as this. Other Cornish producers have won national recognition for "amateur" productions and leading critics have been able to discern musical feeling and artistic merit which prompted such efforts, unendowed though they too might have been with disciplined finesse.

The late great Walter Barnes founded the Penzance Society to encourage those who wished, however feebly at first, to express their musical feelings and the Society has to-day achieved no mean following of musicians and listeners as a result. In Arthur Miners is an example both of the development of local talent and of your Critic's ruthless disapprobation. Why should your Critic disparage a young soloist's efforts which should be warmly welcomed as both courageous and praiseworthy, and which gave the greatest pleasure to scores who hardly expected "the full demands of the music" to be met. Of course the Orchestra has limitations, but I personally cannot see the point or advantage to anyone in making the worst of them. A large audience gave every indication that they were enjoying the concert and there must surely have been some parts of the Mozart Concerto that were not too painful.

There is no question of disputing that in other circumstances all your Critic's strictures might be entirely justified, but Cornwall will be poorly served if such vitroilic comments should damage a deserving Society or dishearten such a valuable artist.

PTO

2

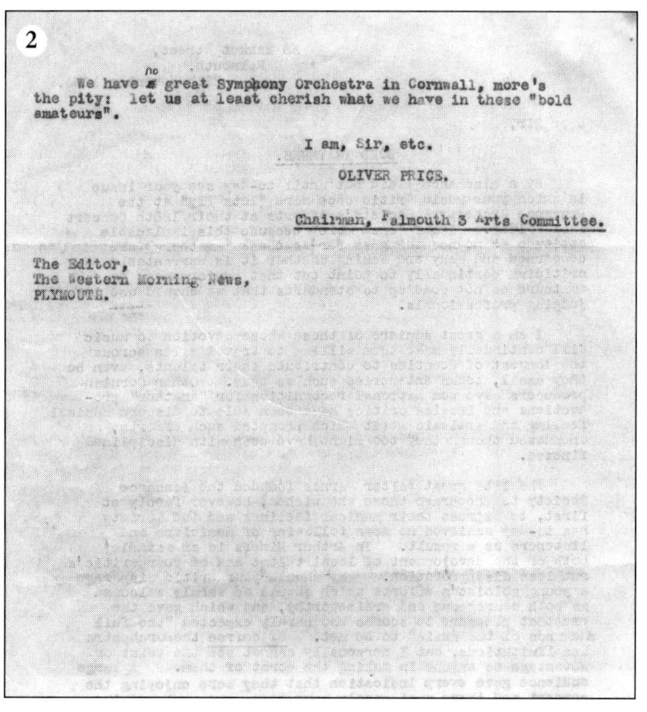

We have no great Symphony Orchestra in Cornwall, more's the pity: let us at least cherish what we have in these "bold amateurs".

I am, Sir, etc.

OLIVER PRICE.

Chairman, Falmouth 3 Arts Committee.

The Editor,
The Western Morning News,
PLYMOUTH.

3

THE WESTERN MORNING NEWS CO LTD.

30th November 1950.

Dear Sir,

I acknowledge receipt of your letter of November 29.

I should have thought that our report of November 25th of Penzance Orchestral Society's concert showed that our critic shares your admiration for "those whose devotion to music will make them willing to travel miles across the longest of counties to contribute their talents, even be they small, to an enterprise such as this"

I cannot understand why you should imagine that because our music critic "once more lest fly" at the Society's efforts, he is guilty of an "implacable attitude". Unless a critic sets a standard by which performances should be judged, surely his criticism is valueless. Presumably the Society desires honest criticism, or it would not invite us to send a representative. The Society must also desire to attain the highest possible standard, and I should have thought that fair criticism would be welcomed as helping to attain that standard. On your own admission the Orchestra has limitations, and I fail to see that our critic has been in any way unkind or unfair in drawing attention to some of those limitations. There is no question of "making the worst of them".

As to the enthusiasm of the audience, there are factors to account for such enthusiasm which the critic would be right to ignore. Anyone who has listened to the Promenade Concerts in London cannot fail to have noticed that the excitement of the audience is by no means also matched by equal enthusiasm on the part of the critics.

Like you I deplore the fact that Cornwall "has no great Symphony Orchestra" and quite frankly the County never will have one if sincere criticism is resented every time it is offered.

Yours faithfully,

Noel A. T. Vinson.

Editor.

4

4th December 1950.

Dear Sir,

"BOLD AMATEURS".

Thank you for your letter of the 30th November.

First, please let it be understood that resentment, if any, has not emanated from those criticised but from a contemporary Society.

May I recapitulate my points as your letter appears not to have indicated that they were understood?

1. The standards selected by your critic were inappropriate to any but first rate professionals: hence the criticsm was unfair.

2. The critical strictures had been so often repeated over a series of concerts as to appear part of a system, that, it is feared cannot fail to have a damaging effect on a Society that relies on their audiences' support for continued existence.

3. The criticism was unrelieved in its destructive tone: not one suggestion was made that was helpful or constructive. In this the Critic was unkind.

While appreciating your point on audiences at Promenade concerts whose immoderate excitement means little to the Critic, I do not see its application here, unless your Critic because of the Prom audience behaviour would rather not have the Proms at all while those present behave that way when (or shortly before) the music ends.

Further I cannot see that the coming into existence of a great Cornish Symphony Orchestra, to which you are not alone in looking hopefully forward, will be hastened by the destruction of amateur aspirations in the meantime.

Could you not accord your Critic space to formulate his views on the future of Orchestral music in Cornwall?

Yours faithfully,

O.F. PRICE.

5

THE WESTERN MORNING NEWS.

5th December 1950.

Dear Sir,

I acknowledge receipt of your letter of December 4th. Let me hasten to assure you that there was no misunderstanding of the points raised by your letter of November 29.

It is obviously a matter of opinion whether the standards selected by our Critic were inappropriate to any but first rate professionals. In fact, he has never expected amateur societies to raise to professional heights, but has always gauged performances on which might be expected from the average musical organisations in the South-West.

The criticism of the Penzance Society was certainly not "part of a system" directed against that Society, but rather "part of a system" to raise the general level of amateur performances throughout our circulation area.

My information is that even members of the Penzance Orchesyral Society are divided in their opinions of our criticism. In my view the realists are those who feel that our Critic's efforts will ppovide the necessary spur to higher achievements.

Yours faithfully,

Noel A. T. Vinson,
Editor.

6

7th December, 1950.

Dear Sir,

BOLD AMATEURS.

Thank you for your letter of the 5th December.

We must, I suppose, agree to differ on your critic's selection of standards and whether a harsh criticism does in fact help an amateur Society. It is, as you say, a matter of opinion.

One thing emerges from this correspondence, however, which seems to me encouraging. We both want a first-rate orchestra in Cornwall. My own feeling is that one way to draw the Penzance Orchestral Society on is by means of the stimulation engendered by the invitation of guest conductors who, it has been my feeling, inspire the members of the Orchestra to be on their mettle. Your critic may have other views which would be more helpful.

My information is that others felt as I did on the subject of your cirtics views. I suppose you cannot afford space for publishing anything in the nature of such correspondence to test public feeling in the matter. Could you not at least, as I said in my last letter, afford space to enable your critic to formulate his method of attaining the end we both desire so much?

I am much obliged to you for all your letters on the subject.

Yours faithfully.

O. F. PRICE.

7

THE WESTERN MORNING NEWS CO. LTD.

8th December, 1950.

Dear Sir,

Without wishing to prolong our correspondence on the subject of the Penzance Orchestral Society, a paragraph in your letter of December 7 does reveal one point on which we are in complete agreement. That is the invitation to guest conductors. In my discussions with our music critic, he made particular reference to the vast difference it made to the Penzance Orchestra when (I think it was) Stanford Robinson conducted them. It is in this direction I feel that great progress is possible. I say this without detriment to the regular conductors of many amateur orchestras, who are doing a fine job obviously for the sheer love of it. But their limitations are, I am afraid, often too obvious.

May I say that I have enjoyed the stimulating exchange of opinions, and assure you that whatever differences there may be on the approach to the matter, our goal appears to be the same.

It might be possible for our music critic to prepare an article on the lines you suggest.

Yours faithfully,

Noel A. T. Vinson

Editor.

Prof Ian Parrott

Mrs Sally Pearson, Pool, Cornwall

Margaret E. Perry, Newlyn, Penzance, Cornwall

Joyce Preston, St Just, Penzance

Phoebe M. Procter (née Nance), Penzance, Cornwall

Mercia Railson, Cwmrheidol, Wales

The Religious Society of Friends,

Mrs A.J. Reynolds, London

Dr E.T.E. Richards, Penzance

Hannah Roberts, Southport

Mr and Mrs G. Robertson

Geoffrey Self, Camborne, Cornwall

Deborah Sharp (née Harrison), Rilla Mill, Cornwall

Elizabeth Smith (Barton), Truro, Cornwall

St Just and Pendeen Old Cornwall Society

Rosemarie Stanley-Jones, Townshend, Cornwall

Mr and Mrs B. Tempest, St Ives

Rose Tempest, St Ives, Cornwall

Audrey Thomas, Newlyn, Penzance

James Treglown

Ann Trevenen Jenkin, Hayle, Cornwall

Mark and Pella Tromans, Sparkford, Somerset

Jean Tunley, Newlyn, Cornwall

Iain and Liz Vosper, Penzance, Cornwall

Averil M. Werngren, Penzance, Cornwall

Anne Williams, Llandeilo, Carmarthenshire

Angela Williams (née Hopwood), Cardiff, Wales

Margaret M. Willis, Truro, Cornwall

Eileen D. Woolmington, St Just, Penzance

Professor Michael Young, Ponterwyd, Mid Wales